Expanding the Lexicon

The Dynamics of Wordplay

Edited by
Esme Winter-Froemel

Editorial Board
Salvatore Attardo, Dirk Delabastita, Dirk Geeraerts, Raymond W. Gibbs,
Alain Rabatel, Monika Schmitz-Emans and Deirdre Wilson

Volume 5

Expanding the Lexicon

Linguistic Innovation, Morphological Productivity, and Ludicity

Edited by
Sabine Arndt-Lappe, Angelika Braun, Claudine Moulin
and Esme Winter-Froemel

DE GRUYTER

This book series was established in connection with the project "The Dynamics of Wordplay" funded by the German Research Foundation (DFG). The present volume is published in cooperation with the "Forum Sprache und Kommunikation Trier". Additional funding was provided by the University of Trier.

Cette collection a été créée dans le cadre du projet « La dynamique du jeu de mots », financé par la Deutsche Forschungsgemeinschaft (DFG). Le présent volume est publié également en collaboration avec le « Forum Sprache und Kommunikation Trier », l'Université de Trèves fournissant un financement complémentaire.

ISBN 978-3-11-068494-0
e-ISBN [PDF] 978-3-11-050193-3
e-ISBN [EPUB] 978-3-11-049816-5

This work is licensed under the Creative Commons Attribution-NonCommercial-NoDerivs 4.0 License. For details go to http://creativecommons.org/licenses/by-nc-nd/4.0/.

Library of Congress Cataloging-in-Publication Data
A CIP catalog record for this book has been applied for at the Library of Congress.

Bibliographic information published by the Deutsche Nationalbibliothek
The Deutsche Nationalbibliothek lists this publication in the Deutsche Nationalbibliografie; detailed bibliographic data are available on the Internet at http://dnb.dnb.de.

© 2019 Sabine Arndt-Lappe, Angelika Braun, Claudine Moulin and Esme Winter-Froemel, published by Walter de Gruyter GmbH, Berlin/Boston
This volume is text- and page-identical with the hardback published in 2018.
Printing: CPI books GmbH, Leck
♾ Printed on acid-free paper
Printed in Germany

www.degruyter.com

Contents

Sabine Arndt-Lappe, Angelika Braun, Claudine Moulin, and Esme Winter-Froemel
Expanding the Lexicon: At the crossroads of innovation, productivity, and ludicity —— 1

I Linguistic Innovation

Natalia Filatkina
Expanding the lexicon through formulaic patterns —— 15

Anette Kremer and Stefanie Stricker
Complex words in the early medieval *Leges Barbarorum* and their contribution to expanding the Old High German lexicon —— 43

Sören Stumpf
Free usage of German unique components —— 67

II Morphological Productivity

Ingo Plag and Sonia Ben Hedia
The phonetics of newly derived words: Testing the effect of morphological segmentability on affix duration —— 93

Marcel Schlechtweg
How stress reflects meaning —— 117

Sabine Arndt-Lappe
Expanding the lexicon by truncation: Variability, recoverability, and productivity —— 141

III Ludicity

Angelika Braun
Approaching wordplay from the angle of phonology and phonetics – examples from German —— 173

Georgette Dal and Fiammetta Namer
Playful nonce-formations in French: Creativity and productivity —— 203

Esme Winter-Froemel
Ludicity in lexical innovation (I) – French —— 229

Claudine Moulin
Ludicity in lexical innovation (II) – German —— 261

Appendix

List of Abstracts / Liste des résumés —— 289

List of Contributors and Editors —— 297

Index —— 301

Sabine Arndt-Lappe, Angelika Braun, Claudine Moulin, and Esme Winter-Froemel
Expanding the Lexicon: At the crossroads of innovation, productivity, and ludicity

1 The dynamic lexicon

Traditionally, the creation of new lexical units and patterns – understood in a wide sense as not being necessarily limited to the word level – has been studied in different research frameworks. Whereas approaches focusing on morphological productivity are directed at system-internal ('grammatical') morphological processes, other approaches have aimed at identifying general types of lexical innovation and describing them in the larger context of lexical change, thus integrating system-external factors related to the historical background of the innovations and their diffusion. In this way, lexical change provides insights into general motives of language change and basic mechanisms of language processing.

The aim of this volume is to discuss fundamental aspects of dynamic processes in the lexicon, including recent and ongoing changes as well as historical processes of change, and to bring new evidence to bear on the traditional dividing line between approaches oriented towards system-internal and system-external aspects.

Current research in language change is marked by a renewed interest in the lexicon, as documented by recent international conferences and publications on structural, typological and cognitive approaches to the lexicon and on regularities of lexical change in the larger context of language change (see, among many others, Blank 1997; Ágel et al. 2002; Brinton and Traugott 2005; Haspelmath and Tadmor 2009; Libben et al. 2012; Zeschel 2012; Ostermann 2015). At the same time, within theoretical linguistics, recent years have seen an increase in more and more psycholinguistically informed work on morphological complexity and productivity, which explicitly relates issues of productivity and modularity in the lexicon to what we know about lexical processing (e.g. Hay 2003; Baayen et al. 2011; Pirelli et al., in press).

The strong interest in this topic was also documented by the high number of submissions we received for the call for papers for our international workshop *Expanding the lexicon / Extensions du lexique / Erweiterungen des Lexikons – Linguistic Innovation, Morphological Productivity, and the Role of Discourse-Related*

∂ Open Access. © 2018 Sabine Arndt-Lappe, Angelika Braun, Claudine Moulin, Esme Winter-Froemel, published by De Gruyter. [(cc) BY-NC-ND] This work is licensed under the Creative Commons Attribution-NonCommercial-NoDerivatives 4.0 License.
https://doi.org/10.1515/9783110501933-003

Factors / Innovation linguistique, productivité morphologique et le rôle de facteurs liés au discours / Sprachliche Innovation, morphologische Produktivität und die Rolle diskursbezogener Faktoren held at Trier University (17–18 November 2016). The workshop brought together participants with different theoretical backgrounds and permitted multilingual discussions and exchange on a wide variety of topics ranging from aspects of the lexicon in medieval times to current innovations in German, English and Romance.

The contributions in this volume go back to papers presented at the workshop as well as to papers presented at the newly created *Forum Sprache und Kommunikation Trier* (www.fsk.uni-trier.de), which aims to foster inter- and transdisciplinary linguistic exchange on a broad range of linguistic phenomena, taking into account the cultural, social and historical contexts in which they are embedded. At the workshop and in the discussions, three main aspects emerged as being of key interest: 1) lexical innovation and conventionalisation, 2) productivity in its interplay with speaker creativity, and 3) the role of ludicity in lexical innovation. These aspects are addressed from different perspectives by various papers in the volume, as will be shown below. It should be stressed that many of the papers touch upon several of the aspects mentioned, thus demonstrating how closely they are interwoven. The following discussion of the three aspects and the papers grouped in each of the main parts of this volume should therefore be interpreted as showing only some of the many links and common lines of investigation. The reader is invited to cross-read the volume and to discover further convergencies, complementary discussions and perspectives for further research.

2 Innovation and conventionalisation

Studying processes of lexical expansion, the notion of lexical innovation and the diachronic evolution of lexical innovations becoming conventionalised and possibly reused in new ways, represent first topics to be dealt with. These issues are addressed from a theoretical perspective in Filatkina's contribution, which is complemented by Kremer and Stricker's investigation of lexical innovation in Old High German and Stumpf's analysis of innovative free usage of unique components in contemporary German. Moreover, the contributions which will be discussed in sections 3 and 4 below also touch upon synchronic and diachronic aspects of specific subtypes of lexical innovations and their subsequent diachronic evolution.

Natalia Filatkina's contribution, *Expanding the lexicon through formulaic patterns: the emergence of formulaicity in language history and modern language use*, approaches the topic of innovation from the perspective of formulaic language. As word-formations, formulaic patterns are considered an important means of lexicon expansion and innovation. Filatkina uncovers substantial differences and characteristics in the way formulaic patterns contribute to lexicon expansion. The differences are particularly clear if studied from a (diachronic) perspective of the emergence of formulaic patterns and against the background of theories of language change. The argument is made that the usual "driving forces" of language change such as regularity / irregularity, codification / normatisation, cultural and contextual / discourse traditions and frequency do not apply to formulaic patterns in the same way as they do, for example, to sound change, grammatical or even lexical change. The emergence of formulaic patterns can best be understood as a process of integration of sometimes controversial aspects, among which frequency and regularity seem to be important accompanying factors but not always driving forces. Irregular, idiosyncratic paths based on conflicts and violation of norms shape the development of formulaicity as well if they are sufficiently supported by the speakers' / hearers' communicative needs and / or embedded into discourse and cultural traditions.

A special dimension of the investigation of lexical expansion and innovation is tackled in the paper by Anette Kremer and Stefanie Stricker (*Selected Complex Words in the Early Medieval* Leges Barbarorum *and their Contribution to Expanding the Old High German Lexicon*), namely the challenges encountered by the exploration of the topic in historical stages of languages for which our textual records provide only a very limited inventory of texts and a very small literary vocabulary. This is the case with Old High German (AD 700–1050) where the exploration of the lexicon is especially complicated due to the fact that extensive monolingual sources are not available on a large scale over the relevant time axis. A larger quantity of complementary Old High German material can be found in vernacular glosses in Latin manuscripts and in the sources explored in the paper for this volume, namely vernacular lexical items present in Latin law codes of the Germanic peoples written in the Early Middle Ages, the so-called *Leges Barbarorum*.

In their paper, the authors analyse a selection of complex lexical items (compounds, derivatives) taken from the Upper German law codes (*Lex Baiuuariorum, Lex Alamannorum, Leges Langobardorum*), as these form a relatively homogeneous tradition. The investigation is carried out with the database of the LegIT project and analyses the formation and use of relevant lexical items in the selected corpus, depicting pathways of expansion of these items in the lexicon of Old High German. Furthermore, the paper focuses on the dynamics of word formation in Old High German, with special attention to complex words not documented outside of the *Leges* tradition. In this context, specific relations between their first and second elements can be traced and related to the specific text genre where they occur. The analysis of derivation cases draws special attention to lexical items resulting from morphological word formation processes that can be considered typical for the law texts, but are no longer productive, and for which we have hardly any evidence in other Old High German sources. Overall the results of the study show the manifold potential of investigation on the lexical level offered by the *Leges* sources for the medieval vernaculars. For further research, the analysis of these sources not only opens a specific reservoir of lexical domains not recorded elsewhere, but will also enable crosslinked analysis with findings in the textual and glossographic domain in order to trace general pathways of lexical development through time.

Sören Stumpf's paper, *Free usage of German unique components: Corpus linguistics, psycholinguistics and lexicographical approaches*, investigates how unique components in phrasemes can be (re-)used outside their original phraseological context and thus contribute to linguistic innovation and expansion of the lexicon. Normally, such unique components can only occur within set phrasemes (e.g. German *ins Fettnäpfchen treten*; an example from English would be *happy as a sandboy*),[1] but as the author shows, they can be reactivated in language use and once usualised, eventually find their way into dictionaries. Exploring this type of lexical innovation through unique components has not yet been approached in a comprehensive way, and the author focuses in his study on findings from corpus studies on the German language and particularly the underlying debonding processes (Norde 2009). Furthermore, he addresses psycholinguistic issues exploring how phrasemes with unique components are processed in the mental lexicon, how their debonding can be grasped and how the motivation of the unique components plays a central role in this process. The author's findings point to the importance of further diachronic investigation of unique components as a source for lexical innovation and open methodological paths for crosslinguistic research. Furthermore, the topic investigated shows close links to aspects of productivity and creativity as well as ludicity in the expansion process, domains that are the subject of the following sections of the volume.

---

[1] For more examples see Dobrovol'skij (1988) or the "List of English Bound Words": https://www.english-linguistics.de/codii/codiibw/en/list-complete.xhtml (accessed 13 September 2017).

3 Productivity

The discussion in section 2 has already indicated that one key means of lexical expansion which languages have at their disposal are productive word-formation processes. Such processes are traditionally defined as regular morphological mechanisms, and determinants of as well as constraints on their productivity have usually been described in terms of the components of the language system: phonology, morphology, syntax, semantics (and, to some extent, pragmatics). The articles that were discussed in section 2 above already point to a well-known delimitation issue here, as we have seen that word-formation in this sense is only one of several mechanisms of lexical expansion that can be productive (compare e.g. the processes described in Kremer and Stricker's paper with the productivity of unique components studied in Stumpf's article). In the present section, however, we limit the discussion of productivity issues to those arising in the synchronic study of word formation processes in the traditional sense.

With respect to traditional notions of productivity, the articles in this volume provide interesting insights in mainly two ways: One concerns the question of the level of description needed to characterize productive processes. There are two articles in this volume, one by Ingo Plag and Sonia Ben Hedia, and one by Marcel Schlechtweg, which essentially show that, if we look at how novel linguistic expressions are used in actual speech (albeit, in Schlechtweg's case, in an experimental setting), it is necessary to take into account more than the system-internal components that traditional analyses have studied. Plag and Ben Hedia's article, *The Phonetics of Newly Derived Words: Some Case Studies*, deals with how prefixed words are realised phonetically in a corpus of English natural speech. They find that the pronunciation of prefixed words reflects the segmentability of that word. Segmentability encompasses both measures of semantic transparency as well as frequency based measures of the competitive activation of morphologically complex words and their bases in language processing (cf. Hay 2003). The findings are highly relevant for the study of lexical innovation: A high degree of segmentability is a characteristic property of productive processes. Building on Plag and Ben Hedia's findings, we can thus expect newly derived words to be pronounced differently (i.e. with longer prefix durations) from older, more lexicalised, derived words. It is an open question whether this type of effect can be captured in terms of the level of granularity that can be formulated with the help of phonological feature systems. Also, Plag and Ben Hedia's findings suggest that the study of newly derived words benefits from integrating the perspective of the speaker and the speech event in the research paradigm. Segmentability and productivity are properties of individual words, as processed by the individual speaker.

Marcel Schlechtweg's contribution, *How stress reflects meaning – The interplay of prosodic prominence and semantic (non-)compositionality in non-lexicalized English adjective-noun combinations*, is concerned with the function of prosodic prominence in novel English adjective-noun constructions. On the basis of acoustic data elicited in a small-scale experimental study, the paper presents evidence that prominence patterns are influenced by both the semantic compositionality of the construct itself and the immediate sentence context in which the adjective-noun construct occurs. Two types of context are tested in the experiment: In the first type, the construct is followed by a relative clause that not only paraphrases the non-compositional meaning but also uses a metalinguistic description to explicitly mark the paraphrase as a definition (*which is called so because*...). In the other type of context provided in the experiment, non-compositionality is merely implied. Unlike in constructs with a compositional semantics, where the noun tends to receive most prominence, in non-compositional constructs the adjective tends to be marked as more prominent. However, the difference between compositional and non-compositional items is only robust in sentence contexts in which the meaning relation between the adjective and the noun is not explicitly provided with the help of a paraphrase. Again, this has implications for the study of productive processes of lexical innovation, as it shows that system-external factors like context influence the formal realisation of newly coined morphological constructs.

A second aspect that characterises discussions of productivity in this volume is the question if and how productive morphological processes are to be delimited from other, specifically creative or playful processes. The article *Expanding the lexicon by truncation: variability, recoverability, and productivity* by Sabine Arndt-Lappe presents an analysis of truncation patterns (mainly patterns of name truncation as in nickname and hypocoristic formation) in three languages (Italian, German, and English), with a focus on two aspects that have traditionally been used as criteria to delimit productive morphology from other processes. One is structural variability: outputs of truncation are shown to provide evidence of the existence of alternative forms, such that different patterns of truncation can be distinguished. Crucially, variability is systematic and determined by both universal and language-specific morphological factors. The other aspect is semantic transparency: it is argued that, even though in truncatory patterns compositionality of meaning does not correspond to compositionality of form, outputs of truncation may still be transparent, in the sense that the regularities that determine the shape of truncatory patterns as well as the way truncatory patterns are used in context are optimally geared towards ensuring that the base forms are recoverable, despite the loss of segmental material. The case of truncations thus challenges traditional assumptions that take the degree of productivity of a morphological process to be correlated with formal predictability and semantic compositionality. Instead, like other articles in the present volume, the truncatory data seem to point towards an approach to productivity that relates this notion in a more integrative way to mechanisms of language processing and contextual factors.

4 Ludicity

The interplay of productivity and the speakers' creativity touched upon in the papers discussed in the preceding section as well as the central role of individual acts of innovation stressed in usage-based approaches to language change (see also Filatkina's contribution discussed in section 2) point to the active role of the speakers in processes of lexical expansion. One type of lexical innovation in which the active role of the speaker is particularly evident are ludic innovations. Although ludicity is obviously an important dimension in lexical expansion, its role has not yet been studied systematically in previous research. This aspect is also linked to the general topic of the book series in which this volume is included and which is dedicated to the dynamics of wordplay, the latter notion being understood in a broad sense, in order, among other things, to precisely include transitions between ludic and "serious" innovation and to explore degrees of ludicity in lexical innovation. In this way, the present volume also presents strong links to the upcoming volume on wordplay and creativity edited by Bettina Full and Michelle Lecolle (in press).

Among the papers of the present volume, the ludic dimension is directly addressed by Braun, Dal and Namer, Winter-Froemel, and Moulin, focusing on different aspects of ludic usage and on different levels of linguistic description.

Angelika Braun's contribution, *Approaching wordplay from the angle of phonology and phonetics – examples from German*, aims to outline the benefits and insights to be gained from a phonetically informed approach to wordplay studies. She argues that various types of wordplay and potentially ludic processes of lexical expansion can be described in a more fine-grained way from a phonetic / phonological perspective. Distinguishing between wordplay which is based on existing lexical items and wordplay involving the creation of new items (most importantly, blending), she proposes a classification of various subtypes of wordplay depending on which part of the syllable is involved and which phonetic processes can be observed. In this way, a fine-grained classification of various subtypes of wordplay and ludic processes of lexical expansion is obtained. This classification is tested by analysing more than 200 items collected by the author from TV shows, newspapers, posted advertisements and previous research papers. All of the examples studied are intended for a German audience, but the material also includes English items, which testifies to the importance of language contact in the domain of wordplay. Moreover, the survey confirms the manageability of the taxonomy proposed and provides first insights into the importance of specific patterns of wordplay. Although the contribution is dedicated to the analysis of specific speech events, the findings thus also shed light on lexical innovation and productive patterns of lexical expansion.

The complex interplay between creativity and productivity is also addressed in Georgette Dal's and Fiammetta Namer's contribution on *Playful nonce-formations in French: creativity and productivity*. While nonce-formations have been in the focus of current research on English and German, there is still a lack of studies on French. In order to fill this gap, the authors draw on corpus data available to identify recurring patterns of the emergence of nonce-formations and distinguish between different subtypes of nonce-formations according to structural features as well as different ways in which the nonce-formations are embedded in the utterance context. Adopting an approach which is based on the speakers' and hearers' perspective on nonce-formations, they argue that nonce-formations represent a micro-system of its own. According to the authors, studying this micro-system requires a complete methodological reversal, focusing on the forms themselves and adopting other criteria of identifying nonce-formations than the standard tools used in morphological studies. In this way, their contribution also provides important general insights into the possibilities and challenges of approaching productivity, combining structural analyses with pragmatic reflections on issues related to the use of the items in individual communication events.

Finally, the contributions by Esme Winter-Froemel and Claudine Moulin, *Ludicity in lexical innovation (I / II) – French / German,* are dedicated to ludicity in the lexicon, taking into account ludic usage and lexicalised items that can convey ludic effects. Lexicographic sources, including contemporary dictionaries as well as historical dictionaries of both languages, are explored to investigate the importance of ludicity across different types of innovations, languages, periods, and contexts of use. Complementing each other, the two contributions argue that ludicity should be recognised as a basic aspect motivating lexical innovation alongside other factors of lexical expansion. At the same time, the authors show that the current lexicographic practice of marking ludic items is still in part unsatisfactory, as labelling of pertinent items is still only unsystematic and not exhaustive.

Moreover, Esme Winter-Froemel's paper focuses on the question of how the lexicographic data can be reinterpreted from a usage-based perspective. These reflections point to basic methodological challenges that need to be dealt with when studying ludicity in the lexicon. In addition, she analyses how the speakers and hearers produce and perceive ludic items, taking into account structural, semantic and pragmatic patterns that emerge from the data provided by the *Petit Robert* 2016 as well as historical dictionaries from the ARTFL database. From the basic features of ludicity identified, markedness emerges as a common denominator that enables speakers and hearers to use the items as a joint action, where both interlocutors demonstrate their linguistic mastery and engage in a game of complicity. A diachronic survey based on the historical dictionaries of French, most importantly different editions of the *Dictionnaire de l'Académie française*, reveals basic patterns of evolution, including the emergence of ludic items from citational uses and from a reinterpretation of obsolete items, patterns of relative stability as well as wearout effects by which the lexical items are retained, but lose their ludic dimension. In this way, ludic items are identified as a highly dynamic domain of the lexicon.

These findings are equally confirmed by Claudine Moulin's paper. Before studying ludic innovations in German, the author presents general methodological reflections on the difficulties of tracing ludic items in lexicographic sources across the history of German, and argues that sources of metalinguistic reflection provide helpful additional information on the ways ludic items are used and perceived in different historical contexts. Particularly interesting in this context are the extensive reflections on wordplay and related phenomena during the Baroque period in linguistic societies such as the *Fruchtbringende Gesellschaft*, with the main actors Justus Georg Schottelius, Georg Philipp Harsdörffer, Philipp von Zesen, and Kaspar Stieler. Historical dictionaries (Kramer, Adelung) and contemporary reference works (most importantly *Duden online* 2017) are analysed with respect to the ways in which ludic items are described and to diachronic patterns that can be observed in the creation and subsequent evolution of ludic items. The author shows that nominal compounds and diminutives play a predominant role in this context. Finally, certain pathways for the evolution of ludic items from the 18th century to current use are identified (+ludic > -ludic [+neutral]; +dialectal > -dialectal > +obsolete; -archaic -ludic > + archaic -ludic > +archaic +ludic). These pathways tie in with some of the pathways identified for French and confirm the strong dynamics that can be observed for ludic items in the lexicon.

In addition to the phenomena studied in the papers summarised here, certain effects of ludicity also appear in other domains, e.g. in the formulaic patterns studied by Natalia Filatkina, which also exhibit playful modifications. It can thus be argued that ludicity represents an important dimension of lexical expansion. At the same time, various contributions highlight the transitions between ludic and non-ludic usage and the necessity to assume a continuum between creative usage and conventionalised items of the lexicon conveying certain stylistic or pragmatic effects. This can be seen as an additional justification for a deliberately broad understanding of wordplay and ludicity, which also takes into account what could be labelled "borderline cases" of wordplay and ludicity. Studying these "marginal" phenomena thus also allows us to gain general insights into the dynamics of the lexicon.

5 Acknowledgements

The workshop *Expanding the lexicon / Extensions du lexique / Erweiterungen des Lexikons* and the preparation of this volume would not have been possible without the financial support which we received from the University of Trier and the German National Research Foundation (Deutsche Forschungsgemeinschaft, DFG). Moreover, we received considerable practical help, and our thanks go to the staff at Trier University – Birgit Imade in particular and also Gabriele Jacobs – as well as to our student assistants Helin Baglar, Simon Eultgen, Samira Jung, Valérie Keppenne, Alistair Plum, Florian Prasch, Sarah Repplinger, Armin Rotzler, and Marie Winter – they all contributed to the success of the workshop with impressive dedication and efficiency.

We would also like to thank the reviewers who evaluated the papers submitted and gave constructive feedback for the contributions to this volume. Moreover, we would like to thank the members of the Editorial Board of the book series *The Dynamics of Wordplay* for accompanying the preparation and publication of this volume in their usual most constructive and efficient way.

We very much enjoyed the discussions at the workshop, which would not have been possible without the contributors' openness to multilingual and interdisciplinary exchange, bringing together different perspectives and approaches to processes of lexical expansion. This also became manifest during the preparation of this volume, as every contribution was commented on by several reviewers with different theoretical backgrounds in order to ensure the interdisciplinary accessibility of the papers.

In addition, we would like to thank our student assistants Sophia Fünfgeld and Constanze Tress for helping us with the French translations of the abstracts and the formatting of the volume, and Martina Bross and Angela Oakeshott for assisting us in the linguistic and stylistic revision of the papers.

Finally, as usual, the editorial team at De Gruyter's has accompanied the various stages of the preparation of this volume most sensitively, providing extremely efficient support at the various stages of its preparation. We would therefore also like to thank Gabrielle Cornefert, Antje-Kristin Mayr, and Ulrike Krauß.

6 References

Ágel, Vilmos, Andreas Gardt, Ulrike Haß-Zumkehr & Thorsten Roelcke (eds.). 2002. *Das Wort – Seine strukturelle und kulturelle Dimension. Festschrift für Oskar Reichmann zum 65. Geburtstag*. Berlin & Boston: De Gruyter.

Baayen, R. Harald, Petar Milin, Dusica Filipović Đurđević, Peter Hendrix & Marco Marelli. 2011. An amorphous model for morphological processing in visual comprehension based on naive discriminative learning. *Psychological Review* 118. 438–482.

Blank, Andreas. 1997. *Prinzipien des lexikalischen Bedeutungswandels am Beispiel der romanischen Sprachen* (Beihefte zur Zeitschrift für romanische Philologie 285). Berlin & Boston: De Gruyter.

Brinton, Laurel J. & Elizabeth Closs Traugott. 2005. *Lexicalization and language change* (Research surveys in linguistics). Cambridge: Cambridge University Press.

Dobrovol'skij, Dmitrij. 1988. *Phraseologie als Objekt der Universalienlinguistik* (Linguistische Studien). Leipzig: Verlag Enzyklopädie.

Full, Bettina & Michelle Lecolle. In press. *Jeux de mots et créativité. Langue(s), discours et littérature* (The Dynamics of Wordplay 4). Berlin & Boston: De Gruyter.

Haspelmath, Martin & Uri Tadmor (eds.) 2009. Loanwords in the world's languages. A comparative handbook. Berlin & Boston: De Gruyter.

Hay, Jennifer. 2003. *Causes and consequences of word structure*. New York & London: Routledge.

LegIT. Der volkssprachige Wortschatz der Leges barbarorum (http://legit.ahd-portal.germling.uni-bamberg.de/, accessed 07 September 2017).

Libben, Gary, Gonia Jarema & Chris Westbury (eds.). 2012. *Methodological and analytic frontiers in lexical research* (Benjamins Current Topics 47). Amsterdam & Philadelphia: John Benjamins.

List of English Bound Words, https://www.english-linguistics.de/codii/codiibw/en/list-complete.xhtml (accessed 05 September 2017).

Norde, Muriel. 2009. *Degrammaticalization*. Oxford: Oxford University Press.

Ostermann, Carolin. 2015. *Cognitive lexicography. A new approach to lexicography making use of cognitive semantics* (Lexicographica. Series Maior 149). Berlin & Boston: De Gruyter.

Pirelli, Vito, Ingo Plag & Wolfgang U. Dressler (eds.). In press. *Word knowledge and word usage: A cross-disciplinary guide to the mental lexicon*. Berlin & New York: De Gruyter.

Zeschel, Arne. 2012. *Incipient productivity. A construction-based approach to linguistic creativity* (Cognitive Linguistics Research 49). Berlin & Boston: De Gruyter.

I **Linguistic Innovation**

Natalia Filatkina
Expanding the lexicon through formulaic patterns

The emergence of formulaicity in language history and modern language use

Abstract: The article aims to study the role of formulaic patterns in the expansion of the lexicon. The notion of formulaic patterns is explained in section 1. It suggests that the formulaic character of human communication overarches single words, polylexical units, sentences and texts. As use of free word combination, formulaic patterns are a constitutive part of human interaction and, therefore, also of lexicon expansion. Section 2 provides a brief sketch of research findings (mostly based on data from standard German) concerning the interaction of formulaic patterns and word-formation products, which have up till now been considered the main tool of lexicon expansion. Here the argument is made that with regard to the new understanding of formulaic patterns, their role in the lexicon expansion process can be revised. Section 3 provides examples of the analysis of the emergence of formulaic patterns in language history and modern language use as an additional tool of lexicon expansion. In contrast to word formation, this has been subject to relatively little investigation so far. In section 3, the analysis is carried out against the background of language change theories. Such "driving forces" of language change as variation / creative modification, regularity / irregularity, codification / normatisation, the role of cultural and contextual / discourse traditions and frequency are applied to the emergence of formulaic patterns. As will be shown, the usual criteria with which we are familiar from existing language (change) theories do not apply to formulaic patterns in the same way as they do for example, to sound change, grammatical or even lexical change. The results of the study are summarized in the concluding section 4. *

---

* I would like to thank two anonymous reviewers, the editors of the volume, and Christian Pfeiffer for many insightful comments on an earlier version of this paper.

∂ Open Access. © 2018 Natalia Filatkina, published by De Gruyter. [CC BY-NC-ND] This work is licensed under the Creative Commons Attribution-NonCommercial-NoDerivatives 4.0 License.
https://doi.org/10.1515/9783110501933-017

1 The notion of formulaic patterns and their status in the lexicon

Speakers of any language generally enjoy considerable freedom in selecting lexical and grammatical items / tools of a given language in order to achieve their communicative goals most effectively. The success of a communicative act depends not only on the successful exploitation of a lexicon (good choice of individual words) and the correct application of grammatical rules, but also on an appropriate combination of words and rules with regard to the pragmatic and conventional aspects of a particular communicative situation. All forms of oral and written human interaction result from a large number of complex choices that Sinclair (1991: 109) described as "the open choice principle".

Nevertheless, Sinclair was also among the first scholars to empirically prove that although some word combinations, sentences and texts are the result of a complex choice based on linguistic freedom, others include "a large number of semi-preconstructed phrases that constitute single choices ("the idiom principle"), even though they might appear to be analysable into segments" (Sinclair 1991: 110). At the end of the 19th and the beginning of the 20th century, similar phenomena were recognized by Paul ([1880] 1995: 25), de Saussure ([1916] 1969: 177) and in Jespersen's concept of the "living grammar" (1968: 17–29). Corpus linguistics, usage-based approaches to language and cognitive sciences called attention to the fact that speakers' linguistic knowledge extends well beyond what can be described in terms of rules of compositional interpretation stated over combinations of single words. In the lexicon of a given language, preconstructed conventionalised items seem to be as productive as free word combinations.[1] This

---

[1] To my knowledge, much research remains to be undertaken as regards the quantification of this proportion in many languages. According to Sinclair, "the open choice principle" is even dominated by the "the idiom principle". For English and German, first figures have been provided in favour of this observation, cf. an overview in Filatkina (forthcoming: 44–48). With regard to a random sample of words starting with the letter *f* in a COBILD dictionary project, Stubbs (2001: 80–81) notes: "One phenomenon, by its sheer frequency, shows the strength of phraseological tendencies across the most frequent words in the language. Suppose we take all 47 wordforms which begin with *f* in the sample. In 41 cases, the following easily recognizable combinations account for the collocation of node and top collocate. [...] [NF: e.g.:] despite the *fact* that; *faded* away; *fair* enough [...]. In the remaining six cases, collocates further down the lists occur in recognizable phrases, such as: natural *fabrics*; animal *feed*, *filing* cabinet [...]. With many words, many more of the top 20 collocates are due to recognizable phrases. [...] I can think of no

idea has just started to find its way into linguistic analysis of modern languages. Depending on the research perspective, the terms *phraseme* or *Phraseologismus* (Burger 2015), *lexical priming* (Hoye 2005), *idiomatische Prägung* (Feilke 1994), *formelhafte Sprache* (Stein 1995), *formulaic language* (Wray 2002), *usuelle Wortverbindungen* (Steyer 2013), *Sprachgebrauchsmuster* (Bubenhofer 2009) or *construction* (Fillmore, Kay, and O'Connor 1988; Goldberg 1995) have been used in order to address this observation.[2]

For any linguistic theory that is based on a view of language as a system of signs *(Systemlinguistik)* or a conglomerate of dynamic grammar rules recruiting a static lexicon into sentence generation *(Generative Grammar)* such items pose a problem because they cannot be clearly attributed to one particular linguistic domain within this system, e.g. to the lexicon. Even though these items are highly lexicalised and conventionalised signs, their function tends rather to be one between grammar, lexicon, syntax and discourse or, as Wray (2008) puts it, they push the boundaries between these domains. Consider example (1a):

(1) a. *to brush one's teeth*
     b. **to wash one's teeth*
     c. **to clean one's teeth*
     d. French: *se laver les dents* lit. 'to wash the teeth'
        German: *sich die Zähne putzen* lit. 'to clean the teeth'
        Italian: *pulire i denti* lit. 'to clean the teeth'
        Russian: чистить зубы *(čistit' zuby)* lit. 'to clean teeth'

The pattern (1a) can be used without any semantic difficulties for addressing a daily morning and evening sanitary activity, but is rather idiosyncratic with regard to the verb constituent: Examples (1b) and (1c) are formed with regard to the (same) rules of English grammar as (1a) and would therefore have to be regarded as correct. Their meaning will also be understood, but it would be confusing for a native speaker of English to hear them being used to name the same sanitary activity as (1a). The meaning in (1b) and (1c) is different from the meaning of example (1a). The explanation for this confusion lies in the fact that the preferred structure of this word combination in English favours the verb *to brush* and does

---

reason why a sample of words beginning with *f* might be untypical of the whole 1,000-word sample. We therefore have initial evidence that all of the most frequent lexical words in the vocabulary have a strong tendency to occur in well-attested phraseological units."
2 For a complete overview and the substantial differences between these approaches cf. Filatkina (forthcoming).

not allow for its substitution without a change of meaning. The preferred structure becomes particularly apparent if compared to other languages (1d) where the preferred structures include a different verb constituent.[3]

Other examples are not only stable in terms of their formal structure. With regard to their form, they are quite regular as they are formed according to the rules of German grammar. However, with regard to their meaning, they are irregular as their holistic meaning is not predictable from the literal meaning of their individual constituents, i.e. it is idiomatic, cf. the modern German example (2a). The substitution of any single constituent even by family-resembling lexemes as in (2b) would destroy the idiomatic meaning.

(2) a. *Perlen vor die Säue werfen*
 lit. "to cast pearls before swine"
 'to offer something valuable to someone who does not know its value'
 b. **Diamanten vor die Schweine werfen*
 lit. "to cast diamonds before pigs"

In order to use (2a) according to the linguistic conventions of modern German, one needs to know that with the preferred structure of this idiom *Das ist / wäre Perlen vor die Säue (geworfen / zu werfen)* lit. "it is / would be pearls (cast) before swine" one can comment on any type of useless action that a person executes and another one does not appreciate, but only in colloquial speech. Within the framework of traditional approaches, formulaic patterns with semantic irregularity such as (2) were considered rare "exceptions" mostly satisfying stylistic or aesthetic, not essential communicative needs. Consequently, they were not a central focus of theoretical linguistic studies.

An extensive attempt to grasp the complex nature of such utterances was undertaken within the framework of phraseology. The complexity was already reflected in the defining criteria of phrasemes. According to Burger (2015), phrasemes are polylexical items that must consist of at least two constituents, have a more or less stable form in which they are frequently reproduced by speakers and can be idiomatic in meaning. Research traditionally focused mainly on one type of polylexical word combination, namely idioms such as in (2) or English *spill the beans* or *break the ice*, because they were considered to be at the centre of the phraseological system. But as usage-based approaches show, the formulaic

---

[3] Though language contact plays a role in lexicon expansion with the help of formulaic patterns, for reasons of space, it cannot be touched upon in this article. The methodological and theoretical importance of a contrastive perspective at such a core level as determining what is formulaic in a historical text is briefly pointed out in footnote 17.

character of human communication reaches far beyond the items that can meet the criteria of phrasemes. It extends beyond single word conventionalised structures such as routine formulae *and?, congratulations!, truly (speaking)*, adverbial / prepositional constructions like *nonwithstanding* or text markers such as Middle High German *firnim* 'remember, memorize, pay attention' on the one hand and formulaic text genres such as contracts, business correspondence, newsletters, recipes, announcements etc. on the other. The texts are formulaic because they can be produced and understood correctly only if they follow the conventionalised traditions of their formulaic matrix. Further examples of frequently used patterns that have largely been excluded from the scope of research into phraseology are listed in (3):

(3) a. German: *allen Grund (haben), allen X zum Trotz, allen Ernstes, auch immer, nicht zuletzt*
lit. "(to have) all the reason, in spite of all X, quite seriously, also always, not least" (Steyer 2013: 239–287)
b. English: *you take, a little bit, one X after another, NP or something* (Langacker 1987: 35–36)

Moreover, the criteria established for phrasemes on the basis of modern languages turn out to be static and therefore not applicable to the study of the diachronic dynamics of formulaic patterns. Polylexicality appears to be problematic from the outset because of the general lack of any (mandatory) spelling norms in the language history. As will be shown in section 3, stability is the exception rather than the rule in historical language use, frequency cannot be employed due to the fragmentary character of historical textual heritage (among other more substantial restraints), and idiomaticity often poses problems resulting from the temporal and cultural distance between today's researcher and the text under investigation.

This is why in Filatkina (forthcoming) typologically heterogeneous units (1–3), single words and whole texts are described as *formulaic patterns* in a wider sense. I will use this term in the following article although it is not yet well-established within linguistic research. Based on the analysis of an extensive data set from Old German, the following definition of formulaic patterns is proposed:

> Formelhaft sind im weitesten Sinn:
> a) Einwortausdrücke, typologisch heterogene Kombinationen aus mehreren Konstituenten bzw. ganze Sätze und / oder Texte,
> b) die holistisch verstanden werden müssen,
> c) sich auf unterschiedlichen (auch noch nicht abgeschlossenen) Stadien der formalen, semantischen und funktionalen Konventionalisierung befinden können,

aber eine stabile zugrundeliegende syntaktische und / oder kognitive Struktur aufweisen,
d) auf Gebrauchskonventionen einer Sprachgemeinschaft beruhen, deren etablierte kulturelle (auch kommunikative) Erfahrungen und Wissensbestände sie tradieren, und
e) die sich durch eine starke Funktionalisierung im Kommunikationsprozess bzw. im Textaufbau auszeichnen können (Filatkina forthcoming: 2–3 and 151–156).

[Formulaic patterns in the broadest sense are:
a) single words, typologically heterogeneous combinations of words, sentences and / or texts
b) that must be understood holistically,
c) can show varying degrees of conventionalisation (ranging from high to low) with regard to their form, meaning and functions, but have a stable underlying syntactic and / or cognitive structure,
d) are based on and reflect the cultural and communicative traditions of the society they are used in, and
e) which can be characterised by a considerable degree of functionalisation in the production and reception of a particular act of oral communication, written text (genre) or discourse (translation: NF)].

Formulaic patterns provide evidence for the necessity of understanding language as a continuum of different linguistic and extra-linguistic domains that have to be described in their entirety. Current usage-based linguistic theories systematically develop the notion of a language as an entirety. Within the paradigm of *Construction Grammar*, for example, formulaic patterns have played a central role from the very beginning (Langacker 1987; Fillmore, Kay, and O'Connor 1988; Goldberg 1995). In fact, it was the inability of other (particularly formal) language theories to describe "exceptions", i.e. formulaic utterances as in (1–3), that led to the establishment of Construction Grammar. One of its major principles is the assumption that a human language consists of signs representing conventionalised form / meaning correspondences that are not strictly predictable from the properties of their component parts or from other constructions. The term *construction* is generally applied to generalisations over typologically very different language instances, regular and irregular, ranging from morphemes and compounds (*door frame* or *lighthouse*) to idioms (*spill the beans*) and degree modifiers (*sort of / kind of*) to abstract constructions such as caused-motion, ditransitive or resultative constructions. They differ with regard to their cognitive representations (from concrete utterances on the language surface to abstract cognitive schemas) but all tend to have a more or less restricted structure that has a certain meaning as well as different lexical slots whose specification can vary depending on the context. All these extremely heterogeneous constructions stand on equal footing in building the basis for human communication and understanding processes, without being ascribed exclusively to core grammar or to the lexicon. The difference between the terms *formulaic patterns* and *constructions* is twofold: the former does not include morphemes but extends its scope to formulaic texts and discourse; the latter prototypically does not include texts (cf. a different approach in Östman 2005), but incorporates morphemes.

The usage-based perspective changes the status of formulaic patterns from peripheral (stylistic or aesthetic) "exceptions" to central means of human interaction. Consequently, it also sheds fresh light on their role as tools of lexicon expansion. Referring to features c), d) and e) from the above definition of formulaic patterns, this point will be made in section 3 and applied to the emergence of formulaic patterns in language history and modern language use.

2 Formulaic patterns, word formation, and lexicon expansion

With regard to their function as a means of lexicon expansion, polylexical word combinations were already studied in early research on phraseology. The term *formulaic pattern* was not used in this paradigm. As noted above, research traditionally focused mainly on idioms. Their contribution to the expansion of the lexicon was compared to that of word-formation products (Fleischer 1992; Barz 2005; Stein 2012). At least for German, there is a vast amount of literature dedicated to this topic.[4] But with a focus on idioms, phraseology was treated as the rarest and least significant path (Barz 2005: 1673; Barz 2007: 30; Stein 2012: 228). Taking into consideration the pivotal role of formulaic patterns in the communication process (cf. section 1), such a conclusion cannot be sustained. The "old" field is opening up for new discussions guided by the assumption that artificial boundaries between single words and formulaic patterns might be a misleading perspective.[5]

---

4 In addition to the above-mentioned work of W. Fleischer cf. Hartmann (1998), Barz (2005, 2007) and Stein (2012).
5 In its turn, research on word-formation has traditionally pursued the idea that the development of new words is formulaic in nature as it generally functions according to specific patterns, e.g. certain productive types of derivation, composition and conversion that may differ in their productivity from language to language. For new insights cf. Arndt-Lappe (2015).

In the traditional research, attention was drawn to the many similarities or "the fuzziness" of the boundaries between compounds and idioms. These were explained by a number of facts. In addition to the shared "naming" function, both tools of lexicon expansion can be products of idiomatisation, e.g. (4):

(4) German: *ein großes Tier*
   lit. "a big animal"
   'an important and influential person'
   German: *Grünschnabel*
   lit. "green beak"
   'a young, inexperienced but often cheeky person'

Consequently, compounds and idioms undergo similar lexicalisation processes with metaphorisation and metonymisation being the most productive. With regard to idiomatisation, compounds and idioms were proclaimed complex lexical signs whose meaning is not derivable from the meaning of their constituents.

It was also pointed out in previous research that sharing the referential function of naming means competition between phrasemes and word-formation products in some cases and complementarity in others (Barz 2007: 27–29). The cases of competition include the coexistence of a phraseme and a word-formation product that both use the same lexical constituents, e.g. idiom (4) *ein großes Tier* 'an important and influential person' versus compound *Großtier* 'a big animal'. Strictly speaking, such utterances do not compete as they differ semantically. Examples of semantically similar utterances can be found as well, cf. German *stark wie ein Bär sein* versus *bärenstark*, *Schwarzer Markt* versus *Schwarzmarkt*. However, they do not seem to be widespread. In cases of complementarity, a word-formation, e.g. *Grünschnabel* (4), does not have an immediate equivalent among phrasemes and vice versa. Due to the fact that the communicative needs of the speakers are met either by a word-formation product or by a phraseme, the simultaneous existence of both appears to be unnecessary. Again, the focus on idioms led previous research to the conclusion that polylexical utterances are particularly productive in negatively connoted target domains such as HUMAN MISBEHAVIOUR (deception), CHARACTER (stupidity), STATE (drunkenness) or INTERPERSONAL RELATIONS (reprehension) (Fleischer 1992, 1996, 1997). Although this seems to be true for idioms, a different understanding of formulaic patterns sheds fresh light on this research question as well. Recent studies that employ the concept of Construction Grammar demonstrate that in the process of name creation lexicalised phrases, e.g. A + N phrases *rote Karte* 'red card', may function as names just as A + N compounds (*Freikarte* 'free ticket') do. The choice between these two forms is governed by the principle of analogy: It is largely dependent on the availability of similar constructions in the mental lexicon of the speakers (Schlücker and Plag 2011: 1539).⁶ Lexicalised phrases and compounds are equally productive constructions that make distinctions between lexicon (compounds) and syntax (phrases) irrelevant for language users.

Another well investigated area of the "joint action" of phrasemes and word-formation as tools of lexicon expansion is the use of phrasemes as a basis for the creation of new words. In Germanic linguistics, the phenomenon has been addressed as *dephrasemische / dephraseologische Wortbildung* (Fleischer 1992; Stein 2012: 231–233). It is illustrated in (5a) by means of an example from modern German. Interestingly, even irregular constituents as in German *Fettnäpfchen* "little pot of fat" in (5b) take part in lexicon expansion. The constituent is irregular because it is obsolete and opaque with regard to the underlying cultural knowledge (an old custom in traditional farmhouses of placing a small pot to collect fat near the stove, cf. Röhrich 2004) for the majority of the native speakers of German. In dictionaries of modern German (duden.de; dwds.de), it is noted as bound to this idiom. However, according to the corpus analysis in Stumpf (2015a: 497), the actual boundness of the constituent to the idiom does not exceed 66%.⁷ This means that in the remaining 34% of all contexts studied in (Stumpf 2015a) *Fettnäpfchen* also occurs in isolation; its meaning, then, is the same as its correspondent meaning in the idiom. Thus, the possibility of re-motivating the compound synchronically without linking it to the underlying cultural knowledge opens up this irregular constituent for "free usage" in the lexicon.

(5) a. *Haare spalten > Haarspalterei*
   lit. "to split hairs" > "hair splitting"
   'to be excessively precise, pedantic'
 b. *bei jemandem ins Fettnäpfchen treten > Fettnäpfchen*
   lit. "to step in in a little pot of fat" > "little pot of fat"
   'to drop a clanger'

---

6 More precisely, Schlücker and Plag (2011: 1539) note: "The larger the number of lexicalized compounds with the same adjective or noun, the higher the probability of the subjects choosing a compound. The larger the number of lexicalized phrases with the same adjective or noun, the higher the probability of the subjects choosing a phrase."
7 For further examples see also the contribution by Stumpf 2017. The role of irregularity in the development of formulaic patterns will be studied in section 3.2.

3 The emergence of formulaic patterns and the principles of language change

An alternative approach to the comparison of word-formation products and formulaic patterns which can help to answer the question of the nature of lexicon expansion is the analysis of the dynamics of the emergence of formulaic patterns in language history and modern language use. In particular, studying diachronic processes of the emergence of what is considered formulaic in modern languages can provide the necessary insights. However, at the present stage of international research, for the majority of languages, the implementation of this approach faces methodological difficulties, a theoretical vacuum and most importantly the lack of empirical data (Filatkina 2012, 2013, forthcoming). Since its establishment in the 19th century, historical linguistics has focused strongly on the analysis of the "open choice principle" and on the description of various but single and isolated linguistic domains such as phonetics, grammar or the lexicon. The historical roots of the other basis of human communication, "the idiom principle", remain without exception a fundamental research question for all languages. The diachronic study of the emergence of formulaic patterns is often neglected entirely, even in publications claiming the status of reference works on language change (for a detailed overview cf. Filatkina, forthcoming). However, the research conducted for Old German (Filatkina 2009, 2012, forthcoming)[8] shows that analysing formulaic patterns can cast new light on the existing language (change) theories and the understanding of lexicon expansion. The main point is that the accepted criteria with which we are familiar from existing theories do not apply to formulaic patterns in the same way as, for example, to sound change, grammatical or even lexical change. Such criteria as variation / creative modification, regularity / irregularity, codification / normatisation as well as the role of cultural and textual / discourse traditions and frequency of use are the subject of discussion in the present section.

---

[8] One possible methodology to detect and extract novel formulaic patterns from modern oral and written texts is shown in Schreiber, Mahlow, and Juska-Bacher (2012).

3.1 Formulaic patterns and the role of variation / creative modification

In any natural language, even pre-constructed formulaic patterns are never absolutely stable and unchangeable, cf. feature c) in the definition of formulaic patterns in section 1. This point has already been made by classical research on phraseology and has led to a shift of paradigms (Burger 2015). Although in the collocation *to brush one's teeth* verb substitution is not allowed, as shown in (1), different types of grammatical and lexical variation do not violate conventional usage: *to brush my teeth, to brush and polish one's teeth, the teeth were brushed, to brush the front teeth*. One of the major achievements of phraseological research in recent years is the understanding that even highly idiomatic units, such as German *Perlen vor die Säue werfen* (2), are not as fixed as has previously been thought. On the other hand, as was pointed out in section 1, computer linguistics, cognitive sciences and most recently Construction Grammar suggest that free entities of a language are not so free but rather pre-constructed. Thus, in any modern language, variation does not contradict but faithfully accompanies formulaicity.

The diachronic investigation of formulaic patterns also supports the view that such patterns are less characterised by syntactic fixedness than has often been assumed. At the historical stages of the language, we see that fixedness or stability can only be attributed to a basic structure underlying a formulaic pattern. As a whole, this pattern possesses a certain meaning, pragmatic function and structure, but both the filling of its lexical slots and grammatical elements are only in the process of being formed. The patterns that might be considered formulaic in a certain language at the current point in time are always products of a process of change, which is inherently enabled by variation – the most natural form of existence of any actively used language and the driving force of any change.[9] As shown in Filatkina (2013), formulaic patterns undergo diachronic changes at all levels: structure, semantics, pragmatics, ways of syntactic contextualisation, distribution in texts, stylistic connotations, frequency of use, degree of familiarity, cultural image component and so on. The idiom *Perlen vor die Säue werfen* (2), for example, occurs 33 times in German texts from the 9th to 16th century (cf. the corpus description in Filatkina, forthcoming). Each time, however, it has a different structure and syntactic contextualization, and moreover it also reveals a semantic change from a very narrow meaning (which can only be found in reli-

---

9 For English, cf. Corrigan, Moravcsik, Ouali, and Wheatley (2009: XVI).

gious contexts) to a much broader one. As regards the pragmatic level, the function of the idiom changes from 'didactic' to 'commentarial', in terms of the stylistic connotation the noble expression of Biblical origin turns into a rather colloquial one. The restriction to religious texts becomes obsolete from the 15th century onwards.

Historical formulaic patterns show a high degree of variation and allow for the conclusion that a pattern becomes formulaic through a complex process of change that takes place in different linguistic domains. It has to be noted though that the changes in one domain (e.g. meaning) do not always cause *immediate* changes in another domain (e.g. form); more common are cases of delayed feature-by-feature change and form / meaning / function-mismatch.[10] This means that only a detailed diachronic analysis of variation processes in all linguistic subsystems and of every single finding can lead to empirically valid generalisations about the paths of formulaicity.

However, the assumption that formulaic patterns emerge as the result of a decline in variation should be reconsidered. Though the pivotal role of the decline in variation has been most clearly demonstrated for orthographical (Kohrt 1998), phonetic (Kohrt 1998) and morphological (Werner 1998) norms, it does not appear to be relevant to formulaic patterns. On the contrary, variation can be an indication of the completion of a conventionalisation process and the establishment of a new utterance: Only after a pattern has reached a high degree of fixedness and conventionalisation, can it become subject to variation and / or modification by language speakers and still remain recognisable and understandable for them. In this sense, variation and to an extent modification are secondary paths of lexicon expansion (cf. example 6a below).

Synchronic mechanisms of variation and / or modification have been studied in detail within the framework of phraseology, particularly using data from standard English(es), German, Russian, French, Italian and Spanish.[11] Despite the numerous studies, no theoretically liable distinction between variation and modification has been proposed so far. The former is generally understood as a regular formal change of a pattern licensed by the norms of a given language, cf. the examples at the beginning of section 3.1. As it has to occur frequently, the varied structure of a pattern might even form a new lexicon entry. In contrast, modification is defined as an irregular, intentional and conscious intervention of

---

10 Cf. Traugott (2014: 8–10) for the diachronic path of the *be going to*-construction.
11 For reasons of space, only a small selection of scholarly work can be given here: Sabban (1998); Langlotz (2006); Dobrovol'skij and Piirainen (2009); Dobrovol'skij (2013), and Burger (2015).

a speaker into the form and / or meaning of a pattern directed at the violation of the existing norms.[12] This intervention is understood as occasional; therefore, it allows for unexpected semantic-pragmatic effects on the part of the hearer and is used creatively as a useful tool for wordplay, e.g. in mass media headlines, fiction or commercials. Due to their occasional character, modifications have been excluded from the pool of means of lexicon expansion. However, Dobrovol'skij and Piirainen (2009: 102–114) show that this is not justified: Playful modifications of existing idioms (6a) or the usage of playful image components for the creation of novel idioms (6b) may become conventionalised and enter the lexicon (see also the contributions by Moulin and Winter-Froemel, this volume).

(6) a. *fix und foxi* modified from *fix und fertig*
  lit. "fixed and foxi" / "fixed and done"
  'to be extremely tired and exhausted'
 b. *blau sein wie ein Veilchen*
  lit. "to be blue as a violet"
  'to be completely drunk'

Though such cases seem to be rather rare, at least in standard German, they resort to a number of various techniques (violation of grammar rules, semantic, syntactic or lexical incompatibility, deconstruction of image consistency through blending, to name just a few) and are (partially) registered in German dictionaries. Dobrovol'skij and Piirainen (2009: 102–114) address such examples with the term *usualisiertes Wortspiel mit Phrasemen* (conventional wordplay with phrasemes). Unfortunately, however, lesser-used languages, oral communication and dialects (Piirainen 1995) continue to be underrepresented in or completely excluded from this research. As they have not undergone normatisation, their contribution to the theoretical distinction between variation and modification appears to be particularly promising. The same holds true for the historical stages of any modern language (cf. example 8 below).

To my knowledge, such cases have not yet been considered within the framework of Construction Grammar. According to this approach, creativity in language arises exclusively from the *free* combination of constructions, subject to there being no conflicts entailed in that combination (Goldberg 2003: 221–222). Variation, on the other hand, is an intrinsic feature of constructions. It is governed by the principles of inheritance, analogy and family resemblance, meaning semantic or phonological similarity between novel and existing forms, relational

---

[12] In my view, this definition comes close to what is understood as wordplay in respective studies (Winter-Froemel 2016).

knowledge and structural alignment. The conflict between these principles should allow for creativity, but this point has yet to be made clear. Bybee (2010: 58) uses the above-mentioned principles for a fine-grained analysis of the variation potential of the construction *it drives me $X_{adj.}$*, but does not discuss a novel utterance *it drives me happy* as a possible creative modification (a construct?) in certain contexts. In her eyes, it is just unlikely because – due to analogy and the family resemblance principle – the *drives*-construction goes with adjectives and phrases indicating madness or insanity. Much research has still to be undertaken into the micro-steps of variation and particularly creative modifications in order to satisfy the far-reaching claim of Construction Grammar as it is formulated in Goldberg (2003: 219):

> Constructionist approaches aim to account for the full range of facts about language, without assuming that a particular subset of the data is part of a privileged 'core'. Researchers in this field argue that unusual constructions shed light on more general issues, and can illuminate what is required for a complete account of language.

3.2 Formulaic patterns and the role of regularity / irregularity

The explanation of the development of formulaic patterns and their variation simply as a case of regularity and analogy would be an oversimplification of the actual state of affairs. Norm conflicts and preservation of lexical and / or grammatical constituents that have to be regarded as obsolete from the point of view of free language use are widespread phenomena in the formation of formulaic patterns. A corpus-based attempt to prove the high degree of irregularity (in terms of norm conflicts and / or preservation of obsolete lexical / grammatical constituents) in the emergence of formulaic patterns is undertaken in Stumpf (2015a, 2015b). In Stumpf (2015b), the novel construction of modern German (7) is analysed:

(7) *können + NP($X_{subject}\ Y_{objectAcc}$)*
 'X is capable of doing / achieving / implementing Y'
 e.g. *Kann Jogi Weltmeister?*
 lit. "Can Jogi [become] world champion?"
 'Can the German national football team under the coach Joachim Löw (Jogi) win the title of world champion?'
 Ägypten kann Demokratie.
 lit. "Egypt can [have / introduce / live in] democracy"
 (Stumpf 2015b)

The formulaic pattern (7) does not occur in this form and meaning before the 21st century and is viewed critically by some native speakers as bad German. This is due to the fact that the conventionalisation process is marked by the violation of two grammatical rules (Stumpf 2015b: 16): a) *können* is an auxiliary verb and prototypically requires a full verb at the end of the construction and b) an (indefinite) article is a compulsory determiner of an object in the accusative in prototypical referential contexts. Neither of these rules is followed in (7). In spite of this, the formulaic pattern currently serves as a basis for numerous occurrences predominantly in situations of oral communicative immediacy where it can be regarded as stylistically neutral. As the corpus data presented in Stumpf (2015b: 10–11) indicates, the pattern is also used in headlines and in the body of mass media articles as an expressive colloquial marker enabling the speakers to convey a complex meaning (cf. the paraphrase in 7) with the help of a rather short form. This is why the pattern differs from similar constructions, e.g. *Olivia kann Mathematik* "Olivia can maths" 'Olivia is good at maths' or *Jeder kann Gitarre [spielen]* "anyone can [play] the guitar" 'anyone knows how to play the guitar' with a much narrower meaning and neutral stylistic connotations. The colloquial expressive connotation prevents the pattern from entering all text genres: At present, it cannot be found in formal fiction, for instance, or academic language. The occupation of the lexical slot *Y* seems to be barely determined at all semantically and / or by family resemblance. Instead, it is occupied by heterogeneous nouns from different semantic fields (profession, title, product, food, occupation, venture, (music) instrument, country etc.) that can be reinterpreted within the pattern (product > production of the product; instrument > ability to play it). *X* cannot be a passive non-animate creature, but any active agent (an individual, a group of individuals, a city, a party, a country, a continent etc.) is licensed by the construction. The holistic meaning of the pattern can be decoded only if the whole context of use is accounted for and included in the interpretation. The uncertainty of native speakers with regard to the "correctness" of the pattern should be interpreted as an indicator of its novel character. The expressiveness achieved by an irregular form leads to (domain specific) frequency, not vice versa.[13]

---

[13] The role of the cultural context, discourse traditions and frequency is studied in more detail in section 3.4.

3.3 Formulaic patterns and the role of codification / normatisation

The decline of variation in the process of arising phonetic, morphological and orthographical conventions in language use has often been attributed to the normative influence of dictionaries and grammar books. This is where the decline predominantly took place as the lack of variation was treated as a necessary characteristic of language norms in historical times. With regard to formulaic patterns, this does not hold true as dictionaries, historical collections of proverbs and idioms as well as chapters dedicated to formulaic patterns in early grammar treaties were and have been compiled with goals rather different from a prescriptive establishment of norms (Hundt 2000; Filatkina 2016; Moulin 2016). Therefore, older texts and collections differ substantially with regard to the formulaic patterns they include. Consider example (8):

(8) a. modern German: *etwas auf dem Kerbholz haben*
     lit. "to have something on a tally"
     'to have done something wrong, to have committed a criminal action'
  b. Early New High German (16th century): *an ain kerbholtz reden*
     lit. "to speak to a tally"
     '1. to lie in order to make financial debts; 2. to make financial debts'
  c. *hab oft an ain kerb geredt*
     lit. "[I] have often spoken to a tally"
  d. *der vil verhaißt an ain kerbholtz*
     lit. "[somebody] who promises a lot to a tally"
  e. *ich schneid oft an ain kerbholtz an*
     lit. "I often make a cut into a tally"
  f. *(er) schrieb mirs an die kerb*
     lit. "(he) wrote it in the tallies"
  g. *so an den kerben zaichnet was*
     lit. "as it was written on the tallies"
  h. *der mich auch an das kerbholtz redt*
     lit. "[somebody] who puts me on the tally as well by speaking"
  i. *kerbredner werden*
     lit. "to become a tally speaker"

In the corpus studied in Filatkina (forthcoming), before 1600, the idiom (8a), which is used in modern German despite the obsolete and therefore irregular constituent *Kerbholz* "tally", occurs in only one text, namely in the "Schelmenzunfft" by Thomas Murner. There, it has a different form and meaning (8b) strongly rooted in the underlying image component – an ancient system of precise counting (Wander [1987] 2001, 2: 1243–1244; Röhrich 2004, 3: 831). Until the 17th century, the system was used in bookkeeping and debt registration when landlords carved debts in a tally, called *Kerbholtz* in German. In only 38 lines of the chapter, the pattern appears eight times, each time with the same meaning but in a different form (8b–i): in the past tense (8c), with different verb constituents (8d–g), in the passive (8g), the noun compound can be reduced to *kerb* (8f) and put into the plural (8g). The whole idiom can be nominalized and serves as a basis for a new compound (8i). In the period between the 15th and 18th centuries, not a single contemporary dictionary of Old German contains this idiom. The first entries can be found only 300 years after the oldest known printing of the "Schelmenzunfft" in 19th century collections of proverbs (Eiselein 1840; Körte [1837] 1974). In striking contrast, they list the idiom with verbal constituents that match neither the present-day nor the historical usage in Murner's text, cf. the examples in (9):

(9) a. *aufs kerbholz losleben*
 lit. "to live to the tally"
 b. *aufs kerbholtz lossündigen*
 lit. "to sin to the tally"
 c. *auf dem kerbholtz stehen*
 lit. "to stand on the tally"
 d. *aufs kerbholtz borgen*
 lit. "to borrow on the tally"
 e. *aufs kerbholtz nehmen*
 lit. "to take on the tally"
 f. *einem etwas aufs Kerbholtz schneiden*
 lit. "to notch something onto someone's tally"
 g. *einem etwas aufs Kerbholtz schreiben*
 lit. "to write something on someone's tally"

Nowadays, one cannot judge in what sense these patterns served as earlier variants (or modifications?) of the idiom (8b) as historical texts known to date provide no evidence of their existence.

3.4 The role of culture, text / discourse traditions, and frequency

The analysis of processes of lexicon expansion by means of the emerging formulaic patterns will be insufficient if the major role of culture is disregarded. Particularly idioms (*to cast pearls before swine*, cf. example (2)) and proverbs (*clothes make the man*) are strongly embedded in culture as they preserve the different types of knowledge of past times in a modern language. This idea corresponds to feature d) in the definition of formulaic patterns in section 1. Different types of knowledge may be culture-specific and are almost always culture-based. The most extensive research dedicated to the classification of cultural phenomena in idioms of modern language varieties was conducted within the project "Widespread Idioms in Europe and Beyond (WI)" (Piirainen 2012, 2016). It had access to 78 modern standard and lesser-used languages from all language families as well as dialects and identified 470 idioms as similar and widely known. A similarly large-scale project devoted to historical languages of the mediaeval and early modern world does not currently exist and would not be possible as scholarly research is completely lacking in such data (cf. an overview in Filatkina, forthcoming).

Two results of the WI-project are of particular importance. Firstly, earlier ideas that the same genetic affiliation of two or more languages could explain a similarity on the level of idioms have been disproven. These ideas disregard the fact that the origin of the majority of idioms does not go back to a common "protolanguage" of an early past. As becomes obvious, distribution crosses genetic boundaries. Secondly, the concept of a "common (European) cultural heritage", which was also often used to explain similarities in earlier works, requires more detailed investigation. Until now, cultural traditions from Classical Antiquity, Christianity (the Bible), the Renaissance, Humanism, and the Enlightenment are included in this term. Though the role of these domains remains central, other cultural domains such as folk narratives, jests and legends appear to be significant as well. They have produced numerous widespread idioms (*to fight like cat and dog, to shed crocodile tears*) and have not yet been listed under the concept of "common (European) cultural heritage". Today's convergence of idioms is the product of an intense exchange of thoughts among educated language users that could only have been based on writing and reading books in historical times. This shared knowledge of widely disseminated texts led to and supported the establishment of cultural memory and many formulaic patterns such as idioms and proverbs. The WI-project describes this phenomenon using the term *intertextuality* and calls for its precise validation in individual languages (Dobrovol'skij and Piirainen 2005; Piirainen 2012: 520).

Cognitive linguistics acknowledges cultural models of human experience, social interaction and embodied experience as important factors in the cognitive categorisation of the world. However, research has tended to repeatedly emphasise the embodied experience. What cognitive research has been lacking to date is a diachronic perspective on the dynamics of the cultural components used in formulaic patterns as, to my knowledge, there are no monograph-length historical studies.[14] Within the framework of the Cognitive Theory of Conventional Figurative Language (Dobrovol'skij and Piirainen 2005), an elaborate classification of cultural domains as they are manifest in modern languages was developed. At present, the question whether formulaic patterns in historical texts are founded on the same source domains (texts, knowledge types) remains unanswered. There is also little knowledge available about the historical target domains that are predominantly verbalised with the help of formulaic patterns. Furthermore, the question still remains as to the impact of historical text / discourse traditions (Coseriu 1988; Blank 1997; Koch 1997) on the emergence of formulaic patterns. This impact can be observed in the development not only of idioms and proverbs but of any type of formulaic patterns. It reduces the role of another driving force of any language change, namely frequency of use. Theories of language change (morphological, typological, lexical and semantic) stress the pivotal role of frequency in any process of emergence of novel items. It is a well-known fact that in the process of lexicon expansion, for example, a sporadic innovation only has a chance to enter into the lexicon if it is supported by a sufficient number of speakers, i.e. if the item is frequently used by them in a new form and / or meaning and function. It is clear that the emergence of formulaic patterns involves frequency. However, another fact has to be taken into account as well: Formulaic patterns are constitutive elements of human communication only with regard to their type frequency; by contrast, their token frequency is generally low. In other words: a certain degree of formulaicity can be attested to absolutely any written text or oral communicative act because any of these sources contain different types of formulaic patterns (*type frequency*). The problem is that each type might occur only once (*token frequency*).

What seems to be a crucial factor for lexicon expansion through formulaic patterns is not so much just the frequent use of a pattern but its frequent use in a specific communication situation or in a specific (cultural) text / discourse tradition. This observation corresponds to the feature e) in the definition of formulaic patterns in section 1. The link between a formulaic pattern and a context ensures that speakers resort to appropriate (even the most irregular!) units in relevant situations. Evidence for such links has already been provided from different research perspectives and various modern languages, most recently within the fine-grained concept of construction discourse and the notion of discourse patterns in Östman (2005, 2015). Feilke (1994: 226) notes that the German formulaic

---

14 One of the first studies of this kind is Geeraerts and Grondelaers (1995).

pattern (10a) is determined by and strongly bound to a formal festive act of celebrating something joyful and cannot be used in a formal funeral ceremony. The pattern is a substantial part of both linguistic knowledge of German native speakers and their general world knowledge about festive acts. The non-conventional variants (10b) and (10c) will not evoke the same knowledge structures as they are – at least at present – neither lexicon entries nor part of the world knowledge.

(10) a. *Ich erhebe mein Glas* [...]
       lit. "I raise my glass to X"
   b. **Wir erheben unsere Sektgläser*
       lit. "we raise our champagne glasses"
   c. **Ich erhebe meinen Krug*
       lit. "I raise my jar / jug / pitcher / mug"
       (Feilke 1994: 226)

Similar ideas based on English data are expressed by Wray (2009: 36) and Wray and Perkins (2000: 7):

> However, it may be premature to judge frequency as a *defining* feature of formulaicity. It has yet to be established that commonness of occurrence is more than a circumstantial associate. There are certainly many formulaic sequences whose culturally-based familiarity belies their comparative rarity in real text (e.g. *That's another fine mess you've gotten me into*; *Time for bed, said Zebedee*; *Here's one I made earlier*) (Wray 2009: 36).[15]

Though frequency is discussed here with regard to its role as a defining feature of formulaic patterns in modern English, the data from Old German in Filatkina (forthcoming) allows for a similar observation in the case of emerging formulaic patterns in language history.

Frequency seems to be a less important factor even in the most recent instances of the development of formulaic patterns. Before 2015, example (11a) could have been considered a completely unmarked routine formulation formed in accordance with the rules of German grammar. But on 31 August 2015, it was used by Chancellor Angela Merkel in her speech during the press conference for the German mass media (*Bundespressekonferenz*) in order to confirm her refugee policy and to appeal to the German population to support the integration of refugees. The pattern is the concluding part of a wider context as quoted in (11b).

---

[15] Hoffmann (2004) questions the role of frequency in the grammaticalisation of complex prepositions such as *by dint of, in conformity with* etc. by drawing a distinction between conceptual and absolute frequency and taking into account the role of analogy.

(11) a. *Wir schaffen das!*
 lit. "We will manage it!"
 b. *Deutschland ist ein starkes Land. Das Motiv, mit dem wir an diese Dinge herangehen, muss sein: Wir haben so vieles geschafft – wir schaffen das!*
 "Germany is a strong country. The motto with which we approach these things has to be: We have managed to do so much – we will manage this!"

Since then, the chancellor has repeated this statement only twice, at the CDU party congress on December 14th 2015 and during her New Year's address to the nation. But the pattern has been more widely cited in the mass media, has initiated a controversial debate about refugee policy and advanced to a key slogan of a new culture of welcome in Germany. It is deeply embedded in the refugee discourse and changes its pragmatic connotation because of this functional strength. As Kreuz and Stumpf (forthcoming) show, most recently the pattern is also used in comics, caricatures and memes that are no longer restricted to the refugee discourse and has become variable with regard to its form, meaning and function. However, the crucial factor in the emergence of this formulaic pattern is not the frequency of use as such but its origin in the refugee discourse and the acute and controversially discussed importance of this discourse for German political and everyday life.[16]

For historical times, frequency presents even more far-reaching (methodological) consequences. When studying the historical dynamics of lexicon expansion through formulaic patterns, not only the low token-frequency of single patterns has to be accounted for.[17] The sporadic, fragmentary and often incomplete records of written texts add to the problem. As was mentioned with regard to the German example (2) *Perlen vor die Säue werfen*, it occurs in historical texts only 33 times, showing a high degree of variation at all levels. But it also contains the noun constituent *Säue* that is completely stable even in modern German though less frequent in the free, non-formulaic usage. Text corpora provide hardly any evidence for its substitution by the more frequent lexeme *Schweine*. The use of the constituent *Säue* in place of *Schweine* must be attested to the use of precisely this constituent by Martin Luther in his translation of the Bible. In my eyes, the

---

16 In my view, the emerging English patterns *Make America great again, fake news* or the older *war on terror* are undergoing similar discourse changes.
17 This is why the decision as to the formulaic character of a certain unit often cannot be made on the basis of one language alone. The cross-linguistic approach becomes an essential method of historical analysis, determining even the decision-making at the core level of definitions. In other words, the existence of a certain formulaic pattern in different historical languages can be considered additional evidence for its formulaic character in the language under investigation (Filatkina, Münch, and Kleine-Engel 2012).

strong involvement with cultural traditions also has to be taken into account in the emergence of the non-frequent formulaic patterns (5b) *bei jemandem ins Fettnäpfchen treten* "to step in a little dish of fat" and (8) *etwas auf dem Kerbholz haben* "to have something on a tally". Despite not being frequent, they are highly lexicalised, opaque with regard to the underlying cultural knowledge and contain the irregular (i.e. obsolete) constituents *Fettnäpfchen* and *Kerbholz*. Therefore, in contrast to morphological or lexical irregularity that can arise through frequent use (e.g. suppletive verb forms), frequency does not necessarily explain formulaic irregularity as (token-wise) formulaic patterns are seldom extremely frequent units.

4 Conclusion

Bearing in mind the aspects analysed, we can conclude that formulaic patterns have to be considered important tools of lexicon expansion both in language history and in present times. As they share a naming function (among others) with, for instance, word-formations, they can contribute to this research field in the same way as the latter do. Formulaic patterns are by no means just a storage area waiting to be recruited into sentence generation but a part of non-static knowledge. Being formulaic does not imply lack of variation or change. From a diachronic point of view, any formulaic pattern undergoes complex variation processes not only with regard to form and meaning but also with regard to all other aspects of pattern use. From a synchronic point of view, variation can even serve as an indicator of a high degree of conventionalisation when established patterns are opened up for variation and (playful) modification by language speakers. Since utterances that can be considered formulaic are extremely heterogeneous in nature, explanations pointing out single factors of their emergence appear to be inconsistent. The emergence of formulaic patterns can best be understood as a process of integration of sometimes controversial aspects, among which frequency and regularity seem to be important accompanying factors but not always driving forces. Irregular, idiosyncratic paths based on conflicts and violation of norms shape the development of formulaicity as well if they are sufficiently supported by the speakers' / hearers' communicative needs and / or embedded into discourse and cultural traditions. Formulaic patterns therefore provide ample proof of the need for comprehensive theories treating language as an entire adaptive system built upon integration and interaction of cognition, culture and discourse.

5 References

Arndt-Lappe, Sabine. 2015. Word-formation and analogy. In Peter O. Müller, Ingeborg Ohnheiser, Susan Olsen & Franz Rainer (eds.), *Word-formation. An international handbook of the languages of Europe* (Handbooks of Linguistics and Communication Science 40.2), 822–841. Berlin & Boston: De Gruyter.

Barz, Irmhild. 2005. Die Wortbildung als Möglichkeit der Wortschatzerweiterung. In D. Alan Cruse, Franz Hundsnurscher, Michael Job & Peter Rolf Lutzeier (eds.), *Lexikologie. Ein internationales Handbuch zur Natur und Struktur von Wörtern und Wortschätzen / Lexicology. An international handbook on the nature and structure of words and vocabularies* (Handbooks of Linguistics and Communication Science 21.2), 1664–1676. Berlin & Boston: De Gruyter.

Barz, Irmhild. 2007. Wortbildung und Phraseologie. In Harald Burger, Dmitrij Dobrovol'skij, Peter Kühn & Neal R. Norrick (eds.), *Phraseologie. Ein internationales Handbuch der zeitgenössischen Forschung / Phraseology. An international handbook of contemporary research* (Handbooks of Linguistics and Communication Science 28.1), 27–36. Berlin & Boston: De Gruyter.

Blank, Andreas. 1997. *Prinzipien des lexikalischen Wandels am Beispiel der romanischen Sprachen* (Beihefte zur Zeitschrift für romanische Philologie 285). Tübingen: Niemeyer.

Bubenhofer, Noah. 2009. *Sprachgebrauchsmuster. Korpuslinguistik als Methode der Diskurs- und Kulturanalyse* (Sprache und Wissen 4). Berlin & New York: De Gruyter.

Burger, Harald. ^{5}2015. *Phraseologie. Eine Einführung am Beispiel des Deutschen* (Grundlagen der Germanistik 36). Berlin: Erich Schmidt.

Bybee, Joan. 2010. *Language, usage and cognition*. Cambridge: Cambridge University Press.

Corrigan, Roberta, Edith A. Moravcsik, Hamid Ouali & Kathleen M. Wheatley. 2009. Introduction. Approaches to the study of formulae. In Roberta Corrigan, Edith A. Moravcsik, Hamid Ouali & Kathleen M. Wheatley (eds.), *Formulaic language* (Typological Studies in Language 82), vol. 1 (Distribution and historical change), xi–xxiv. Amsterdam & Philadelphia: Benjamins.

Coseriu, Eugenio. 1988. Die Ebenen des sprachlichen Wissens. Der Ort des "Korrekten" in der Bewertungsskala des Gesprochenen. In Jörn Albrecht, Jens Lüdtke & Harald Thun (eds.), *Energeia und Ergon. Sprachliche Variation – Sprachgeschichte – Sprachtypologie. Studia in honorem Eugenio Coseriu* (Tübinger Beiträge zur Linguistik 300), vol. 1, 327–364. Tübingen: Niemeyer.

Dobrovol'skij, Dmitrij. 2013. *Besedy o nemezkom slove / Studien zur deutschen Lexik* (Studia philologica). Moskva: Yazyki slavjanskoj kul'tury.

Dobrvol'skij, Dmitrij & Elisabeth Piirainen. 2005. *Figurative language: Cross-cultural and cross-linguistic perspectives* (Current research in the semantics / pragmatics interface 13). Amsterdam & Oxford: Elsevier.

Dobrovol'skij, Dmitrij & Elisabeth Piirainen. 2009. *Zur Theorie der Phraseologie. Kognitive und kulturelle Aspekte* (Stauffenburg Linguistik 49). Tübingen: Stauffenburg.

Eiselein, Joseph. 1840. *Die Sprichwörter und Sinnreden des deutschen Volkes in alter und neuer Zeit*. Freiburg: Friedrich Wagnerische Buchhandlung.

Feilke, Helmuth. 1994. *Common sense-Kompetenz. Überlegungen zu einer Theorie "sympathischen" und "natürlichen" Meinens und Verstehens*. Frankfurt a.M.: Suhrkamp.

Filatkina, Natalia. 2009. Historical phraseology of German: Regional and global. In Jarmo Korhonen, Wolfgang Mieder, Elisabeth Piirainen & Rosa Piñel (eds.), *Phraseologie global - areal - regional. Akten der Konferenz Europhras 2008 vom 13.-16.8.2008 in Helsinki*, 143–151. Tübingen: Niemeyer.
Filatkina, Natalia. 2012. "Wan wer beschreibt der welte stat / der muoß wol sagen wie es gat". Manifestation, functions and dynamics of formulaic patterns in Thomas Murner's "Schelmenzunft" revisited. In Natalia Filatkina, Ane Kleine-Engel, Marcel Dräger & Harald Burger (eds.), *Aspekte der historischen Phraseologie und Phraseographie* (Germanistische Bibliothek 46), 21–44. Heidelberg: Universitätsverlag Winter.
Filatkina, Natalia. 2013. Wandel im Bereich der historischen formelhaften Sprache und seine Reflexe im Neuhochdeutschen: Eine neue Perspektive für moderne Sprachwandeltheorien. In Petra M. Vogel (ed.), *Sprachwandel im Neuhochdeutschen* (Jahrbuch für germanistische Sprachgeschichte 4), 34–51. Berlin & New York: De Gruyter.
Filatkina, Natalia. 2016. Wie fest sind feste Strukturen? Beobachtungen zu Varianz in (historischen) Wörterbüchern und Texten. In Luise Borek & Andrea Rapp (eds.), *Vielfalt und Varianz interdisziplinär: Wörter und Strukturen*, 7–27. Mannheim: Institut für deutsche Sprache. http://pub.ids-mannheim.de/laufend/opal/pdf/opal2016-2.pdf (accessed 21 March 2017).
Filatkina, Natalia. Forthcoming. *Historische formelhafte Sprache: Theoretische Grundlagen und methodische Herausforderungen*. Trier: Trier University habilitation.
Filatkina, Natalia, Birgit U. Münch & Ane Kleine-Engel. 2012. Anstelle einer Einleitung: "Große Fische fressen die Kleinen". Zur Notwendigkeit der interdisziplinären Untersuchung der historischen Formelhaftigkeit. In Natalia Filatkina, Birgit U. Münch & Ane Kleine-Engel (eds.), *Formelhaftigkeit in Text und Bild* (Trierer Beiträge zu den historischen Kulturwissenschaften 2), 1–12. Wiesbaden: Ludwig Reichert.
Fillmore, Charles J., Paul Kay & Mary Catherine O'Connor. 1988. Regularity and idiomaticity in grammatical constructions. The case of *let alone*. *Language* 64. 501–538.
Fleischer, Wolfgang. 1992. Konvergenz und Divergenz von Wortbildung und Phraseologie. In Jarmo Korhonen (ed.), *Phraseologie und Wortbildung – Aspekte der Lexikonerweiterung* (Linguistische Arbeiten), 53–65. Tübingen: Niemeyer.
Fleischer, Wolfgang. 1996. Zum Verhältnis von Wortbildung und Phraseologie im Deutschen. In Jarmo Korhonen (ed.), *Studien zur Phraseologie des Deutschen und des Finnischen II* (Studien zur Phraseologie und Parömiologie), 333–343. Bochum: Brockmeyer.
Fleischer, Wolfgang. 1997. Das Zusammenwirken von Wortbildung und Phraseologisierung in der Entwicklung des Wortschatzes. In Rainer Wimmer & Franz Josef Berens (eds.), *Wortbildung und Phraseologie* (Studien zur deutschen Sprache. Forschungen des Instituts für deutsche Sprache), 9–24. Tübingen: Narr.
Geeraerts, Dirk & Stefan Grondelaers. 1995. Looking back at anger: Cultural traditions and metaphorical patterns. In John Taylor & Robert E. MacLaury (eds.), *Language and the cognitive construal of the world* (Trends in Linguistics. Studies and Monographs 82), 153–180. Berlin & New York: De Gruyter.
Goldberg, Adele E. 1995. *Constructions. A construction grammar approach to argument structure*. Chicago: University of Chicago Press.
Goldberg, Adele E. 2003. Constructions: A new theoretical approach to language. *Trends in Cognitive Sciences* 7(5). 219–224.
Hartmann, Dirk. 1998. Lexikalische Felder als Untersuchungsrahmen für Phraseologismen und deren Leistungen für den Wortschatz. In Dietrich Hartmann (ed.), *"Das geht auf keine*

Kuhhaut". Arbeitsfelder der Phraseologie (Studien zur Phraseologie und Parömiologie), 127–147. Bochum: Brockmeyer.
Hoey, Michael. 2005. *Lexical priming. A new theory of words and language.* London & New York: Routledge.
Hoffmann, Sebastian. 2004. Are low-frequency complex prepositions grammaticalized? On the limits of corpus data – and the importance of intuition. In Hans Lindquist & Christian Mair (eds.), *Corpus approaches to grammaticalization in English* (Studies in Corpus Linguistics 13), 171–210. Amsterdam: John Benjamins.
Hundt, Markus. 2000. *"Spracharbeit" im 17. Jahrhundert. Studien zu Georg Philipp Harsdörffer, Justus Georg Schottelius und Christian Gueintz* (Studia Linguistica Germanica 57). Berlin & New York: De Gruyter.
Jespersen, Otto. [10]1968. Living grammar. In Otto Jespersen, *The philosophy of grammar*, 17–29. London: Allen & Unwin.
Koch, Peter. 1997. Diskurstraditionen: zu ihrem sprachtheoretischen Status und ihrer Dynamik. In Barbara Frank, Thomas Haye & Doris Tophinke (eds.), *Gattungen mittelalterlicher Schriftlichkeit* (ScriptOralia 99), 43–79. Tübingen: Narr.
Kohrt, Manfred. [2]1998. Historische Phonologie und Graphematik. In Werner Besch, Anne Betten, Oskar Reichmann & Stefan Sonderegger (eds.), *Sprachgeschichte. Ein Handbuch zur Geschichte der deutschen Sprache und ihrer Erforschung* (Handbooks of Linguistics and Communication Science 2.1), vol. 1, 551–572. Berlin & New York: De Gruyter.
Körte, Wilhelm. [1837] 1974. *Die Sprichwörter und sprichwörtlichen Redensarten der Deutschen nebst den Redensarten der deutschen Zechbrüder und aller Praktik Grossmutter, d.i. der Sprichwörter ewigem Wetterkalender.* Hildesheim: Olms.
Kreuz, Christian & Sören Stumpf. Forthcoming. Phrasem-Bilder im Diskurs. Theoretische Überlegungen und methodische Herangehensweisen zur multimodalen und diskursiven Phrasem-Analyse. To appear in Natalia Filatkina & Sören Stumpf (eds.), *Formelhafte Sprache in Text und Diskurs* (Formelhafte Sprache / Formulaic Language 1). Berlin & Boston: De Gruyter.
Langacker, Ronald W. 1987. *Foundations of cognitive grammar.* Stanford: Stanford University Press.
Langlotz, Andreas. 2006. *Idiomatic creativity. A cognitive-linguistic model of idiom-representation and idiom-variation in English* (Human Cognitive Processing 17). Amsterdam & Philadelphia: Benjamins.
Moulin, Claudine. 2016. "Nach dem die Gäste sind, nach dem ist das Gespräch". Spracharbeit und barocke Tischkultur bei Georg Philipp Harsdörffer. In Nina Bartsch & Simone Schultz-Balluff (eds.), *PerspektivWechsel oder: Die Wiederentdeckung der Philologie*, vol. 2 (Grenzgänge und Grenzüberschreitungen. Zusammenspiele von Sprache und Literatur in Mittelalter und Früher Neuzeit), 261–287. Berlin: Erich Schmidt.
Östman, Jan-Ola. 2005. Construction discourse. A prolegomenon. In Jan-Ola Östman & Miriam Fried (eds.), *Construction grammars: Cognitive grounding and theoretical extensions* (Constructional Approaches to Language 3), 121–144. Amsterdam & Philadelphia: Benjamins.
Östman, Jan-Ola. 2015. From construction grammar to construction discourse ... and back. In Jörg Bücker, Susanne Günthner & Wolfgang Imo (eds.), *Konstruktionsgrammatik V. Konstruktionen im Spannungsfeld von sequenziellen Mustern, kommunikativen Gattungen und Textsorten*, 15–43. Tübingen: Stauffenburg.
Paul, Hermann. [1880] 1995. *Prinzipien der Sprachgeschichte.* Tübingen: Niemeyer.

Piirainen, Elisabeth. 1995. Mänden häbbt groote Aorne un könnt doch nich häörn. Zum usualisierten Wortspiel im Westmünsterländischen. *Niederdeutsches Wort. Beiträge zur niederdeutschen Philologie* 35. 177–204.
Piirainen, Elisabeth. 2012. *Widespread idioms in Europe and beyond. Towards a lexicon of common figurative units*, vol. 1. New York: Peter Lang.
Piirainen, Elisabeth. 2016. *Lexicon of common figurative units. Widespread idioms in Europe and* beyond, vol. 2. New York: Peter Lang.
Röhrich, Lutz. [7]2004. *Lexikon der sprichwörtlichen Redensarten*. Darmstadt: Wissenschaftliche Buchgesellschaft.
Sabban, Annette. 1998. *Okkasionelle Variationen sprachlicher Schematismen. Eine Analyse französischer und deutscher Presse- und Werbetexte*. Tübingen: Narr.
Saussure, Ferdinand de. [1916] 1969. *Cours de linguistique générale*. Publié par Charles Bally et Albert Sechehaye. Paris: Payot.
Schlücker, Barbara & Ingo Plag. 2011. Compound or phrase? Analogy in naming. *Lingua* 121. 1539–1551.
Schreiber, David, Cerstin Mahlow & Britta Juska-Bacher. 2012. Phraseologische Neologismen: Identifikation und Validierung. *Yearbook of Phraseology* 3. 3–30.
Sinclair, John. 1991. *Corpus, concordance, collocation* (Describing English language). Oxford: Oxford University Press.
Stein, Stephan. 1995. *Formelhafte Sprache. Untersuchungen zu ihren pragmatischen und kognitiven Funktionen im gegenwärtigen Deutsch* (Sprache in der Gesellschaft: Beiträge zur Sprachwissenschaft 22). Frankfurt a.M.: Peter Lang.
Stein, Stephan. 2012. Phraseologie und Wortbildung des Deutschen. Ein Vergleich von Äpfeln mit Birnen? In Michael Prinz & Ulrike Richter-Vapaatalo (eds.), *Idiome, Konstruktionen, "verblümte rede". Beiträge zur Geschichte der germanistischen Phraseologieforschung* (Beiträge zur Geschichte der Germanistik), 225–240. Stuttgart: Hirzel.
Steyer, Kathrin. 2013. *Usuelle Wortverbindungen. Zentrale Muster des Sprachgebrauchs aus korpusanalytischer Sicht* (Studien zur Deutschen Sprache. Forschungen des Instituts für Deutsche Sprache). Tübingen: Narr.
Stubbs, Michael. 2001. *Words and phrases. Corpus studies of lexical semantics*. Oxford: Oxford University Press.
Stumpf, Sören. 2015a. *Formelhafte (Ir-)Regularitäten. Korpuslinguistische Befunde und sprachtheoretische Überlegungen* (Sprache – System und Tätigkeit 67). Frankfurt a. M.: Peter Lang.
Stumpf, Sören. 2015b. "Kann Jogi Weltmeister?" – Phraseologische und konstruktionsgrammatische Überlegungen zu einer aus (laien-)sprachkritischer Sicht "agrammatischen" Konstruktion. *Aptum. Zeitschrift für Sprachkritik und Sprachkultur* 11. 1–20.
Traugott, Elizabeth C. 2014. Toward a constructional framework for research on language change. *Cognitive Linguistic Studies* 1(1). 3–21.
Wander, Karl Friedrich Wilhelm. [1987] 2001. *Deutsches Sprichwörter-Lexikon: ein Hausschatz für das deutsche Volk*. Printed edition 1987, Augsburg: Weltbild; digital edition 2001. Berlin: Digitale Bibliothek 62.
Werner, Otmar. [2]1998. Historische Morphologie. In Werner Besch, Anne Betten, Oskar Reichmann & Stefan Sonderegger (eds.), *Sprachgeschichte. Ein Handbuch zur Geschichte der deutschen Sprache und ihrer Erforschung* (Handbooks of Linguistics and Communication Science 2.1), 572–596. Berlin & New York: De Gruyter.

Winter-Froemel, Esme. 2016. Approaching wordplay. In Sebastian Knospe, Alexander Onysko & Maik Goth (eds.), *Crossing languages to play with words. Multidisciplinary perspectives* (Dynamics of Wordplay 3), 11–46. Berlin & Boston: De Gruyter.
Wray, Alison. 2002. *Formulaic language and the lexicon*. Cambridge: Cambridge University Press.
Wray, Alison. 2008. *Formulaic language: Pushing the boundaries* (Oxford Applied Linguistics). Oxford: Oxford University Press.
Wray, Alison. 2009. Identifying formulaic language: Persistent challenges and new opportunities. In Roberta Corrigan, Edith A. Moravcsik, Hamid Ouali & Kathleen M. Wheatley (eds.), *Formulaic language* (Typological Studies in Language 82), vol. 1 (Distribution and historical change), 27–51. Amsterdam & Philadelphia: Benjamins.
Wray, Alison & Michael R. Perkins. 2000. The functions of formulaic language: An integrated model. *Language and communication* 20(1). 1–28.

Anette Kremer and Stefanie Stricker
Complex words in the early medieval *Leges Barbarorum* and their contribution to expanding the Old High German lexicon

Abstract: This article examines selected complex words (compounds, derivatives) taken from the early *Leges barbarorum* and illustrates how these words expanded the lexicon of Old High German. The examples are taken from the Upper German laws (*Lex Baiuvariorum, Lex Alamannorum, Leges Langobardorum*) which form a relatively homogeneous tradition. In the area of compounding, complex words unattested outside of the *Leges* tradition are examined which exhibit specific relations between their first and second elements. In the area of derivation, focus is placed in particular on lexemes resulting from a word formation process which is productive in the type of text examined but which is hardly seen elsewhere in Old High German and is no longer productive. The data presented in this article come from the LegIT database which has been studied since 2012 within the scope of a research project at the University of Bamberg.

1 Introduction

The vernacular words that appear in the medieval law codes of various Germanic peoples, the so-called laws of the barbarians (Latin: *Leges barbarorum*),[1] are among the earliest records of the German language. The *Leges* are mainly written in Latin, but numerous vernacular words are inserted in the Latin text. Commonly referred to as inserts, these words were integrated into the text at the time it was written and were not entered subsequently, as was the case with Old High German glosses in Latin manuscripts (Stricker 2009: 31–32).[2] The inserts are essential elements of the text and serve a specific meaning within the legal practices of the various Germanic tribes, as they contribute to providing the most compact and precise information about a legal case.

---

[1] This is the general term established for all continental Germanic laws known to date (Kroeschell 2008: 23).
[2] For further information about the term *insert* see Prinz (2010: 292–322).

∂ Open Access. © 2018 Anette Kremer, Stefanie Stricker, published by De Gruyter. [CC BY-NC-ND] This work is licensed under the Creative Commons Attribution-NonCommercial-NoDerivatives 4.0 License.
https://doi.org/10.1515/9783110501933-045

When comparing the *Leges barbarorum* with other forms of Old High German traditions, such as the texts and glosses, the number of vernacular words contained in them is rather low: The Germanic laws contain about 1,200 vernacular lemmata (types) and more than 42,000 tokens. The contribution to the overall tradition of Old High German is approximately three percent.[3] At the same time, the *Leges* represent a very old type of text (for comparative data on the gloss tradition cf. Stricker 2009: 31–32; regarding text tradition cf. Meineke and Schwerdt 2001: 99–165). The first laws were written down in the fifth century, in a period when Old High German (OHG), the earliest known stage of German, was only a fragmentarily attested language. Besides the vernacular *Leges* inserts, only a small number of runic inscriptions and proper nouns from this time have survived (Untermann 1989: 15–18; Sonderegger 2003: 83–85). The tradition of the Upper German *Leges* examined here began (with the exception of *Edictum Rothari* in a manuscript from the seventh century) in the latter half of the eighth century. The *Leges* are ultimately also of importance because they offer "a direct link with the language and life" (Bostock 1976: 83) of the various Germanic tribes. The inserts are extremely precious evidence for the earliest testimonies of German, and of great importance not only for linguists but also for historical grammarians, historical lexicographers, historical pragmaticians, legal and medical historians and cultural scholars.

The low frequency of lexemes and tokens in the *Leges* compared to Old High German texts and particularly to glosses, is accounted for by their functional limitation. The lexemes and tokens are encountered exclusively in a specific type of text, the Germanic laws, and within this type of text above all in the keyword-type labels of legally relevant facts, such as crimes, violations, legal facts, etc. They are encountered indeed not only in the legal lexicon but also in the lexicon of everyday life, albeit with a relatively modest overall distribution.

Due to their long and heterogeneous process of emergence, the vernacular lexicon of these sources is disparate, containing not only younger Old High German lexemes but also older Germanic lexemes that had been transferred into Medieval Latin. The latter will not be examined in this article. Here, we intend to illustrate how, in the early Middle Ages, the Old High German lexicon within the Upper German *Leges* was expanded. To this end, we will concentrate on a selection of complex words, namely compounds and suffix derivatives, in particular

---

3 The data published in Stricker and Kremer (2014: 239) and Stricker, Kremer, and Schwab (2014: 285) have been updated. Current status according to the Bamberg gloss database *BStK Online:* https://glossen.ahd-portal.germ-ling.uni-bamberg.de/pages/1 (accessed 21 June 2017); see also Bergmann (2005: 49).

on those which appear exclusively or are concentrated in these laws. Prior to this explorative qualitative analysis, we will provide some notes on the state of research and above all, on the function and meaning of vernacular words from the *Leges* which have been attributed to this specific type of text.

2 The state of research

Previous linguistic works have investigated other selected aspects: Baesecke's (1935) work, for example, is dedicated to etymological aspects and the manuscript filiations, while Schmidt-Wiegand and her academic followers primarily discussed semantical issues from a semasiological perspective (Hüpper-Dröge 1983; Niederhellmann 1983; von Olberg 1983, 1991; Schmidt-Wiegand 1991). Tiefenbach (2004) analysed grammatical characteristics of the vernacular vocabulary of the Bavarian laws regarding not only phonological and lexical but also morphological specificities, as we have done in this article.

Apart from these fundamental works, the *Leges* vocabulary is seldom found in historical German grammars and dictionaries. Exceptions to this are the inserts in Graff's *Althochdeutscher Sprachschatz* ('Old High German Thesaurus', 1834–1842, *Deutsches Rechtswörterbuch* ('German Legal Dictionary'; since 1914) and Seebold's *Chronologisches Wörterbuch des deutschen Wortschatzes* ('Chronological Dictionary of German'; 2001). The entry selection of all of the aforementioned dictionaries is based on the editions of the *Monumenta Germaniae Historica* (1863–1926), which also do not include the overall tradition (Stricker, Kremer, and Schwab 2014: 287). The vocabulary is missing in the comprehensive *Althochdeutsches Wörterbuch* ('Old High German Dictionary') edited by Karg-Gasterstädt and Frings (since 1952, KFW), in the *Etymologisches Wörterbuch des Althochdeutschen* ('Etymological Dictionary of Old High German') edited by Lloyd, Springer, and Lühr (since 1988) as well as in Schützeichel's dictionaries (Schützeichel 2012, SchGW), which aim to register the complete vocabulary of the Old High German glosses and texts. The reason why the vernacular inserts have been neglected in these essential linguistic works of reference is that these words have not yet been collected systematically, as the corpus is not easily accessible in either direction, formally and semantically (Tiefenbach 2009: 975). Consequently, they are mostly omitted in historical linguistic follow-up studies (Tiefenbach 2004: 263).

3 The emergence and the function of vernacular words in the *Leges barbarorum*

Latin was the lingua franca of the written culture in Medieval Europe. As such, it also served as the common legal language used since the Germanic tribes made contact with the Roman Empire during the Migration Period and adopted the tradition of written legal statutes, as well as the practice of codifying the law, also assimilated from the Romans. Nevertheless, there remained a co-existing, primarily oral legal tradition maintained by each of the various Germanic tribes from their pre-literary custom law. Although the Roman influence on the individual laws of the barbarians obviously varies according to the intensity of contact between the Germanic peoples and the Empire, we may notice a general change in the basic Germanic legal system, by which the primarily oral customary law was transformed into a written record of legal practice. This change was largely motivated by a desire for legal certainty, a desire which all Germanic tribes had shared (Frassetto 2003: 231–232; Schmidt-Wiegand 2006: 143; Oliver 2011: 8–10; Hähnchen 2012: 108–109).

The use of vernacular vocabulary in the ancient laws reflects the persisting importance of oral tradition, even within written legal authority. The vernacular lexemes may have already been established in the oral legal tradition as technical terms. They may, however, have also been transferred from everyday language into the legal language without having acquired a specific legal meaning until used in the context of a legal text. This transfer process did not cause the creation of whole lexical inventories within the *Leges* tradition, but it did provide a small selection of technical terms (See 1964: 2; Poethe 2000: 203). This kind of transfer of single, everyday language lexemes to coin a new term in a language for special purposes is closely linked to partially undocumented phenomena of language change. In many cases, a semantic change – primarily a reinterpretation – can be observed when a specific meaning is developed to name a referent related to the legal context in a more precise and nuanced manner (See 1964: 20).

For instance, the noun OHG *marach*, which is known as *Mähre* 'female horse of minor value' in contemporary German, was commonly used until the sixteenth century as a general reference to a 'female horse, mare' (DWB, VI: 1467–1471). Thus, it appears in the gloss tradition as the vernacular equivalent to the Latin words *equa* and *iumenta* (Graff 1963, II: 844; KFW, VI: 478). In the *Leges* manuscripts, however, *marach* is reinterpreted as a 'valuable charger'; it no longer describes the sex, but rather the quality of a horse. On the one hand, the striking position of a *marach* becomes apparent through the contrast with less valuable horses, such as *wilz* '(mediocre, regularly used) Wendish horse', and *angargnago* 'rejected grazing horse' (see below). On the other hand, its value is further confirmed by examples such as the extraordinarily high penalty fee that, according to Bavarian law, had to be paid for its injury (Nótári 2013: 274; Schwab, forthcoming).

During the process of writing down the Germanic laws, scribes preserved the vernacular terms, which were already known from the oral law tradition, in the Latin text (Lühr 1989: 46). In many cases, however, they could not rely on widely established vernacular terms to express specific criminal offences or injured parties, particularly if there was no appropriate German equivalent available. Thus, they were forced to create a new technical term in order to summarise the details of a legal case, which could otherwise be described comprehensively by a Latin sentence. Hence, the vernacular inserts functioned as lexical tags in the Latin text (Tiefenbach 2004: 263; Tiefenbach 2009: 960). To highlight the vernacular inserts within the Latin text, as well as to raise awareness of the following change from Latin to vernacular language, the scribes used specific meta-communicative markers, formulaic phrases such as e.g. *quod Alamanni / Baiuvarii ... dicunt* 'which the Alamans / Bavarians call ...', *quod ... vocant / vocamus / vocatur* or *quod ... dicunt / dicimus / dicitur /* 'which they / we call / is called ...'.

One such tagging term which is introduced by a meta-communicative marker is the noun OHG *pulislac*, an insert that can typically be found in the Upper German laws, for example in the Alemannic law:

> *Lex Alamannorum*, LVII, 1: *Si quis alium per iram percusserit, quod Alamanni* **pulislac** *dicunt, cum uno solido conponat* (MGH LL nat. germ. I,5,1: 116a). 'If anyone strikes another in anger, which the Alamans call **pulislac**, let him compensate with one solidus' (Rivers 1977: 85).

This endocentric determinative compound is described by the determinant *puli-* (< OHG *būl(l)a* 'bump') and the determinatum OHG *slag* 'blow' (KFW I: 1487; Schützeichel 2012: 296). The meaning of the compound can be described as 'a blow that causes a bump'. The determinant represents the consequences suffered by the injured party resulting from a serious crime of passion. This kind of relation between both elements of the compound is not documented beyond the *Leges* tradition. Other Old High German compounds that contain the determinatum *slac* express different kinds of relations between the two stems: *hantslag* 'a blow struck by the hand' and *hamarslag* 'a blow struck by the hammer', for instance, which involve the instrument used to strike a blow. The nouns *bruodersleggo*, *fatersleggo* and *kindsleggo* 'a blow against the brother / father / child' specify the person that was hit (Schwab, forthcoming). These examples illustrate the important role that word formation plays in the creation of new signifiers intended to become valid and binding terms within the legal practice.

Dealing with such lexical tags in a philological analysis means dealing with semantic ambiguities; it is often difficult to grasp the specific meaning of the insert in the different Germanic laws. In this regard, semantic analysis of the inserts is a more complex matter than the analysis of the Old High German glosses. The glossation method allows the provision of a one-to-one correspondence between the Latin and the German word, and is often accomplished without any major issues. When we examined the vernacular *Leges* vocabulary, we observed that there is often a larger scope of interpretation and a lack of formal and semantic symmetry between Latin and German. On the one hand, these problems are caused by the divergent syntactic, morphological and semantic structures of Latin and German. On the other hand, the Latin text refers to the description of complex legal circumstances. In some cases, this description renders the distinction in the use of the vernacular to tag an entire sentence, a single syntagm, or even a single word of the Latin sentence unclear.

An example of this is the noun *marach* cited above:

> Lex Alamannorum, LXI, 2: *Et si ille talem involaverit equum, quod Alamanni* **marach** *dicunt, sic eum solvat sicut et illo amissario* (MGH LL nat. germ. I,5,1: 131a). 'And if he steals such a horse as the Alamans call **marach**, let him pay for it just as for the stallion' (Rivers 1977: 91).

In the Alemannic laws, *marach* is closely related to the Latin noun *equus*, which generally means 'horse, steed'. It is clear in the text passage that the insert refers to a male horse, but it does not explicitly identify it as a valuable steed, leading us to further analysis and discussion about the use of *marach* in similar contexts (see the details above). As a further consequence, the New High German semantic paraphrases vary widely, ranging from a single word to a highly complex syntagm (Schwab, forthcoming).

The lexical tagging of essential legal facts by means of the vernacular vocabulary is vital in forming a connection between the written Latin text and the oral vernacular language of each Germanic tribe. It ensured that all members of the tribe, particularly criminal suspects or defendants, could face accusations at trial and comprehend details relating to the injured party even without an understanding of Latin (Schmidt-Wiegand 1989: 550).

In this particular genre, legal words form a substantial part of the overall vernacular vocabulary. They are predominantly used to label various kinds of

criminal offences and the persons or animals that are involved in a crime, for example as an injured party. However, as the following overview illustrates, whilst legal terms may represent the bulk of the vocabulary, there remains a broad range of other semantic fields to which the words refer, as they are used in legal context. They are listed in their present entirety as follows:
1. legal vocabulary (209 types, e.g. *gezunfti* 'agreement, alliance')
2. medicine (145 types, e.g. *ādargrāti* 'wire section')
3. social structure (92 types, *frīgilāz* 'freed man')
4. animals (72 types, e.g. *leitihund* 'leading dog')
5. agriculture (52 types, e.g. *zurft* 'clod of earth')
6. art of warfare (52 types, e.g. *sahs* 'sword')
7. architecture (48 types, e.g. *winkilsūl* 'corner column')
8. measurement and currency (43 types, e.g. *fant* 'pledge')
9. everyday life (24 types, e.g. *fuora* 'journey')
10. myths and religion (21 types, e.g. *grapworf* 'throwing a dead body out of the grave')
11. craft (11 types, e.g. *handegawerc* 'handicraft')
12. proper names (57 types; *Godofrid*, *Fresia* 'Frisia').

The vernacular *Leges* words cover completely different semantic fields than those in the Old High German glosses or texts. As the glosses and texts are predominantly associated with religious and theological contents, lexemes from the aforementioned semantic fields would be less likely to appear there (Tiefenbach 2004: 263).

4 Word formation in Old High German

In contemporary German, the most important patterns of word formation are composition and derivation. Compounds are formed by a combination of (prototypically two) stems represented by simple or complex words, whereas the central model of a derivative is characterised by the addition of a simple or a complex word (= base) to an affix (Fleischer and Barz 2012: 84–87).

The central role of Old High German compounding and derivation is demonstrated clearly in works by Meineke (1994), Splett (2000), Meineke and Schwerdt (2001), and Müller (2016).[4] The distribution of these two models, or

---

4 Additional literature referring to word formation in Old High German can also be found here.

rather, of their subtypes "differs with respect to word classes" (Müller 2016: 1880). Most Old High German compounds are nominal endocentric determinative compounds with a simple nominal stem as first and second elements (e. g. OHG *bluom-garto* 'flower garden', *bior-faz* 'beer barrel'). Furthermore, there are complex words with a determinant which indicates an inflectional marker, e.g. the genitive marker *-es* in OHG *tag-es-zīt* 'day time'. Such words are usually referred to as case compounds (German: *unechte / uneigentliche Komposita*). There are only a few adjective determinative compounds, e.g. OHG *gold-faro* 'golden' (Splett 2000: 1213–1214; Meineke and Schwerdt 2001: 290; Müller 2016: 1870 and 1880), whereas the formation of new verbs by compounding is "an atypical means" (Müller 2016: 1880).

The semantic relationship between the substantive determinant and the substantive determinatum is variable, depending on the context, whereas the relationship for an adjective determinans in Old High German is usually attributive (OHG *junc-man* 'young man') and a verbal determinant often represents the purpose for which the determinatum is being used (OHG *blās-balc* 'bellows') (Splett 2000: 1215).

As for derivation in Old High German, the patterns of prefixation and suffixation are indeed relevant. Since the pattern of "suffixation is much more pronounced" (Müller 2016: 1886) and only suffixation is relevant for our article, only this will be briefly introduced here.[5] Focus is placed on our priority accordingly in the case of the following examples of adjectival and substantive derivatives. Particularly in Old High German, the latter are prominently represented in the form of abstract nouns[6] which have verbal, adjectival or substantive bases (Meineke and Schwerdt 2001: 295–296). More productive still are suffixes which form nouns, including *-ī(n)*, *-ida*, *-unga*, *-āri* and *-nissi*. Those which only appear sporadically, or are no longer productive at all include *-il*, *-t* and *-idi*. Adjective derivatives arise predominantly out of substantive or adjectival bases in conjunction with inherited suffixes (e.g. *-īg*, *-isc*, *-īn*) or through morphological means which in Old High German still do not hold the confirmed status of a suffix, but which also appear as free words, e.g. *līh*[7] 'body, shape, form', *haft* 'bound', *samo* 'same' (Splett 2000: 1218–1219; Meineke and Schwerdt 2001: 299–301).

---

5 For more information about prefixation in Old High German, see Splett (2000: 1216–1218) and Müller (2016: 1885–1886, 1890–1891, 1894–1898).
6 For more detailed information, see also Meineke (1994).
7 For a comprehensive summary, see also Schmid (1998).

It is, in many cases, impossible to determine beyond any doubt whether Old High German compounds and derivatives are new formations of productive or simply active patterns of word formation and whether inherited lexemes originate from the pre-Old High German era. What is in many cases all the more problematic is the question of the degree of semantic motivation and morphemic transparency, i.e. it is not always possible to say unequivocally whether individual lexemes should remain classified as semantically transparent morpheme combinations, or rather as simplexes (Splett 2000: 1213).

5 The contribution of word formation to the vernacular *Leges* vocabulary

Morphological aspects of word formation have been of only marginal relevance to date, mostly in connection with semantic-etymological problems and analyses of the vernacular *Leges* vocabulary. Thus, until now, a relatively modest number of *Leges* inserts has been investigated regarding their word formation patterns. A somewhat more extensive grammatical investigation of the word formation patterns occurring in the *Leges* and their productivity is offered by Tiefenbach (2004) with regard to the *Lex Baiuvariorum*. His explanations there serve as the basis and starting point of reference for our article. For our analysis, we have chosen examples of compounding and derivation taken from the Upper German laws, particularly the Alemannic and Bavarian laws, to illustrate the diversity of occurring formation patterns. All of the examples are Old High German words taken from the semantic field of legal vocabulary.

5.1 Compounds

Compounds are used in the *Leges*[8] as a central opportunity for compressing information. They are characterised by a high level of expressivity, which is why

---

[8] The complex words found in the *Leges* are recorded in the LegIT database. The database is related to the LegIT project, which started at the University of Bamberg in 2012. It is supervised by Professor Stefanie Stricker and funded by the *German Research Foundation* (DFG). The project aims to collect the vernacular vocabulary found in the set of continental West-Germanic law manuscripts. Furthermore, it seeks to analyse the Germanic lexemes according to a determined number of formal and semantic criteria, whereby the main focus is set on the grammatical approach. All of the vocabulary and the results of our analysis will be made available

they play such a crucial role, specifically in the formation of technical terms. These compounds feature consistently throughout a range of languages for special purposes, with particular meaning found in contemporary German, as well as throughout its history. In that regard, the early medieval legal language is an illustrative example of these preferences (Schmidt-Wiegand 1999: 77; Stein 2000: 286; Tiefenbach 2004: 278).

We identified a high number of compounds in the *Leges*, the most frequent of which consisted of two stems, which may be either simplexes or complex words. According to our recent lemma inventory of the LegIT database, a considerable number of them occur exclusively in the *Leges*, either to label a crime or to name a person or animal involved in an offence. The nouns *angargnago* and *taudragil* exemplify the characteristics of compounds mentioned above.

Angargnago, which is part of the semantic field of animals, is only recorded in the Bavarian laws. *Taudragil*, which we linked to the semantic field of medicine, is found in the Alemannic and Bavarian laws. Both compounds represent the injured party of a criminal offence:

(1) OHG *angargnago*
Lex Baiuvariorum, XIIII, 12: *Et si deterior fuerit[,] quod* **angargnago** *dicimus, qui in hoste utilis non est, cum tremissa conponat* (MGH LL nat. germ. I,5,2: 418). 'And if it [= a horse] is of inferior value, which we call **angargnago**, which is unsuitable for military campaigns, let him compensate with one tremissis' (Rivers 1977: 157).

(2) OHG *taudragil*
Lex Alamannorum, LXV, 34: *Si quis in genuculo transpunctus fuerit aut plagatus, ita ut claudus permaneat, ut pes eius ros tangat, quod Alamanni* **taudragil** *dicunt, cum 12 solidis conponat* (MGH LL nat. germ. I,5,1: 127). 'If, however, one injures another in the knee so that he remains lame and his foot drags [...] through the dew, which the Alamans call **tautragil**, let him compensate with twelve solidi' (Rivers 1977: 89).

Angargnago literally means 'rodent of the meadow'. As the aforementioned Bavarian law excerpt in (1) demonstrates, this term describes an inferior horse that is no longer fit for military or agricultural use. It is barely fed by its owner and spends its days gnawing at the grass of a meadow, waiting to die (Tiefenbach 1980: 300; Nótári 2013: 274).

---

through our web-service. Because the project is still a work in progress, access to the database is password protected. The LegIT website, which offers background information about our project and the laws, is available without any restrictions, see http://legit.ahd-portal.germling.uni-bamberg.de/. Detailed information about the LegIT database is also provided in Stricker, Kremer, and Schwab (2014) and Stricker and Kremer (2014).

The determinant of the compound is the masculine noun OHG *angar* 'meadow'; the determinatum is the masculine noun OHG *gnago*, which is an agent noun formed by suffixation with *-o* on the strong verb OHG *gnagan* 'to gnaw'. The derivative *gnago* provides the earliest record of *gnagan*, occurring for the first time in Bavarian law manuscripts written in the second half of the eighth century.[9] Further early records of this verb appear in the tradition of Old High German glosses, though these do not occur until the ninth century (SchGW, III: 481).

In Alemannic and Bavarian law, *taudragil* refers to a male person who drags a lame foot through the morning dew after being injured in the knee. The determinant component of *taudragil* is the noun OHG *tau, tou* 'dew' (Schützeichel 2012: 333). The determinatum is the masculine agent noun OHD *dragil* or, with primary umlaut *a > e*, *dregil* 'someone who drags (something)' < Germanic **þregila*. It is formed by the addition of the derivational suffix *-il* to the gothic strong verb *þragjan* 'to run', which has its origin in the Germanic root **þrag-*, **þrāg-* 'to drag, to slide on the ground' (Meineke 1982: 257; Walde and Hofmann 1972: 698f.). In early Old High German, the suffix *-il* is no longer productive and is replaced by *-āri* (Meineke and Schwerdt 2001: 296). The single component *tau, tou* occurs frequently in Old High German glosses and texts. It is the vernacular equivalent to the Latin noun *ros* and is found, for example, in the Old High German *Isidor* and in the *Murbach Hymns* (SchGW, X: 10). The noun *dragil*, however, was already archaic in early Old High German (Meineke 1982: 257). Therefore, it is certainly a possibility that the complex word was already no longer morphemically transparent in Old High German. The compound itself is found exclusively in Alemannic and Bavarian laws, with no further records in the gloss or literary tradition, rendering it perfectly suited to illustrate the uniqueness of the *Leges* inserts.

As both of the aforementioned compounds are characterised by a metonymic character and a near-poetic expressivity, they are fitting examples of the lexical richness and variation of the early medieval legal language.

Apart from such singular phenomena, there are numerous word families that emerged through compounding, with one such example based on the adjective determinatum *wunt* 'wounded', an element of the semantic field of medicine. It consists of four endocentric compounds that appear in the Alemannic and Bavarian laws.

---

9 Munich, University Library. Cim 7 (= 8° Cod. ms. 132).

(3) OHG *(h)rev(a)wunt*
    Lex Baiuvariorum, V, 5: *Si quis eum percusserit, ut cervella eius appareant, vel in interiora membra vulneraverit, quod **hrevavunt** dicunt, vel eum ligaverit contra legem, cum VI sold conponat* (MGH LL nat. germ. I,5,2: 340). 'If anyone strikes him so that his brain appears, or injures the internal organs, which they call **hrevavunt**, or binds him contrary to law, let him compensate with six solidi' (Rivers 1977: 135).

The determinant of the adjective *(h)rev(a)wunt* is the strong masculine noun OHG *(h)ref / (h)rev* 'uterus, mother's womb' (Schützeichel 2012: 255). The *Leges* context clearly indicates that the determinant provides information on the site of the injury, as the adjective is used to refer to wounds inflicted upon the internal organs of the (lower) abdominal area (Riecke 2004: 405). Because *(h)rev(a)wunt* occurs in a manuscript of the *Leges Baiuvariorum* that was written down in the second half of the eighth century,[10] it constitutes the first record of the adjective *wunt* in Old High German. Other records in Old High German glosses and literature appear later, for instance in the *Muspilli* (Hellgardt 2013: 288).

Furthermore, we can find one of the oldest records of the German noun *Wunde* 'wound' (< OHG *wunta*) (Schützeichel 2012: 400) in the same manuscript, where it occurs with the determinant *(h)rev(a)*:

(4) OHG *(h)revawunt(a)*
    Lex Baiuvariorum, X, 4: *Si autem ignem posuerit in domo ita, ut flamma eructuat et non perarserit et a familiis liberata fuerit: unumquemque de liberis cum sua **hreuauunti** conponat, eo quod illos inunuuan, quod dicunt, in disperationem vitae fecerit* (MGH LL nat. germ. I,5,2: 387). 'However, if he starts a fire in a house so that the flame bursts forth, and it is not burned down and is saved by the domestic slaves, let him compensate for each one of the freemen with his **hrevawunta**, since he did those things in inunuuam, which they say endangers life' (Rivers 1977: 147).

This noun stands for various kinds of bodily wounds, in particular, chest wounds, abdominal wounds or injuries to internal organs (Niederhellmann 1983: 249–250; Tiefenbach 2004: 281).

In some of the tituli of numerous manuscripts of the Alemannic and Bavarian laws, we observed that there are synonyms for the adjective *(h)rev(a)wunt*, which are used to describe an injury to the internal organs:

(5) OHG *ferahwunt* and

(6) OHG *gorawunt*

---

[10] Munich, University Library. Cim 7 (= 8° Cod. ms. 132).

Lex Alamannorum, LXV, 27: *Si autem interiora membra vulneratus fuerit, quod* **'refvunt'** *{**ferhvunt**[11], **gorovunt**[12]} dicunt, cum 12 solidos conponat* (MGH LL nat. germ. I,5,1: 126, 12b). 'If, however, the internal organs are injured, which they call **'refvunt'** {**ferhvunt, gorovunt**}, let him compensate with twelve solidi' (Rivers 1977: 89).

The adjective *ferahwunt* is documented in manuscripts of the *Lex Alamannorum* and *Baiuvariorum*, which emerged between the tenth and the twelfth century.[13] The determinant is the strong neuter noun OHG *ferah* 'life, soul, heart'. This compound means 'critically or even mortally wounded', by which the determinant refers to the consequences the wound has for the injured party (Niederhellmann 1983: 207).

The adjective *gorawunt* is the result of an occasional word formation documented in the Alemannic laws. It can be found in manuscripts written between the second half of the ninth century and the first half of the tenth century.[14] It contains the strong neuter OHG *gor* 'faeces (presumably only of animals), manure' (KFW, IV: 331) as determinant, which describes the site of the injury in such a way that it refers to a wound on the intestines or on the intestinal wall (Niederhellmann 1983: 252; Riecke 2004: 338).

5.2 Suffix derivatives

The Germanic laws contain several vernacular derivatives created by suffixation. One of the typical suffixes, which frequently occur in the *Leges*, is *-ī(n)*. When attached to verbal bases, *-ī(n)* produces feminine abstract nouns. This deverbal pattern has ceased to be productive in Old High German but still appears in the works of the glossator and translator Notker (Schatz 1927: § 364, 369; Wilmanns 1967: § 237–239; Tiefenbach 2004: 280–282). New Old High German words with *-ī(n)* show adjectives or participles as bases (Splett 2000: 1218). A particularly unique accumulation of this pattern is noticeable in the Bavarian laws, where it predominantly forms nouns based on phrases, for example

(7) OHG *firstfallī*

Lex Baiuvariorum, X, 3: *Si quis desertaverit aut culmen eicerit, quod sepe contingit, aut incendio tradiderit, uniuscuiusque, quod **firstfalli** dicunt, quae per se constructa sunt, id est*

---

11 Stuttgart, State Library of Württemberg. Cod. iur. 4° 134.
12 Leiden, University Library. Voss. lat. qu. 119; Vienna, Austrian National Library. Cod. 502.
13 Munich, Bavarian State Library. Clm 5260; Munich, Bavarian State Library. Clm 5260; Munich, Bavarian State Library. Clm 5260.
14 Leiden, University Library. Voss. lat. qu. 119; Vienna, Austrian National Library. Cod. 502.

balnearius pistoria coquina vel cetera huiusmodi, cum III sold conponat et restituat dissipata vel incensa (MGH LL nat. germ. I,5,2: 387). 'If anyone destroys or knocks down a roof, which often occurs, or burns it, which they call **firstfalli**, let him compensate with three solidi for each no matter how it is constructed, that is, a bakery, bath, kitchen or other of this kind, and let him restore what he destroyed or burned' (Rivers 1977: 147).

The noun is based on a phrase consisting of the noun OHG *first* 'roof ridge' and the strong verb OHG *fallan* 'to fall' (KFW, III: 917, 542–546). According to the text passage above, it represents 'the falling (by which destruction is meant) of a roof by knocking it down or burning it'.

(8) OHG *marchfallī*
    Lex Baiuvariorum, IV, 18: *Si quis aliquem de equo suo deposuerit, quod **marachfalli** vocant, cum VI sold conponat* (MGH LL nat. germ. I,5,2: 329). 'If anyone pulls someone from his horse, which they call **marachfalli**, let him compensate with six solidi' (Rivers 1977: 132).

The noun is based on a phrase consisting of the noun OHG *march / marah* 'charger' and the strong verb OHG *fallan* 'to fall' (Schwab, forthcoming; KFW, III: 542–546). As described in the text passage above, this represents the falling from a horse (more specifically, a charger).

(9) OHG *kepolsceinī*
    Lex Baiuvariorum, IV, 4: *Si in eo venam percusserit, ut sine igne sanguinem stagnare non possit, quod adargrati dicunt, vel in capite testa appareat quod **kepolsceini** vocant, et si os fregerit et pellem non fregit quod palcprust dicunt, et si talis plaga ei fuerit, quod tumens sit: si aliquid de istis contigerit, cum VI sold conponat* (MGH LL nat. germ. I,5,2: 318). 'If he cuts through his vein so that he cannot stop [the blood] without a cauterizing iron, which they call adarcrati; if the skull appears on the head, which they call **kepolsceini**; if he breaks a bone and the skin is not broken, which they call palcbrust; and if he causes such an injury that a swelling results: if any of these things happen, let him compensate with six solidi' (Rivers 1977: 130).

The noun is based on a phrase consisting of the noun OHG *gebal* 'skull' and the strong verb OHG *skīnan* 'to shine' (Seebold 2001: 372b; Tiefenbach 2004: 281). As the passage above illustrates, this stands for an injury which implies the exposure of the cranial bone.

Apart from this particular phrase-based pattern, derivatives with *-ī(n)* appear in the Alemannic and Bavarian laws, where they function primarily as determinata within endocentric determinative compounds. An example of this is the noun *scartī* 'gash, deep cut in the skin' (Tiefenbach 2004: 287–289; Schwab, forthcoming). The base of the term is the adjective OHG *scart*, derived from the strong verb OHG *sceran* 'to cut, to shear' (Kluge 2011: 796, 801). According to Kluge (2011: 796), there is no textual evidence of this noun as a single word until the thirteenth century. Investigating the *Leges*, however, we can report to the contrary, as *scartī* occurs in two manuscripts of the Alemannic law, which were written down in the eighth and ninth centuries.[15] On the basis of this, the etymological information for the lemma *scartī* or, in contemporary German, *Scharte,* should be corrected in future editions of the dictionary.

Apart from the limited evidence of the single noun that can be found in the laws, there are numerous records citing its occurrence in endocentric determinative compounds, where it functions as the determinatum, namely in

(10) OHG *lidiscartī*
'mutilation of a part of the body' with the determinant OHG *lid* 'part of the body' (Riecke 2004: 383).
In the *Lex Baivariorum*, the noun describes a deep cut in the skin of an ear:
Lex Baiuvariorum, IV, 14: *Si aurem maculaverit, ut exinde turpis appareat, quod* **lidiscarti** *vocant, cum VI sold conponat* (MGH LL nat. germ. I,5,2: 326). 'If he mutilates the ear so that it appears disfigured, which they call **lidiscart[i]**, let him compensate with six solidi' (Rivers 1977: 132).

In Alemannic law, a synonym for *lidiscartī* is

(11) OHG *ōrscartī*
'cutting off (a half of) the ear' with the determinant OHG *ōr(a)* 'ear' (Schützeichel 2012: 245)
Lex Alamannororum, LX, 3: *Si enim medietatem auris absciderit, quod* **orscardi** *Alamanni dicunt, cum 6 solidis conponat* (MGH LL nat. germ. I,5,1: 118b). 'Furthermore, if he cuts off half [of] the ear, which the Alamans call **[or]scardi**, let him compensate with six solidi' (Rivers 1977: 86).

(12) OHG *aranscartī*
Lex Baiuvariorum, XIII, 8: *Si quis messem alterius initiaverit maleficis artibus et inventus fuerit, cum XII solidis conponat, quod* **aranscarti** *dicunt, et familiam eius et omnem substantiam eius vel pecora eius habeat in cura usque ad annum* (MGH LL nat. germ. I,5,2: 411). 'If anyone performs magic on another's crops through witchcraft, which they call **aranscarti**, and he is discovered, let him compensate with twelve solidi. And let him [the latter] have the former's domestic slaves and all his property and livestock in his care for a year' (Rivers 1977: 154–155).

In *aranscartī*, the determinant is OHG noun *ar(a)n* 'harvest' (KFW, I: 618; Graff 1963, I: 528; Tiefenbach 2004: 287). As illustrated above, in the Bavarian

---

[15] Wolfenbüttel, Herzog August Library. Cod. Guelf. 513 Helmstadiensis; Paris, Bibliothèque Nationale. lat. 10753.

laws, *aranscartī* is linked to the destruction of harvest (perhaps by cutting it down?) supposed to have ensued under the influence of magic.

Meineke (1994, 133–198) presents only two records of the suffix *-ī(n)* within the parallel tradition of the Old High German glosses and texts, namely *fliukōnuuerī* 'fly whisk' (StSG, I: 147, 1) and *kirihuuigī* 'parish fair' ("Laubhüttenfest") (StSG, I: 253, 12). Both have nominal bases and are taken from the German–Latin *Abrogans* glossary, the earliest preserved manuscript of which emerged at around 790.[16] When compared with the variety of evidence in the *Leges* manuscripts, it becomes apparent that the suffixation with *-ī(n)* is a pattern of word formation highly related to the early medieval legal language, particularly the legal language of Bavarian law.

Moreover, a wide range of feminine abstract nouns was created by the old Germanic suffixes *-(s)ti / -tu*, which were added to strong verbs. These are no longer productive in Old High German (Bergmann 1991: 243–246, 251; Tiefenbach 2004: 280). Nevertheless, several words formed by these suffixes have been preserved in contemporary German, "which are still recognizable as corresponding derivations" (Müller 2016: 1875), for example, *Fahrt* 'drive, journey' or *Sicht* 'sight'. The types that are recorded in the *Leges*, more precisely in the Bavarian and Lombard laws, frequently "have a relation to a morphological-semantic base which has become more or less unclear, and have taken on the character of simplex forms" (Müller 2016: 1875). These usually occur as determinata within endocentric determinative compounds. The examples (13) to (15) demonstrate clearly once again how semantic change and reinterpretation are affecting the lexemes, as is seen in their progression from words of everyday language into technical terms:

(13) OHG *zuht*

This noun is based on the strong verb OHG *ziohan* 'to move; to raise; to pull'. The meaning of *zuht* depends on the context; it stands for 'move', 'raising', or 'food' (Meineke 1994: 331–397). In the *Leges*, *zuht* only occurs as a determinatum e.g. in *heimzuht* 'sudden move towards someone, ambush', which contains the noun determinant OHG *heim* 'home'[17]:

> Lex Baiuvariorum, IV, 24: *Si autem minus fuerint scuta, verumtamen ita per vim iniuste cincxerit, quod **heimzuht** vocant, cum XII sold conponat* (MGH LL nat. germ. I,5,2: 332). 'If, however, there are fewer men [literally, shields], by whom he is unjustly and forcibly sur-

---

16 St. Gall, Abbey Library. Cod. Sang. 911.
17 See also the New High German noun *Heimsuchung* 'ambush' (Saar 1999: 247).

rounded, which they call **heimzuht**, let him be compensated with twelve solidi' (Rivers 1977: 133).

(14) OHG *runst*

Runst is based on the strong verb OHG *rinnan* 'to gutter'. Its meaning can be described as a 'trickle', 'stream', or 'flow'. In the *Leges*, the noun can only be found as a determinatum e. g. in *hovarunst / hoverunst* 'illegal, violent access to a farmstead' with the noun determinant OHG *hov / hof* 'courtyard, property' and in *bluotruns(t)* 'bleeding injury' with the noun determinant OHG *bluot* 'blood' (SchGW, VIII: 23–25; Bulitta and Schmidt-Wiegand 2000: 60; Kluge 2011: 136):

> *Lex Baiuvariorum*, XI, 1: *Si quis in curtem alterius per vim contra legem intraverit, quod* **hoverunst** *vocatur, cum III sold. conponat* (MGH LL nat. germ. I,5,2: 396). 'If anyone enters another's courtyard by force contrary to law, [which they call **hoverunst**], let him compensate with three solidi' (Rivers 1977: 150).

> *Lex Baiuvariorum*, IV, 2: *Si ei sanguinem fuderit, quod* **plotruns** *vocant, solidum I et semi conponat* (MGH LL nat. germ. I,5,2: 317). 'If he spills his blood, which they call **plotruns**, let him compensate with one and one-half solidi' (Rivers 1977: 130).

(15) OHG *grif(t)*

Grif(t) is based on the strong verb OHG *grīfan* 'to grip'. It means 'grip; handful'. *Leges* compounds in which this noun occurs are e. g. *huorgrif(t) / horcrift* 'indecent assault of a woman' with the noun determinant *huor* 'fornication; prostitute' and *anagrif(t)* 'attack' with the prepositional determinant OHG *ana* 'against' (KFW, IV: 1018, 1383–1385; Graff 1963, IV: 319; Schützeichel 2012: 34):

> *Lex Baiuvariorum*, VIII, 3: *Si quis propter libidinem liberae manum iniecerit aut virgini seu uxori alterius, quod Baiuuarii* **horcrift** *vocant, cum VI solidis conponat* (MGH LL nat. germ. I,5,2: 355). 'If anyone lays a hand on a freewoman because of lust, or on a virgin or on another's wife, which the Bavarians call **horcrif[t]**, let him compensate with six solidi' (Rivers 1977: 139).

> *Leges Langobardorum* (Rothair's Edict), 214: *Si quis liberam puellam absque consilio parentum aut voluntate duxerit uxorem, conponat, ut supra,* **anagrift** *solidos XX et propter faida alios vigenti* (MGH LL IV: 52). 'He who takes to wife a free girl without the advice and consent of her relatives shall pay twenty solidi as composition for the **seizure**, as above, and another twenty solidi to avert the feud' (Fischer Drew 1973: 93–94).

When examining the patterns of suffixation within the vernacular *Leges* vocabulary, it is interesting to note that suffixes which are productive in Old High

German rarely occur in the legal codes. Frequently occurring productive suffixes such as *-līh*, *-unga* and *-ida*, for instance, are recorded only sporadically:

(16) OHG *haiftlīch*
> Lex Alamannorum, IX: *Si quis in curtem episcopi armatus contra legem intraverit, quod Alamanni haistera handi {Bawari **haiftlichen**} dicunt, 18 solidos conponat* (MGH LL nat. germ. I,5,1: 76b). 'If anyone armed enters the courtyard of a bishop contrary to law, [...] which the Alamans call haistera handi {the Bavarians call **haiftlichen**}, [let him compensate with eighteen solidi]' (Rivers 1977: 70).

The adjective is a *hapax legomenon* within both the Alemannic law and the entire tradition of Old High German (Schmid 1998: 445). It is formed by the Old High German adjective base *haift* 'vehement' and the suffix *-līch*, which is one of the most popular adjective suffixes in German, especially in combination with substantive and adjective bases (Meineke and Schwerdt 2001: 301). In the text passage above, action is marked as 'vehement', especially when referring to the level of violence which is used by the actor. There is hardly any difference in meaning between the base *haift* and the suffix derivative *haiftlīch*, something which is often observed in Old High German adjective derivatives with an adjective base (Splett 2000: 1219).

(17) OHG *murdrida*
> Lex Baiuvariorum, XIX, 2: *Si quis liberum occiderit furtivo modo et in flumine eiecerit vel in talem locum eiecerit, ut cadaver reddere non quiverit, quod Baiuuarii **murdrida** dicunt, inprimis cum XL sold conponat eo quod funus ad dignas obsequias reddere non valet* (MGH LL nat. germ. I,5,2: 455). 'If anyone kills a freeman in a secret manner and throws him into a river or throws him into such a place that the corpse cannot be recovered, which the Bavarians call **murdrida**, in the first place let him compensate with forty solidi, since he cannot recover the corpse for a worthy burial' (Rivers 1977: 167).

Based on the legal context described above, this noun can be described as 'secret murder' (Weisweiler and Betz 1974: 75; Tiefenbach 2004: 279). As a common element in Old High German (Splett 2000: 1218), the suffix *-ida* is combined with a verbal base, OHG *murd(i)ren* 'to murder' (KFW VI, 12: 916).

(18) OHG *himilzorunga*
> Lex Baiuvariorum, VIII, 4: *Si indumenta super genucula elevaverit, quod **himilzorun[ga]** vocant, cum XII solidis conponat* (MGH LL nat. germ. I,5,2: 355). 'If he lifts her garments above the knees, which they call **himilzorunga**, let him compensate with twelve solidi' (Rivers 1977: 139).

Himilzorunga is an endocentric determinative compound formed by the elements OHG *himil* 'sky, ceiling' and the suffix derivative *zorunga*, which is one of the earliest records for -*unga* in German. According to Nótári (2013: 277) "the morpheme *himil* can be understood with the help of the German and the Anglo-Saxon word *hama* and the Middle High German words *ham*, *heme* with the meaning *dress*. However, this requires presumption of a *hem* form in order to deduce *himil* from it by the addition of the suffix -*ila*."[18] *Zorunga* is based on the strong verb OHG *zeran* 'to tear'. Thus, in referring to the text passage above, the noun can be described as 'indecent tearing at a woman's garments' (Tiefenbach 2004: 279–280).

The derivatives mentioned above appear primarily in Upper German laws, the origins of which reach back to the eighth century. They therefore pertain to the earliest records of the suffixes presented here, which were productive not only in the Germanic period but, to some extent, also in early Old High German, even up to contemporary German. Likewise, the suffixes -*lich* and -*ung* are used today to form new signifiers in everyday language as well as to coin technical terms in languages for special purposes.

6 Conclusion

Compounding and suffixation are highly productive and indispensable patterns of word formation in the early legal language of the Germanic tribes. Primarily, they are used to create lexemes that provide compact and condensed information pertaining to significant legal facts, such as the criminal offences, which are negotiated in court, and the injured parties. The complex words contribute to the expansion of the lexicon in various aspects. Two particular findings have been investigated in this article, for which, due to lack of space, admittedly only a few examples could be given: (1) word formation via compounding is used rather broadly, whereby it not uncommonly produces complex words which were exclusively identified in the *Leges*. Additionally, compounds can exhibit an exclusive semantic relationship between their first and second elements. (2) In the case of derivation, it may be observed that the Upper German *Leges* productively use the suffix -*ī(n)*, whereas this is only found sporadically elsewhere in Old High German in a number of complex words.

---

[18] The Old High German noun *hamo* and the Middle High German successor *ham*, which are related to the contemporary German *Hemd* 'shirt', belong to Germanic **hama-*, **haman-* 'shell, skin', which is related to the Indo-European stem **k̂em-* 'to cover'. OHG *himil* is likely to be a part of this word family (https://www.dwds.de/wb/Hemd#et-1, accessed 21 June 2017).

The systematic investigation of the word formation patterns of all complex vernacular *Leges* words remains an endeavour for future research. However, this will only be possible following a comprehensive inventory of the inserts.

The tradition of the laws of the barbarians contains numerous other semantic, lexical and morphological peculiarities that demand urgent, detailed examination by historical linguists. Moreover, because the lexemes have spread into several Germanic and Old High German dialects, they provide a very interesting corpus that can be used in more intense linguistic analysis, for example for a phonological and graphemic investigation. Its results would certainly serve to further enrich our knowledge about historical German grammar.

7 References

Editions

Leges Alamannorum, MGH LL nat. germ. I,5,1. http://www.dmgh.de/de/fs1/object/display/bsb00000857_meta:titlePage.html?sortIndex=020:020:0005:010:01:00 (accessed 15 February 2017).

Lex Baiuvariorum, MGH LL nat. germ. I,5,2. http://www.dmgh.de/de/fs1/object/display/bsb00000861_meta:titlePage.html?sortIndex=020:020:0005:010:02:00 (accessed 15 February 2017).

Leges Langobardorum, MGH LL IV. http://www.dmgh.de/de/fs1/object/display/bsb00000878_meta:titlePage.html?sortIndex=020:010:0004:010:00:00 (accessed 17 June 2017).

Dictionaries

Bergmann, Rolf. 1991. *Rückläufiges Morphologisches Wörterbuch des Althochdeutschen*. Tübingen: Niemeyer.

Deutsches Rechtswörterbuch. Wörterbuch der älteren deutschen Rechtssprache, vol. I–XIII. Since 1914. Weimar: Böhlau. https://www.rzuser.uni-heidelberg.de/~cd2/drw/ (accessed 12 March 2017).

DWB = Grimm, Jacob & Wilhelm Grimm. 1885. *Deutsches Wörterbuch*, vol. VI. Leipzig: Hirzel. http://woerterbuchnetz.de/DWB/?sigle=DWB&mode=Vernetzung&lemid=GM00433#XGM00433 (accessed 25 February 2017).
https://www.dwds.de/wb/Hemd#et-1 (accessed 21 June 2017).

Graff, Eberhard Gottlieb. 1963 [1834–1842]. *Althochdeutscher Sprachschatz oder Wörterbuch der althochdeutschen Sprache. Etymologisch und grammatisch bearbeitet*, vol. I–VII. Darmstadt: Wissenschaftliche Buchgesellschaft.

KFW = Karg-Gasterstädt, Elisabeth & Theodor Frings (eds.). Since 1952. *Althochdeutsches Wörterbuch. Auf Grund der von Elias von Steinmeyer hinterlassenen Sammlungen im Auf-*

trag der Sächsischen Akademie der Wissenschaften zu Leipzig, vol. I–VII. Berlin: Akademie.
Kluge, Friedrich. ²⁵2011. *Etymologisches Wörterbuch der deutschen Sprache*. Edited by Elmar Seebold. Berlin & New York: De Gruyter.
Lloyd, Albert Larry, Otto Springer & Rosemarie Lühr (eds.). Since 1988. *Etymologisches Wörterbuch des Althochdeutschen*, vol. I–IV. Göttingen: Vandenhoeck & Ruprecht.
SchGW = Schützeichel, Rudolf. 2004. *Althochdeutscher und altsächsischer Glossenwortschatz*, vol. I–XII. Tübingen: Niemeyer.
Schützeichel, Rudolf. ⁷2012. *Althochdeutsches Wörterbuch*. Berlin & New York: De Gruyter.
Seebold, Elmar. 2001. *Chronologisches Wörterbuch des deutschen Wortschatzes. Der Wortschatz des 8. Jahrhunderts (und früherer Quellen)*. Berlin & New York: De Gruyter.
StSG = Steinmeyer, Elias & Eduard Sievers. 1968–1969 [1879–1922]. *Die althochdeutschen Glossen*, vol. I–V. Berlin, Dublin & Zürich: Weidmann.
Walde, Alois & Johann Baptist Hofmann. ⁵1972. *Lateinisches Etymologisches Wörterbuch*, vol. 2: *M–Z*. Heidelberg: Winter.

Literature

Baesecke, Georg. 1935. Die deutschen worte der germanischen gesetze. *Beiträge zur Geschichte der deutschen Sprache und Literatur* 59. 1–101.
Bergmann, Rolf. 2005. Kulturgeschichtliche Aspekte des althochdeutschen Glossenwortschatzes. In Isolde Hausner, Peter Wiesinger & Katharina Korecky-Kröll (eds.), *Deutsche Wortforschung als Kulturgeschichte. Beiträge des Internationalen Symposiums aus Anlass des 90-jährigen Bestandes der Wörterbuchkanzlei der Österreichischen Akademie der Wissenschaften Wien, 25.–27. September 2003*, 49–76. Wien: Verlag der Österreichischen Akademie der Wissenschaften.
Bostock, J. Knight. ²1976. *A Handbook on Old High German Literature*. Oxford: Clarendon Press.
Bulitta, Brigitte & Ruth Schmidt-Wiegand. 2000. Hof. In Heinrich Beck, Dieter Geuenich & Heiko Steuer (eds.), *Reallexikon der germanischen Altertumskunde,* vol. 15: *Hobel–Iznik*, 59–63. Berlin & New York: De Gruyter.
Fischer Drew, Katherine. 1973. *The Lombard Laws*. Philadelphia: University of Pennsylvania Press.
Fleischer, Wolfgang & Irmhild Barz. ⁴2012. *Wortbildung der deutschen Gegenwartssprache*. Berlin & Boston: De Gruyter.
Frassetto, Michael. 2003. *Encyclopedia of Barbarian Europe. Society in Transformation*. Santa Barbara, Denver & Oxford: ABC Clio.
Hähnchen, Susanne. 2012. *Rechtsgeschichte. Von der Römischen Antike bis zur Neuzeit*. Heidelberg, München, Landsberg, Frechen & Hamburg: Müller.
Hellgardt, Ernst. 2013. Muspilli. In Rolf Bergmann (ed.), *Althochdeutsche und altsächsische Literatur. Ein Handbuch*, 288–292. Berlin & New York: De Gruyter.
Hüpper-Dröge, Dagmar. 1983. *Schild und Speer. Waffen und ihre Bezeichnungen im frühen Mittelalter* (Germanistische Arbeiten zu Sprache und Kulturgeschichte 3). Frankfurt am Main & Bern: Peter Lang.
Kroeschell, Karl. 2008. *Deutsche Rechtsgeschichte,* vol. 1: *Bis 1250*. Köln & Wien: Böhlau.
Lühr, Rosemarie. 1989. Zum Sprachtod einer Restsprache: Zwei ausgestorbene Wörter aus der Lex Baiuvariorum. In Heinrich Beck (ed.), *Germanische Rest- und Trümmersprachen* (Real-

lexikon der Germanischen Altertumskunde – Ergänzungsbände 3), 45–67. Berlin & New York: De Gruyter.
Meineke, Eckhard. 1982. trikil. In Rudolf Schützeichel (ed.), *Addenda und Corrigenda zu Steinmeyers Glossensammlung* (Nachrichten der Akademie der Wissenschaften in Göttingen. I. Philologisch-Historische Klasse 1982, 6), 18–36. Göttingen: Vandenhoeck & Ruprecht.
Meineke, Eckhard. 1994. *Abstraktbildungen im Althochdeutschen. Wege zu ihrer Erschließung* (Studien zum Althochdeutschen 23). Göttingen: Vandenhoeck & Ruprecht.
Meineke, Eckhard & Judith Schwerdt. 2001. *Einführung in das Althochdeutsche*. Paderborn, München, Wien & Zürich: Schöningh.
Müller, Peter O. 2016. Historical word-formation in German. In Peter O. Müller, Ingeborg Ohnheiser, Susan Olsen & Franz Rainer (eds.), *Word-formation. An international handbook of the languages of Europe* (Handbücher zur Sprach- und Kommunikationswissenschaft 40.5), 1867–1914. Berlin & Boston: De Gruyter.
Niederhellmann, Annette. 1983. *Arzt und Heilkunde in den frühmittelalterlichen Leges. Eine wort- und sachkundliche Untersuchung* (Arbeiten zur Frühmittelalterforschung 12; die volkssprachigen Wörter der Leges barbarorum III). Berlin & New York: De Gruyter.
Nótári, Tamás. 2013. Bavarian Linguistic Elements in Lex Baiuvariorum. *Acta Juridia Hungarica* 54(3). 272–285.
Olberg, Gabriele von. 1983. *Freie, Nachbarn und Gefolgsleute. Volkssprachige Bezeichnungen aus dem sozialen Bereich in den frühmittelalterlichen Leges* (Germanistische Arbeiten zu Sprache und Kulturgeschichte 2). Frankfurt am Main, Bern & New York: Peter Lang.
Olberg, Gabriele von. 1991. *Die Bezeichnungen für soziale Stände, Schichten und Gruppen in den Leges Barbarorum* (Arbeiten zur Frühmittelalterforschung 11; Die volkssprachigen Wörter der Leges barbarorum II). Berlin & New York: De Gruyter.
Oliver, Lisi. 2011. *The Body Legal in Barbarian Law* (Toronto Anglo-Saxon Series). Toronto: University of Toronto Press.
Poethe, Hannelore. 2000. Fachsprachliche Aspekte der Wortbildung. Die Leistung der Wortbildung für Fachsprache und Fachtext. In Irmhild Barz, Marianne Schröder & Ulla Fix (eds.), *Praxis- und Integrationsfelder der Wortbildungsforschung* (Sprache, Literatur und Geschichte: Studien zur Linguistik und Germanistik 18), 199–218. Heidelberg: Winter.
Prinz, Michael. 2010. Vergessene Wörter. Frühe volkssprachliche Lexik in lateinischen Urkunden und Amtsbüchern. *Jahrbuch für germanistische Sprachgeschichte* 1. 292–322.
Riecke, Jörg. 2004. *Die Frühgeschichte der mittelalterlichen medizinischen Fachsprache im Deutschen*, vol. II: *Wörterbuch*. Berlin & New York: De Gruyter.
Rivers, Theodore John (ed.). 1977. *Laws of the Alamans and Bavarians* (The Middle Ages Series). Philadelphia: University of Pennsylvania Press.
Saar, Stefan Christoph. 1999. Heimsuchung. In Heinrich Beck, Dieter Geuenich & Heiko Steuer (eds.), *Reallexikon der Germanischen Altertumskunde*, vol. 14, 247–250. Berlin & New York: De Gruyter.
Schatz, Josef. 1927. *Althochdeutsche Grammatik* (Göttinger Sammlung indogermanischer Grammatiken und Wörterbücher 6). Göttingen: Vandenhoeck & Ruprecht.
Schmid, Hans Ulrich. 1998. *-lîh-Bildungen. Vergleichende Untersuchungen zu Herkunft, Entwicklung und Funktion eines althochdeutschen Suffixes* (Studien zum Althochdeutschen 35). Göttingen: Vandenhoeck & Ruprecht.
Schmidt-Wiegand, Ruth. 1989. Rechtsvorstellungen bei den Franken und Alemannen vor 500. In Dieter Geuenich (ed.), *Die Franken und die Alemannen bis zur Schlacht bei Zülpich*

(496 / 7) (Reallexikon der Germanischen Altertumskunde – Ergänzungsbände 19), 545–557. Berlin & New York: De Gruyter.

Schmidt-Wiegand, Ruth. 1991. Die volkssprachigen Wörter der Leges barbarorum als Ausdruck sprachlicher Interferenz. In: Dagmar Hüpper & Clausdieter Schott (eds.), *Stammesrecht und Volkssprache. Ausgewählte Aufsätze zu den Leges barbarorum. Festgabe für Ruth Schmidt-Wiegand zum 1.1.1991*, 181–212. Weinheim: VCH Acta Humaniora.

Schmidt-Wiegand, Ruth. 1999. Rechtssprache im Althochdeutschen und ihre Erfassung: eine Übersicht. In Lothar Hoffmann, Hartwig Kalverkämper & Herbert Ernst Wiegand (eds.), *Fachsprachen / Languages for special purposes. Ein internationales Handbuch zur Fachsprachenforschung* und *Terminologiewissenschaft / An international handbook of special-language and terminology research* (Handbücher zur Sprach- und Kommunikationswissenschaft 14.2), 2309–2319. Berlin & New York: De Gruyter.

Schmidt-Wiegand, Ruth. 2006. Sprache, Recht, Rechtssprache bei Franken und Alemannen vom 6. bis zum 8. Jahrhundert. In Gerhard Dilcher (ed.), *Leges – Gentes – Regna. Zur Rolle von germanischen Rechtsgewohnheiten und lateinischer Schriftkultur bei der Ausbildung der frühgermanischen Rechtskultur*, 141–158. Berlin: Schmidt.

Schwab, Vincenz. forthcoming. *Volkssprachige Wörter in Pactus und Lex Alamannorum*. Bamberg: University of Bamberg dissertation 2017.

See, Klaus. 1964. *Altnordische Rechtswörter. Philologische Studien zur Rechtsauffassung und Rechtsgesinnung der Germanen* (Hermaea. Germanistische Forschungen. Neue Folge 16). Tübingen: Niemeyer.

Sonderegger, Stefan. [3]2003. *Althochdeutsche Sprache und Literatur. Eine Einführung in das älteste Deutsch. Darstellung und Grammatik* (De Gruyter Studienbuch). Berlin & New York: De Gruyter.

Splett, Jochen. [2]2000. Wortbildung des Althochdeutschen. In Werner Besch, Anne Betten, Oskar Reichmann & Stefan Sonderegger (eds.), *Sprachgeschichte. Ein Handbuch zur Geschichte der deutschen Sprache und ihrer Erforschung* (Handbücher zur Sprach- und Kommunikationswissenschaft 2.2), 1213–1222. Berlin & New York: De Gruyter.

Stein, Gabriele. 2000. The function of word-formation and the case of English *-cum-*. In Christiane Dalton-Puffer & Nikolaus Ritt (eds.), *Words: Structure, meaning, function: A festschrift for Dieter Kastovsky*, 277–288. Berlin & New York: Mouton de Gruyter.

Stricker, Stefanie. 2009. Definitorische Vorklärungen. In Rolf Bergmann & Stefanie Stricker (eds.), *Die althochdeutsche und altsächsische Glossographie. Ein Handbuch*, vol. 1, 20–32. Berlin & New York: De Gruyter.

Stricker, Stefanie & Anette Kremer. 2014. Das Bamberger LegIT-Projekt. Zur Erfassung des volkssprachigen Wortschatzes der Leges barbarorum in einer Datenbank. *Sprachwissenschaft* 39(3). 237–263.

Stricker, Stefanie, Anette Kremer & Vincenz Schwab. 2014. Der volkssprachige Wortschatz der *Leges Barbarorum*. Zum Projekt einer Online-Datenbank. In Bettina Bock & Maria Kozianka (eds.), *Weiland Wörter Welten – Akten der 6. Internationalen Konferenz zur Historischen Lexikographie und Lexikologie (Jena, 25.–27. Juli 2012). Whilom Worlds of Words – Proceedings of the 6th International Conference on Historical Lexicography and Lexicology (Jena, 25–27 July 2012)*, 285–294. Hamburg: Dr. Kovač.

Tiefenbach, Heinrich. 1980. Bezeichnungen für Fluren im Althochdeutschen, Altsächsischen und Altniederfränkischen. In Heinrich Beck, Dietrich Denecke & Herbert Jankuhn (eds.), *Untersuchungen zur eisenzeitlichen und frühmittelalterlichen Flur in Mitteleuropa und ihrer Nutzung, II. Bericht über die Kolloquien der Kommission für die Altertumskunde Mittel-*

und Nordeuropas in den Jahren 1975 und 1976 (Abhandlungen der Akademie der Wissenschaften in Göttingen. Philologisch-historische Klasse III, 115), 287–322. Göttingen: Vandenhoeck & Ruprecht.

Tiefenbach, Heinrich. 2004. *Quod Paiuuuarii dicunt* – Das altbairische Wortmaterial der Lex Baiuvariorum. In Albrecht Greule, Rupert Hochholzer & Alfred Wildfeuer (eds.), *Die bairische Sprache. Studien zu ihrer Geographie, Grammatik, Lexik und Pragmatik. Festschrift Ludwig Zehetner*, 263–290. Regensburg: edition vulpes.

Tiefenbach, Heinrich. 2009. Volkssprachige Wörter innerhalb lateinischer Texte. Rechtstexte: Leges, Kapitularien, Urkunden. In Rolf Bergmann & Stefanie Stricker (eds.), *Die althochdeutsche und altsächsische Glossographie. Ein Handbuch*, vol. 1, 958–975. Berlin & New York: De Gruyter.

Untermann, Jürgen. 1989. Zu den Begriffen 'Restsprache' und 'Trümmersprache'. In Heinrich Beck (ed.), *Germanische Rest- und Trümmersprachen* (Reallexikon der Germanischen Altertumskunde – Ergänzungsbände 3), 15–20. Berlin & New York: De Gruyter.

Weisweiler, Josef & Werner Betz. ³1974. Deutsche Frühzeit. In Friedrich Maurer & Heinz Rupp (eds.), *Deutsche Wortgeschichte*, vol. 1, 55–133. Berlin & New York: De Gruyter.

Wilmanns, Wilhelm. ²1967. *Deutsche Grammatik. Gotisch, Alt-, Mittel- und Neuhochdeutsch*, vol. II: Wortbildung. Berlin: De Gruyter.

Sören Stumpf
Free usage of German unique components
Corpus linguistics, psycholinguistics and lexicographical approaches

Abstract: In phraseological research, unique components are words that only occur within phrasemes (e.g. in *jmdn. an den **Pranger** stellen* TO PUT SOMEBODY IN THE UC [= unique component] (*Pranger* PILLORY) 'to pillory somebody' and *im **Handumdrehen*** IN A UC (*Handumdrehen* HAND'S TURNING) 'immediately, in the twinkling of an eye'. Still, observations of actual language use show that seemingly unique components can also be (re-)used outside of phraseological contexts and that they can contribute to the expansion of the lexicon. This paper deals with this free usage of unique components and focuses on corpus analytical, psycholinguistic and lexicographical approaches. It addresses questions about how the free usage of unique components can be ascertained with the help of corpus linguistics, how this usage can be explained from a psycholinguistic perspective and to what extent freely used unique components are recorded in German dictionaries. *

1 Introduction

Within phraseological research it seems to be a well-investigated fact that phrasemes can be the origin of lexical-semantic innovations by functioning as source units for secondary words and meanings as well as for the respective formation processes / products (e.g. *Haare spalten* → *Haarspalterei*) (cf. Stein 2012: 231–233). This paper deals with a phenomenon which at first sight seems paradoxical and has not received much attention up to now: Lexical expansion through unique components.[1] This seems to be especially paradoxical in view of the fact that unique components are words which (nowadays) only occur in formulaic expressions and can therefore, by definition, not be used as autonomous lexical units (as in: ***klipp** und klar* UC AND CLEAR 'very clearly'; ***Fersengeld** geben* TO GIVE UC (*Ferse* HEEL + *Geld* MONEY) 'to escape, to take to one's heels'; *etw.*

---

* I would like to thank Viola Kämmer for translating this article into English.
1 These elements are also called "unique elements" (Jaki 2014), "bound words" (Soehn 2004, 2006; Trawiński, Sailer, and Soehn 2005) or "cranberry words" (Richter and Sailer 2003).

*auf dem **Kerbholz** haben* TO HAVE SOMETHING ON THE UC (*Kerbe* TALLY + *Holz* STICK) 'somebody has committed a crime, to not have a clean record') (cf. Häcki Buhofer 1998: 162).[2] This is why they are often referred to as lexical irregularities in phraseological research (see Stumpf 2015; in print a; in print b).

Looking at this from the point of view of corpus linguistics, it becomes apparent that many of the words research has previously classified as unique components can be found not only in phraseological contexts but also increasingly in free contexts (see Stumpf 2014; accepted) such as:

(1) Ein **Fettnäpfchen** war den Mächtigen des Verbandes offenbar genug. Vor Wochenfrist hatte sich Assistenztrainer Hansi Flick (Foto) verbal vergaloppiert, als er das Rezept gegen Freistöße von Portugals Cristiano Ronaldo benannte: "Stahlhelme aufsetzen und groß machen." (Hamburger Morgenpost, 15 June 2012)
[One single blunder was apparently enough for those who have the say in the association. Before the week was out, assistant coach Hansi Flick (photo) had taken the wrong verbal track when he called the recipe for dealing with Portugal's Cristiano Ronaldo's free kicks: "putting on steel helmets and making ourselves great."]

Here, the unique component *Fettnäpfchen* is used as an autonomous unit and is separated from its phraseological context of *ins **Fettnäpfchen** treten / tappen* TO STEP INTO THE UC (*Fett* FAT + *Näpfchen* LITTLE POT) 'to displease somebody because of an inconsiderate comment / behavior, to blunder'.

This paper deals with this specific usage of unique components and focuses on the question in what way and to what extent freely used unique components can contribute to lexical expansion. Among others, the following questions can be considered relevant:
1. What methods could be applied in order to empirically prove the usage of components outside of phraseology? (section 3)
2. How can it be explained that seemingly unique components defy their phraseological fixedness? (section 4)

---

[2] Throughout this article, the German phrasemes and their meaning will be translated into English wherever possible. If the morphemes of a unique component are opaque and occur only within the scope of phraseological boundedness, no English equivalents can be given. If the unique component is a compound, the individual constituents of this compound will be translated. Translated constituents are written in small capital letters; the phraseological meaning is written in single quotation marks.

3. How can this usage outside of phraseology and the process of debonding[3] unique components be explained from a psycholinguistic point of view? (section 5)
4. What are the criteria for categorizing a unique component used outside of phraseology as an autonomous lexical unit? (as opposed to unique components that are occasionally freely used in the sense of phraseological modifications) (section 6)
5. How and to what extent are unique components which have become free lexemes dealt with in German dictionaries? (section 7)

These questions will be answered empirically with the help of extensive corpus-based analysis (drawing on the Deutsche Referenzkorpus / DeReKo and the analysis tool COSMAS-II).[4] From a theoretical point of view, the concept of semantic decomposability will be used to explain the usage of unique components outside of phraseology.

2 The current state of research

In previous research unique components have been defined as words that can only be found in the constituent inventory of phrasemes (e.g. *im **Brustton** der Überzeugung* WITH THE UC (*Brust* CHEST + *Ton* TONE) OF CONVICTION 'with complete and utter conviction' and *seit **Menschengedenken*** SINCE UC (*Mensch* HUMAN + *Gedenken* MEMORY) 'as long as anyone can remember') (cf. Dobrovol'skij 1989: 57; Fleischer 1997a: 37; Häcki Buhofer 2002a: 429; Čermák 2007: 21 and Crudu 2016: 113). Unique components are mainly considered phenomena that prototypically reveal the fixedness of phrasemes (cf. Korhonen 1992: 49 and Häcki Buhofer 2002b: 129). In many cases they are lexical units which have

---

3 By using the term "(phraseological) bonding" I refer to the phenomenon that certain words only occur in formulaic expressions and that they more or less disappear from free language use. Furthermore, the "process of bonding" (German: *Unikalisierung(sprozess)*) refers to the process of a free lexeme becoming phraseologically bound. "(Phraseological) debonding" indicates the reverse process: Phraseologically bound components are separated from their formulaic expression and are used as autonomous lexemes of the lexicon again. I have taken the term from research on (de-)grammaticalization. Here, "debonding" means "a composite change whereby a bound morpheme in a specific linguistic context becomes a free morpheme" (Norde 2009: 186). Thus, I adopted the term which is usually used with morphemes and applied it to lexemes.
4 https://cosmas2.ids-mannheim.de/cosmas2-web/ (accessed 27 March 2017).

become rare or even obsolete and which can no longer be found in free use but only in formulaic language. The fossilization of these elements in phrasemes shows their phraseological boundedness and can be regarded as a sign of the stabilizing effect of phrasemes (cf. Palm 1997: 30). This is the reason why phrasemes – due to their fixedness – can be considered repositories for archaic parts of a language.[5] Previous attempts at categorization were based on theory and included various levels of description (structural, semantic, etymological etc.). Nevertheless, their weak spot lies both in conveying the idea of an easy distinction between "phraseologically bound" and "non-phraseologically bound" elements and in compiling an exhaustive and representative list of phraseologically bound components (see Dobrovol'skij 1978; Feyaerts 1994 and Dobrovol'skij and Piirainen 1994a, 1994b). Previous classification models proceed on the assumption that categorization must be dichotomous: Either a component is phraseologically bound or it is not. However, an attentive observer might see that words which have been classified as unique by research can, in fact, occur outside of phraseological contexts, as is the case with the following three examples taken from the DeReKo:

(2) Der Nationalismus der korsischen Separatisten mit seinem Bombenterror gegen "Überfremdung" und für die Abtrennung vom französischen Mutterland ist oft nur der **Deckmantel** für Korruption und Verbrechen. (Salzburger Nachrichten, 31 October 1992)
[The Corsican separatists' nationalism with its terror bombing against "foreign infiltration" and for separation from the French mother country often serves as a pretext for corruption and crime.]

(3) Man kann ja über alles nachdenken und planen, bloß sollten **Luftschlösser** ausgeschlossen bleiben. (Niederösterreichische Nachrichten, 15 March 2012)
[Of course it is legitimate to think about everything and anything and make plans, but castles in the air should be excluded.]

(4) Der "glücklichste Formulierer" [...] ist der bayerische Ministerpräsident Edmund Stoiber noch nie gewesen. [...] Nun schien wieder so ein Tag eines Stoiber'schen **Bärendienstes** zu sein. (Rhein-Zeitung, 11 August 2005)
[Bavaria's premier Edmund Stoiber has never had the "most fortunate turn of phrase". [...] And today seemed to be another day of Stoiberian disservice.]

---

[5] However, it should be emphasized that even with unique-components-expressions there can sometimes be considerable structural variation (as in *aussehen / geschmückt / herausgeputzt / vorgeführt werden wie ein* **Pfingstochse** TO LOOK LIKE / TO BE DECORATED / TO BE PRIMPED UP / TO BE PRESENTED LIKE A UC (*Pfingsten* PENTECOST + *Ochse* OX) 'to look like / to be decorated / to be primped up / to be presented in a grossly overstated way').

With such examples, the crucial point is that they contradict the rigid and dichotomous definition of unique components by exhibiting the free usage of exactly those components that had previously been classified as unique. The observation that some unique components may occur in free usage is not a new one in unique component research. Häcki Buhofer (2002b: 154) finds that every lexeme in phrasemes (with unique components) whose meaning can more or less be derived from its form can also be used as an individual lexeme. Thus, she concludes that in most cases it is very difficult to draw a clear and reasonable line between uniqueness and non-uniqueness in a synchronous language system (cf. Häcki Buhofer 2002b: 155).

The problematic initial situation is as follows: On the one hand, there are the prevailing dichotomous definitions of previous phraseological research and the ensuing attempts at classification. On the other hand, there are examples and researchers' affirmative opinions about a usage outside of phrasemes that contradict this approach. Thus, the question arises as to how this situation should be dealt with and in how far this contradiction can be resolved. In my opinion, this should be done with the help of empirical analysis, as this approach is the only way to react to the previous, mainly intuitive and theoretical research into unique components.

3 Corpus analysis of unique components: unique components as a prototypical category

In order to empirically examine or even disprove a dichotomous distinction between unique components and free lexemes, corpus analysis would appear to be a suitable approach. It is only through a systematic and corpus analytical method that the actual usage of (seemingly) unique components can be ascertained and the essence of this uniqueness be described on an empirical level. It is this corpus-based method of examination that Steyer (2000: annotation 16) draws attention to when she writes that even supposedly unique components and thus, an element's boundedness to the respective phrase as well as a 'no-longer-existence' outside of the phrase, can be assessed through corpus analysis.[6]

The empirical section centers around the question as to what extent the elements can be considered phraseologically bound (also see Barz 2007a). The

---

6 However, this method has rarely been used in previous research on unique components.

underlying basis for the analysis is the DeReKo, with which it is possible to search for words in millions of texts and to ascertain and describe their usage with the help of mass data (cf. Steyer 2004: 94). Using the results from the corpus analysis, the concept of uniqueness can then be drafted.

The evaluation is based on a corpus of 1,909 components presumed to be unique components. The corpus was compiled with examples taken from previous unique component research and from the phraseological dictionaries of Röhrich (2006), Duden (2008), Quasthoff (2010) and Schemann (2011). The result is a list of phrasemes containing words that one might suppose to be unique. Within the scope of this corpus analysis, 1,318 components were assessed.

The quantitative analysis consists of the following three steps:

1. Determination of the **absolute quantity** of unique components: The first task is to determine the absolute quantity of the single lexemes (e.g. searching for *Gängelband*). The result reveals the absolute occurrence of the constituent: At the time of retrieval, *Gängelband* can be found 848 times in the DeReKo. Self-evidently, this set of results contains phraseologically bound lexemes as well as free realizations.

2. Determination of the unique components' **extra-phraseological usage**: This second step of the procedure centers on how many cases there are where the unique component is used in a non-phraseological context. In order to make this free usage more apparent, differentiated queries are used to exclude cases where the lexeme is used in a phraseological unit. To determine the basic form of a „unique component"-idiom, co-occurrence analysis are conducted in which those words are rendered visible that are frequently used in combination with the search word and that can therefore be seen as variants of the same phraseme (e.g. *jmdn. am **Gängelband** führen / haben / halten* 'to keep somebody on a leash, to keep somebody tied to one's apron strings' // *jmdn. vom **Gängelband** befreien / lösen* 'to let somebody off the leash, cut somebody loose from one's apron strings'). The results show that there are 91 instances where *Gängelband* is not used in the word combinations *jmdn. am **Gängelband** führen / haben / halten* // *jmdn. vom **Gängelband** befreien / lösen*. The full text display shows these free realizations; for example:

(5) Dabei wären viele Firmen in Mittelfranken bereit, Behinderte ihren Fähigkeiten entsprechend einzusetzen, "wenn das **Gängelband** der Politik nicht wäre". Es sei schließlich "gesellschaftliche Pflicht, etwas für die Menschen zu tun, die nicht auf der Sonnenseite des Lebens stehen." (Nürnberger Nachrichten, 01 May 2003)

[Yet many companies in Middle Franconia would be prepared to employ disabled people according to their abilities, if politics didn't have them (the companies) on a leash. After all, it was a social obligation to do something for those who don't live on the sunny side of life.]

3. **Calculation of phraseological boundedness:** In a third and final step the percentage proportions of instances of free usage are compared with those of phraseological usage. The word *Gängelband* can be found 848 times (= 100%). 91 of these 848 instances occur within an extra-phraseological context (= approx. 11%). Thus, the component *Gängelband* (only) occurs in phraseological word combinations in about 89% of all instances.

The analysis reveals that these instances are rather heterogeneous with regard to their phraseological boundedness, which is why the components can be ranked by the degree of their phraseological boundedness (cf. Stumpf 2015: 479–525). Apart from words that are only used in formulaic contexts (e.g. *Schnippchen* in *jmdm. ein Schnippchen schlagen* 'to trick / outwit somebody'), corpus analysis also brings to light those lexemes that are (phraseologically) bound only to a lesser extent (e.g. *Gardinenpredigt* in *jmdm. eine Gardinenpredigt halten* TO GIVE SOMEBODY A UC (*Gardine* CURTAIN + *Predigt* SERMON) 'to give somebody a lecture'). However, the most interesting aspect is that there are many words located in the "intermediate zone" between these two points (e.g. *Schokoladenseite* CHOCOLATE + SIDE and *Armutszeugnis* POVERTY + CERTIFICATE). From a corpus analytical point of view, there is a gradual distribution ranging from strongly phraseological to almost non-phraseological constituents. The empirical approach disproves the prevailing dichotomy of previous research: A component is not "either – or" but "more or less" phraseologically bound. Therefore the dichotomous division of unique components and free lexemes has to be relativized and replaced by a more dynamic concept.

Unique components embody a prototypical category, which can be visualized by a center-periphery model (see Figure 1).[7] Lexemes which possess a strong phraseological boundedness (e.g. *Kieker*) can be regarded as prototypical representatives of the whole category and are thus located in the center as opposed to lexemes that possess a weaker phraseological boundedness (e.g. *Zwickmühle* DOUBLE + MILL 'quandary', *Denkzettel* THINK + NOTE / REMINDER 'a lesson taught' and *Irrweg* ERRING + PATH 'wrong track'). Outside of the peripheral

---

7 Cf. also Holzinger (2013: 64), who refers to this as a continuum.

bounds there are those lexemes that are not bound to a formulaic context (e.g. *Garage* 'garage').

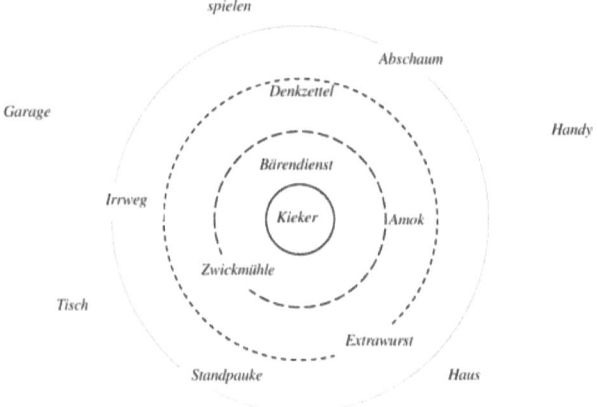

Fig. 1: The center-periphery model of unique components

4 Semantic decomposability as a determining factor of free usage

Given the relative boundedness of unique components, the question arises as to what kind of factors lead to the free usage of unique components. In fact, the semantic decomposability / analyzability[8] of the idioms which contain unique components plays a decisive role. It is the principle of compositionality that can be considered the basis of the theory of semantic decomposability (see Frege 1923) as it claims that the meaning of a complex expression is determined by the meanings and the composition of its parts (cf. Rabanus et al. 2008: 28):

> Contrary to the traditional view that idioms are non-compositional, many idiomatic phrases appear to be decomposable or analyzable with the meaning of their parts contributing independently to their overall figurative meanings [...]. (Gibbs 1990: 422)

---

8 See Gibbs and Nayak (1989); Gibbs, Nayak, and Cutting (1989); Gibbs et al. (1989) and Gibbs (1990). In German "semantically decomposable / analyzable phrasemes" are known as *semantisch teilbare Idiome* (cf. Dobrovol'skij 1997: 23–27).

In the case of phraseological word combinations, semantic decomposability is closely connected to a parallelism in the segmentation of the lexical and semantic structure of an idiom and, thus, also to the semantic status of the single components (cf. Dobrovol'skij and Piirainen 2009: 46). Semantic decomposability applies to those idioms whose constituents or constituent groups can act as relatively autonomous units that carry meaning, as is the case with the idiom *(leeres) Stroh dreschen*, in which the phraseological component *Stroh* could stand for 'dummes, inhaltsloses Zeug' (Engl.: 'stupid, meaningless stuff') (cf. Dobrovol'skij 1988: 131–132):

Tab. 1: Semantic decomposability of *(leeres) Stroh dreschen*

(leeres) Stroh	*dreschen*
'dummes, inhaltsloses Zeug	reden'
(EMPTY) STRAW	TO THRESH
'stupid, meaningless stuff	to talk'

The dissolution of uniqueness caused by semantic decomposability is also emphasized in the research:

> Da die Konstituenten der sekundär motivierten, semantisch teilbaren Phraseologismen eine selbstständige Bedeutung haben, tendieren sie besonders zur Autonomisierung [...]. Die semantische Teilbarkeit der Phraseologismen ist demzufolge [...] eine Voraussetzung für das Auftreten neuer Sememe bei einem Wort, die einem Phraseologismus entsprungen sind. (Földes and Györke 1988: 105; see also Földes 1988: 71 and Ptashnyk 2005: 92–93)
> [As the constituents of the secondarily motivated, semantically decomposable phrasemes possess an independent meaning, they are prone to autonomization [...]. Thus, the semantic decomposability of the phrasemes is [...] a premise for the occurrence of new sememes which stem from a phraseme.]

I then subjected this assumption, which has previously only been illustrated with the help of a few examples, to empirical analysis. 153 expressions, taken from the list of "living" unique-components-idioms compiled by Dobrovol'skij and Piirainen (1994a, 1994b), were examined with regard to their semantic decomposability. Here, the central question is how the semantic decomposability of a unique component is linked to its phraseological boundedness.

In order to determine decomposability, I included not only the comparison between the structure of an idiom and the structure of its semantic equivalent but also an analysis of syntactic transformations[9] such as 1) "relative clause" transformation, 2) "interrogative sentence" transformation and 3) the possibility of replacing the unique component with a demonstrative pronoun (Dobrovol'skij 2004: 67):

(6) Die gestern an den Tag gelegte Geschlossenheit lässt daher an die disziplinarische **Gardinenpredigt** denken, die Parteipräsident Fulvio Pelli seinen Delegierten vor zwei Monaten in Rapperswil hielt. (Die Südostschweiz, 14 March 2008)
[The unity that was displayed yesterday reminds us of the disciplinary lecture the party's president Fulvio Pelli gave his delegates two months ago in Rapperswil.]

(7) Ach Valentin, hättest Du je gedacht, welch große **Werbetrommel** in Deinem Namen einst gerührt werden würde? (Braunschweiger Zeitung, 14 February 2008)
[Oh, Valentine, would you ever have thought that so much would be drummed up in your name one day?]

(8) Der nationale Verband verhehlt nicht, dass er an die Unschuld seiner prominentesten Athletin glaubt und ihr durchaus dieses **Hintertürchen** offen halten wird. (Nürnberger Nachrichten, 14 December 2009)
[The national association makes no secret of the fact that it believes its most prominent female athlete to be innocent and that it will keep this loophole open for her.]

Overall, 59 (39%) out of 153 unique-component-idioms are semantically decomposable (e.g. *jmdm. eine* **Standpauke** *halten* TO GIVE SOMEBODY A UC (*Stand* STANDING + *Pauke* KETTLEDRUM) 'to give somebody a (real) dressing-down'). Figure 2 illustrates the relationship between semantic decomposability and the degree of phraseological boundedness of the respective unique-component-idioms.

As can be seen from the overview, there seems to be a connection between semantic decomposability and phraseological boundedness. The empirical analysis shows that the number of semantically decomposable unique-component-idioms decreases with the increase of phraseological boundedness. Semantically decomposable unique components are usually less phraseologically bound because they possess a certain meaning of their own, which allows them to be used outside of the phraseme. For example, 90% of the unique components which have a phraseological boundedness of 0–29% are semantically decomposable. Conversely, about 6% of the unique components that occur almost only in phrasemes (those that are phraseologically bound in 96% of all cases) possess semantic decomposability. Thus, semantic decomposability decreases with increasing phraseological boundedness.

---

9 Transformation tests provide proof of decomposability by giving the component a referential status and, thus, an autonomous meaning (cf. Dobrovol'skij 2000: 118).

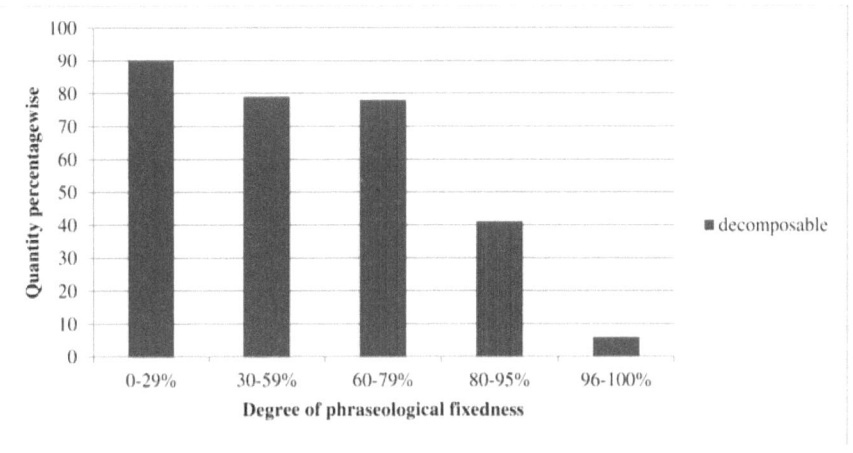

Fig. 2: Quantitative distribution of semantic decomposability of unique components

It can therefore be concluded that the most important feature for the process of autonomization is semantic decomposability, through which phraseological meaning can be allocated to the single constituents (cf. Barz 2007a: 16). In this way, the unique components gain morphosyntactic autonomy and develop semantic-associative potency (cf. Fleischer 1997a: 240).[10] Semantic decomposability leads to a free usage of the unique components with a phraseologically motivated meaning (cf. Barz 2007b: 33).

---

[10] This morphosyntactic autonomy also becomes apparent in forms of use usually reserved for free words. In the following text, for example, the (unique) substantival component of the phraseme **Luftschlösser** bauen TO BUILD UC (*Luft* AIR + *Schlösser* CASTLES) 'to make unrealistic plans' is used in the singular form and with the function of a genitive attribute: Auch der Einsturz des **Luftschlosses** "Einkaufszentrum" wird in Lampertheim kein großes Bedauern auslösen. (Mannheimer Morgen, 20 December 2000).

5 Psycholinguistic reflections on the free usage of unique components

The free usage of unique components can also be explained using psycholinguistic evidence. Here, it is especially research in the field of language processing that draws attention to the important relationship between phrasemes and lexemes and between phrasemes and free syntagmata: Although phrasemes – like words – are represented mentally as units, they are not necessarily treated as connected units by the speaker or hearer (cf. Burger, Häcki Buhofer, and Sialm 1982: 187), but are subject to the mechanisms governing the usage of free syntagmata (cf. Barz 2007a: 9). From a psycholinguistic point of view, phraseological variants are clues which suggest that phrasemes are not necessarily stored as complete and solid units but that they might be cognitive units, brought into being through certain production processes (cf. Häcki Buhofer 1999: 71). Through this variability, the syntactical-semantical unit of the phraseme is broken down, which – at least to some extent – makes it seem like a structured unit that is composed of autonomous parts (cf. Sabban 1998: 108). Unique-components-idioms, too, are processed as semantically (relatively) autonomous entities in the mental lexicon (cf. Dobrovol'skij 1995: 24). Although the speaker stores them as a whole, he is also capable of understanding their single constituents as autonomous words with a specific meaning. According to this assumption, the relevant unique-components-idioms are perceived as lexical units produced in line with the rules of semantic composition (cf. Dobrovol'skij 1995: 25), which benefits their autonomization and, thus, also their usage outside of phraseology.

Often speakers are not aware of the phraseological boundedness of the single constituents. Burger (2015: 92) points out that test subjects are able to visualize certain unique components (e.g. *Hungertuch* HUNGER + CLOTH, *Kerbholz* TALLY + STICK and *Maulaffen* MOUTH + MONKEYS) and are even capable of indicating features associated with these words.[11] From a cognitivist perspective, the "necrotic" character of unique components, which also calls into question whether these elements, because of their lack of meaning, can still be called words, has to be strongly relativized. Cognitive tests show that – despite their phraseological isolation – meaning can be attributed to the unique components (cf. Dobrovol'skij and Piirainen 1994b: 449). It can therefore be noted – as Hallsteinsdóttir (2001: 278) puts it:

---

11 Cf. also Burger (1973: 27).

> Eine unikale Komponente wird isoliert nicht als bedeutungslos angesehen, sondern ihr wird eine Bedeutung zugeordnet, die als die wörtliche Bedeutung aufgefasst wird. Auch wenn die etymologisch korrekte Bedeutung nicht bekannt ist, können Sprecher bei unikalen Komponenten – durch eine Quasimotivierung [...] – eine wörtliche Bedeutung konstruieren.
> [Taken by itself, a unique component is not regarded as meaningless, but is attributed a meaning that is considered literal. Even if the etymologically correct meaning is unknown, speakers can construct unique components' literal meanings through a quasimotivation.]

Regarding the free use of unique components, the process of phraseological bonding as well as the reverse process have to be brought into focus. The bonding can be seen as a kind of terminal point through which phraseologically bound components lose their status of autonomous elements in the lexicon (cf. Fleischer 1997b: 12). However, corpus analysis also proves the reverse case to be true: Through both an elliptic formation of meaning (see section 6) and through "cognitive processes of re-motivation" (Häcki Buhofer 2002a: 432) phraseologically bound constituents can regain their status as autonomous semantic elements in the lexicon. Thus, the terminal point of the bonding process can be overcome and unique components can once more gain a meaning (even if it is probably a slightly different one) (cf. Häcki Buhofer 2002a: 432f).

According to Häcki Buhofer (2002a: 432), the benefit of a cognitivist perspective lies in the fact that it enables us to describe and explain why unique components can be taken out of their phraseological boundedness and why they can be used freely with a (re-)motivated meaning. Speakers possess a strong cognitive tendency to attribute meaning to constituents which could stem from correct as well as incorrect knowledge (from the point of view of historical linguistics) or from synchronic and contemporary processes of motivation (cf. Häcki Buhofer 2002b: 156). According to Häcki Buhofer's (2002b: 135) understanding of the psycholinguistic perspective and psycholinguistic findings, the concept of uniqueness is a contradiction per se and would therefore lose its legitimization almost completely.

6 Freely used unique components as a contribution to the expansion of the lexicon

The question arises as to what kind of (lexical) status can be ascribed to unique components: Primarily, this is about the connection between phraseology and word formation, which is especially characterized by the fact that the formation potential in both word formation and phraseology are a source of lexical-semantic innovations (cf. Stein 2012: 230). Phrasemes can function as source units for secondary / derivative words and meanings as well as for the respective formation processes and products (cf. Barz 2007a: 8). In the case of unique components, so-called "de-phraseological derivation" plays the essential role in their autonomization. Földes (1988: 69) describes de-phraseological derivation as the development of word formations on the basis of a phraseme. This process, which takes place when unique components autonomize, can be defined as "elliptical meaning formation" (cf. Stein 2012: 235).

Tab. 2: *Sitzfleisch* (phraseological boundedness 35%)

kein	Sitzfleisch	haben
'keine	Ausdauer	haben'
NO	SITTING + MEAT	TO HAVE
'no	stamina	to have'

As Barz (2007a: 13) points out, this phraseological meaning formation is based on the principle of elliptical language use. According to this principle, parts of a complex expression can be left out if the communication partners share a sufficient amount of foreknowledge (cf. Fritz 2006: 51). Thus, the left-out expressions are a form of content which is not included in the verbal expression but which has to be mentally added (cf. von Polenz 2008: 302). Unique components that are freely used can therefore contribute to the expansion of the lexicon while they take on the meaning of the phraseme they are taken from (cf. Barz 2007a: 7). Földes (1988: 71) already draws attention to this special variety of lexical expansion by emphasizing that the extracted element gains formal-syntactical autonomy and absorbs the semantics of the whole construction. This "absorption" of the phraseme's meaning is seen clearly in the following examples:[12]

(9) Strapazierfähiges **Sitzfleisch** ist neben guter Kondition wichtig, wenn 35 Mitglieder des RV Wanderlust Beddingen am Montag, 17. Juli, sich auf den Weg zum Bundestreffen in Kiel machen. Vor den Radsportlern liegen 375 Kilometer, die an sechs Tagen auf den Zweirädern bewältigt werden müssen. (Braunschweiger Zeitung, 13 July 2006)

---

[12] The individual meaning specifications are taken from Duden (2013).

[Besides being in good shape, iron stamina / a resilient butt will be important for the 35 members of the RV Wanderlust Beddingen who will start out for their national meeting in Kiel on Monday, 17th July. The cyclists will have to tackle 375 kilometres in six days.]

Tab. 3: *Kohldampf* (phraseological boundedness 57%)

Kohldampf '(großen) Hunger	*schieben* haben'
CABBAGE + STEAM '(ravenous) hunger	TO SHOVE to have'

(10) Mächtiger **Kohldampf** muß einen jungen Mann in Berlin verleitet haben, den Ausdruck Schnellimbiß zu wörtlich zu nehmen. (Rhein-Zeitung, 28 January 1998)
[Ravenous hunger must have driven the young man in Berlin to take the expression fast food restaurant literally.]

Tab. 4: *Daumenschraube(n)* (phraseological boundedness 72%)

die 'den	*Daumenschrauben* Druck '(mehr) Zwang	*anziehen* erhöhen' ausüben'
THE 'the	THUMB + SCREWS pressure '(more) coercion	TO TIGHTEN to increase' to exercise'

(11) Auch Großbritannien und Frankreich, die im UN-Sicherheitsrat wie die USA, Russland und China ein Vetorecht haben, forderten weitere **Daumenschrauben** für die Führung in Teheran. (Hannoversche Allgemeine, 05 December 2007)
[Great Britain and France, who – like the US, Russia and China – have the right of veto in the UN Security Council, demanded that further pressure be put on the leadership in Teheran.]

In the examples quoted, *Sitzfleisch* has the meaning of 'Ausdauer / Durchhaltevermögen' (Engl.: 'stamina / perseverance / endurance'), *Kohldampf* means '(großer) Hunger' (Engl.: '(ravenous) hunger') and *Daumenschrauben* means 'Druck / Zwang / Sanktionen' (Engl.: 'pressure / coercion / sanctions'). As a result of the constituents' separation from their phraseological context, there exists a free usage which is motivated by the phraseological meaning (cf. Häcki Buhofer 2002b: 135). In the case of unique components, a new – since the item was no longer part of current usage outside of the phraseme – lexeme can develop in this way (cf. Barz 2007a: 14 and Häcki Buhofer 2002b: 155).

In the case of elliptical meaning formation on a phraseological basis, Barz (2007b: 33) comes to the conclusion that, compared to meaning formation on the basis of word formation, it does not lead to the expansion of the lexicon that frequently, as most instances of a free use of unique components are occasional in nature. My own corpus analysis, however, illustrates that freely used unique components can by no means be reduced to occasional modifications. Some unique components contribute to lexical expansion because they have undergone the process of lexicalization completely and are thus available to the speaker as free lexemes with a distinct meaning. The crucial question is when a unique component that is used outside of phraseological contexts gains the status of an autonomous lexeme. For this purpose, the quantitative analysis of the degree of phraseological boundedness conducted in the present paper can be extremely helpful. In my opinion, unique components which are semantically decomposable and also freely used in more than 50% of all cases cannot be denied a certain meaning of their own and, thus, they can also not be denied the status of a lexeme (e.g. *Denkzettel* THINKING + NOTE / REMINDER and *Krokodilsträne(n)* CROCODILE + TEAR(S)).

7 Inclusion of debonded words in the online Duden

Needless to say, for lexicography the previously illustrated process of debonding involves the inclusion of the relevant elements in the dictionary. As part of the present paper, the inclusion of 81 unique components, which range from a low to a high degree of phraseological boundedness, will be further examined. As can be seen from the online Duden,[13] although more and more of the freely used unique components have their own entries in the dictionary, the lemmatization does not seem to take place systematically. Table 5 shows a summarized segment of this analysis:

---

13 http://www.duden.de/ (accessed 27 March 2017).

Tab. 5: Inclusion of the debonded words in Duden online

Boundedness	Component	Meaning specification in Duden online
10%	*Gardinenpredigt* (CURTAIN + SERMON)	'Vorhaltungen in strafendem Ton, durch die jemand seine Verärgerung zu erkennen gibt' 'Remonstrances in a punitive tone, that display somebody's annoyance'
11%	*Armutszeugnis* (POVERTY + CERTIFICATE)	---
23%	*Extrawurst* (EXTRA + SAUSAGE)	---
26%	*Luftschloss* (AIR + PALACE)	'etwas Erwünschtes, was sich jemand in seiner Fantasie ausmalt, was aber nicht zu realisieren ist' 'something wished for that somebody pictures in his / her imagination but that cannot be realized'
35%	*Sitzfleisch* (SITTING + MEAT)	(umgangssprachlich scherzhaft) '[mit geistiger Trägheit verbundene] Ausdauer bei einer sitzenden Tätigkeit' (colloquially jocular) 'stamina in a sendentary occupation [often associated with mental sluggishness]'
46%	*Denkzettel* (THINKING + NOTE / REMINDER)	'exemplarische Strafe oder als Warnung angesehene unangenehme Erfahrung' 'Exemplary punishment or unpleasant experience that is seen as a warning'
57%	*Kohldampf* (CABBAGE + STEAM)	'starkes Hungergefühl; großer Hunger, von dem jemand befallen ist' 'Ravenous hunger; somebody is ravenously hungry'
66%	*Fettnäpfchen* (FAT + LITTLE POT)	---
72%	*Daumenschraube* (THUMB + SCREW)	---
78%	*Zwickmühle* (DOUBLE + MILL)	(umgangssprachlich) 'schwierige, verzwickte Lage, aus der es keinen Ausweg zu geben scheint' (colloquial) 'difficult, precarious situation / dilemma in which there seems to be no way out'
82%	*Bärendienst* (BEAR + SERVICE)	---

Boundedness	Component	Meaning specification in Duden online
83%	*Schattendasein* (SHADOW + EXISTENCE)	'Zustand geringer Bedeutung, weitgehender Vergessenheit' 'status of little (social) importance, obscurity'

The table demonstrates that debonded lemmata can be found in the online Duden, for example *Schattendasein* with a phraseological boundedness of 83% and the meaning of 'Zustand geringer Bedeutung, weitgehender Vergessenheit' (Engl.: 'status of little (social) importance, obscurity')[14] or *Luftschloss* which means 'etwas Erwünschtes, was sich jemand in seiner Fantasie ausmalt, was aber nicht zu realisieren ist' (Engl.: 'something wished for that somebody pictures in his / her imagination but cannot be realized')[15] and possesses a phraseological boundedness of 26%. By way of contrast, there are no entries for the words *Bärendienst* (82%) and *Extrawurst* (23%), which could be attributed a certain autonomy due to their gradual phraseological boundedness (similar to *Schattendasein* and *Luftschloss*) and their semantic decomposability. Thus, it seems to be rather inconsistent to have a separate dictionary entry for a strongly (phraseologically) bound word like *Schattendasein* while at the same time leaving out a word with a very weak phraseological boundedness like *Armutszeugnis* (11%). There is reason to assume that the lemmatization of freely used unique components is not based on empirical research.

Yet, the unique components which possess no further specification in Table 5 could very easily be given a meaning specification on the basis of their phraseologically motivated semantics. *Armutszeugnis* could be paraphrased with 'Beweis für jmds. Unfähigkeit / Unvermögen' (Engl.: 'proof of sb.'s incompetence / inability'), *Extrawurst* with 'ein Extrawunsch, eine bevorzugte Behandlung' (Engl.: 'a (granted) additional wish, preferential treatment'), *Fettnäpfchen* with 'ungeschicktes / unbedachtes / unkluges Verhalten / Fauxpas' (Engl.: 'clumsy / inconsiderate / ill-advised behavior / faux pas'), *Daumenschraube(n)* with 'starker Druck / Zwang (der auf eine Regierung o.ä. ausgeübt wird) / Sanktionen' (Engl.: 'strong pressure (put on sb. (e.g. the government)) / sanctions') and *Bärendienst* could be paraphrased with 'eine gute Absicht, die jedoch jemand anderem schadet' (Engl.: 'a good intention that nevertheless harms somebody').

---

14 http://www.duden.de/rechtschreibung/Schattendasein (accessed 27 March 2017).
15 http://www.duden.de/rechtschreibung/Luftschloss (accessed 27 March 2017).

8 Summary and perspectives

As corpus analysis shows, the category of unique components is a prototypical one. A word is not "either – or" but "more or less" phraseologically bound. This is why unique components can occur as or develop into autonomous and free lexemes, despite their apparent phraseological boundedness. In doing so, they acquire an independent, phraseme-motivated meaning, which is derived from their semantic decomposability.

The free usage of unique components can also be explained from a psycholinguistic perspective. Unique-components-phrasemes are processed as (more or less) semantically autonomous entities in the mental lexicon. Although speakers store these fixed expressions as a whole, they are capable of understanding their single constituents as autonomous words with specific meanings.

Thus, the process of phraseological bonding is not a unidirectional one. In actual language use, several debonding processes can be ascertained. Unique components can therefore contribute to the expansion of the lexicon as words that were seemingly restricted to a phraseological context can now again be used independently. From a lexicographical point of view, debonded words should find their way into the dictionaries.

For future research, it might be interesting to trace the debonding processes of single unique components diachronically and to determine further influential factors that promote the separation from the respective phrasemes. The motivation of the unique components undoubtedly plays a decisive role here. Within the scope of this corpus analysis, the words that occurred frequently in free usage were almost always compound words whose structure could be described as being relatively transparent (e.g. *Deckmantel* PROTECTING + COAT, *Lebensnerv* LIFE + NERVE or *Schokoladenseite* CHOCOLATE + SIDE):

> Die grosse Zahl der zusammengesetzten Wörter mit unikalen Elementen bietet von der Zusammensetzung her oft Anhaltspunkte für eine Motivation (die keine Remotivation im sprachgeschichtlichen Sinn ist), aber eine Aufteilung der phraseologischen Bedeutung auf die verschiedenen Komponenten einschliesslich der ‚unikalen' erlaubt. (Häcki Buhofer 2002b: 155)
> [From the point of view of their composition, the huge number of compound words with unique elements can often be an indication of a motivation (which is not a remotivation in the historical linguistics sense), but which permits an allocation of the phraseological meaning to the different components, including the 'unique' ones.]

The free usage of phraseologically bound word formations is therefore facilitated by the fact that they are composed of commonly used elements and according to regular word formation rules (e.g. *Lauf-feuer* RUNNING + FIRE, *Hinter-hand*

BEHIND + HAND, *Tanz-bein* DANCING + LEG) (cf. Häcki Buhofer 1998: 168, 2002b: 134). Thus, they can be motivated more easily than (for example) unique components whose morphemes only occur within the scope of phraseological boundedness such as in *klipp*, *Tapet* or *Kieker*.

9 References

Barz, Irmhild. 2007a. Die Phraseologie als Quelle lexikalischer Neuerungen. In Hans Ulrich Schmid (ed.), *Beiträge zur synchronen und diachronen Sprachwissenschaft* (Abhandlungen der Sächsischen Akademie der Wissenschaften zu Leipzig, Philologisch-Historische Klasse 80,4), 7–20. Leipzig: Verlag der Sächsischen Akademie der Wissenschaften.

Barz, Irmhild. 2007b. Wortbildung und Phraseologie. In Harald Burger, Dmitrij Dobrovol'skij, Peter Kühn & Neal R. Norrick (eds.), *Phraseologie / Phraseology. Ein internationales Handbuch der zeitgenössischen Forschung / An international handbook of contemporary research* (Handbücher zur Sprach- und Kommunikationswissenschaft 28.1), 27–36. Berlin & New York: De Gruyter.

Burger, Harald. 1973. *Idiomatik des Deutschen* (Germanistische Arbeitshefte 16). Tübingen: Niemeyer.

Burger, Harald. ⁵2015. *Phraseologie. Eine Einführung am Beispiel des Deutschen* (Grundlagen der Germanistik 36). Berlin: Erich Schmidt.

Burger, Harald, Annelies Häcki Buhofer & Ambros Sialm. 1982. *Handbuch der Phraseologie.* Berlin & New York: De Gruyter.

Čermák, František. 2007. Idioms and morphology. In Harald Burger, Dmitrij Dobrovol'skij, Peter Kühn & Neal R. Norrick (eds.), *Phraseologie / Phraseology. Ein internationales Handbuch der zeitgenössischen Forschung / An international handbook of contemporary research* (Handbücher zur Sprach- und Kommunikationswissenschaft 28.1), 20–26. Berlin & New York: De Gruyter.

Crudu, Mihai. 2016. *Sprachliche Unikalia im Phraseolexikon des Deutschen und Rumänischen.* Berlin: Wissenschaftlicher Verlag.

Dobrovol'skij, Dmitrij. 1978. *Phraseologisch gebundene lexikalische Elemente der deutschen Gegenwartssprache.* Leipzig: University of Leipzig dissertation.

Dobrovol'skij, Dmitrij. 1988. *Phraseologie als Objekt der Universalienlinguistik.* Leipzig: Verlag Enzyklopädie.

Dobrovol'skij, Dmitrij. 1989. Formal gebundene phraseologische Konstituenten. Klassifikationsgrundlagen und typologische Analyse. *Beiträge zur Erforschung der deutschen Sprache* 9. 57–78.

Dobrovol'skij, Dmitrij. 1995. *Kognitive Aspekte der Idiom-Semantik* (Eurogermanistik 8). Tübingen: Narr.

Dobrovol'skij, Dmitrij. 1997. *Idiome im mentalen Lexikon. Ziele und Methoden der kognitiv basierten Phraseologieforschung* (Fokus 18). Trier: Wissenschaftlicher Verlag Trier.

Dobrovol'skij, Dmitrij. 2000. Ist die Semantik von Idiomen nichtkompositionell? In Susanne Beckmann, Peter-Paul König & Georg Wolf (eds.), *Sprachspiel und Bedeutung. Festschrift für Franz Hundsnurscher zum 65. Geburtstag*, 113–124. Tübingen: Niemeyer.

Dobrovol'skij, Dmitrij. 2004. Semantische Teilbarkeit der Idiomstruktur. Zu operationalen Kriterien. In Christine Palm-Meister (ed.), *EUROPHRAS 2000. Internationale Tagung zur Phraseologie vom 15.–18. Juni 2000 in Aske / Schweden* (Stauffenburg Linguistik 25), 61–68. Tübingen: Stauffenburg.
Dobrovol'skij, Dmitrij & Elisabeth Piirainen. 1994a. Phraseologisch gebundene Formative: auf dem Präsentierteller oder auf dem Abstellgleis? *Zeitschrift für Germanistik* 4 (Neue Folge). 65–77.
Dobrovol'skij, Dmitrij & Elisabeth Piirainen. 1994b. Sprachliche Unikalia im Deutschen. Zum Phänomen phraseologisch gebundener Formative. *Folia Linguistica. Acta Societatis Linguisticae Europaeae* 28. 449–473.
Dobrovol'skij, Dmitrij & Elisabeth Piirainen. 2009. *Zur Theorie der Phraseologie. Kognitive und kulturelle Aspekte* (Stauffenburg Linguistik 49). Tübingen: Stauffenburg.
Duden. ³2008. *Redewendungen. Wörterbuch der deutschen Idiomatik*. Mannheim: Dudenverlag.
Duden. ⁴2013. *Redewendungen. Wörterbuch der deutschen Idiomatik*. Berlin: Dudenverlag.
Feyaerts, Kurt. 1994. Zur lexikalisch-semantischen Komplexität der Phraseologismen mit phraseologisch gebundenen Formativen. In Christoph Chlosta, Peter Grzybek & Elisabeth Piirainen (eds.), *Sprachbilder zwischen Theorie und Praxis. Akten des Westfälischen Arbeitskreises "Phraseologie / Parömiologie" (1991 / 1992)* (Studien zur Phraseologie und Parömiologie 2), 133–162. Bochum: Brockmeyer.
Fleischer, Wolfgang. ²1997a. *Phraseologie der deutschen Gegenwartssprache*. Tübingen: Niemeyer.
Fleischer, Wolfgang. 1997b. Das Zusammenwirken von Wortbildung und Phraseologisierung in der Entwicklung des Wortschatzes. In Rainer Wimmer & Franz-Josef Behrens (eds.), *Wortbildung und Phraseologie* (Studien zur deutschen Sprache 9), 9–24. Tübingen: Narr.
Földes, Csaba. 1988. Erscheinungsformen und Tendenzen der dephraseologischen Derivation in der deutschen und ungarischen Gegenwartssprache. *Deutsche Sprache* 16. 68–78.
Földes, Csaba & Zoltan Györke. 1988. Wortbildung auf der Grundlage von Phraseologismen in der deutschen, russischen und ungarischen Sprache. *Zeitschrift für Phonetik, Sprachwissenschaft und Kommunikationsforschung* 41. 102–112.
Frege, Gottlob. 1923. Logische Untersuchungen. Dritter Teil: Gedankengefüge. *Beiträge zu Philosophie des deutschen Idealismus* 3. 36–51.
Fritz, Gerd. ²2006. *Historische Semantik* (Sammlung Metzler 313). Stuttgart: Metzler.
Gibbs, Raymond W. 1990. Psycholinguistic studies on the conceptual basis of idiomaticity. *Cognitive Linguistics* 1. 417–451.
Gibbs, Raymond W. & Nandini P. Nayak. 1989. Psycholinguistic studies on the syntactic behavior of idioms. *Cognitive Psychology* 21, 100–138.
Gibbs, Raymond W., Nandini P. Nayak, John L. Bolton & Melissa E. Keppel. 1989. Speakers' assumptions about the lexical flexibility of idioms. *Memory & Cognition* 16. 58–68.
Gibbs, Raymond W., Nandini P. Nayak & Copper Cutting. 1989. How to kick the bucket and not decompose. Analyzability and idiom processing. *Journal of Memory and Language* 28. 576–593.
Häcki Buhofer, Annelies. 1998. Processes of idiomaticity – idioms with unique components. In Peter Ďurčo (ed.), *Europhras '97. Phraseology and Paremiology. International Symposium, 2–5 September 1997*, 162–169. Bratislava: Akadémia PZ.

Häcki Buhofer, Annelies. 1999. Psycholinguistik der Phraseologie. In Nicole Fernandez Bravo, Irmtraud Behr & Claire Rozier (eds.), *Phraseme und typisierte Rede* (Eurogermanistik 15), 63–75. Tübingen: Stauffenburg.

Häcki Buhofer, Annelies. 2002a. Phraseologisch isolierte Wörter und Wortformen. In David Alan Cruse, Franz Hundsnurscher, Michael Job & Peter Rolf Lutzeier (eds.), *Lexikologie. Ein internationales Handbuch zur Natur und Struktur von Wörtern und Wortschätzen* (Handbücher zur Sprach- und Kommunikationswissenschaft 21.1), 429–433. Berlin & New York: De Gruyter.

Häcki Buhofer, Annelies. 2002b. „Unikalia" im Sprachwandel: phraseologisch gebundene Wörter und ihre lexikographische Erfassung. In Elisabeth Piirainen & Ilpo Tapani Piirainen (eds.), *Phraseologie in Raum und Zeit. Akten der 10. Tagung des Westfälischen Arbeitskreises "Phraseologie / Parömiologie" (Münster 2001)* (Phraseologie und Parömiologie 10), 125–160. Baltmannsweiler: Schneider Verlag Hohengehren.

Hallsteinsdóttir, Erla. 2001. *Das Verstehen idiomatischer Phraseologismen in der Fremdsprache Deutsch* (Philologia – Sprachwissenschaftliche Forschungsergebnisse 49). Hamburg: Kovač.

Holzinger, Herbert J. 2013. Unikale Elemente: Eine Herausforderung für Lexikologie und Lexikografie. *Aussiger Beiträge. Germanistische Schriftenreihe aus Forschung und Lehre* 7. 53–66.

Jaki, Sylvia. 2014. *Phraseological Substitutions in Newspaper Headlines. "More than Meats the Eye"* (Human Cognitive Processing 46). Amsterdam & Philadelphia: John Benjamins.

Korhonen, Jarmo. 1992. Morphosyntaktische Variabilität von Verbidiomen. In Csaba Földes (ed.), *Deutsche Phraseologie in Sprachsystem und Sprachverwendung*, 49–87. Wien: Praesens.

Norde, Muriel. 2009. *Degrammaticalization* (Oxford linguistics). Oxford: Oxford University Press.

Palm, Christine. ²1997. *Phraseologie. Eine Einführung* (Narr-Studienbücher). Tübingen: Narr.

von Polenz, Peter. ³2008. *Deutsche Satzsemantik. Grundbegriffe des Zwischen-den-Zeilen-Lesens* (De-Gruyter-Studienbuch). Berlin: De Gruyter.

Ptashnyk, Stefaniya. 2005. "Unstabile" feste Wortverbindungen. Zur Dynamik des phraseologischen Sprachbestandes. *Hermes* 35. 77–95.

Quasthoff, Uwe. 2010. *Wörterbuch der Kollokationen im Deutschen*. Berlin & New York: De Gruyter.

Rabanus, Stefan, Eva Smolka, Judith Sterb & Frank Rösler. 2008. Die mentale Verarbeitung von Verben in idiomatischen Konstruktionen. *Zeitschrift für germanistische Linguistik* 36. 27–47.

Richter, Frank & Manfred Sailer. 2003. Cranberry Words in Formal Grammar. In Clarie Beyssade, Olivier Bonami, Patricia Cabredo Hofherr & Francis Corblin (eds.), *Empirical Issues in Formal Syntax and Semantics*, vol. 4, 155–171. Paris: Presses de l'Université Paris-Sorbonne.

Röhrich, Lutz. ⁷2006. *Lexikon der sprichwörtlichen Redensarten*, 3 vols. (Herder-Spektrum 5400). Freiburg: Herder.

Sabban, Annette. 1998. *Okkasionelle Variationen sprachlicher Schematismen. Eine Analyse französischer und deutscher Presse- und Werbetexte* (Romanica Monacensia 53). Tübingen: Narr.

Schemann, Hans. ²2011. *Deutsche Idiomatik. Wörterbuch der deutschen Redewendungen im Kontext*. Berlin & Boston: De Gruyter.

Soehn, Jan-Philipp. 2004. License to COLL. How to bind bound words and readings to their contexts. In Stefan Müller (ed.), *The proceedings of the 11th International Conference on Head-Driven Phrase Structure Grammar, Center for Computational Linguistics*, 261–273. Leuven: CSLI Publications.

Soehn, Jan-Philipp. 2006. *Über Bärendienste und erstaunte Bauklötze. Idiome ohne freie Lesart in der HPSG* (Europäische Hochschulschriften Reihe 1, Deutsche Sprache und Literatur 1930). Frankfurt am Main: Peter Lang.

Stein, Stephan. 2012. Phraseologie und Wortbildung des Deutschen. Ein Vergleich von Äpfeln mit Birnen? In Michael Prinz & Ulrike Richter-Vapaatalo (eds.), *Idiome, Konstruktionen, „verblümte Rede". Beiträge zur Geschichte der germanistischen Phraseologieforschung* (Beiträge zur Geschichte der Germanistik 3), 225–240. Stuttgart: Hirzel.

Steyer, Kathrin. 2000. Usuelle Wortverbindungen des Deutschen. Linguistisches Konzept und lexikografische Möglichkeiten. *Deutsche Sprache* 28. 101–125.

Steyer, Kathrin. 2004. Kookkurrenz. Korpusmethodik, linguistisches Modell, lexikografische Perspektiven. In Kathrin Steyer (ed.), *Wortverbindungen – mehr oder weniger fest*, 87–116. Berlin: De Gruyter.

Stumpf, Sören. 2014. *Mit Fug und Recht* – Korpusbasierte Erkenntnisse zu phraseologisch gebundenen Formativen. *Sprachwissenschaft* 39. 85–114.

Stumpf, Sören. 2015. *Formelhafte (Ir-)Regularitäten. Korpuslinguistische Befunde und sprachtheoretische Überlegungen* (Sprache – System und Tätigkeit 67). Frankfurt am Main: Peter Lang.

Stumpf, Sören. In print a. Formelhafte (Ir-)Regularitäten. Theoretische Begriffsbestimmung und empirische Beispielanalyse. In Maurice Kauffer & Yvon Keromnes (eds.), *Approches théoriques et empiriques en phraséologie*. Tübingen: Stauffenburg.

Stumpf, Sören. In print b. Formulaic (ir-)regularities in German. Corpus linguistics and construction grammar approaches. In Natalia Filatkina & Sören Stumpf (eds.), *Konventionalisierung und Variation / Conventionalization and variation*. Franfurt am Main: Peter Lang.

Stumpf, Sören. Accepted. A corpus analysis of German unique components. In Salah Mejri, Inès Sfar & Olivier Soutet (eds.), *Phraséologie et discours*.

Trawiński, Beata, Manfred Sailer & Jan-Philipp Soehn. 2005. Combinatorial aspects of collocational prepositional phrases. In Patrick Sain-Dizier (ed.), *Computational linguistics dimensions of syntax and semantics of prepositions* (Text, Speech and Language Technology), 181–196. Dordrecht: Springer.

II Morphological Productivity

Ingo Plag and Sonia Ben Hedia
The phonetics of newly derived words: Testing the effect of morphological segmentability on affix duration

Abstract: Newly derived morphologically complex words have played a prominent role in research on morphological productivity and lexical innovation (e.g. Baayen 1989, 1996; Plag 1999; Mühleisen 2010). Most of the attention concerning the properties of such words has been devoted to their phonological, morphological, semantic and syntactic properties (see, for example, Bauer et al. 2013 for such analyses). This paper takes a look at the phonetic properties of affixed words, testing Hay's (2003) 'segmentability hypothesis', according to which newly derived words are expected to show less phonetic integration, hence less phonetic reduction, of the affix involved than established forms. This hypothesis is based on the idea that morphological segmentability negatively correlates with phonological integration. To date there is only one study that clearly confirmed the segmentability hypothesis (i.e. Hay 2007), while other studies have failed to replicate the effect (see Hanique and Ernestus 2012 for an overview). The present study investigates the issue with data from the Switchboard corpus for five affixes of English: *un-*, locative *in-*, negative *in-*, *Dis-* and adverbial *-ly*. Using different measures of morphological segmentability, we demonstrate that the durations of the two prefixes *un-* and *dis-* (unlike the durations of *in-* and *-ly*) largely support the segmentability hypothesis. With *un-* and *dis-* prefixed words, prefixes that are more easily segmentable have longer durations. *

---

* The authors wish to thank the editors and the reviewers for their constructive feedback on an earlier version. We are also grateful for comments to the members of the DFG Research Unit FOR2373 and to the audiences at the Workshop on Expanding the Lexicon, Trier, 17–18 November 2016 and at the Old World Conference on Phonology, Düsseldorf, 20–22 February 2017. The usual disclaimers apply. This research was partially funded by the Deutsche Forschungsgemeinschaft (Research Unit FOR2373 'Spoken Morphology', Projects PL 151/7–1 and PL 151/8–1) and the Strategischer Forschungsfonds der Heinrich-Heine-Universität Düsseldorf, which we gratefully acknowledge.

∂ Open Access. © 2018 Ingo Plag, Sonia Ben Hedia, published by De Gruyter. [CC BY-NC-ND] This work is licensed under the Creative Commons Attribution-NonCommercial-NoDerivatives 4.0 License.
https://doi.org/10.1515/9783110501933-095

1 Introduction

Neologisms and rare words have played a prominent role in research on morphological productivity (e.g. Baayen 1989, 1996; Plag 1999; Mühleisen 2010). Most of the attention concerning the properties of such lexical innovations has been devoted to their phonological, morphological, semantic and syntactic properties. For example, Plag (1999) provides a detailed analysis of the complex phonological alternations observable with 20th century neologisms in *-ize*, *-ify* and *-ate*. Work on morphological properties has been devoted, among other things, to possible and impossible affix combinations (e.g. Hay and Plag 2004; Plag and Baayen 2009). The semantics and syntax of newly derived words has been investigated, for instance, in Plag (1998), Barker (1998), Mühleisen (2010) and Schulte (2015). Bauer, Lieber, and Plag (2013) provide analyses at all four levels of description of a plethora of productive derivational processes in English.

Recently, another level of description has come under the radar of morphologists, phonetics (see, for example, Hanique and Ernestus 2012; Plag 2014 for overviews). There is some work that shows that, at least for some morphological categories, phonetic detail can tell us something about the morphological structure of a word. Morphologically complex words are often phonetically reduced (or otherwise phonetically variable) as compared to their citation forms (e.g. Pluymaekers, Ernestus, and Baayen 2005). And bases of complex words are phonetically different from the same form pronounced as a free morpheme outside the derived word in question (Kemps et al. 2005a, 2005b; Blazej and Cohen-Goldberg 2015). The extent and nature of such phonetic variability and its theoretical significance are still largely unclear, but it seems that phonetic detail may also be relevant for the question of how newly derived words and established words may differ.

Consider the word *government*. It is mostly pronounced [gʌvmənt] or [gʌvəmənt], not [gʌvərnmənt]. This phonological opacity goes together with semantic opacity: *government* does not primarily denote 'action of VERBing' (as is standardly the case with *-ment* derivatives), but rather denotes the people who govern, or, more generally, 'political authorities'. Other pertinent cases are *restless* and *exactly*, which are words that are often pronounced without a /t/. It has been suggested (e.g. by Hay 2003) that such cases of phonological opacity may not be idiosyncratic, but reflect different degrees of morphological segmentabilty, which in turn is influenced by the frequential properties of base and derivative (Hay 2001, 2003). *Government* is far more frequent than its base *govern* and is therefore less easily segmented than, for example, *enjoyment*, whose base is far more frequent than its derivative (see Plag 2003: Chapter 4 for an introduction to the notion of morphological segmentability). Similarly, *exactly* is far more frequent than its base and easily loses its /t/, while, for example, *abstractly* is much less frequent than its base and is unlikely to occur without its base-final /t/.

Phonetic variability may affect not only bases but also affixes. For example, Hay (2007) finds that the vowel of the prefix *un-* may be realized as a full vowel, as a schwa, or even be completely absent in running speech. The prefix may be realized with variable acoustic duration (measured in milliseconds) within and across speakers, and across different derivatives, even at the same speech rate. Hay (2001, 2003) demonstrates that this kind of phonetic variation is not random, and her results suggest that factors facilitating morphological decomposition (e.g. boundary-like phonotactics or low frequency of the derived form relative to the base) lead to phonetically longer pronunciations. In other words, according to Hay (2002, 2003), the degree of phonetic reduction is at least partially determined by the degree of morphological segmentability of the word in question. We will call this the 'segmentability hypothesis'.

Newly derived words are usually easily decomposable[1] since, crucially, this allows the hearer to access the constituent morphemes and compute the meaning of the word unknown to him / her on the basis of the individual morphemes (and / or the pertinent word-formation rule). It can thus be predicted that a newly derived word, or the affix that derives it, is phonetically less reduced than the same affix in an established form which is less easily decomposed. It is, however, very difficult to analyze the phonetic properties of newly derived words for two reasons. First, one does not know whether a given word that a given speaker uses is new to this speaker, even if it is new for other speakers. Second, in order to observe phonetic reduction, words should be observed in their natural context, i.e. in natural conversational speech (Tucker and Ernestus 2016). Unfortunately, existing speech corpora are usually rather small, and new coinages are rather rare events. Whether affixes in newly derived words are less reduced can, however, be indirectly tested by examining the effects of segmentability on all words. If there is a general effect of segmentability in the predicted direction, newly derived words will show the largest effects, as they are at the end of the segmentability scale.

The present paper tests the segmentability hypothesis with data from the Switchboard corpus (Godfrey and Holliman 1997) for five affixes of English: *un-*, negative *in-*, locative *in-*, *dis-* and adverbial *-ly*. Different measures of morpholog-

---

[1] We use the term 'decomposable' when we refer to words, and the term 'segmentable' when we refer to affixes.

ical segmentability are investigated, and the results demonstrate that the durations of the prefixes *un-* and *dis-* largely support the segmentability hypothesis. With *un-* and *dis-* prefixed words, prefixes that are more easily segmentable have longer durations. This is indirect evidence that newly derived words, which necessarily rely on morphological decomposition, may have phonetic properties different from those of established forms. The suffixed words and the words derived with *in-*, as collected in our data set, do not show this effect, however, which raises interesting new research questions.

2 Phonetic implementation and morphological segmentability

As mentioned in the introduction, it has been claimed (e.g. by Hay 2003) that phonetic reduction in morphologically complex words reflects the degree of morphological segmentability. We have labeled this the 'segmentability hypothesis'. If true, this means that new morphologically derived words should show less phonetic reduction than existing words. This is due to the fact that neologisms derived by affixation need to be morphologically decomposed in order to allow the listener to come up with an interpretation of the new word, based on the meaning of the affix, the meaning of the base, and the context.

Hay (2007) presents evidence from English words derived with the prefix *un-* that such a reduction effect can indeed be found. In that study, relative frequency is used as a measure of segmentability. This measure is computed as the ratio of the frequency of the derivative and the frequency of the base. The rationale behind this ratio builds on dual route models of lexical storage and access, i.e. whole word vs. decomposed. Complex words with a high frequency of the derivatives vis-à-vis a low frequency of the base will have a very strong representation of the derived word in the mental lexicon, as against a rather weak representation of the base. This will lead to a whole-word bias in lexical processing. Conversely, having a derivative with low frequency and a corresponding base with a high frequency, this will support morphological decomposition since the base representation is strong, and the representation of the derivative is weak. In the extreme case of neologisms, there is no representation of the derived word yet, and decomposition is the only possibility.

Hay (2007) finds an effect of relative frequency, such that *un-* words that have a lower relative frequency (and thus are more easily segmented) show longer prefix durations. One problem with Hay's result is that many studies have failed to replicate the effect of relative frequency or of other measures of segmentability on durational properties of complex words. Apart from relative frequency, semantic and structural measures have been used to test the segmentability hypothesis. Semantic measures use some operationalized notion of semantic transparency. The more semantically transparent a derivative, the more easily it can be segmented. Measures of semantic transparency are standardly gathered through rating experiments with ordinary language users, or, alternatively, through ratings by trained experts. Structural measures make recourse to structural distinctions based on boundary strength (e.g. phrase-boundary vs. word boundary vs. affix boundary), types of bases (e.g. phrases vs. words vs. roots), or prosodic domains (phrase boundary vs. word boundary vs. foot boundary vs. syllable boundary).

Research on the acoustic correlates of segmentability is still scarce, and is not exclusively limited to features that encode reduction. Table 1 summarizes various pertinent studies and their results, ordered by the columns 'Effect found' and 'Predictor'.

Tab. 1: Overview of pertinent studies

Author	Language	Affix	Dependent variable	Predictor	Effect found
Sproat and Fujimura 1993; Lee-Kim, Davidson, and Hwang 2013	English	coda /l/	velarization	boundary strength	yes
Ben Hedia and Plag 2017	English	un-, negative in-, locative in-, negative	duration of prefixal nasal	boundary strength	yes
Smith, Baker, and Hawkins 2012	English	dis-, mis-	duration	boundary strength	yes
Plag, Homann, and Kunter 2017	English	-s	duration	boundary strength	yes
Hay 2003	English	-ly	duration	relative frequency	yes
Hay 2007	English	un-	duration	relative frequency	yes
Pluymakers et al. 2011	Dutch	-igheid	duration	boundary strength	no

Author	Language	Affix	Dependent variable	Predictor	Effect found
Bürki et al. 2011	French	re-	presence / absence of schwa	boundary strength ratings	no
Schuppler et al. 2013	Dutch	-t	presence / absence	relative frequency	no
Pluymaekers, Ernestus, and Baayen 2005	Dutch	ge-, ont-, ver-, -lijk	duration	relative frequency	no
Smith, Baker, and Hawkins 2012	English	dis-, mis-	duration	relative frequency	no
Plag, Homann, and Kunter 2017	English	-s	duration	relative frequency	no

Only four languages have been investigated so far, Dutch, English, French and German. Only two studies, both based on English, have found evidence for an effect of relative frequency. Four other studies have failed to find this effect. A number of studies have looked at effects of structurally-based boundary strength, sometimes finding effects, sometimes not finding them. In general, it seems impossible at this stage to say which factor may be responsible for the presence or absence of the expected effect in a given study.

It should also be noted that the studies listed in Table 1 approached the problem from two different angles, word-based or category-based. While relative frequency is a word-based measure, i.e. a measure that pertains to a particular word, measures of boundary strength are often averaged over sets of derivatives to compare affixes. For example, Smith, Baker, and Hawkins (2012) investigated whether pseudo-prefixes (which have a weaker boundary) show more reduction than real prefixes. Similarly, Plag, Homann, and Kunter (2017) found durational differences between different types of final /s/ and /z/ in English (non-morphemic vs. suffix vs. clitic). Ben Hedia and Plag (2017) compared the duration of the prefixal nasal across three prefixes that vary in their average boundary strength (*un-* having a stronger boundary than negative *in-*, which in turn has a stronger boundary than locative *in-*). Since the present paper focuses on properties of individual words we will only use word-based measures of segmentability.

In order to shed more light on the potential effects of segmentability on the phonetic properties of derived words, the present study will investigate five affixes of English, *un-*, negative *in-*, locative *in-*, *dis-* and adverbial *-ly*. The negative prefix *un-* is highly productive and creates highly transparent derivatives, usually on the basis of words. Both *in-* prefixes have different allomorphs that show place assimilation with the base-initial consonant. The negative prefix *in-* (as in *impossible*) is a bit less productive, has some less transparent derivatives (e.g. *insane*) and is often based on bound roots. The locative prefix *in-* (as in *implant, immigration*) has many opaque derivatives and is often attached to bound roots. Based on frequential and semantic measures, Ben Hedia and Plag (2017) show that of the three prefixes, *un-* is the most easily segmentable, followed by negative *in-*, followed by locative *in-*. The negative prefix *dis-* is highly productive, but also has some less transparent derivatives in its category. Finally, the suffix *-ly* derives adverbs from adjectives. Its status as inflectional or derivational is debated (see Plag 2003: 195–196; Payne, Huddleston, and Pullum 2010; Giegerich 2012), but everybody agrees that the suffix is fully productive and, apart from very few exceptions (such as *hardly*), there are only fully transparent formations.

3 Methodology

3.1 Data

In order to investigate the kinds of questions raised in the previous sections, it is necessary to investigate natural conversations because it is in this type of speech that reduction processes are most likely to occur (see Tucker and Ernestus 2016 for discussion). All words for this study were taken from the Switchboard Corpus (Godfrey and Holliman 1997). This is a collection of about 2400 two-sided phone conversations among North American speakers of English, with over 3 million word tokens. The data were originally extracted from the corpus for a study of gemination effects of consonants across the morphemic boundary, e.g. with words such as *un-necessary, im-mobile, im-migrate, dis-similar, oral-ly* (Ben Hedia in preparation; Ben Hedia and Plag 2017). The data set can, however, also be fruitfully employed for the purposes of this study by using a different acoustic measurement, i.e. affix duration instead of duration of the consonant at the morphemic boundary.

We investigate four different subsets of data. One subset contains *un-*prefixed words, one *dis-*prefixed words, one *in-*prefixed words and one *-ly*-suffixed words. The *in-*data set is composed of *in-*prefixed words with allomorph /ɪm/. This was necessary for the purposes of the gemination study because words with the allomorph /ɪn/ and a following base-initial /n/ are extremely rare.

The morphological status of a word was defined by using established criteria (cf. e.g. Plag 1999: Chapter 5; Bauer, Lieber, and Plag 2013: Chapter 3.2.2; Schulte

2015: Chapter 6). All words that show the affixational meaning and whose base is attested outside the derivative with a similar meaning, counted as morphologically complex. It did not matter whether the base occurs as a free morpheme (e.g. *natural* in *unnatural*) or as a bound morpheme (e.g. *-plicit* in *implicit* and *explicit*).

Each data set includes up to 160 tokens. We included as many different types as possible for each affix with the restriction that for each affix a sufficient number of words with a singleton (e.g. *unfit*), as well as with a double consonant at the morphological boundary had to be included (e.g. *unnatural*). Since morphological geminates are extremely rare with some affixes (e.g. only six different types for the prefix *un-* in the whole corpus), some types were included several times in the data set. Table 2 shows the number of different types and tokens for each data set.

Tab. 2: Overview of the data

Affixes	Types	Tokens
un-	101	158
in-	83	156
negative *in-*	29	86
locative *in-*	54	70
dis-	58	108
-ly	146	150
Total	398	596

3.2 Acoustic segmentation

After all sound files were extracted from the corpus, text grids were generated with a Python script for all sound files. The segmentation and transcription of the data was carried out manually using the software Praat (Boersma and Weenink 2014). We annotated the word and the affix in question, as well as the segments of the syllable adjacent to the affix. Double consonants straddling the morphemic boundary were segmented as one segment, since in most cases no boundary between the two consonants was discernible.

The criteria for the segmentation were developed by consulting the relevant phonetic literature (cf. Ladefoged and Maddieson 1996; Johnson 1997; Ladefoged

2003; Machač and Skarnitzl 2009; Ladefoged and Johnson 2011) and were optimized during the segmentation process. The beginning of the prefixed word was marked at the point where the waveform as well as the spectrogram visibly displayed the features of the word initial segment, in the case of *un-* and *in-* a vowel, in the case of *dis-* a stop. Vowels are characterized by a high amplitude, as well as a clear and distinct formant structure. The occlusion of /d/ marked the beginning of *dis*-prefixed words. The end of *-ly*-suffixed words was marked where the clear formant structure of the word-final vowel diminished and the amplitude of the waveform decreased. In the case of a following vowel, the boundary between the two vowels was set where the formant structure visibly changed.

To set the boundary between affix and base, the spectral and amplitudinal features of nasals (for *un-* and *in-*), fricatives (for *dis-*) and laterals (for *-ly*) were considered. Nasals have a regular waveform which has a lower amplitude than the waveform of vowels. Formants of nasals are quite low and faint in comparison to those of vowels. Boundaries between the nasal and a following vowel were marked at the point where the amplitude increases in the waveform and the formants become clearly visible. Approximants following the nasal were identified in a similar way as following vowels, since, like vowels, they have a higher amplitude than nasals, as well as more acoustic energy. If a stop followed the nasal, the boundary was marked at the beginning of the occlusion, which was identified by the abrupt decrease of the waveform and the sudden diminishment of the formants. In the case of a following fricative, the boundary was set where the waveform became visibly irregular and the energy was concentrated in the upper part of the spectrogram with no distinct formants visible.

Fricatives are characterized by an irregular waveform, which is very easy to distinguish from the regular waveform of vowels. Furthermore, for fricatives, there is energy throughout the whole spectrogram and no separate formant bands are visible. Most energy is visible in the upper part of the spectrogram. This is even more pronounced for voiceless fricatives, i.e. all of the *dis*-prefixed words in the data set. The boundary between /s/ and the following vowel was set where the waveform became regular and a distinct formant structure became visible. In the case of a following approximant, the same criteria were followed. If a stop followed the fricative, the boundary was marked at the beginning of the occlusion. There were no fricatives immediately following the prefixal /s/ in the datasets.

Laterals are very similar to vowels regarding their acoustical properties. Thus, it is quite challenging to set a boundary between vowels and laterals. However, there are some aspects in which /l/ can be distinguished from vowels. There is less amplitude in the waveforms of laterals than in those of vowels. Furthermore, their formant structure, in contrast to that of vowels, is constant. Due to less energy in the speech signal, the formants of /l/ are in general fainter. For intervocalic /l/ a visible decrease in the waveform, as well as the change in formant structure was used to mark the beginning of /l/. All boundaries were set at the nearest zero crossing of the waveform.

The reliability of the segmentation criteria was verified by trial segmentations in which it was ensured that all annotators placed all boundaries with only small variations. For the final measurement, each annotator worked on a disjunct set of items. After the segmentation process was completed, a script was used to measure and extract word duration, the number of segments in the word, the duration of the nasal in question, and the duration of its preceding and following segments in milliseconds.

3.3 Predictor variables

The duration of segments in natural speech is subject to a variety of different influences, and in order to address our research question these influences need to be controlled for. This can be done by coding the pertinent variables and using them as independent variables in a multiple regression model. We can distinguish variables of interest and noise variables. In our case, the variables of interest are the morphological segmentability measures. In addition to the variables of interest there are of course many other factors that might influence the duration of segments in speech production, such as speech rate or the following segment. In the following, we will describe all variables which were included in the models. First the variables of interest, i.e. the segmentability measures, will be explained. Then we will turn to the noise variables.

Segmentability. We used four different measures of segmentability: two measures of semantic transparency, relative frequency and type of base. We will discuss each in turn.

Semantic transparency has been used extensively in psycholinguistic research to investigate the question of whether words are processed as wholes or whether they are decomposed into their constituent morphemes (see, for example, Marslen-Wilson 2009 for an overview). These studies have shown that transparent words are more easily decomposed than non-transparent words. We created two variables to test semantic transparency. The first one is SEMANTICTRANSPARENCYBINARY, in which we coded for each word whether its meaning was transparent or opaque. If the meaning of the derivative was fully compositional, it was categorized as transparent. We checked the meaning of the derivatives and their bases in the online version of the *Oxford English Dictionary* (OED 2013). We coded those words as fully compositional in which the meaning of the derived word is straightforwardly computed by combining the meaning of the affix with the meaning of the base. Examples of transparent words are *unnatural* and *impossible*, whose meanings can be paraphrased as combining the prefixal meaning 'not' with the meaning of the base. Words that did not meet this strict criterion were categorized as opaque, as, for example, *impression* or *imposed*.

The second variable we used to measure semantic transparency is SEMANTICTRANSPARENCYRATING. We conducted a survey in which all the complex words included in this study were rated for their decomposability. In an online experiment using LimeSurvey (https://www.limesurvey.org/) native speakers of American English were asked how easy it is to decompose a given word into two meaningful parts on a scale from 1 ("very easy to decompose") to 4 ("very difficult to decompose"). The prefixes *un-* and *in-* were rated in one rating survey, for the affixes *dis-* and *-ly* separate rating surveys were conducted. A total of 110 participants between the ages of 16 and 63 rated the items. The reliability of the judgements was checked by a thorough inspection of the data (including the calculation of item-total correlations), as well as by computing Cronbach's α (Cronbach 1951) for each rating. After all ratings turned out to be reliable ($\alpha \geq 0.97$), we coded the median of the ratings for each word (i.e. type) in the variable SEMANTICTRANSPARENCYRATING.

Another measure of decomposability is probabilistic in nature: relative frequency (Hay 2002, 2003). Relative frequency is defined as the ratio of the frequency of a derived word to the frequency of its base. The more frequent a derivative is in comparison to its base, the higher its relative frequency and the less decomposable it is. We computed the variable RELATIVEFREQUENCY by dividing a word's lemma frequency by its base lemma frequency.[2] Frequencies were extracted from the DVD version of the Corpus of Contemporary American English (COCA, Davies 2008), using the query tool Coquery (Kunter 2016). We consider COCA an appropriate source for the frequency counts because the data in this corpus come from the same variety of English as the speech data in the Switchboard Corpus, i.e. North American English. Following standard procedures relative frequency was log-transformed to reduce the potentially harmful effect of skewed distributions in linear regression models.

The fourth measure of segmentability is structural in nature and concerns the distinction between bound roots and words as bases. Derivatives with words as

---

[2] Bound roots do not occur outside of the words whose base they are. In accordance with common practice, bound roots were therefore assigned the lowest possible frequency, i.e. 1.

bases can be assumed to be more easily decomposed than words that have a bound root as their base. This distinction was coded for each derivative in the variable TYPEOFBASE.

Affix. We coded the factor AFFIX, using the five levels un, inNeg, inLoc, dis and ly. Since we devised separate analyses for each affix, this factor plays a role only in the analysis of *in-*.

Affix-adjacent segment. Phonetic studies have shown that the duration of consonants depends heavily on the following segment. For nasals, following vowels lead to shorter durations, while following consonants increase duration. For voiceless fricatives, a following vowel leads to longer durations than a following consonant (Umeda 1977: 854). For the three prefixes, it is therefore important to account for the difference between a following vowel and a following consonant. We coded the variable FOLLOWINGSEGMENT with the two levels consonant and vowel to account for possible effects of the following segment on the duration of the prefix.

Umeda (1977) also showed that the preceding segment influences the duration of consonants. For laterals, a preceding consonant leads to shortening (Umeda 1977: 851). This is of relevance for the suffix *-ly*, which can be preceded by a consonant or a vowel. Therefore, we coded the variable PRECEDINGSEGMENT with the two levels consonant and vowel in the *-ly*-dataset.

Number of consonants. As shown in a previous study on a subset of this data (Ben Hedia and Plag 2017), morphological geminates display longer durations than singletons, i.e. for *un-* and *in-*prefixed words a double nasal (e.g. /nn/ in *unnatural*) is longer than a singleton (/n/ in *uneasy*). In such cases it is impossible to tell where the morphological boundary would be located inside the stretch of two adjacent identical consonants straddling that boundary. Hence, in order to account for the influence of the number of cross-boundary consonants in the word, we simply coded the variable NUMBEROFCONSONANTS with the two levels single and double. Words such as *un-necessary, im-mobile, im-migrate, dis-similar, oral-ly* are coded with the value double, words such as *im-possible* or *sad-ly* are coded as single.

Speech rate. We coded the variable SPEECHRATE for each word by dividing the number of segments included in the word by the total word duration in seconds. It is expected that the more segments are produced per second, i.e. the higher the speech rate, the shorter the duration of the affix will be.

Stress.[3] Stressed syllables tend to have a longer duration than unstressed syllables (e.g. Fry 1955, 1958; Lieberman 1960; Beckman 1986; Harrington et al. 1998; see also Laver 1994 for an overview). Thus, if an affix bears stress, it might be longer. Coding affix stress is however quite challenging. While the suffix -*ly* is never stressed, the presence or absence of stress is a potential problem with the prefixes investigated in this paper. This is because the stress status of prefixes is difficult to determine and not well researched. While it seems uncontroversial that prefixes bear (secondary) stress when followed by an unstressed syllable, it is often unclear whether they are stressed or unstressed when followed by a stressed syllable. In pronunciation dictionaries, such as Wells (2008), the prefix in those cases is sometimes stressed, sometimes unstressed and sometimes variably stressed. However, as shown by Hanote et al. (2010: 2ff.) for the prefix *un-*, the stress assignment in Wells (2008) does not follow any systematic pattern. Furthermore, in conversational speech (as found in our data), additional contextual factors might influence the stress status of the prefixes (cf. Videau and Hanote 2015). The matter is further complicated by the difficulty in determining the relative prominence relation between the prefix and a following stressed syllable, i.e. coding prefix stress is quite challenging. Because of the difficulty coding prefix stress (unsystematic annotation in dictionaries, potential contextual influences, difficulty of determining prefixal stress based on acoustic properties) we did not code prefix stress in one of our variables. Instead we coded base-initial stress. As explained above, only when the base-initial syllable is stressed can a prefix be unstressed. If the base-initial syllable is unstressed, the prefix must be stressed. Therefore, we can at least partially account for prefixal stress by coding for the stress status of the base-initial syllable of a prefixed word. Coding for base-initial stress is also relevant in view of Umeda's (1977) finding that consonants before unstressed vowels are shorter, i.e. there might be an independent effect of the presence or absence of stress in the base-initial syllable on prefix duration. A possible explanation for this effect is that the lengthening of the adjacent stressed syllable spills over to the prefix. The variable STRESSPATTERN was therefore coded with regard to the base-initial syllable, with the levels beforeStressed and beforeUnstressed.

Syllabicity. In words ending in the suffix -*ly*, the lateral is sometimes syllabic. This occurs quite often when the suffix -*al* precedes -*ly* (e.g. in words like *educationally* or *mentally*). The schwa preceding /l/ is deleted, and /l/ becomes

---

[3] Note that another potentially confounding factor for the coding of stress is that in English primary stress may shift to the prefix for emphatic purposes. None of the prefixes in our data, however, bears such primary stress.

syllabic. It is claimed in the literature that syllabic consonants are longer than non-syllabic consonants (see, e.g. Jones 1959: 136; Price 1981; Clark and Yallop 1995: 67). To consider possible effects of syllabicity on duration, we coded the variable SYLLABICITY for the suffix -*ly*, with the two levels yes and no.

Utterance Position. Words uttered at the end of an utterance or phrase have been shown to be pronounced with a longer duration than words in mid-positions (e.g. Oller 1973; Berkovits 1993). Some studies found the lengthening effect to be restricted to the final syllable of a word. For example, utterance-final position of *un*-prefixed words did not have a lengthening effect on prefixal /n/ (Hay 2007). But there is also evidence that segments occurring in the first syllable of a word participate in phrase- or utterance-final lengthening processes (Oller 1973). We therefore included the variable POSITION in which we coded whether the item was utterance final, followed by a pause or produced in mid position, i.e. immediately followed by the next word.

Word Form Frequency. Frequency has been shown to affect the duration of a word. More frequent words tend to have shorter durations (see, e.g. Aylett and Turk 2004; Gahl 2008). One would therefore expect shorter affix durations with more frequent words. To account for this effect we included Word Form Frequency (taken from COCA) as a covariate (WORDFORMFREQUENCY). We log-transformed this variable before it entered the models.

3.4 Statistical analysis

To see whether the segmentability affects the duration of the affixes in our data set we fitted linear regression models to each of the data sets. In all models the absolute duration of the affix in seconds was used as the dependent variable.

Given that many factors may play a role in the production of sounds, a multivariate method of analysis is called for. We opted for multiple regression because it allows the researcher to look at the effect of one predictor in the presence of other, potentially intervening, predictors. The use of mixed effects models was precluded by the data's unnestedness. The vast majority of items is produced by a different speaker and many items occur only once in the corpus, so that it did not make sense to use these variables as random effects.

As a general strategy, in order to avoid overfitting, we started the analyses of the different data sets with a baseline model that had only a rather small number of pertinent predictors: SPEECHRATE and NUMBEROFCONSONANTS. Both of these predictors can be expected to have a straightforward effect on the duration of the affix in question and can serve as a reality check on our data. We then added additional predictors individually and in different orders. In total, there were never more than three predictors that survived in our final models. In general, if a predictor showed a p-value lower than or equal to 0.05, and if the Akaike Information Criterion (AIC) of the model including the predictor was lower than when the predictor was not included, the predictor was kept in the model. Non-significant predictors were eliminated. The particulars of the modeling procedure specific to each affix are described in the pertinent result section below.

There are a number of measurements that we would want to use in our analysis that are correlated with each other. This can lead to serious problems in regression models ('multicollinearity', e.g. Baayen 2008: Chapter 6). This holds in particular for the four measures of segmentability which tend to go together. For example, words with a higher relative frequency (or those with bound roots) also tend to be semantically less transparent. One strategy to deal with collinearity is to include only one of the correlating variables. This is a conservative and safe strategy, which may, however, decrease the power of the model. If collinearity only affects noise variables, another option is to keep the correlating variables in the model but not interpret their individual contribution to the model (cf. Wurm and Fisicaro 2014). Another strategy to address collinearity issues is principal component regression (see, e.g., Baayen 2008: Chapter 5; Venables and Ripley 2011). This method will be used in the analysis of the prefix *dis-*.

For the statistical analyses presented in this paper, we used R (R Development Core Team 2014). The regression analyses were done with the MASS package (Venables and Ripley 2011). The plots of the models were generated with the visreg package (Breheny and Burchett 2015). For a plot showing the effect of a variable, all other variables are held constant at the median (for numeric variables) or at the most common category (for factors).

4 Results

4.1 The prefix *un-*

This prefix is characterized by the fact that its derivatives in general, and in our data set, are semantically highly transparent and that its bases are words, not bound roots. Of the four segmentability measurements, only RELATIVEFREQUENCY was distributed with enough variation to be used as a predictor. To the baseline model we added the following predictors according to the procedure described in section 3.4: RELATIVEFREQUENCY, WORDFORMFREQUENCY, STRESSPATTERN, POSITION, and FOLLOWINGSEGMENT.

In the final model only three predictors survive as significant, RELATIVE-FREQUENCY, SPEECHRATE and NUMBEROFCONSONANTS. The regression model is documented in Table 3.

Tab. 3: Final regression model for *un-*; Adjusted R-squared = 0.45

	Estimate	Std.Error	t-value	Pr(>|t|)
(Intercept)	-1.238	0.083	-14.996	<2e-16
RelativeFrequency	-0.014	0.007	-2.027	0.044
SpeechRate	-0.057	0.006	-9.592	<2e-16
numberOfConsonantsdouble	0.165	0.051	3.244	0.001

The negative coefficient of RELATIVEFREQUENCY tells us that the higher the relative frequency, the shorter the duration of the prefix. This result is in accordance with the segmentability hypothesis and replicates for North American English the findings in Hay (2007), which investigated New Zealand English.

Unsurprisingly, a higher speech rate leads to shorter prefix durations. For NUMBEROFCONSONANTS we also find the expected effect: a double nasal across the morphemic boundary has a longer duration. Figure 1 illustrates the effects.

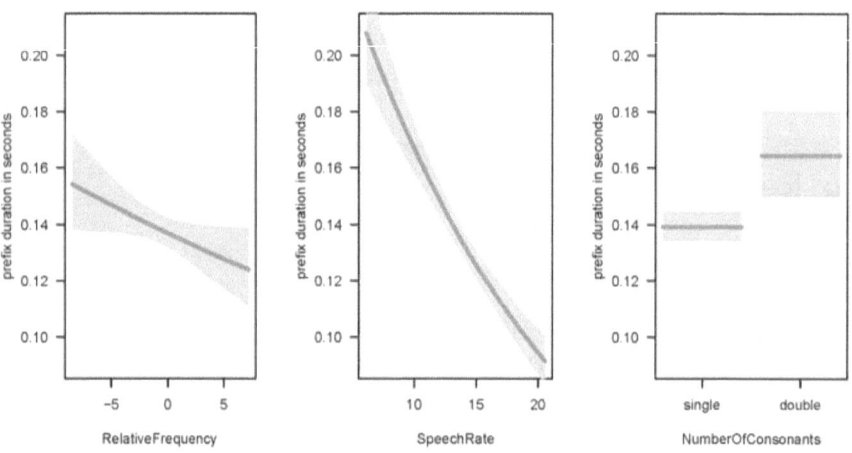

Fig. 1: Partial effects of final regression model for *un-*. The grey areas indicate the 95 percent confidence interval

4.2 The prefix *in*-

For the prefix *in*-, the following predictors were added to the baseline model: AFFIX, WORDFORMFREQUENCY, STRESSPATTERN, POSITION, and one of the four segmentability measures at a time. None of the four segmentability measures turned out to have a significant effect on prefix duration, only speech rate and the number of consonants turned out to be significant predictors.

4.3 The prefix *dis*-

Initial explorations of this data set showed significant correlations between the four segmentability measures. It was therefore not advisable to include them simultaneously in one regression. We therefore fitted four different models, each with one of the segmentability measures. In each of these models, the segmentability measures turned out to have a significant effect on prefix duration. Table 4 gives the statistics for the segmentability measures. In accordance with the segmentability hypothesis, words with a higher relative frequency show shorter durations (as shown by the negative coefficient in Table 4). Semantically transparent words have longer prefixes than semantically opaque words (shown by the positive coefficient of SEMANTICTRANSPARENCYBINARY and the negative coefficient of SEMANTICTRANSPARENCYRATING). Words with free bases have longer prefix durations than words with bound roots.

Tab. 4: Effects of segmentability measures in models with only one segmentability measure in addition to speech rate and number of consonants.

	Estimate	Std. Error	t value	Pr(>|t|)
RelativeFrequency	-0.003	0.001	-2.73	0.008
SemanticTransp.Binarytransparent	0.022	0.007	3.30	0.001
SemanticTransp.Rating	-0.011	0.003	-3.27	0.002
TypeOfBasefree	0.023	0.008	2.76	0.007

In addition to devising individual models each with one of the four segmentability measures we decided to use principal component analysis to derive a single segmentability measure, and then use this measure in a regression model to predict prefix duration. In a principal component analysis, the dimensionality of the data is reduced by transforming the different variables into so-called principal components. The transformation results in linear combinations of the predictors that are orthogonal to each other. The uncorrelated new linear predictors are called 'principal components'.

In order not to overfit our models we first tested which of the noise variables had a significant influence. Apart from NUMBEROFCONSONANTS and SPEECHRATE (which were already in the baseline model), none of the noise variables had an effect on prefix duration. We then fitted a principal components regression model (using the `pcr` function of the `pls` package, Mevik and Wehrens 2007) with the four segmentability measures, NUMBEROFCONSONANTS and SPEECHRATE as predictors.

In the first step of this analysis the model yields six principal components. In a second step a regression model is fitted with all principal components as predictors. This model explains 43.2 percent of the overall variance. The first three components do most of the work, they explain 41.9 percent of the overall variance.

But what do these components mean? For the interpretation of the principal components it is useful to look at the correlations of the principal components with the original predictors. We therefore looked at how the first three components in our model relate to the original predictors. Table 5 gives the loadings of the original predictor variables on the first three principal components. The loadings are proportional to the correlations of the original variables to the principal components. In the table the most relevant loadings are given in bold print; very small loadings are not printed.

Tab. 5: Loadings of original predictor variables on the three most important principal components in the principal component regression model. ('PC' = principal component).

	PC1	PC2	PC3
RelativeFrequency	-0.426	0.150	-0.191
SemanticTransparencyBinarytransparent	**0.514**	0.220	
TypeofBasefree	**0.475**		-0.313
SemanticTransparencyRating	**-0.547**		
NumberOfConsonantsdouble	0.165	**-0.624**	**0.672**
SpeechRate		**0.733**	**0.635**

Principal component 1 (PC1) can be straightforwardly interpreted as tapping into morphological segmentability, as it correlates most strongly with all four segmentability measures (see top four rows of the table). The second and third components, i.e. PC2 and PC3, represent the effects of SPEECHRATE and NUMBEROFCONSONANTS.

In the regression model, PC2 is the strongest predictor, accounting for 28.5 percent of the overall variance. PC1, i.e. segmentability, comes in second, accounting for 8.3 percent of the overall variance. This shows that a combined measure of segmentability, as expressed by PC1, is indeed predictive of prefix duration, even in the presence of other influences. The effect of segmentability goes in the expected direction. As is clear from the correlations as given in Table 5, higher values of PC1 indicate a greater degree of segmentability. In the model, PC1 has a positive coefficient (estimate=0.007, standard error= 0.002, t=3.84, p<0.001), which means that increased segmentability goes together with increased prefix duration. Figure 2 plots the partial effect of segmentability. Derivatives that are more easily segmentable show longer prefix durations, in accordance with the segmentability hypothesis.

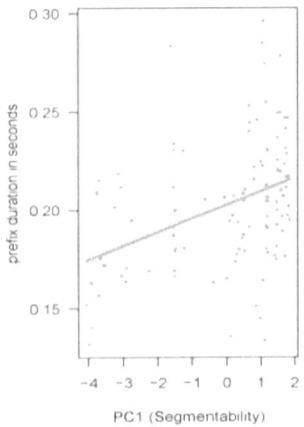

Fig. 2: Partial effect of segmentability (PC1) on prefix duration

4.4 The suffix -ly

For this affix relative frequency is the only segmentability measure that we can use since all -ly derivatives in the data set are fully transparent. Including relative frequency into the baseline model shows a non-significant effect of this variable (t=0.071, p=0.94). In other words, we do not find support for the segmentability hypothesis with words of this morphological category.

5 Summary and conclusion

Let us summarize our findings. Words with the prefixes *un-* and *dis-* show robust effects of segmentability in the predicted direction. For *un-* derivatives the only available segmentability measure was relative frequency. This measure turned out to have a significant effect on the duration of the prefix, such that more easily segmentable words showed longer prefix durations, in accordance with the segmentability hypothesis. With *dis-*, all four measures showed a significant effect on prefix duration individually. For this prefix we also devised a principal component analysis to derive a combined measure of segmentability. This combined measure was predictive for prefix duration in the way expected by the segmentability hypothesis. Based on the consideration that the interpretation of newly derived words needs to rely on morphological decomposition, we have indirect evidence that with these two prefixes newly derived words will tend to have longer prefixes in speech, and that, therefore, neologisms of these two morphological categories tend to differ phonetically from established words of that category.

The results for *un-* replicate Hay's (2007) results with a different data set and for a different variety of English. Our results for *dis-* are in line with those of Smith, Baker, and Hawkins (2012), in so far as these authors found longer prefix durations for prefixed words (e.g. *displeased*) as against pseudo-prefixed words (e.g. *displayed*). However, Smith, Baker, and Hawkins (2012) did not test for a potential effect of relative frequency.

The segmentability effect was not found for the two *in-* prefixes, nor for the suffix *-ly*. Overall, the present study thus replicates the mixed results obtained in previous studies. It is unclear which factors may be responsible for the non-emergence of durational effects of segmentability. Speculating on the basis of only these affixes, one could venture the hypothesis that such effects may only emerge beyond a certain threshold of decomposability. Both *un-* and *dis-* seem to be prefixes that are easily segmentable with the vast majority of their derivatives, while *in-* and *-ly* seem phonologically more integrated. For example, Raffelsiefen (1999) consistently assigns prosodic word status to *un-*, while *in-* is treated variably as either forming a prosodic word, or as being integrated into the prosodic word of its base, depending on the word in question. To our knowledge, the prosodic word status of *-ly* is not treated in the literature, but we see no evidence for this suffix building a prosodic word of its own. Further research is necessary to investigate potential causes for the emergence or non-emergence of the segmentability effect in a given case.

To summarize, our results demonstrate that phonetic detail may help us to gain insight into aspects of lexical innovation that have been underexplored.

There is a continuum between highly idiosyncratic stored words at one end, and newly created words at the other end, and the innovation may manifest itself also at the level of phonetics, i.e. through the durational patterns of the words in question.

The present findings also have implications for morphological theory and morphological processing. The gradient effects of segmentability support theories in which morphological structure is conceived as gradient (see, for example, Hay and Baayen 2005; Plag and Balling, in press for discussion). Furthermore, our results call for processing models that are able to accommodate the presence of phonetic correlates of morphological structure in speech.

6 References

Aylett, Matthew & Alice Turk. 2004. The smooth signal redundancy hypothesis: A functional explanation for relationships between redundancy, prosodic prominence, and duration in spontaneous speech. *Language and Speech* 47(1). 31–56.

Baayen, Harald. 1989. *A corpus-based study of morphological productivity. Statistical analysis and psycholinguistic interpretation*. Amsterdam: Vrije Universiteit dissertation.

Baayen, Harald. 1996. The effect of lexical specialization on the growth curve of the vocabulary. *Computational Linguistics* 22. 455–480.

Baayen, Harald. 2008. *Analyzing linguistic data: A practical introduction to statistics using R*. Cambridge: Cambridge University Press.

Barker, Chris. 1998. Episodic -ee in English: A thematic role constraint on a new word formation. *Language* 74(4). 695–727.

Bauer, Laurie, Rochelle Lieber & Ingo Plag. 2013. *The Oxford reference guide to English morphology*. Oxford: Oxford University Press.

Beckman, Mary. 1986. *Stress and non-stress accent* (Netherlands phonetic archives 7). Dordrecht: Foris Publications.

Ben Hedia, Sonia & Ingo Plag. 2017. Gemination and degemination in English prefixation: Phonetic evidence for morphological organization. *Journal of Phonetics* 62. 34–49.

Ben Hedia, Sonia. In preparation. *Gemination and degemination in English affixation*. Düsseldorf: Heinrich-Heine-Universität Düsseldorf dissertation.

Berkovits, Rochele. 1993. Progressive utterance-final lengthening in syllables with final fricatives. *Language and Speech* 36(1). 89–98.

Blazej, Laura J. & Ariel M. Cohen-Goldberg. 2015. Can we hear morphological complexity before words are complex? *Journal of Experimental Psychology: Human Perception and Performance* 41(1). 50–68.

Boersma, Paul & David Weenink. 2014. *Praat: Doing phonetics by computer*. Version 5.4.04. http://www.fon.hum.uva.nl/praat/ (accessed 07 June 2017).

Breheny, Patrick & Woodrow Burchett. 2015. *Visreg: visualization of regression models*. https://CRAN.R-project.org/package=visreg (accessed 07 June 2017).

Bürki, Audrey, Mirjam Ernestus, Cédric Gendrot, Cécile Fougeron & Ulrich H. Frauenfelder. 2011. What affects the presence versus absence of schwa and its duration: A corpus analysis of French connected speech. *The Journal of the Acoustical Society of America* 130(6). 3980–3991.

Clark, John E. & Colin Yallop. ²1995. *An introduction to phonetics and phonology* (Blackwell Textbooks in Linguistics 9). Oxford: Blackwell.

Cronbach, Lee J. 1951. Coefficient alpha and the internal structure of tests. *Psychometrika* 16(3). 297–334.

Davies, Mark. 2008. *The corpus of contemporary American English: 400+ million words, 1990–present.* http://www.americancorpus.org/ (accessed 07 June 2017).

Fry, Dennis B. 1955. Duration and intensity as physical correlates of linguistic stress. *The Journal of the Acoustical Society of America* 27(4). 765–768.

Fry, Dennis B. 1958. Experiments in the perception of stress. *Language and Speech* 1. 126–152.

Gahl, Susanne. 2008. Time and thyme are not homophones: The effect of lemma frequency on word durations in spontaneous speech. *Language* 84(3). 474–496.

Giegerich, Heinz J. 2012. The morphology of -*ly* and the categorial status of 'adverbs' in English. *English Language and Linguistics* 16(3). 341–359.

Godfrey, John J. & Edward Holliman. 1997. *Switchboard-1 Release 2*. Philadelphia: Linguistic Data Consortium. https://catalog.ldc.upenn.edu/ldc97s62 (accessed 07 June 2017).

Hanique, Iris & Mirjam Ernestus. 2012. The role of morphology in acoustic reduction. *Lingue e Linguaggio* 11. 147–164.

Hanote, Sylvie, Nicolas Videau, Franck Zumstein & Philippe Carré. 2010. Les préfixes anglais *un-* et *de-*: Etude phonétique et acoustique. *Corela. Cognition, représentation, langage* HS-9. http://corela.revues.org/1081 (accessed 07 June 2017).

Harrington, Jonathan, Mary Beckman, Janet Fletcher & Sallyanne Palethorpe. 1998. An electropalatographic, kinematic, and acoustic analysis of supralaryngeal correlates of word and utterance-level prominence contrasts in English. In Robert H. Mannell & Jordi Robert-Ribes (eds.), *Proceedings of the 5th International Conference on Spoken Language Processing (ICSLP), 30 November –4 December, Sydney, Australia*, vol. 5, 1851–1854. Canberra: ASSTA.

Hay, Jennifer. 2001. Lexical frequency in morphology: Is everything relative? *Linguistics* 39(6). 1041–1070.

Hay, Jennifer. 2002. From speech perception to morphology: Affix-ordering revisited. *Language* 78. 527–555.

Hay, Jennifer. 2003. *Causes and consequences of word structure*. New York & London: Routledge.

Hay, Jennifer. 2007. The phonetics of *un-*. In Judith Munat (ed.), *Lexical creativity, texts and contexts* (Studies in Functional and Structural Linguistics 58), 39–57. Amsterdam & Philadelphia: John Benjamins.

Hay, Jennifer & Harald Baayen. 2005. Shifting paradigms: Gradient structure in morphology. *Trends in Cognitive Sciences* 9. 342–348.

Hay, Jennifer & Ingo Plag. 2004. What constrains possible suffix combinations? On the interaction of grammatical and processing restrictions in derivational morphology. *Natural Language & Linguistic Theory* 22(3). 565–596.

Johnson, Keith. 1997. *Acoustic and auditory phonetics*. Malden, Oxford & Victoria: Blackwell.

Jones, Daniel. 1959. The use of syllabic and non-syllabic *l* and *n* in derivatives of English words ending in syllabic *l* and *n*. *STUF - Language Typology and Universals* 12(1–4). 136–144.

Kemps, Rachèl, Mirjam Ernestus, Robert Schreuder & Harald Baayen. 2005a. Prosodic cues for morphological complexity: The case of Dutch plural nouns. *Memory & Cognition* 33(3). 430–446.
Kemps, Rachèl, Lee H. Wurm, Mirjam Ernestus, Robert Schreuder & Harald Baayen. 2005b. Prosodic cues for morphological complexity in Dutch and English. *Language and Cognitive Processes* 20. 43–73.
Kunter, Gero. 2016. *Coquery: A free corpus query tool.* http://www.coquery.org (accessed 07 June 2017).
Ladefoged, Peter. 2003. *Phonetic data analysis: An introduction to fieldwork and instrumental techniques.* Malden, Oxford & Victoria: Blackwell.
Ladefoged, Peter & Keith Johnson. [6]2011. *A course in phonetics.* Boston: Wadsworth Cengage Learning.
Ladefoged, Peter & Ian Maddieson. 1996. *The sounds of the world's languages. Phonological theory.* Oxford & Malden: Blackwell.
Laver, John. 1994. *Principles of phonetics* (Cambridge Textbooks in Linguistics). Cambridge: Cambridge University Press.
Lee-Kim, Sang-Im, Lisa Davidson & Sangjin Hwang. 2013. Morphological effects on the darkness of English intervocalic /l/. *Laboratory Phonology* 4(2). 475–511.
Lieberman, Philip. 1960. Some acoustic correlates of word stress in American English. *Journal of the Acoustical Society of America* 32(4). 451–454.
LimeSurvey Project Team & Carsten Schmitz. 2015. *LimeSurvey: An Open Source survey tool.* Hamburg: LimeSurvey Project. https://www.limesurvey.org/ (accessed 07 June 2017)
Machač, Pavel & Radek Skarnitzl. 2009. *Principles of phonetic segmentation* (Erudica 14). Prague: Epocha.
Marslen-Wilson, William D. 2009. Morphological processes in language comprehension. In M. Gareth Gaskell (ed.), *The Oxford handbook of psycholinguistics*, 175–193. Oxford: Oxford University Press.
Mevik, Bjørn-Helge & Ron Wehrens. 2007. The pls package: Principal component and partial least squares regression in R. *Journal of Statistical Software* 18(2). 1–24.
Mühleisen, Susanne. 2010. *Heterogeneity in word-formation patterns.* Amsterdam & Philadelphia: John Benjamins.
OED. 2013. *The Oxford English Dictionary online.* Oxford: Oxford University Press.
Oller, D. Kimbrough. 1973. The effect of position in utterance on speech segment duration in English. *The Journal of the Acoustical Society of America* 54(5). 1235–1247.
Payne, John, Rodney Huddleston & Geoffrey K. Pullum. 2010. The distribution and category status of adjectives and adverbs. *Word Structure* 3(1). 31–81.
Plag, Ingo. 1998. The polysemy of *-ize* derivatives: On the role of semantics in word formation. *Yearbook of Morphology* 1997. 219–242.
Plag, Ingo. 1999. *Morphological productivity: Structural constraints in English derivation* (Topics in English Linguistics 28). Berlin & New York: Mouton de Gruyter.
Plag, Ingo. 2003. *Word-formation in English* (Cambridge Textbooks in Linguistics). Cambridge: Cambridge University Press.
Plag, Ingo. 2014. Phonological and phonetic variability in complex words: An uncharted territory. *Italian Journal of Linguistics* 26(2). 209–228.
Plag, Ingo & Harald Baayen. 2009. Suffix ordering and morphological processing. *Language* 85(1). 109–152.

Plag, Ingo & Laura W. Balling. In press. Derivational morphology: An integrated perspective. In Vito Pirrelli, Wolfgang U. Dressler & Ingo Plag (eds.), *Word knowledge and word usage: A cross-disciplinary guide to the mental lexicon*. Berlin & New York: Mouton de Gruyter.

Plag, Ingo, Julia Homann & Gero Kunter. 2017. Homophony and morphology: The acoustics of word-final S in English. *Journal of Linguistics* 53(1). 181–216.

Pluymaekers, Mark, Mirjam Ernestus & Harald Baayen. 2005. Lexical frequency and acoustic reduction in spoken Dutch. *Journal of the Acoustical Society of America* 118(4). 2561–2569.

Pluymaekers, Mark, Mirjam Ernestus, Harald Baayen & Geert Booij. 2010. Morphological effects in fine phonetic detail: The case of Dutch *-igheid*. *Laboratory Phonology* 10. 511–531.

Price, Patti J. 1981. Sonority and syllabicity: Acoustic correlates of perception. *Phonetica* 37(5–6). 327–343.

R Development Core Team. 2014. *R: A language and environment for statistical computing*. Vienna: R Foundation for Statistical Computing. https://www.r-project.org/ (accessed 07 June 2017).

Raffelsiefen, Renate. 1999. Diagnostics for prosodic words revisited: The case of historically prefixed words in English. In Tracy Alan Hall & Ursula Kleinhenz (eds.), *Studies on the phonological word* (Current Issues in Linguistic Theory 174), 133–201. Amsterdam & Philadelphia: John Benjamins.

Schulte, Marion. 2015. *The semantics of derivational morphology: A synchronic and diachronic investigation of the suffixes -age and -ery in English* (Language in Performance). Tübingen: Narr.

Schuppler, Barbara, Wim A. van Dommelen, Jacques Koreman & Mirjam Ernestus. 2012. How linguistic and probabilistic properties of a word affect the realization of its final /t/: Studies at the phonemic and sub-phonemic level. *Journal of Phonetics* 40(4). 595–607.

Smith, Rachel, Rachel Baker & Sarah Hawkins. 2012. Phonetic detail that distinguishes prefixed from pseudo-prefixed words. *Journal of Phonetics* 40(5). 689–705.

Sproat, Richard & Osamu Fujimura. 1993. Allophonic variation in English /l/ and its implications for phonetic implementation. *Journal of Phonetics* 21. 291–311.

Tucker, Benjamin V. & Mirjam Ernestus. 2016. Why we need to investigate casual speech to truly understand language production, processing and the mental lexicon. *The Mental Lexicon* 11(3). 375–400.

Umeda, Noriko. 1977. Consonant duration in American English. *The Journal of the Acoustical Society of America* 61(3). 846–858.

Venables, William N. & Brian D. Ripley. [4]2011. *Modern applied statistics with S* (Statistics and Computing). New York, Berlin & Heidelberg: Springer.

Videau, Nicolas & Sylvie Hanote. 2015. Pronunciation of prefixed words in speech: The importance of semantic and intersubjective parameters. *Lexis. Journal in English Lexicology* 9. http://lexis.revues.org/pdf/982 (accessed 07 June 2017).

Wells, John C. [3]2008. *Longman pronunciation dictionary*. Harlow: Pearson Education.

Wurm, Lee H. & Sebastiano A. Fisicaro. 2014. What residualizing predictors in regression analyses does (and what it does not do). *Journal of Memory and Language* 72. 37–48.

Marcel Schlechtweg
How stress reflects meaning

The interplay of prosodic prominence and semantic (non-) compositionality in non-lexicalized English adjective-noun combinations

Abstract: The paper discusses the relation between stress and meaning in *non-lexicalized* English adjective-noun (AN) combinations. Native speakers of American English were recorded in a production study while reading sentences containing AN constructions such as *black tram*. These items could be interpreted in either a compositional (e.g., a tram that is black) or a non-compositional way (e.g., a tram that runs only during the night). The objective of the experiment was twofold. First, it aimed at examining whether non-lexicalized constructions with a non-compositional meaning were stressed differently than their compositional counterparts. Second, it was investigated whether stress assignment in non-compositional items further depended on whether the non-compositional meaning was explicitly marked by the immediate context. Possible acoustic correlates of stress, i.e., fundamental frequency, duration, and intensity were measured and analyzed. Overall, while the items with implied non-compositional semantics showed a clear tendency towards initial stress, the combinations with compositional meanings did not. Moreover, the constructions whose non-compositional semantics were explicitly marked by the immediate context tended not to carry initial stress either. I argue that initial stress seems to mark non-compositional semantics only if the non-compositional meaning is not explicitly marked by a different means already. The results are interpreted against the background of the interaction of semantic and phonetic aspects in language production.

1 Introduction

It is well known that some English AN constructions have different meanings. For instance, while *green house* is semantically compositional because its entire meaning is the sum of its constituent meanings, *greenhouse* is non-compositional because parts of its meaning are hidden, i.e., not overtly given (see, e.g., Zwitserlood 1994: 366). Although the overall meanings of *green house* and *greenhouse* differ, the same constituents are combined. Nevertheless, the two forms are not identical because they can be distinguished on, for example, prosodic grounds, i.e., the main prominence is placed on the adjective in *greenhouse* but not in *green house* (see Gussenhoven 2004: 19).

While the prosody of lexicalized English AN constructions has been the subject of both comprehension and production research (e.g., McCauley, Hestvik, and Vogel 2012; Morrill 2012; Vogel and Raimy 2002), the prosody of *non-lexicalized* constructions has been investigated in comprehension (e.g., Schlechtweg 2018) but not in production experiments. The current analysis is a first pilot study to fill this gap and aims at contributing to the understanding of how prosodic and semantic aspects interact. The first question to be answered is whether the main prominence appears on the adjective if a construction is semantically non-compositional. If this is the case, the second issue to be addressed is whether initial stress is also used if the non-compositional semantics are explicitly marked by the immediate context.

The article is structured as follows. Section 2 presents the theoretical foundations of the paper. Semantic non-compositionality and means that explicitly mark it are discussed before we turn to the notion of stress, functions of stress, and reasons for stress variation in complex items in English. Section 3 describes a production study, which is still exploratory in nature but provides first evidence for the interplay of the semantic characteristics and the phonetic form of non-lexicalized AN combinations. Section 4 concludes the present paper.

2 Theoretical foundations

2.1 Semantic non-compositionality and means to mark it in English

As mentioned above, some English AN combinations have different meanings. The examples in (1) illustrate the phenomenon:

(1) a. *a green house*
       'a house that is green'
    b. *a greenhouse*
       'a house made of glass that is used for growing plants'

The two spoken versions are distinguished; i.e., in (1a), both *green* and *house* carry an accent but in (1b) only *green* does so (Gussenhoven 2004: 277). Note that orthographic differences are ignored here as the paper focuses on prosodic contrasts. The question arises, however, what language users do if they deal with non-lexicalized constructions. Consider (2):

(2) a. *a black tram*
'a tram that is black'
b. *a black tram*
'a tram that runs only during the night'

How could one mark the non-compositional semantics of *black tram* (see 2b), which differ from the compositional meaning (see 2a)? On the one hand, the immediate context can explicitly mark a non-compositional meaning. One way of marking non-compositionality of meaning is by explicitly referring to the first constituent as a naming unit (see Härtl 2016). An example of an explicit marker is the phrase *called so because* (see 3a). On the other hand, prosodic modifications can be used in spoken language. For instance, as shown in (3b), while *black tram* with the compositional meaning would probably carry an accent on both constituents, the accent on the noun might be deleted if the non-compositional reading is intended, leaving only the accent on the adjective (see Gussenhoven 2004: 277).

(3) a. A black tram is called so because it is a tram that runs only during the night.
b. A BLACK tram is a tram that runs only during the night.

So far, however, no study has investigated whether this is actually the case. That means we can only speculate that the prosodic structure is changed as in (3b) to mark the non-compositional meaning, but we do not know for sure. The present paper aims at filling this gap. Moreover, another interesting question remains if one considers (3a): What is the prosodic structure of *black tram* here? Put differently, do speakers also adjust the prosodic structure of non-compositional constructions if their meaning is explicitly marked as non-compositional by the immediate context? Answering this question represents the second objective of the current article. If non-compositional semantics trigger initial stress, this might happen independently of the immediate context. Alternatively, however, initial stress might be used only if the non-compositional meaning is not marked explicitly. The latter scenario would mean that language users avoid, so to speak, redundancy while producing non-lexicalized constructions and rely on a single means to explicitly mark non-compositionality. This would be compatible with results discussed in Härtl (2016), who found that non-compositional German AN compounds were less likely to occur with *sogenannt* ('so-called') or quotation marks than non-compositional AN phrases. German compounds are marked by their nature because they lack the inflectional adjectival suffix of phrases and have initial rather than non-initial, phrasal stress. Therefore, in contrast to phrases, they do not seem to depend on additional means that mark their non-compositional meaning.

2.2 Stress in complex constructions in English

2.2.1 Abstract versus concrete approaches to prosody

As Ladd and Cutler (1983) illustrate, prosody research can be roughly classified into two approaches. On the one hand, abstract approaches theoretically describe prosody and its connection to other domains of grammar. On the other hand, concrete approaches examine the physical characteristics of prosody by investigating its different acoustic correlates such as fundamental frequency (F0), duration, and intensity. The present article combines the two perspectives. That is, the influence of semantics on the prominence pattern of complex constructions is discussed, and it is assumed that prominence can be expressed through the physical variables F0, duration, and intensity (see also, e.g., Kunter 2011; Lehiste 1970; Plag, et al. 2008).

2.2.2 Stress versus accent

It has often been claimed that complex constructions in English are stressed either on the first or on the second element. Chomsky and Halle (1968: 94), for instance, argue that primary stress in phrases is assigned "to the rightmost sonority peak in the string under consideration" (= Nuclear Stress Rule). In contrast, primary stress in compounds is located on "the leftmost sonority peak" (= Compound Rule) (see also, e.g., Liberman and Prince 1977: 257). Gussenhoven (2004: 19) takes up the distinction between the two prominence patterns but defines them differently. He states that both elements of a complex construction are stressed; however, while only the first element of a compound is accented, both elements of a phrase are accented. Gussenhoven's differentiation connects to the view that unstressed syllables are never accented but stressed syllables are accented or not (Bolinger 1958, 1986; Vanderslice and Ladefoged 1972). Stress represents here a feature of the lexical level, and pitch-accents are "added" at the phrasal level. In the present article, the term "stress" is used to mean main prominence, and it is measured in terms of its acoustic correlates F0, duration, and intensity. The study remains agnostic as to whether the relevant level of grammatical computation is lexical or phrasal. Throughout the present paper, the term "initial stress" refers to what is usually known as "compound stress / prominence" and the term "non-initial stress" refers to what is usually known as "phrasal / nuclear stress / prominence".

2.2.3 Functions of stress and reasons for stress variation

Assuming that English AN constructions have either initial or non-initial stress, we must ask what determines whether a specific combination is stressed in one or the other way. One basic function of stress is to structure the information of an utterance according to the speaker's and listener's needs at a specific moment in their communication (see, e.g., Bell and Plag 2013; Ladd 1984). That means, for instance, while information that is in focus or has not been introduced before during a conversation is typically prominent, non-focused or given information is usually not. Stress can also be used to contrast several alternatives. The example in (4) shows that stress serves to, first, contrast different colors and, second, introduce new information, namely the color red, to the current communication.

(4) Speaker A: *I know that you wore the green shirt yesterday night.*
     Speaker B: *No, I wore the RED shirt.*

Furthermore, initial stress in phrasal or compound constructs is often considered to be a reflex of lexicalization (see, e.g., Plag et al. 2008). For example, while the lexicalized *greenhouse* has initial stress, the non-lexicalized *green house* bears non-initial stress. Apart from the aforementioned factors, several other reasons for stress variation exist. These include within- and across-speaker-related factors (see, e.g., Kunter 2011: Chapter 8), dialectal influences (see, e.g., Trudgill and Hannah 2008: 57), sentence type (see, e.g., Morrill 2012), sentence position (see, e.g., Farnetani, Torsello, and Cosi 1988), the surrounding material (see, e.g., Gussenhoven 2004), and analogy (see, e.g., Plag 2006; Plag, Kunter, and Lappe 2007). In the experiment to be reported later, all the factors mentioned so far are controlled for (see Section 3) in order to examine whether another factor, namely semantic (non-)compositionality, has an influence on the stress pattern of non-lexicalized AN constructions in English.

Considering all English AN constructions, i.e., both lexicalized and non-lexicalized ones, we observe that, first, non-initial stress is more frequent than initial stress and, second, that compositionality is more common than non-compositionality as AN combinations typically fulfill a simple descriptive function (see, e.g., Liberman and Sproat 1992: 134). Hence, on the one hand, there seems to be a connection between non-initial stress and semantic compositionality. The idea finds further support in Giegerich (2004), who argues that noun-noun (NN) attribute-head constructions, whose semantics overlap with those of prototypical AN items to a large extent, usually carry non-initial stress. On the other hand, NN constructions in particular show that initial stress seems to be linked to semantic non-compositionality. Since the semantic relation between the two nouns is not overtly expressed, parts of the semantics are hidden and, thus, the meaning of NN combinations is non-compositional (see, e.g., Zwitserlood 1994). Apart from being non-compositional, NN constructions typically bear initial stress: Based on the investigation of different corpora, several authors claim that approximately 67 percent (Plag and Kunter 2010: 357), around 75 percent (Liberman and Sproat 1992: 134), almost 90 percent (Plag and Kunter 2010: 357; Plag et al. 2007: 207–208) or even approximately 94 percent (Berg 2012: 11; Plag and Kunter 2010: 357) of English NN constructions have initial stress. The aforementioned observations point to the connection both between initial stress and non-compositionality and between non-initial stress and compositionality, which has also been investigated in further experimental studies. Using a lexical-decision task, McCauley et al. (2012) showed that non-compositional AN items in English were responded to more accurately if they were presented with initial stress in comparison to non-initial stress. Compositional constructions, however, showed higher accuracy rates with non-initial stress. Vogel and Raimy (2002) and Hall and Moore (1997) observed that adults were more likely to select a picture representing a non-compositional interpretation when they heard English AN combinations with initial stress. In contrast, hearing non-initial stress, participants favored pictures expressing compositional meanings. Focusing on production rather than comprehension, Farnetani et al. (1988) and Morrill (2012) found that compounds, i.e., non-compositional constructions, were typically pronounced with initial stress, but phrases, i.e., compositional items, with non-initial stress. Overall, the findings of these studies underline the link between stress and semantic compositionality. However, previous research generally suffers from the fact that the non-compositional items were not only non-compositional but also lexicalized. Therefore, it is difficult, if not impossible, to state that semantics, rather than lexicalization, is really responsible for the effects. Investigating non-lexicalized constructions represents an appropriate alternative that enables us to concentrate on semantics while controlling for lexicalization. In Schlechtweg (2018), for instance, only non-lexicalized items were tested in a lexical-decision experiment and it was shown that non-compositional AN combinations in English were perceived more efficiently with initial than with non-initial stress. The major concern of the current article is to see whether the connection between semantics and stress in non-lexicalized constructions can be confirmed in a production study.

3 (Non-)compositionality and stress in non-lexicalized English AN combinations: Insights from a production study

3.1 Objectives and hypotheses

The study asks, first, whether non-lexicalized and semantically non-compositional AN constructions in English are pronounced with initial stress, as opposed to their compositional counterparts. If this is the case, the experiment further aims at investigating whether non-compositional combinations also have initial stress if their meaning is explicitly marked as non-compositional by the immediate context. Specifically, *called so because* is used in the present study for this purpose. It is examined whether initial stress occurs independently of the immediate context or whether the explicit marker *called so because* inhibits the realization of initial stress (see also Section 2.1). In order to address these issues, the three conditions given in Table 1 are investigated (for further examples, see Table 6).

Tab. 1: The three conditions of the study

Condition	Example
Implied compositional semantics	Thomas took a black tram again, which has a color he likes.
Implied non-compositional semantics	Thomas took a black tram again, which is a tram that runs only during the night.
Explicitly marked non-compositional semantics	Thomas took a black tram again, which is called so because it is a tram that runs only during the night.

The study was designed to test the following hypotheses:
1. The items with implied non-compositional semantics, but not the items with implied compositional semantics, were expected to show initial stress

because this prosodic pattern is regarded as a means to mark non-compositionality. The hypotheses further below are formulated under the assumption that Hypothesis (1) is met. If Hypothesis (1) is not met, it must be concluded that semantic (non-)compositionality does not seem to have an influence on the stress pattern.
2. With regard to the comparison of the items with implied non-compositional semantics and the same items whose non-compositional meaning is explicitly marked, the following outcomes are possible:
   a. There is no effect, and items in both conditions have initial stress. This would mean that non-compositional semantics always trigger initial stress, independently of how explicitly non-compositionality in meaning is marked in the immediate context.
   b. The items with implied non-compositional semantics have initial stress but the items whose non-compositional semantics are explicitly marked do not. This would mean that non-compositionality triggers initial stress only if no other explicit marker of non-compositionality is present. Since *called so because* already explicitly marks the non-compositional semantics, it would be redundant to, additionally, modify the stress pattern.
3. With respect to the comparison of the items whose non-compositional semantics are explicitly marked and the items with implied compositional semantics, the following outcomes are possible:
   a. As opposed to the items with implied compositional semantics, the items whose semantics are explicitly marked were expected to have initial stress if Hypothesis (2a), in addition to Hypothesis (1), was correct.
   b. If Hypothesis (2b) was correct, the items whose non-compositional semantics are explicitly marked would, like the items with implied compositional semantics, carry non-initial stress.

3.2 Method

3.2.1 Participants

Six native speakers of American English, four females and two males, were tested in the study. Their mean age was 26 years (age range: 21–36, standard deviation: 5.9), and they were university students.

3.2.2 Materials

Six non-lexicalized complex AN constructions were created. Each AN combination was embedded in three different sentences and conditions (see Table 1 above and Table 6). The compositional version of an item was always tested prior to the non-compositional variants of the same item because it seemed likely that the compositional interpretation was less accessible once the new non-compositional one had been introduced. The version with implied non-compositional semantics preceded the one whose non-compositional meaning was explicitly marked in 50 percent of the items; in the remaining 50 percent, the order was reversed.

Several potentially confounding variables were controlled for in the experiment (see also Section 2.2.3). In order to reduce the influence of analogy, the non-compositional meanings were based on non-existent relations between the adjective and the noun. For instance, *black tram* with non-compositional semantics refers to a tram that runs only during the night. Although lexicalized AN constructions with the adjective *black* exist in English, there is no combination in which *black* represents the concept NIGHT. The nouns, in turn, did not appear in any lexicalized AN construction anyway. Furthermore, lexicalization effects were ruled out by investigating non-lexicalized items only. Moreover, since the same combinations were used in the three conditions, the informativity of the constituents and the phonetic environment were identical across conditions. The AN items were embedded in the same sentence type and position in each condition. That means, for instance, that *black tram* always occurred in the main clause *Thomas took a black tram again*, which, in turn, was followed by a relative clause starting with *which*. In order to minimize the influence of individual differences between language users and dialects, all subjects spoke each AN item in each condition and all were American speakers. Finally, as will be explained below Table 2, information structure was controlled for as well.

Apart from the 18 test sentences, 42 filler sentences, which increased the distance between the test items in one condition and the same items in another condition, were included in the experiment. Subjects always read at least 20 other sentences between the sentence with an item in one condition and the sentence with the same item in another condition.

3.2.3 Procedure

Subjects sat in a silent room approximately 40 centimeters (16 inches) from a large diaphragm condenser USB microphone and 70 centimeters (28 inches) from a computer screen. Participants saw one sentence from Table 1 or Table 6 at a time on the screen, read it silently first, and said "Okay" once they had read and understood it. After their reaction, a yes-no comprehension question referring to the sentence was shown on the screen and participants were asked to give the correct answer. Table 2 gives the respective questions for the sentences already presented in Table 1. The overall accuracy rate was 97 percent; only sentences associated with correct answers were later analyzed. After the response, the sentence appeared on the screen again, subjects read it aloud, and were recorded with Praat (Boersma and Weenink 2016).

Tab. 2: The yes-no questions

Sentence	Yes-no question
Thomas took a black tram again, which has a color he likes.	Is a black tram a tram that is bright? (Answer: No)
Thomas took a black tram again, which is a tram that runs only during the night.	Is a black tram a tram that goes to the graveyard? (Answer: No)
Thomas took a black tram again, which is called so because it is a tram that runs only during the night.	Is a black tram called so because it is a tram that goes to the graveyard? (Answer: No)

It is well known that information structure can have an influence on prosody (see Section 2.2.3). Therefore, the three conditions under investigation must be comparable with regard to information structure. Apart from the presence / absence of *called so because it is*, the sentences and questions used in the two non-compositional conditions were identical and, hence, information structure was controlled for. It was, however, equally important to ensure that information structure did not vary between the compositional and non-compositional conditions. The yes-no questions played a decisive role in this respect. As Table 2 shows, the focus always laid on the same element, for example, on the noun *tram*. Moreover, the amount of given and new information was identical across the conditions. For instance, *black* was used once and *tram* twice in the question of each condition. Hence, *black* was, so to speak, less given in the context of each condition. Generally speaking, this might increase the likelihood of initial stress because new, but not given, information is normally made prominent (Ladd 1984); however, the crucial point is that the information structure is balanced across all conditions.

3.3 Data analysis

A vital question in a production study is how one determines whether a construction has initial or non-initial stress. The present analysis is based on the measurement of three potential acoustic correlates of stress, namely F0, duration, and intensity. Generally speaking, higher F0, longer duration, and higher intensity have been traditionally associated with stressed syllables (see Lehiste 1970). Since the present paper cannot give a detailed and general discussion of these parameters (for a review, see, e.g., Kunter 2011: 57–69; Terken and Hermes 2000), we focus on three studies whose methodology is similar to that of the experiment reported in the present section. Plag (2006) analyzed the F0 in compounds. The author defined initial and non-initial stress in the following way: He first calculated the F0 difference between the first and second element of different compound types and then compared these differences. If compound type A showed a greater difference than compound type B, compound type A was considered to have initial stress and compound type B to carry non-initial stress. Farnetani et al. (1988) and Morrill (2012) not only looked at F0 but also at duration and intensity. Further, they used not only differences but also ratios. That means, for instance, that the authors examined minimal pairs and regarded greater F0 differences, higher duration ratios, and / or greater intensity differences between the first and second element of one construction in comparison to another construction as an indication of initial stress in the first and non-initial stress in the second construction. The present experiment adopts and slightly expands this approach, following previous work that has shown that the methodology can be successfully applied to the study of prominence in complex constructions. That is, it is assumed here that a statistically significant difference between the ratios (adjective values divided by noun values) and differences (adjective values minus noun values) of two conditions reflects the phonological categorical distinction between initial and non-initial stress. For instance, if construction A shows a greater F0 ratio and difference than construction B, this can be an indication that construction A carries a pitch accent on the first constituent only, i.e., it has initial stress, and construction B bears a pitch accent on both the first and the second constituent, i.e., it has non-initial stress (see Gussenhoven 2004: 277).

Before one can calculate ratios and differences, however, one has to measure the acoustics of the adjectives and nouns. The vowels of these constituents together with, if available in an item, liquids and glides were separated from the rest of the recordings and used as the intervals for the following measurements (for a detailed overview of segmentation criteria, see Turk, Nakai, and Sugahara 2006). The duration (= D) of each interval was obtained from the oscillogram and the maximum intensity (= I) was measured with the "Get maximum intensity" function in Praat. Moreover, the maximum F0 (= F0) was retrieved with the "Get maximum pitch" function and Praat's autocorrelation method. A pitch range of 75 to 300 Hertz (Hz) (males) and 100 to 500 Hz (females) was chosen and individually adjusted if necessary. Since extreme outliers were excluded from the analyses and since the constituents of the AN items were not associated with boundary tones, maximum F0s were used because they reflect the pitch contour more appropriately than mean F0s or F0s at the mid-points of vowels (Kunter 2011: 74–75). The target items were not placed in clause-, statement-, or question-final position; instead, each item was put before the word *again*, "which was expected to carry all boundary-related tonal elements" (Plag, Kunter, and Schramm 2011: 364).

For all adjectives and nouns, F0, D, and I were obtained. Afterwards, the ratio and difference of the adjective and noun value was calculated resulting in the six dependent variables fundamental frequency ratio ($F0_r$), fundamental frequency difference ($F0_d$), duration ratio (D_r), duration difference (D_d), intensity ratio (I_r), and intensity difference (I_d). Repeated-measures ANOVAs by subject (F_1) and by item (F_2) were conducted using $F0_r$, $F0_d$, D_r, D_d, I_r, and I_d as dependent variables. Homogeneity of variances, an assumption of the ANOVA, was given in F_1 and F_2 in the analyses of D_r, D_d, I_r, and I_d; both the Bartlett test, which assumes a normal distribution of the data, and the Levene test, which does not assume a normal distribution of the data, showed that the variances were equal ($p > .05$). In the analysis of $F0_r$, these tests revealed equal variances at least in F_1. In the analysis of $F0_d$, at least the Levene test indicated equal variances in both F_1 and F_2. The independent and fixed variable, SEMANTIC COMPOSITIONALITY, was a within-subject / item factor and had the three levels implied compositional semantics, implied non-compositional semantics, and explicitly marked non-compositional semantics. SUBJECT and ITEM were included as random variables.

3.4 Results

Note that, in this result section, the three conditions are abbreviated in the following way: C = implied compositional semantics, N = implied non-compositional semantics, S = explicitly marked non-compositional semantics.

3.4.1 Fundamental frequency

The analysis of $F0_r$ revealed a significant main effect of SEMANTIC COMPOSITIONALITY ($F_1(2,10) = 6.83$, $p < .05$; $F_2(2,10) = 5.66$, $p < .05$). Post-hoc comparisons showed that N and C significantly differed (Difference of means $[DM]_1 = 0.104$, $t_1 = 2.79$, $p_1 < .05$; $DM_2 = 0.137$, $t_2 = 2.56$, $p_2 < .05$). Significance was also reached in the comparison of S and N ($DM_1 = -0.130$, $t_1 = -3.50$, $p_1 < .01$; $DM_2 = -0.170$, $t_2 = -3.17$, $p_2 = .01$), but not between S and C.

The analysis of $F0_d$ showed a significant main effect of SEMANTIC COMPOSITIONALITY ($F_1(2,10) = 7.45$, $p = .01$; $F_2(2,10) = 6.50$, $p < .05$). Not only N and C ($DM_1 = 20.63$, $t_1 = 3.40$, $p_1 < .01$; $DM_2 = 25.33$, $t_2 = 3.11$, $p_2 < .05$) but also S and N significantly differed ($DM_1 = -19.88$, $t_1 = -3.28$, $p_1 < .01$; $DM_2 = -25.48$, $t_2 = -3.13$, $p_2 < .05$). The difference between S and C did not reach significance. Overall, Hypotheses 1, 2b, and 3b were confirmed. Descriptive statistics are summarized in Table 3 ($F0_r$ and $F0_d$) and displayed in Figure 1 (only $F0_d$).

Tab. 3: Descriptive statistics of $F0_r$ / $F0_d$, subject analysis (F_1) (item analysis [F_2] in brackets)[1]

	C	N	S
N of $F0_r$	6 (6)	6 (6)	6 (6)
N of $F0_d$	6 (6)	6 (6)	6 (6)
M of $F0_r$	1.003 (1.001)	1.106 (1.138)	0.976 (0.968)
M of $F0_d$	-4.61 (-5.05)	16.03 (20.28)	-3.85 (-5.20)
SD of $F0_r$	0.091 (0.147)	0.145 (0.136)	0.044 (0.039)
SD of $F0_d$	6.68 (21.73)	21.32 (21.81)	5.86 (6.59)

---

[1] N (in first column) = Number of observations, M = Mean, SD = Standard deviation.

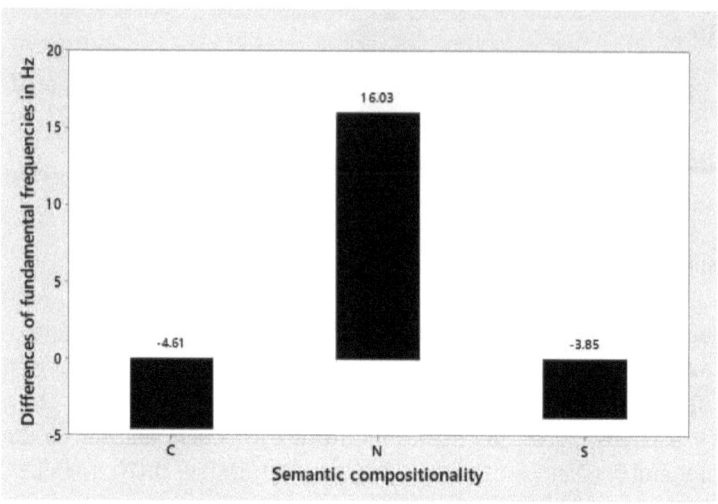

Fig. 1: Mean F0$_d$ in subject analysis (F$_1$)

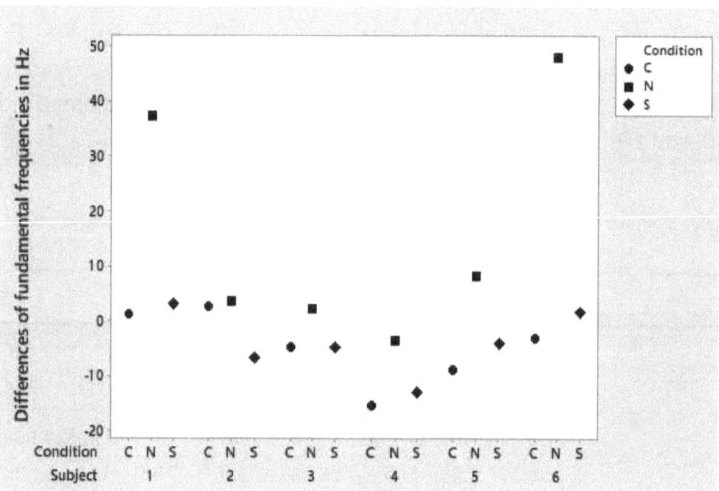

Fig. 2: Distribution of values of F0$_d$ in subject analysis (F$_1$)

Figures 2 and 3 illustrate that the individual values that contributed to the overall means given in Table 3 were higher in condition N than in conditions C and S, which, in turn, were often closer together, for all subjects and items. Since the analysis of $F0_r$ revealed a similar pattern, the distributions are not presented here.

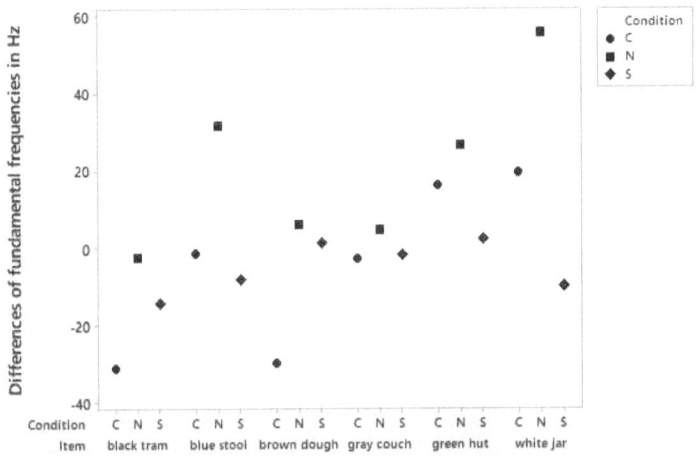

Fig. 3: Distribution of values of $F0_d$ in item analysis (F_2)

3.4.2 Duration

The analysis of D_r showed a significant main effect of SEMANTIC COMPOSITIONALITY ($F_1(2,10) = 11.57$, $p < .01$; $F_2(2,10) = 8.20$, $p < .01$). Post-hoc comparisons revealed a significant difference between N and C ($DM_1 = 0.257$, $t_1 = 4.77$, $p_1 = .001$; $DM_2 = 0.214$, $t_2 = 4.05$, $p_2 < .01$). The difference between S and N was significant in the subject analysis and marginally significant in the item analysis ($DM_1 = -0.157$, $t_1 = -2.91$, $p_1 < .05$; $DM_2 = -0.109$, $t_2 = -2.05$, $p_2 = .067$). S and C did not significantly differ.

The analysis of D_d showed a significant main effect of SEMANTIC COMPOSITIONALITY ($F_1(2,10) = 10.29$, $p < .01$; $F_2(2,10) = 9.87$, $p < .01$). N and C significantly differed ($DM_1 = 35.60$, $t_1 = 4.44$, $p_1 = .001$; $DM_2 = 31.45$, $t_2 = 4.38$, $p_2 = .001$). A significant difference was also detected between S and N ($DM_1 = -24.41$, $t_1 = -3.04$, $p_1 < .05$; $DM_2 = -20.27$, $t_2 = -2.82$, $p_2 < .05$) but not between S and C. Overall, again, Hypotheses 1, 2b, and 3b were confirmed. Descriptive statistics are summarized in Table 4 (D_r and D_d) and displayed in Figure 4 (D_d only).

Tab. 4: Descriptive statistics of D_r / D_d, subject analysis (F_1) (item analysis [F_2] in brackets)

	C	N	S
N of D_r	6 (6)	6 (6)	6 (6)
N of D_d	6 (6)	6 (6)	6 (6)
M of D_r	1.173 (1.181)	1.430 (1.395)	1.273 (1.287)
M of D_d	19.53 (20.49)	55.13 (51.95)	30.72 (31.68)
SD of D_r	0.103 (0.326)	0.111 (0.424)	0.171 (0.384)
SD of D_d	18.25 (61.40)	9.23 (60.40)	26.40 (65.50)

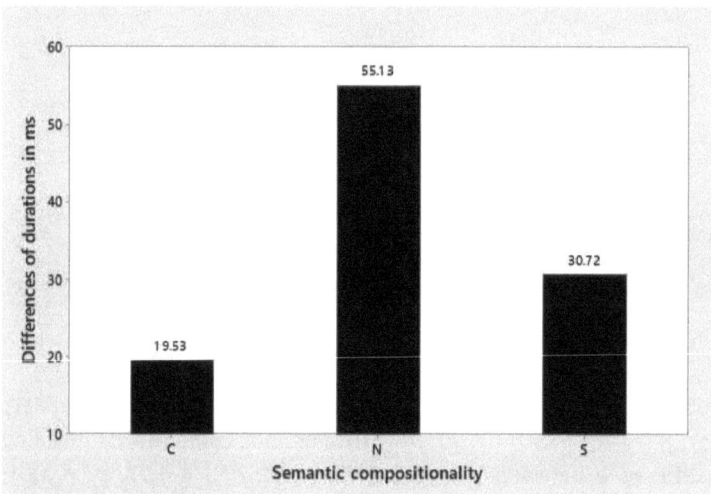

Fig. 4: Mean D_d in subject analysis (F_1)

Some of the standard deviations in Table 4 are high. Figures 5 and 6 present the distributions of the values included in the calculation of the means of D_d. The graphs illustrate that D_d of N is higher than that of C and S for five of the six subjects and items. The analysis of D_r revealed a similar pattern. Figure 5 also shows that N was the most stable condition across subjects. Figure 6 illustrates that the large standard deviations are based on the different phonetic nature of the items and that the standard deviations of all conditions are similar.

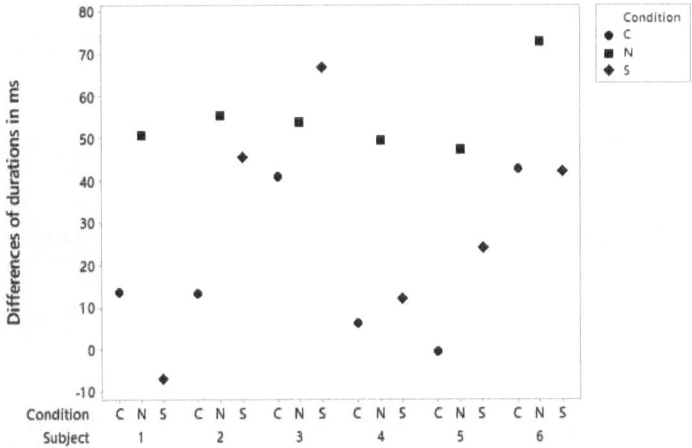

Fig. 5: Distribution of values of D_d in subject analysis (F_1)

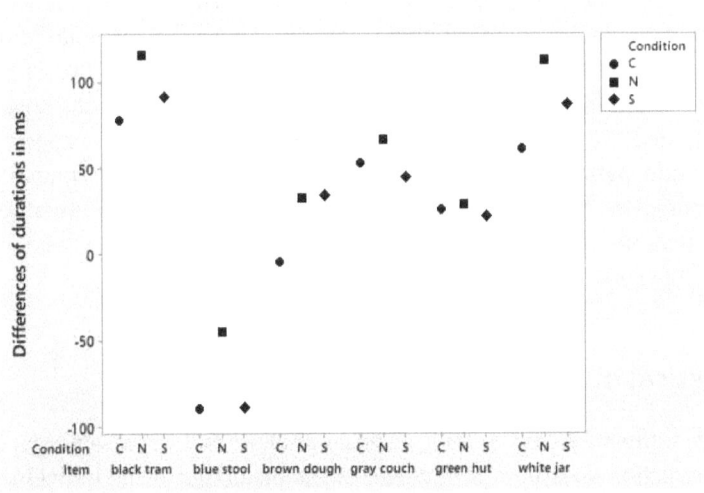

Fig. 6: Distribution of values of D_d in item analysis (F_2)

3.4.3 Intensity

The analyses of I_r and I_d did not show a main effect of SEMANTIC COMPOSITIONALITY. Descriptive statistics are presented in Table 5.

Tab. 5: Descriptive statistics of l_r / l_d, subject analysis (F_1) (item analysis [F_2] in brackets)

	C	N	S
N of l_r	6 (6)	6 (6)	6 (6)
N of l_d	6 (6)	6 (6)	6 (6)
M of l_r	1.012 (1.012)	1.020 (1.021)	1.012 (1.010)
M of l_d	0.76 (0.74)	1.26 (1.30)	0.81 (0.60)
SD of l_r	0.012 (0.010)	0.016 (0.020)	0.015 (0.012)
SD of l_d	0.69 (0.66)	0.98 (1.39)	1.03 (0.78)

3.4.4 Summary of results

In sum, only the AN constructions with implied non-compositional semantics showed a clear tendency towards initial stress. In contrast, the combinations with explicitly marked non-compositional semantics, as well as the items with implied compositional semantics, tended to carry non-initial stress. Crucially, both measures taken (ratios and differences) for two of the three acoustic parameters measured (F0 and duration) showed robust effects in the expected direction. The only parameter that did not show an effect of semantic compositionality was intensity; this, however, is in line with evidence from the literature that suggests that intensity may in fact not always be a reliable cue to stress (for a review, see Cutler 2005).

3.5 Theoretical discussion

Speakers have different means at their disposal to mark that the meaning of a complex construction goes beyond the sum of the meanings of the individual constituents. On the prosodic side, initial stress represents a typical marker of semantic non-compositionality in English. The findings of the present pilot study support the idea that language users place more prosodic prominence on the initial constituent if the semantics of a complex construction deviate from the compositional interpretation. Specifically, it is shown that native speakers of English lengthen the initial syllables and pronounce them at a higher pitch level. The latter finding is compatible with Gussenhoven's (2004: 277) proposal that non-compositional items such as compounds carry an accent only on the first constituent but compositional constructions such as phrases bear an accent on both constituents. On the non-prosodic level, *called so because* is one way to explicitly mark a non-compositional meaning. The analyses of the current experiment indicate that speakers, if exposed to a non-lexicalized complex construction whose non-compositional semantics are explicitly marked, tend not to use initial stress and, instead, seem to favor the standard prosodic structure of compositional semantics. Therefore, this first pilot study suggests that native speakers of English might rely on either a prosodic or a non-prosodic means, but not on both, to mark meaning deviations when they produce non-lexicalized constructions in their language.

Overall, the present findings are, on the one hand, similar to the results of previous studies such as Farnetani et al. (1988) and Morrill (2012). That means specifically that F0 and duration turned out to be reliable correlates in the distinction between initial and non-initial stress. For example, Morrill's (2012) analysis revealed a greater duration ratio for compounds compared to phrases, indicating that the former carry initial stress but the latter non-initial stress. Keeping in mind that the compounds of her study were non-compositional and the phrases compositional, one can see that the findings are similar to those of the present experiment. On the other hand, however, three differences have to be emphasized as well. First, the other authors investigated lexicalized items and, thus, their effects might also be based on lexicalization rather than semantic non-compositionality. Second, intensity played a much greater role in the other two studies than in the present experiment. A potential explanation is the low number of participants and items examined in my study. Third, some of the other authors' results are connected to the fact that they looked at different sentence positions such as subject position, question-, statement-, or clause-final position. For instance, Morrill (2012) found a higher F0 in the second constituent in comparison to the first one in compounds in question-final position. This effect has its roots in the rising intonation of this environment. In contrast, the present study focused on a single position in which the acoustic properties of items were not influenced by boundary phenomena found in final positions.

A result of the analysis reported here is that only items with implied non-compositional semantics but not items whose non-compositional meaning was explicitly marked by the immediate context showed a clear tendency to carry initial stress. This finding partly connects to the study described in Härtl (2016), who investigated German AN compounds and phrases of comparable frequencies and found that phrases occurred more often with *sogenannt* ('so-called') than compounds. Crucially, the German AN compounds of Härtl's experiment resemble the items with implied non-compositional semantics of the present study in two respects: First, both are non-compositional and, second, both carry initial stress. The German AN phrases examined by Härtl and the non-compositional constructions that occurred with *called so because* in the current experiment share two characteristics as well: First, and again, both are non-compositional and, second, both have non-initial stress. Taken together, both Härtl's and my own study show that the non-compositional semantics of AN constructions are less likely to be marked by means of initial stress if an explicit and non-prosodic marker such as *sogenannt* or *called so because* is present. Nevertheless, these issues have to be investigated further because, strictly speaking, *sogenannt* and *called so because* differ in crucial respects. The latter, but not the former, has to be followed by an expression that explains the function of the modifier. Further, while *called so because* in the present study focuses on the contribution of the adjectival semantics to the entire meaning only, *sogenannt* refers to the whole AN construction. Whether these syntactic and semantic differences affect stress has not been tackled in the current work.

Finally, it has to be emphasized again that the number of participants and items was, in comparison to other studies such as Morrill (2012), quite small. As a consequence, the results are still rather exploratory in nature and have to be confirmed in subsequent and more comprehensive studies.

4 Conclusion

The current paper investigated non-lexicalized AN combinations in English and addressed two questions: Are non-compositional constructions stressed differently in comparison to compositional items and, if so, does the explicit marking of non-compositionality in the immediate context have an influence on stress distribution? Although the dataset is rather small, this analysis suggests that the answer to both of these questions might be "Yes": Non-compositionality seems to trigger initial stress in non-lexicalized items, but only if no other device to mark non-compositionality, such as *called so because*, is used.

5 References

Bell, Melanie J. & Ingo Plag. 2013. Informativity and analogy in English compound stress. *Word Structure* 6(2). 129–155.

Berg, Thomas. 2012. The cohesiveness of English and German compounds. *The Mental Lexicon* 7(1). 1–31.

Boersma, Paul & David Weenink. 2016. *Praat: doing phonetics by computer [Computer program]: Version 6.0.21*. http://www.praat.org/ (accessed 20 October 2016).

Bolinger, Dwight. 1958. A theory of pitch accent in English. *Word* 14. 109–149.

Bolinger, Dwight. 1986. *Intonation and its parts: The melody of language*. Stanford, CA: Stanford University Press.

Chomsky, Noam & Morris Halle. 1968. *The sound pattern of English*. New York, NY: Harper & Row.

Cutler, Anne. 2005. Word stress. In David B. Pisoni & Robert E. Remez (eds.), *The handbook of speech perception*, 264–289. Malden, MA: Blackwell.

Farnetani, Edda, Carol Taylor Torsello & Piero Cosi. 1988. English compounds versus non-compound noun phrases in discourse: An acoustic and perceptual study. *Language and Speech* 31(2). 157–180.

Giegerich, Heinz J. 2004. Compound or phrase? English noun-plus-noun constructions and the stress criterion. *English Language and Linguistics* 8(1). 1–24.

Gussenhoven, Carlos. 2004. *The phonology of tone and intonation*. Cambridge: Cambridge University Press.

Hall, D. Geoffrey & Catherine E. Moore. 1997. Red bluebirds and black greenflies: Preschoolers' understanding of the semantics of adjectives and count nouns. *Journal of Experimental Child Psychology* 67(2). 236–267.

Härtl, Holden. 2016. Normality at the boundary between word-formation and syntax. *Linguistische Berichte*. Sonderheft 22. 71–98.

Kunter, Gero. 2011. *Compound stress in English: The phonetics and phonology of prosodic prominence* (Linguistische Arbeiten 539). Berlin: De Gruyter.

Ladd, D. Robert. 1984. English compound stress. In Dafydd Gibbon & Helmut Richter (eds.), *Intonation, accent and rhythm: Studies in discourse phonology* (Research in Text Theory 8), 253–266. Berlin: Walter de Gruyter.

Ladd, D. Robert & Anne Cutler. 1983. Introduction: Models and measurements in the study of prosody. In D. Robert Ladd & Anne Cutler (eds.), *Models and measurements in the study of prosody* (Springer Series in Language and Communication 14), 1–10. Berlin: Springer.

Lehiste, Ilse. 1970. *Suprasegmentals*. Cambridge, MA: MIT Press.

Liberman, Mark & Alan Prince. 1977. On stress and linguistic rhythm. *Linguistic Inquiry* 8(2). 249–336.

Liberman, Mark & Richard Sproat. 1992. The stress and structure of modified noun phrases in English. In Ivan A. Sag & Anna Szabolcsi (eds.), *Lexical matters*, 131–181. Leland Stanford Junior University: Center for the Study of Language and Information.

McCauley, Stewart M., Arild Hestvik & Irene Vogel. 2012. Perception and bias in the processing of compound versus phrasal stress: Evidence from event-related brain potentials. *Language and Speech* 56(1). 23–44.

Morrill, Tuuli. 2012. Acoustic correlates of stress in English adjective-noun compounds. *Language and Speech* 55(2). 167–201.

Plag, Ingo. 2006. The variability of compound stress in English: Structural, semantic, and analogical factors. *English Language and Linguistics* 10(1). 143–172.

Plag, Ingo & Gero Kunter. 2010. Constituent family size and compound stress assignment in English. In Susan Olsen (ed.), *New impulses in word-formation* (Linguistische Berichte, Sonderheft 17), 349–382. Hamburg: Buske.

Plag, Ingo, Gero Kunter & Sabine Lappe. 2007. Testing hypotheses about compound stress assignment in English: A corpus-based investigation. *Corpus Linguistics and Linguistic Theory* 3(2). 199–232.

Plag, Ingo, Gero Kunter, Sabine Lappe & Maria Braun. 2008. The role of semantics, argument structure, and lexicalization in compound stress assignment in English. *Language* 84(4). 760–794.

Plag, Ingo, Gero Kunter & Mareile Schramm. 2011. Acoustic correlates of primary and secondary stress in North American English. *Journal of Phonetics* 39(3). 362–374.

Schlechtweg, Marcel. 2018. *Memorization and the compound-phrase distinction: An investigation of complex constructions in German, French and English* (Studia Grammatica 82). Berlin: De Gruyter.

Terken, Jacques & Dirk J. Hermes. 2000. The perception of prosodic prominence. In Merle Horne (ed.), *Prosody: Theory and experiment: Studies presented to Gösta Bruce*, 89–127. Dordrecht: Kluwer Academic Publishers.

Trudgill, Peter & Jean Hannah. ⁵2008. *International English: A guide to the varieties of Standard English*. London: Routledge.

Turk, Alice, Satsuki Nakai & Mariko Sugahara. 2006. Acoustic segment durations in prosodic research: A practical guide. In Stefan Sudhoff, Denisa Lenertová, Roland Meyer, Sandra Pappert, Petra Augurzky, Ina Mleinek, Nicole Richter & Johannes Schließer (eds.), *Methods in empirical prosody research* (Language, Context, and Cognition 3), 1–28. Berlin: Walter de Gruyter.

Vanderslice, Ralph & Peter Ladefoged. 1972. Binary suprasegmental features and transformational word-accentuation rules. *Language* 48. 819–838.

Vogel, Irene & Eric Raimy. 2002. The acquisition of compound vs. phrasal stress: The role of prosodic constituents. *Journal of Child Language* 29(2). 225–250.

Zwitserlood, Pienie. 1994. The role of semantic transparency in the processing and representation of Dutch compounds. *Language and Cognitive Processes* 9(3). 341–368.

Appendix: Remaining test sentences in the three conditions

Tab. 6: Remaining test sentences in the three conditions[2]

Condition	Test sentence
Compositionality (C)	Nicole used a white jar again, which has a nice color.
Non-compositionality (N, S)	Nicole used a white jar again, which (is called so because it) is a jar used to store sugar.
Compositionality (C)	Lucy sat on a blue stool again, which has a color she likes.
Non-compositionality (N, S)	Lucy sat on a blue stool again, which (is called so because it) is a stool used for therapies in the water.
Compositionality (C)	Sarah slept in a green hut again, which has a color she likes.
Non-compositionality (N, S)	Sarah slept in a green hut again, which (is called so because it) is a hut we find in a garden.
Compositionality (C)	Steven made a brown dough again, which has a nice color.
Non-compositionality (N, S)	Steven made a brown dough again, which (is called so because it) is a dough made of chocolate.
Compositionality (C)	Sally relaxed on a gray couch again, which has a color she likes.
Non-compositionality (N, S)	Sally relaxed on a gray couch again, which (is called so because it) is a couch made of cement.

---

[2] The two non-compositional conditions are given in the same lines. What appears between brackets belongs to the condition with *called so because* (= S) only.

Sabine Arndt-Lappe
Expanding the lexicon by truncation: Variability, recoverability, and productivity

Abstract: Two issues have posed a challenge for morphological theories to account for how and why patterns of name truncation and clipping are so productive as a means of expanding the lexicon in many languages, and have fuelled the debate about whether or not such truncation patterns should be considered regular word-formation (e.g. Lappe 2007; Ronneberger-Sibold 2010; Alber and Arndt-Lappe 2012; Mattiello 2013; Manova 2016). These are (a) the variability of observed output forms, and (b) their functional indeterminacy and lack of semantic transparency. The present article presents case studies from Italian, German and English to bear on these issues. With respect to (a), it is argued that variability arises from the existence of different, systematic truncation patterns both within and across languages, and discusses the available evidence on how the formal distinctions correspond to the functional differentiation of patterns. With respect to (b), it is argued that productive truncation patterns are optimised for recoverability, and evidence is discussed to suggest that discourse context plays a crucial role in establishing transparent base-derivative relations. On a theoretical level, I will argue that excluding truncation from grammatical morphology on the grounds of the scope of formal variation in outputs and their lack of transparency may be premature, and is not helpful in accounting for the productivity of truncatory patterns observed in language. Instead, the findings of the present study suggest an agenda for future research that will study patterns and usage of truncation both within and across languages in more detail. *

1 Introduction

This article is concerned with two types of truncatory processes: truncated personal names as they are used in many languages to form vocatives and hypocoristics, and truncated non-names. I will use the term 'truncated names' to refer to the former and 'clippings' to refer to the latter. Both truncated names and

---

* I am grateful to Birgit Alber, Ingo Plag, and Elke Ronneberger-Sibold for many inspiring discussions and constructive feedback on earlier versions of this paper. Thanks also to two anonymous reviewers for their helpful comments. Needless to say, all remaining errors are mine.

clippings can occur with or without suffixes. Examples of the different types of truncation are given in (1)–(3).[1]

(1) Name truncations, without suffix
    a. German
        Katha   ◆ Katharina
        Seba   ◆ Sebastian
        Manu   ◆ Manuela
    b. Central Alaskan Yup'ik (McCarthy and Prince [1986] 1996)
        Aŋ, Aŋuk   ◆ Aŋukaynaq
        Aŋif   ◆ Aŋivyan
        Kał, Kalik ◆ Kalixtuq
    c. English
        Pat, Trish   ◆ Patricia
        Abe   ◆ Abraham
        Liz, Beth, Bess ◆ Elisabeth

(2) Name truncations, with suffix
    a. German I
        Kat-i   ◆ Katharina
        Gab-i   ◆ Gabriele
        Rolf-i   ◆ Rolf
    b. German II
        Woll-e   ◆ Wolfgang
        Ed-e   ◆ Eduard
        Rall-e   ◆ Ralf
    c. English
        Patt-y, Trish-y ◆ Patricia
        Ab-y   ◆ Abraham
        Lizz-y, Bett-y ◆ Elisabeth

(3) Clippings, without suffix
    a. German
        Mathe   ◆ Mathematik
        Psycho   ◆ Psychologie
        Päda   ◆ Pädagogik
        Abi   ◆ Abitur

---

1 Note that (1)–(3) are not meant to provide exhaustive sets of attested truncations for each base form. In some cases more than one truncation is cited to illustrate the variation found in attested output forms. Such variation will be discussed in detail in section 2 below.

b. French (Kilani-Schoch 1996)
    appart   ♦ appartement
    manif   ♦ manifestation
    formid   ♦ formidable
    bac   ♦ baccalauréat
c. Swedish (Nübling 2001)
    el   ♦ elektricitet
    raff   ♦ raffinaderi
    rea   ♦ realisation
d. English
    maths   ♦ mathematics
    geog   ♦ geography
    bio   ♦ biology
    lab   ♦ laboratory

As becomes evident from the examples cited, 'truncation' is actually a misnomer for the processes exemplified. Especially among the suffixed forms, derivative forms[2] are not necessarily shorter than their base forms (compare e.g. *Rolf-i* ♦ *Rolf*). What we see, instead, is that most truncation is templatic, which means that the formal properties of the process are best described in terms of the resulting output structure (in the examples in (1)–(3): a monosyllabic or a disyllabic word) rather than in terms of what and how much material is deleted from the base word (cf. Alber and Arndt-Lappe 2012; Manova 2016 for discussion). If we accept that truncation is best described in terms of such an output-oriented perspective, it becomes clear that forms like *Rolfi* (♦ *Rolf*), in spite of the fact that no truncation in a literal sense is involved, belong to the same kind of morphological category: Like *Kati* (♦ *Katharina*), the output form *Rolf-i* corresponds to a disyllabic template. Also functionally, there is no difference between forms like *Rolfi* and forms like *Kati*.

In terms of the topic of this volume, truncations constitute an interesting case, as their form and meaning straddle the boundaries of what is considered regular word-formation in many frameworks (cf. e.g. Ronneberger-Sibold 2015a for a recent summary). At the same time many truncation processes undoubtedly display a high degree of productivity, in the sense that a lot of new forms are being coined, with a both regular and predictable form and function. This is particularly true of name truncations in many languages (on form cf. e.g. Alber and Arndt-Lappe 2012 for a summary of the literature; on function cf. e.g.

---

2 The terminology used here, referring to outputs of truncation as 'derivative forms' and to full forms as their 'bases', suggests that truncation is considered a regular word-formation process. Cf. below for discussion.

Schneider 1993, 2003 on German and English name truncations, respectively, Lappe 2007 on English; Alber 2010 on Italian). What I want to argue in this paper, on a general level, is that looking at productive truncation patterns can teach us something about what regular word-formation is like. On a more specific level, this paper is meant as a step towards laying out a research agenda that may help to develop a better understanding of how, in spite of the analytical challenges, truncation works as a regular and productive mechanism of lexical expansion.

In terms of formal aspects, the challenge that has made it difficult for some frameworks to classify truncation as a regular word-formation process is that truncatory patterns seem to involve a greater variety of options than other morphological processes, giving the impression that outputs are, in essence, unpredictable (cf. e.g. Ronneberger-Sibold 2015a). With respect to some formal aspects, the unpredictability assumption has been challenged in work set in the framework of Prosodic Morphology (McCarthy and Prince 1993, 1996). In this research program, truncatory patterns have often been cited as evidence for the claim that prosodic categories (esp. the syllable and the metrical foot) play an important role in determining the structure of outputs of morphology. Thus, many languages have truncatory patterns in which the output of truncation regularly corresponds to a metrical foot of that language (e.g. Bat-El 2005 for Hebrew; Piñeros 2000 for Spanish; Féry 1997 and Wiese 2001 for German *i*-suffixed forms like those in (2a) above). One problem with many studies in Prosodic Morphology, however, is that, given the interest of the research program, their focus is necessarily limited. Thus, several studies look only at prosodic restrictions on the size of truncated forms. Only much more rarely do they discuss the question as to which part of the base is retained in the truncation. The same is true for effects such as segmental changes and substitution phenomena, which are often cited as evidence for the alleged unpredictability of truncation. Lappe (2007) is a comprehensive empirical study of major truncation patterns in English within Prosodic Morphology, but for many other languages we are lacking important data. Another problem with analyses of the form of truncations is that it is unclear what underlies the patterns we observe. Thus, the fact that there are many crosslinguistic similarities between the formal properties of truncation patterns has been modelled in optimality-theoretic studies as an effect of the ranking and interaction of universal markedness constraints, which, crucially, form an integral part of grammar. The very same crosslinguistic similarities, however, have also been interpreted as grounded in universal, cognitive principles that are not grammatical (Berg 2011; Ronneberger-Sibold 2015a). Finally, it is unclear if and in how far it is justified to think of different truncation patterns within a given language as different morphological categories of that language.

With respect to the meaning of truncations, one important challenge is that it is unclear how a transparent form-meaning relationship can be achieved in truncated forms. As a consequence of these problems, truncatory processes are in some frameworks considered to be instances of marginal morphology, extragrammatical morphology or creative processes (esp. within a Natural Morphology context, e.g. Mattiello 2013). Another challenge is the formalisation of the meaning of truncated forms, given that they share their denotational meaning with their bases, but differ from their bases in terms of affective meaning components that vary with the way they are used pragmatically in discourse (cf. esp. Schneider 2003 for an analysis).

Interestingly, both challenges (formal variability, and the indeterminacy of meaning) come across as particularly urgent in the analysis of truncation, but are in fact a matter of current debate in other, catenative morphological processes as well (for discussion of universal vs. category specific variation in catenative morpho-phonology cf. e.g. Steriade 1999; Carlson and Gerfen 2011; Bermúdez-Otero, to appear; for discussion of the nature of morphological transparency cf. e.g. Bell and Schäfer 2016; Schäfer 2017 on compounding).

In the present paper I will argue that excluding truncation from grammatical morphology on the grounds of the scope of formal variation in outputs and their lack of transparency may be premature, and is not helpful in accounting for the productivity of many truncatory patterns observed in language. Building on previous work on English (especially Lappe 2007) and crosslinguistic work (esp. Alber and Arndt-Lappe 2012), I will present case studies to show that, with respect to structural predictability, a more appropriate analysis of the investigated patterns crucially involves taking into account the systematic and highly constrained variability of the structural properties of truncatory patterns. The available evidence seems to suggest that both universal and morphological factors interact to produce the observed variation. With respect to semantic transparency, the evidence from truncation suggests a notion of morphological transparency that makes crucial reference to psycholinguistic notions of the recoverability of the base-derivative relation. The paper will discuss relevant structural properties of truncations in the light of psycholinguistic evidence about factors that facilitate or impede word recognition and lexical access. The available evidence for name truncation and clipping suggests that, despite the loss of transparency, the truncatory patterns under investigation strive to preserve recoverability.[3] In more general terms, the study of truncation sheds interesting light on the question of how transparency is in fact related to recoverability.

Towards the end of this section, two disclaimers are in order. First, as we will see in the course of the paper, there is by far not yet enough evidence available to allow us to come to definite conclusions. Rather, the goal of the paper is to show that the existing evidence opens up interesting new avenues for research, which will study pattern variability and the meaning of truncated words, identifying regular patterns and studying the relationship between productivity and regularity in these patterns.

Second, it is important to note that the paper will only look at productive truncatory patterns. There is a wealth of literature that deals with other types of truncation, whose status for the language system is less clear. Prominent instances are, for example, brand names and the use of truncation in advertising language (cf. e.g. Ronneberger-Sibold and Wahl 2014; Ronneberger-Sibold 2015b).

The paper is structured as follows. Section 2 will discuss formal predictability and variability, section 3 will be devoted to transparency and recoverability. The paper will end with a concluding section (section 4).

2 Formal predictability and variability

A general problem in assessing the predictability of output structures of truncatory processes is that, in much of the pertinent literature, the degree of predictability is not in the focus of investigation. A further problem is that major work on truncation comes from very different theoretical frameworks, which happen to make radically different claims about the predictability of truncatory patterns (cf. Manova 2016 for a recent overview).

In what follows I will present case studies that investigate aspects of the formal predictability of truncatory patterns. The data come from German, Italian, and English. Section 2.2 will look at the question of how many subpatterns there may be, and review some of the evidence that there may be functional differences between them. Section 2.3 will be concerned with structural differ-

---

[3] This is contrary to claims in the literature that argue that truncation is motivated by the aim to obscure recoverability (e.g. Ronneberger-Sibold 2001), which may hold for some patterns of truncation, but will be shown to be problematic for the productive patterns to be discussed in this paper.

ences between subpatterns that can be captured in terms of different degrees of optimisation.

2.1 Patterns distinguished by word structure and anchoring

One thing that is striking about truncation when studied across languages is that there seem to be general constraints on the formal properties of truncation that seem to hold across languages, to the effect that truncatory patterns, even in typologically distinct languages, look strikingly similar (for pertinent data and a theoretical account cf. Alber and Arndt-Lappe 2012). Such constraints pertain to the general word structure of truncated forms (measured in terms of the number of syllables and the stress pattern) and the question as to which part of the base survives in the truncation. The latter will be referred to as 'anchoring' in this paper. Within the bounds of these universal constraints, languages differ systematically in what functional use they make of such options. Furthermore, languages differ in how they map the different possibilities onto different functions.

In order to explore systematic differences between languages, we turn to name truncations. In what follows I will describe word structure and anchoring patterns in Italian and German on the basis of two parallel surveys that were conducted in 2002 at the universities of Verona and Trento (for Italian; in collaboration with Birgit Alber) and in 2007 at the university of Siegen (for German). In both cases informants, who were undergraduate students participating in general linguistics courses, were asked to supply (in written form) nicknames of names of people they know. All data come from native speakers of the language in question. The surveys yielded 244 different Italian and 544 different German base-derivative pairs. Orthographic variants, nicknames that bear no formal relation to the original name, and anglicised versions of names and nicknames were excluded.[4] A detailed structural analysis of the Italian data that were collected in Verona can be found in Alber (2010), which also served as a model for the classification of the Italian data in the present study.

Table 1 provides an overview of word structures in the Italian data. 'S' stands for a 'strong', i.e. (main-) stressed syllable, 'w' stands for a 'weak', i.e. unstressed, syllable.

---

4 The latter occurred only in the German data.

Tab. 1: Word structure in the Italian sample

	N	%	examples
S w	82	33.6	Anto (♦ Antonella)
S w, with a reduplicated consonant	20	8.2	Pippo (♦ Filippo)
S w, other fixed segments	7	2.9	Pine (♦ Giuseppina)
S w, *i*-final[5]	94	38.5	Andri (♦ Andrea)
S	35	14.3	Giò (♦ Giovanni)
w S	5	2.0	Milé (♦ Milena)
Other	1	0.4	Eleo (♦ Eleonora)
Total	**244**	**100**	

The data fall into five distinct patterns: There are two highly frequent disyllabic patterns, one of which takes two syllables from the base word and ends in an open syllable, and one of which involves a fixed segment, *-i*, which may be analysed as a suffix.

Among the rarer patterns, we find a monosyllabic pattern that comprises an open syllable, a disyllabic pattern that resembles the first disyllabic pattern but involves reduplication of the second onset consonant (cf. Alber 2010 for a detailed description), and, interestingly, a disyllabic pattern with iambic stress. Four of the five iambic forms are apparently exponents of a pattern reported by in Alber (2007, 2010) for Southern varieties of Italian, where the truncated form preserves the stretch from the initial to the main-stressed syllable of the base, regardless of the number of syllables involved. The forms are *Marí* (♦ *María*), *Milé* (♦ *Miléna*), *Sofí* (♦ *Sofía*), and *Moré* (♦ *Moréno*). More examples of the Southern Italian pattern are given in (4), from Alber (2010).

(4)   Ba   ♦ Bárbara
      Francé   ♦ Francésca
      Antoné   ♦ Antonélla

Tables 2–4 look at anchoring in the three major Italian patterns: the unsuffixed disyllabic pattern ('Sw-truncations'), the *i*-final disyllabic pattern ('*i*-final Sw-

---

5 This group comprises S w forms where *-i* is not part of the base name (e.g. *Andri* (♦ *Andrea*) and S w forms in which *-i* is present also in the base (e.g. *Ori* (♦ *Orielta*). The reason why the latter have been categorised as 'S w, *i*-final' and not as 'S w' is that they show the same anchoring pattern as other *i*-final forms (cf. Tables 2 and 3 below).

truncations'), and the monosyllabic pattern. In order to be able to distinguish between the two anchoring patterns, only bases are considered in which main stress is non-initial.

Tab. 2: Anchoring in Sw-truncations for bases where main stress is non-initial

	N	%	examples
initial syllable	44	55.0	Marghe (♦ Margherita)
main-stressed syllable	29	36.3	Betta (♦ Elisabetta)
other or unclear	7	8.8	Nico (♦ Domenico), Benza (♦ Benzina)
Total	80	100	

Tab. 3: Anchoring in *i*-final Sw-truncations for bases where main stress is non-initial

	N	%	examples
initial syllable	71	89.9	Albi (♦ Alberto)
main-stressed syllable, noninitial	7	8.9	Resy (♦ Teresa)
unclear	1	1.3	Tessy (♦ Stefania)
Total	79	100	

Tab. 4: Anchoring in monosyllabic truncations for bases where main stress is non-initial

	N	%	examples
initial syllable	19	95.0	Ste (♦ Stefania)
main-stressed syllable, noninitial	1	5.0	Cè (♦ Francesca)
Total	20	100	

Anchoring is surprisingly uniform. The portion of the base that survives in the truncated form begins with the beginning of the initial or the main stressed syllable of the base and ends when the disyllabic or monosyllabic structure that characterises the word structure of the truncatory pattern is satisfied. Other types of anchoring are extremely marginal. I will henceforth refer to the two major anchoring patterns as 'initial' and 'stress' anchoring, respectively. Note that truncatory patterns that differ in word structure also differ in anchoring:

Simplex (i.e. unsuffixed) disyllabic names may anchor to the initial or the mainstressed syllable of their bases (cf. Table 2). *i*-suffixed disyllables, however, as well as monosyllables, seem to almost exclusively anchor to the initial syllable of their bases, and not to the main-stressed syllable (cf. Tables 3 and 4). By contrast, 18 of the 20 forms that involve reduplication of a consonant (e.g. *Pippo* ♦ *Filippo*) anchor to the main-stressed vowel of their bases (cf. Alber 2010).

Table 5 provides a survey of word structures in the German data. The format of the table is the same as in Table 1. As in the Italian dataset, I assume that final sounds which occur as non-etymological segments in some of the data can be analysed as suffixes. In these cases, all forms ending in these segments are classified as '*x*-final', regardless of the etymological status of the final segment.

Tab. 5: Word structure in German name truncations

	N	%	examples
S w	128	23.5	Karo (♦ Karolin)
S	68	12.5	Jo (♦ Johann)
S, *s*-final	7	1.3	Fabs (♦ Fabian)
S w, *i*-final	251	46.1	Wolfi (♦ Wolfgang)
S w, *e*-final	35	6.4	Wolle (♦ Wolfgang)
S w, *e(r)l*-final	12	2.2	Naddel (♦ Nadine)
S w, *chen*-final	8	1.5	Inchen (♦ Ina)
S w, other fixed segments	31	5.7	Nico (♦ Niclas)
other	4	0.7	Elisa (♦ Elisabeth)
Total	544	100	

We see that *i*-suffixed forms make up about half of the data (46.1%) provided by the German students. This is the pattern that has received most attention in the literature on German truncation (cf. e.g. Ronneberger-Sibold 1992, 1995; Féry 1997; Steinhauer 2000, 2007; Wiese 2001; Köpcke 2002; Alber 2007). However, the data in Table 5 show that German has at least two more productive, unsuffixed patterns of name truncation. These are unsuffixed disyllables (with an open final syllable) and unsuffixed monosyllables. Both patterns together account for some 36% of the data. Also, the *i*-suffixed pattern is not the only suffixed pattern. In the data we also find a set of 36 *e*-final forms (-*e* is phonologically realised as [ə]): Compare e.g. *Wolle* ♦ *Wolfgang*, *Ede* ♦ *Edmund*, or *Domme* ♦ *Dominik*). Furthermore, there is a group of Sw forms involving other fixed segments. Finally, there is a small number of forms which involve diminutive suffixes which have traditionally not been analysed as truncatory suffixes (-*chen*, -*e(r)l*), but which did involve truncation to a disyllabic form in all cases in the dataset,[6] and a very small number of truncated forms which do not correspond to any of the major word-structure patterns. As in the other languages discussed, the latter make up only a very small proportion of the data (0.7%).

Tables 6–8 provide an overview of anchoring patterns found in the three major patterns attested in the data: unsuffixed monosyllabic and disyllabic forms (the latter will be referred to as 'Sw-truncations'), and *i*-suffixed disyllabic forms (*i*-suffixed Sw-truncations). As in the previous discussion, the relevant dataset will be restricted to those forms where main stress in the base form is non-initial. Note also that *e*-final disyllables will not be discussed any further. As stress is initial in all base names in the dataset, it is not possible to distinguish anchoring patterns for this type.

Tab. 6: Anchoring in unsuffixed Sw-truncations for bases where main stress is non-initial

	N	%	examples
initial syllable	30	30.3	Manu (♦ Manuéla)
main-stressed syllable, noninitial	62	62.6	Ela (♦ Manuéla)
other	7	7.1	Lilo (♦ Lieselotte)
Total	99	100	

---

[6] For reasons of methodological consistency, derivatives ending in -*chen* and -*e(r)l* have been kept in the database, but will not be considered any further in the analysis. But cf. Moulin (this volume) for a discussion of the function of -*chen* in 18th century German, which seems to imply that diminutive function is actually quite close to the function of nicknames. Cf. also Schneider (2003) for a pertinent proposal for English, which considers the nickname marker -*y* to be part of the diminutive system of the language.

Tab. 7: Anchoring in *i*-suffixed Sw-truncations for bases where main stress is non-initial

	N	%	examples
initial syllable	84	71.2	Brunni (♦ Brunhílde)
main-stressed syllable, non-initial	32	27.1	Tini (♦ Bettína)
other	2	1.7	Betty (♦ Elísabeth)
Total	118	100	

Tab. 8: Anchoring in monosyllabic truncations for bases where main stress is non-initial

	N	%	examples
initial syllable	13	81.3	Lu (♦ Luísa)
main-stressed syllable, noninitial	3	18.8	Nel (♦ Cornélia)
Total	16	100	

Like their Italian counterparts, German *i*-suffixed name truncations show a clear tendency to anchor to the initial rather than the main-stressed syllable of the base. The same seems to be true for monosyllabic truncations in the two languages. Unsuffixed disyllabic patterns show slightly different anchoring preferences in the two datasets. In the German data, stress anchoring is the majority choice; in the Italian data both anchoring possibilities are used to about the same extent. Future research may substantiate whether these differences indeed reflect systemic differences between languages. Another clear difference between name truncation patterns in the two languages is that, unlike Italian, German does not have a name truncation pattern that anchors to both the initial and the main-stressed syllable: Thus, *Miléna* can become *Milé* in (Southern?) Italian, but names like *Sabíne* cannot become *Sabí* in German.[7]

2.2 Universal vs. morphological determinants of patterns

A question that has not yet received much attention in the literature is whether and in how far different truncatory patterns can be distinguished by their func-

---

[7] Attested German truncated names for the base *Sabine* are *Bíne* and, less commonly, *Sábi*.

tion. The existing evidence points to two dimensions here: one is that name truncation patterns differ from patterns of non-name truncation ('clippings'); the other is that languages seem to vary in terms of which pattern they use for a given function.

Two large-scale empirical studies of English name and non-name truncation patterns, Lappe (2007) and Berg (2011), provide independent evidence for differences between name truncation and word clipping patterns. One such difference concerns anchoring patterns. Word clippings show significantly more initial anchoring than name truncation.[8] Tables 9 and 10 illustrate this by providing the relevant figures for English monosyllabic name truncations and monosyllabic clippings from Lappe's (2007) study. The tables have the same format as the tables provided in section 2.1 on Italian and German, considering only bases in the dataset in which main stress is non-initial. The total dataset comprises 948 base-derivative pairs that were extracted from a website providing resources for genealogical research (truncated names, various patterns) and 702 base-derivative pairs that were extracted from dictionaries (clippings, various patterns; for details cf. Lappe 2007: 59–60).

Tab. 9: Anchoring in monosyllabic names for bases where main stress is non-initial

	N	%	examples
initial syllable	63	53.0	Hez (♦ Hezekiah)
main-stressed syllable	50	42.0	Kye (♦ Hezekiah)
other	6	5.0	Beth (♦ Elisabeth)
Total	119	100	

---

[8] Lappe's (2007) and Berg's (2011) studies differ in terms of how they classify anchoring patterns. Berg (2011) makes a traditional distinction between fore-clipping and back-clipping; Lappe (2007) uses initial anchoring and stress anchoring. The difference between these two classification systems does not bear on the issues discussed in this article. Recent research indicates that we need a tripartite classification (initial, stress, and final anchoring) to account for anchoring patterns found in truncations crosslinguistically (Alber 2017).

Tab. 10: Anchoring in monosyllabic clippings for bases where main stress is non-initial

	N	%	examples
initial syllable	123	90.4	ack (♦ acknowledge)
main-stressed syllable	10	7.4	sheen (♦ machine)
other	3	2.2	droid (♦ android)
Total	137	100	

English monosyllabic name truncations may anchor either to the initial or to the main-stressed syllable of their bases. Together, these two anchoring patterns account for 95% of the data. By contrast, non-initial anchoring is extremely rare among clippings (less than 10%).

English monosyllabic name truncations and clippings similarly differ in terms of how faithful they are to the sound structure of their bases. For example, the substitution of the dental fricatives, [θ] and [ð], by corresponding stops, [t] and [d], is systematically observed in name truncation, but not in clippings. (5) provides examples, again from Lappe (2007).

(5) a. name truncations
　　　　Martha　　　♦ Mart, Marth
　　　　Cynthia　　 ♦ Cynt, Cynth
　　　　Bertha　　　♦ Bert, Berth
　　　　Nathaniel　♦ Nat, Nath
　　b. clippings
　　　　mathematics　♦ maths
　　　　catheter　　 ♦ cath
　　　　methedrine　 ♦ meth
　　　　synthesiser　♦ synth
　　　　thespian　　 ♦ thesp

The evidence cited from English in this section seems to suggest that clippings and truncated names differ in terms of the degree to which their structure is geared towards optimising recoverability of their base lexeme. Clippings are more faithful to the segmental structure of their bases, and they preserve the initial part of the base, which, from a psycholinguistic perspective, is the part that is most relevant for word recognition (cf. below). This raises the question of whether the variability that we observe is an effect of universal mechanisms (as argued in Berg 2011), or whether it is morphological in a similar way to how other morphological processes are. One piece of evidence that there is at least some morphological aspect to the variation is that languages differ in terms of which patterns they exploit for which functions. The doubly anchored pattern documented for Southern Italian in section 2.2 is a case in point. Pertinent examples are repeated in (6) for convenience.

(6) Ba ♦ Bárbara
Francé ♦ Francésca
Antoné ♦ Antonélla

The pattern gives rise to truncated names of different lengths, depending on the position of the main-stressed syllable in the base. Such a pattern is used only for names in Italian (cf. (6)): Truncated forms always preserve the stretch from the beginning to the main-stressed syllable of the base. By contrast, for English the same pattern, also preserving the stretch from the beginning to the main-stressed syllable of the base, has recently been documented for clippings (Spradlin and Jones 2016 where the pattern is referred to as 'totes truncation'[9]). Examples are given in (7).

(7) 'totes truncation' (Spradlin and Jones 2016)
bluebs ♦ blúeberries
emósh ♦ emotional
inapróp ♦ inappropriate
clarificásh ♦ clarification

English *bluebs* (♦ *blueberries*) is like Italian *Ba* (♦ *Bárbara*), *emósh* is like *Francé*, *inapróp* is like *Antoné*. Note that there are also differences between the two patterns: The Italian names always end in an open syllable, the English clippings end in a closed syllable.

Another piece of evidence that suggests that morphological category co-determines variability in truncatory patterns is that formal variability seems systematic and predictable. For example, the discussion of word structure and anchoring patterns in German, Italian, and English truncations in this section already showed that there are only very few cases which form exceptions to the major patterns. For English, it is argued in Lappe (2007) that productive patterns can be systematically distinguished from exceptional forms also if not only word structure and anchoring, but also the segmental properties of truncated forms are taken into account. A good example is the consonantal makeup of English monosyllabic name truncations. We have already seen in (5) that the

---

9 The name 'totes truncation' is based on the fact that in those cases in which pertinent forms are adjectives, they are often modified by the adverb *totes* (♦ *totally*). However, the pattern is by no means restricted to adjectives (Spradlin and Jones 2016).

pattern systematically allows dental fricatives to be substituted by corresponding plosives. What is important now is that other consonant changes that are occasionally observed in existing truncated forms are not systematic (and extremely rare). For example, in the truncated name *Bill*, which is well-established for the base *William*, [w] in *William* corresponds to [b] in *Bill*. The same segmental change is also observed in truncations for bases like *Willis* and *Wilbert*, for which also *Bill* is an attested truncated name. However, the alternation ([w] ~ [b]) is crucially restricted to cases in which the output form is *Bill*, and does not occur in other contexts. For example, *Winfield*, *Wendy*, and *Webster* cannot become *Bin, *Bend, or *Beb, but only (and regularly) *Win*, *Wen*, and *Web*. It thus seems that whereas the morphological category systematically allows alternations concerning the dental fricatives, it does not systematically allow other types of (optimising) alternations.

3 Semantic transparency and base recoverability

The assumption that semantic transparency is a characteristic of productive morphological processes is commonplace in much of the morphological literature (cf. e.g. Ronneberger-Sibold 2001; Braun and Plag 2003; Bell and Schäfer 2016). Nevertheless, we find that the term is used in slightly different senses in the literature. In the psycholinguistic literature on morphological processing the term 'transparency' is often employed to refer to the degree to which morphemes in a morphologically complex word are formally and semantically related to the base morphemes from which they derive (cf. e.g. Libben et al. 2003 for discussion). In the theoretical morphological literature we find that in some approaches also the aspect of compositionality, i.e. predictability of meaning resulting from the combination of morphemes, is important. For example, Ronneberger-Sibold defines transparency as "the possibility of inferring a meaning from the parts of such a word or phrase and *the way they are combined*." (Ronneberger-Sibold 2001: 98, my emphasis).

According to this latter view, then, truncatory processes are not transparent by definition because here formal compositionality does not correspond to semantic compositionality. As an example, consider the English truncated name *Ed*, derived from the base *Edward*. We may argue that *Ed* has a diminutive meaning component and, thus, differs semantically from *Edward* (cf. esp. Schneider 2003; Alber and Arndt-Lappe 2012 for discussion). The meaning of *Ed* as a complex meaning is, however, not reflected in the form *Ed*, which is clearly not compositional.

However, in terms of a definition of transparency as a measure of recoverability of bases within the truncation, the issue of how transparent outputs of truncation are becomes less trivial. Crucially, then, base recoverability in truncation is a process that must be very similar to word recognition from word fragments. It is this type of transparency that I will discuss in this section, relating, where possible, relevant structural properties of truncation to pertinent findings from psycholinguistic research. To avoid ambiguity, I will henceforth use the term 'base recoverability' to refer to the phenomenon. The purpose of this section is to show that rules governing the formation of truncated words in productive patterns of truncation seem to be geared towards facilitating recoverability of the base. In what follows we will look at anchoring in truncation and relate the attested productive patterns to findings that have emerged from the psycholinguistic literature on properties of words that play a role in lexical access and word recognition. In section 3.3 we will then discuss the problem that, because of the reduction of phonological form, truncation may lead to homonymous truncated forms for different base words (to be referred to as 'the homonymy problem'). A large number of homonymous truncations can be seen as a factor obstructing base recoverability because, given homonymous truncations, speakers cannot know which is the right base form. We will discuss some preliminary evidence about how recoverable bases are when truncations are used in discourse context. The pertinent data will again come from English.

3.1 Anchoring and word recognition

An important problem that we face when investigating crosslinguistic regularities in anchoring patterns is that very few empirical studies systematically investigate anchoring. Still, we often find that authors comment on observed generalisations, even if it is assumed that anchoring is, in general, variable and unsystematic. For example, for French clippings Scullen (1997: 97) basically assumes that "establishing a single site for the mapping of elements to a template [...] appears to be futile". Still, she admits that left anchoring is "the standard case" (Scullen 1997: 97). A similar comment can be found in Bat-El's (2005) study of Hebrew hypocoristics. Focussing on regularities in output structure of truncated names, she notes that "THs [templatic hypocoristics; SAL] come in various forms when their correspondence to their base is considered: left-anchored, *misanchored* [sic!], and reduplicated, again, either left-anchored or misanchored." (Bat-El 2005: 126, my emphasis). Finally, in her comparative study of German and Swedish truncations Nübling (2001) notes that, in principle, different anchoring patterns are attested, those where the initial part of the base lexeme is retained ('Kopfwörter'), and those where the final part is retained ('Endwörter'). For the latter type, however, she notes:

> Dieser Typ ist ist in beiden Sprachen [Schwedisch und Deutsch, SAL] *kaum vertreten, wobei das Schwedische immerhin drei Beispiele aufweist*. Dabei handelt es sich um fremdsprachige Vorlagen mit Nichtinitialakzent. (Nübling 2001: 174–175, my emphasis)
> [This type is hardly represented in the two languages [Swedish and German, SAL]. *In Swedish, at least, there are three examples*. All of them are modelled on non-native words with non-initial stress. (Translation: SAL, my emphasis)]

The examples cited indicate that, even in studies which do not focus explicitly on anchoring or which do not presuppose that anchoring is systematic, it has frequently been noted that anchoring does not appear to be arbitrary, but that there are at least very strong tendencies.

In the case studies on English name truncation and clipping, and German and Italian name truncation that were discussed in section 2.2 we saw the same phenomenon. Whereas truncatory patterns differ in terms of which anchoring types they allow, anchoring is surprisingly uniform. We find that all patterns allow anchoring to material that is initial in the base. Additionally, some patterns allow anchoring to material that is main-stressed in the base. Together, initial anchoring and main-stress anchoring account for more than 90% of all data collected in these pilot studies.

Alber and Arndt-Lappe (2012) systematically investigate which anchoring patterns (and word structure patterns) are attested crosslinguistically. The survey is based on published work on truncation set in different frameworks. Their findings show that what we saw in the pilots in section 2.2, can well be extended to other languages: The predominant anchoring pattern is left-edge anchoring, followed by main-stress anchoring. In addition, there are patterns which preserve both initial and main-stressed material from their bases.

In sum, there is converging evidence that the overwhelming majority of truncatory patterns preserve initial and main-stressed material of their bases. Furthermore, there is evidence that anchoring to base-initial material is more widespread than anchoring to main-stressed material. These two facts are interesting because they can be directly related to well-known findings in the psycholinguistic literature about the role of initial material and stress-related information in word recognition.

The central role of word-initial material in word recognition has been demonstrated in experimental research across different languages and using an array of different tasks. Thus, for example, in experiments in which participants are put into a tip-of-the-tongue state, it turns out that initial parts of words are among those that speakers are more likely to remember than other parts (cf.

Brown and McNeill 1966 for a classic experiment). There is, furthermore, a type of psycholinguistic experiments that is very relevant to our present discussion, because the task almost simulates the task that hearers of truncated words face, i.e. that of decoding bases. This type of experiments investigates word identification from word fragments. For example, in Nooteboom (1981) Dutch speakers were presented with two different types of Dutch word fragments: word-initial fragments and word-final fragments. Both types of fragment shared the characteristic that they uniquely identified their source words. Interestingly, even in this configuration the initial word part served as a much better cue to correct word identification than the final part. The results of Nooteboom's study thus not only show that the initial part of a word plays a key role in word recognition; it also demonstrates that the initial portion of a word often suffices to lead to correct identification (95% of Nooteboom's stimulus words).

The role of stress-related information in word-recognition is less straightforward than that of initial material. Whereas there is abundant evidence to show that stress is important in word recognition in many languages, it is not so clear whether what is relevant for word recognition is the stressed syllable itself, or the prominence pattern of the whole word, and how differences between individual stress-based languages with respect to the role of stress in word recognition are to be explained (cf. esp. Cutler and Pasveer 2006 for an overview of the relevant findings). In addition, there is an ongoing debate about whether and how stress information is confounded by segmental information (e.g. vowel quality and length, cf. esp. Cutler 2015 on English). A number of studies have shown that stress information can be exploited for word recognition. For example, van Donselaar, Koster, and Cutler (2005) and Soto-Faraco, Sebastián-Gallés, and Cutler (2001) have shown for Dutch and Spanish, respectively, that in priming experiments, primes consisting of the first two syllables of the target words lead to faster reaction times and fewer errors in lexical decision tasks if the fragments used as primes contain the right stress information, as compared to if the fragments have a different stress pattern. The latter even inhibits word access. Reinisch, Jesse, and McQueen (2010) have convincingly shown in an eye-tracking experiment that Dutch listeners indeed use stress information already in very early stages of word recognition to disambiguate between segmentally identical, but prosodically different competitors (e.g. upon hearing the first two syllables [ɔkto] of Dutch *Október* vs. *Óctopus*). Their findings suggest that the moment a word fragment becomes available for auditory word recognition, listeners use not only the segmental makeup of that fragment for their word search, but also the information on whether or not that fragment bears stress. Crucially, relevant stress information seems to reside not only in the perception of the acoustic difference between successive strong and weak syllables, but also in the perception of strong syllables themselves. Thus, on the basis of an acoustic analysis of their stimuli and a correlation of these with the fixation data, Reinisch, Jesse, and McQueen (2010) found that perception of a strong syllable leads to a decline in the number of fixations on competitors with a weak syllable in this position. The relevant acoustic parameter for their Dutch informants was the duration of the vowel in the syllabic nucleus.

Stress has also been shown to be important in stages of auditory processing prior to word recognition. In stress-based languages like English and Dutch, stress is used by listeners as a segmentation cue. Evidence from misperception of word junctures and word-spotting experiments, in particular, suggests that the set of competing lexical items activated upon hearing a target word with non-initial main stress includes words starting with the syllable that is stressed in the target word (e.g. Cutler and Norris 1988 et seq. for English; Vroomen, van Zon, and de Gelder 1996 for Dutch).

In sum, we know that lexical stress plays an important role in word recognition in many languages. Likewise, evidence from studies investigating segmentation suggests that in languages such as English and Dutch, the expectation of listeners seems to be that words begin with strong syllables. For the recoverability of bases in truncation in such languages this suggests the following interpretation: For stress-anchored truncatory patterns, base recoverability is more difficult if the base does not bear initial stress than if it does. This is due to speakers' biases in segmentation. However, findings like those of Reinisch, Jesse, and McQueen (2010) for Dutch suggest that stress-anchoring for bases with non-initial stress also has advantages over initial-syllable anchoring: The advantage is that this way the truncated form preserves the stressed syllable of the base as a stressed syllable, preserving the stress cue that is relevant for word recognition. This is not always the case if a truncated form anchors to the initial syllable of a base form.

3.2 The homonymy problem

In this section we will look at the question of how strongly recoverability of bases of truncated forms is influenced by the potential of truncation to create homonymous forms. I will again base my discussion on examples from English. It has often been noted that truncation may lead to a large number of homonymous forms. For example, names like *Alonzo*, *Alfred*, *Alvina*, etc. may all be truncated to become *Al*. Similarly, among clippings, there are at least three homonymous forms *mag*, which are derived from *magazine*, *magnesium*, or *magnet*, respectively. For obvious reasons, then, the potential of truncatory processes to lead to homonymous forms creates problems for base recoverability. This raises the question of how speakers and hearers cope with the homonymy problem in language use.

A standard assumption in the morphological literature is that truncations arise in circumstances in which contextual factors are tightly constrained so that base recoverability is possible (cf. e.g. Jespersen [1949] 1965: 538–551, and Marchand 1960: 363–364 on English). These are, specifically, in-group slang, all kinds of specialised language, and, for names, 'the narrow family circle' (Jespersen 1965: 540). It is, however, important to note that the use of truncation is by no means confined to such contexts. For English, both Marchand and Jespersen interpret this as a secondary development, where outputs of truncation, which have originated in the tightly knit situational contexts just described, come to be used also outside these circles.

No matter what exactly lexicalisation or conventionalisation paths of truncations look like, it is interesting to investigate how truncations are used when they are used outside the narrow contexts mentioned by Jespersen and Marchand. Here we can observe the use of truncations in situations in which speakers or writers assume that hearers and readers without specialised contextual knowledge will be able to decode them, and, hence, in many cases, that hearers and readers will be able to recover bases of truncated words from their lexicon. Apart from theoretical assumptions made in the literature, there is, to my knowledge, no systematic empirical research that addresses this issue to date. Therefore, this section will be confined to a presentation of preliminary evidence gathered mainly from my own collected materials. The conclusions to be drawn from this discussion are necessarily tentative, leaving it to future research to test them against larger amounts of data.

An interesting test case for the question of how truncations are used in such contexts is the use of clippings, i.e. truncated non-names, in media that are aimed at a wide and, crucially, non-specialised audience. Here we can approximate the lexical resources that hearers and readers have at their disposal for decoding bases using standard dictionaries and electronic corpora. In what follows we will look at a small selection of English clippings that have appeared in the *Time Magazine* within the last two decades. They are provided in (8), together with the immediate sentence context in which they are used in the source.

(8) A sample of clippings from the *Time Magazine* (clippings are italicized)
   a. Even more robust than the lowbrow *merch* trade is the market for knockoffs of items worn by the future princess [...] (25 April 2011, p. 48, in an article about the royal wedding of Prince William and Kate Middleton)
   b. Think Tank [a band] is often experimental but never jarring, mixing *synth* and acoustic picking (12 May 2003, p. 57)
   c. the latest news on how your body handles carbs vs. fats [...] Should you count calories or *carbs*? (07 July 2003, p. 50)
   d. Last Thursday, when Arnold Schwarzenegger arrived at the county government building in Norwalk, Calif., you could tell with no trouble that he was one of the biggest stars in Hollywood – and not just if you measure *lat* spread. (18 August 2003, p. 18)
   e. His private life, like that of most Delta Force *vets*, is largely hidden... (03 November 2003, p. 27)

With the exception of *merch*, all clippings cited in (8) are attested as lemmas in the Oxford English Dictionary (OED). As earliest attestations, the OED cites the dates 1891 (*vet* ♦ *veteran*), 1939 (*lat* ♦ *latissimus dorsi*), 1976 (*synth* ♦ *synthesizer*), and 1981 (*carbs* ♦ *carbohydrates*). For all clippings cited, we may hypothesise that base recoverability does in some sense play a role in decoding the meaning of the sentence. Thus, three of the five clippings are listed by the OED as homonymous clippings for different base words: *carb* is attested as a clipping of *carbohydrate* and *carburettor*, *lat* is a clipping of *latissimus dorsi* and *latrine*, and *vet* is listed as a clipping of *veteran* and *veterinary* (*surgeon*). Interestingly, the meanings of these homonymous pairs are so unrelated that it is hard to think of a context in which homonymous forms could be confused. For at least another three of the five clippings, we have evidence that they have their origin in specialised language in the sense of Jespersen (1965: 538–551) and Marchand (1960), which means that it is unlikely that the writers of the articles cited in (8) can safely assume that the clippings are lexicalised for all readers of the *Time Magazine*. *Merch* (8.a) is not attested in the OED, which is an indication that the clipping is quite recent. A Google© search for *merch* on US American websites reveals that *merch* is mainly used to refer to merchandise articles sold, in particular, to young fans of movies, rock'n roll music and related arts. *Synth* (8.b) is a word that originates also from specialised language in the music and pop culture. The OED lists three attestations for *synth*: Two of them (1976 in the Liverpool Echo, 1983 in the Yellow Advertiser) are private ads advertising secondhand synthesizers, and one is a review of a band's performance in the music magazine Sounds, 1977). Finally, the OED marks the clipping *lat(s)* (s.v.) explicitely as a term from bodybuilding language and specifically mentions the attributive use of *lat* in *lat spread* as referring to a bodybuilding pose.

What we see in the examples cited is that the immediate context in which the clipping occurs can be used to identify the base forms of the clippings. Thus, in all but one cases (*synth*, 8.b), the syntactic context makes it clear that both the clipping and its base must be a noun. For *synth*, the context is ambiguous, allowing for an analysis as a noun or as a verb, respectively.

We also see that readers of the sentences are given strong semantic cues in the immediate environment of the clipping that serve to constrain the search for base words. In the cases of *merch trade*, *lat spread*, and *Delta Force vets*, clippings are embedded in a nominal compound where the meaning of the other elements already defines the semantic field within which the base of the truncation is to be found, and, in the cases of *lat* and *vets*, excludes the homonymous competitors of these clippings. The clippings *synth* (8.b) and *carbs* (8.c) are embedded in coordinating constructions, where the clipping is coordinated with an antonym, *acoustic* for *synth* and *fats* and *calories* for *carbs*, respectively. Again, the construction thus excludes the homonymous competitor for *carbs*, *carburettor*, and constrains the semantics of *carbs* and *synth* to antonyms of *acoustic* and *fat* or *calories*. This, for example, immediately precludes the possibility that any of the many English words or senses of words starting with <synth> and referring to concepts from philosophical (e.g. *synthesis*, *synthetic*, *synthesist*) or chemical (e.g. *synthalin*, *synthase*, *synthetic*, *synthesise*) semantic fields, would act as bases of *synth*. Similarly, it excludes all words starting with <carb> and referring to chemical compounds which are, at least to lay wisdom, not relevant to dieting, such as, for example, *carbon*, *carbon dioxide*, *carbonium*, or *carbonate*.

Apart from providing semantic cues, it may also be the case that the context in which clippings occur facilitates base recovery on a much more simple, straightforward level. Thus, it is known that speakers and listeners keep some sort of statistical record of cooccurrence probabilities of words and constructions in discourse (cf. e.g. Jurafsky 2003 for a summary of evidence and for pertinent references). It is therefore possible that, on a mere formal level, the immediate context in which a (potentially unknown) clipping occurs already influences base recovery on the basis of a probabilistic estimation of the chances that any of the potential competitors for a base occur in a given formal environment. Methodologically, we can test this hypothesis by approximating cooccurrence probabilities in large electronic corpora that are balanced to reflect a (broadly) representative sample of the contemporary language as it is written or spoken.

As an example, we will apply the procedure to the clipping *merch* in (8.a). Recall from the discussion above that *merch* is (a) not attested in the OED and

(b) that it has its origins in the special language of a very narrowly defined community. This makes *merch* a good candidate here, because, of all examples in (8), *merch* seems to have the lowest degree of lexicalisation. In addition, recall that in our attestation in (8.a) *merch* occurs in a very tight compound construction, which makes it easy to define the context over which we would want to determine cooccurrence probabilities.

We will first take the OED as a reference point for what potential candidates for bases of the clipping *merch* could be. A search in the OED for nouns that are in current usage (i.e. non-obsolete) starting with the letter sequence <merch> yields 23 hits. Although all 23 words are, with one exception (*merchet*), members of the same word family, we may still assume that recovery of a base of *merch* in the given context involves singling out one of several competitors, such as, for example, *merchant, merchandise, merchandiser, merchantability, merchanting*.

In order to estimate how the immediate context of *merch* in our example (8.a) provides a cue to its base, we will use the Corpus of Contemporary American English (COCA, 425 million words, BYU interface at http://corpus.byu.edu/coca/, accessed 02 September 2017) to determine the likelihood that any of the competitors starting with <merch> occurs in the same construction. The search targeted words starting with the sequence <merch>, and immediately preceding the noun *trade*.

The first finding is that, like in the OED, the combination *merch trade*, involving the clipping, is unattested among all 425 million words in the COCA. This supports the assumption that *merch* is indeed very recent. The second finding is that if we look at the distribution of competitors cooccurring with *trade*, we see that indeed the given context is very well suited to biasing the base search for *merch* towards the intended competitor, *merchandise*. Thus, of the 23 competitors for a base for *merch* that we found in the OED, only two different words are attested as cooccurring with *trade*. These are *merchandise* and *merchant*, which occur in 72 places in the corpus in total. Of these, 69 attestations (i.e. 95.83%) involve *merchandise trade*. The facts for *merch* thus suggest the following: Clippings seem to often occur in contexts in which also their bases are highly frequent. More specifically, their bases are more frequent in these contexts than the bases of their competitors. Given what we know about the use of cooccurrence probabilities in speech processing, this insight, if verifiable by future research, has strong implications for an interpretation of base recoverability in word clipping.

A third, related type of contextual cue that is likely to play an important role for base recoverability in truncation is frequency of use of the base of the truncated word itself, within the speech community in which the truncated word is used. Thus, for English it has been shown that the meaning of (most) truncatory patterns involves signalling familiarity and closeness with the referent of the base (e.g. Wierzbicka 1984; Quirk et al. 1985; Schneider 2003; Plag 2003: 117, 121; Alber and Arndt-Lappe 2012). We can therefore assume that the base as well as the derivative are highly frequent for speakers using truncated words. Crucially, for these speakers, the base form is presumably more frequent than competing other base forms. To take again our example *merch* (8.a), we may assume that within the pertinent speech community in which *merch* is used regularly (young fans of movies, rock'n roll music and related arts, cf. above), the base *merchandise* is more frequent than its most serious competitor, *merchant*. Likewise, for name truncation, it is plausible to assume that among close acquaintances of the person referred to, the base name for a given truncated name will be used more frequently than its potential competitors. For example, among close friends and family of a person named *Lucinda* whose conventionalised nickname is *Cindy*, the name *Lucinda* will be used more frequently than other potential bases of *Cindy*, such as *Cinderella* or *Cynthia*. This high relative frequency of the base form will in itself be another factor that enhances recoverability. The reason is that we know that high frequency of a word facilitates lexical access (cf. esp. Segui et al. 1982).

To sum up this section, we see that our findings concerning the role of context in enhancing base recoverability is similar to what we found for anchoring: The conditions under which truncations occur in context are optimal conditions when it comes to facilitating word recognition and lexical access. We also see, however, that much more research is needed to explore the exact interaction between contextual factors and the use of truncation. Furthermore, on a theoretical level, it remains an open question if and in how far the conditions of use of truncation in context are different from those of other word-formation processes.

4 Conclusion

On the basis of a selection of case studies, this paper investigated structural predictability and base recoverability in productive processes of name truncation and clipping. With respect to structural predictability, the paper presented new data on Italian and German patterns, as well as a discussion and evaluation of the empirical literature on English (Lappe 2007; Berg 2011; Spradlin and Jones 2016 to show that structural variability is systematic. Patterns can be distinguished on the basis of word structure and anchoring. Productive segmental changes seem to be tied to specific truncatory patterns and, hence, seem to be morphologised. Also, such systematic segmental patterns can be distinguished from unsystematic, idiosyncratic patterns that are attested in isolated forms. Furthermore, there is evidence that patterns can be distinguished functionally. Here we find crosslinguistic similarities (esp. when comparing truncation of names and non-names, cf. Berg 2011 for English), but also interesting differences that suggest that languages differ in terms of how exactly they make use of the available patterns. More research is certainly needed to explore crosslinguistic similarities and differences here.[10]

On a theoretical level, then, the findings on structural predictability challenge the view sometimes found in the literature that outputs of truncation are, in general, unpredictable. Furthermore, it suggests that the sharp line that some approaches assume to exist between grammatical word-formation and extragrammatical processes (as defended e.g. in Dressler 2000, 2005; Ronneberger-Sibold 2010, 2015a) cannot be upheld (cf. Dal and Namer, this volume, for a similar argument with respect to nonce formations).

The second part of the paper was concerned with the question of base recoverability, an aspect of morphological processes that is related to transparency. First, it was shown that this is a notoriously understudied area, where many of the pertinent issues have not been addressed by empirical research in a systematic fashion. We then discussed two types of evidence that can tell us something about base recoverability in truncation: anchoring patterns and the role of the discourse context in resolving the homonymy problem.

Due to the way it is often defined in the literature (involving a compositional element), the notion of transparency is difficult to apply to truncation. It thus proved helpful to reformulate the question of whether or not truncations are transparent, in terms of base recoverability, and to relate issues of base recoverability to the psycholinguistic issues of word recognition and lexical access. Truncations are thus different from other, compositional morphological processes in that establishing a relation between a truncated form and a base is, essentially, word recognition on the basis of a fragment. The evidence discussed then clearly suggests that, in spite of all the problems that truncation theoreti-

---

[10] Another obvious source of crosslinguistic similarities between truncatory patterns is of course language contact. One example, contributed by an anonymous reviewer, is that the English <-y> spelling seems to be becoming increasingly popular in German suffixed truncations. The traditional spelling of the suffix in German is <-i>. The morphological status of <-y> (as a new German suffix or as a new spelling variant) is unclear, but could be explored in a detailed comparative study of the structural and functional properties of the two types of form.

cally poses for base recovery, truncations are actually formed (in terms of anchoring and homonymy avoidance) and used (in terms of contextual cues) in such a way as to create ideal conditions for word recognition. With respect to the relevance of contextual cues, the findings of the small pilot study presented in this article suggest a promising perspective for further research, looking in more systematic terms and on a larger scale at how novel truncations are used in discourse context (cf. e.g. Dal and Namer, this volume, for a typology of stylistic strategies).

To conclude, the available evidence suggests that the patterns of truncation that we discussed in this paper are structurally predictable and functionally differentiated; base-derivative relations are recoverable. Truncation processes can hence be classified as formally and semantically regular morphological processes, provided one's morphological theory allows morphological processes to display systematic variability, and systematically grounds semantic transparency in the (psycholinguistic) recoverability of base-derivative relationships. Both provisos seem to be independently needed to account for many other, concatenative processes as well (on variation in concatenative morphophonology cf. e.g. Zuraw 2010; Carlson and Gerfen 2011; on the psycholinguistic grounding of semantic transparency cf. e.g. Hay 2003; Bell and Schäfer 2016; Schäfer 2017). It therefore does not come as a surprise that patterns of truncation are highly productive, in the sense employed by many morphological theories, in many languages.

5 References

Alber, Birgit. 2010. An exploration of truncation in Italian. In Peter Staroverov, Daniel Altshuler, Aaron Braver, Carlos A. Fasola & Sarah Murray (eds.), *Rutgers working papers in linguistics 3*, 1–30. New Brunswick: LGSA.
Alber, Birgit. 2017. *Typological analysis in optimality theory*. Paper presented at the 25th Manchester Phonology Meeting, Manchester, 25–27 May.
Alber, Birgit & Sabine Arndt-Lappe. 2012. Templatic and subtractive truncation. In Jochen Trommer (ed.), *The phonology and morphology of exponence - the state of the art* (Oxford Studies in Theoretical Linguistics), 289–325. Oxford: Oxford University Press.
Bat-El, Outi. 2005. The emergence of the binary trochaic foot in Hebrew hypocoristics. *Phonology* 22(2). 115–143.
Bell, Melanie J. & Martin Schäfer. 2016. Modelling semantic transparency. *Morphology* 26(2). 157–199.
Berg, Thomas. 2011. The clipping of common and proper nouns. *Word Structure* 4(1). 1–19.
Bermúdez-Otero, Ricardo. To appear. Stratal phonology. In S. J. Hannahs & Anna R. K. Bosch (eds.), *The Routledge handbook of phonological theory*. Abingdon, OX: Routledge.

Braun, Maria & Ingo Plag. 2003. How transparent is Creole morphology? A study of early Sranan word formation. In Geert Booij & Jaap van Marle (eds.), *Yearbook of morphology 2002*, 81–104. Dordrecht: Kluwer.
Brown, Roger & David McNeill. 1966. The 'tip of the tongue' phenomenon. *Journal of Verbal Learning and Verbal Behaviour* 5. 325–337.
Carlson, Matthew T. & Chip Gerfen. 2011. Productivity is the key: Morphophonology and the riddle of alternating diphthongs in Spanish. *Language* 87(3). 510–538.
Cutler, Anne. 2015. Lexical stress and English pronunciation. In Marnie Reed & John Levis (eds.), *The handbook of English pronunciation*, 106–124. Malden, Oxford & Chichester: Wiley.
Cutler, Anne & Dennis Norris. 1988. The role of strong syllables in segmentation for lexical access. *Journal of Experimental Psychology: Human Perception and Performance* 14. 113–121.
Cutler, Anne & Dennis Pasveer. 2006. Explaining crosslinguistic differences in effects of lexical stress on spoken word recognition. In Rüdiger Hoffmann & Hansjörg Mixdorff (eds.), *Speech prosody: 3rd international conference. Dresden, May 2–5, 2006*, 237–400. Dresden: TUDpress.
Donselaar, Wilma van, Mariëtte Koster & Anne Cutler. 2005. Exploring the role of lexical stress in lexical recognition. *The Quarterly Journal of Experimental Psychology Section A* 58(2). 251–273.
Dressler, Wolfgang U. 2000. Extragrammatical vs. marginal morphology. In Ursula Doleschal & Anna M. Thornton (eds.), *Extragrammatical and marginal morphology* (LINCOM Studies in Theoretical Linguistics 12), 1–10. München: LINCOM Europa.
Dressler, Wolfgang U. 2005. Word-formation in natural morphology. In Pavol Štekauer & Rochelle Lieber (eds.), *Handbook of word-formation* (Studies in Natural Language & Linguistic Theory), 267–284. Dordrecht: Springer.
Féry, Caroline. 1997. Uni und Studis: Die besten Wörter des Deutschen. *Linguistische Berichte* 172. 461–490.
Hay, Jennifer. 2003. *Causes and consequences of word structure*. New York: Routledge.
Jespersen, Otto. 1965 [1949]. *A modern English grammar. Part 6: Morphology*. London: Allen & Unwin.
Jurafsky, Dan. 2003. Probabilistic modeling in psycholinguistics: Linguistic comprehension and production. In Rens Bod, Jennifer Hay & Stefanie Jannedy (eds.), *Probabilistic linguistics*, 39–95. Cambridge, MA: MIT Press.
Kilani-Schoch, Marianne. 1996. Syllable and foot in French clipping. In Bernhard Hurch & Richard A. Rhodes (eds.), *Natural phonology: The state of the art* (Trends in Linguistics. Studies and Monographs), 135–152. Berlin & New York: Mouton de Gruyter.
Köpcke, Michael. 2002. Die sogenannte *i*-Derivation in der deutschen Gegenwartssprache. Ein Fall für outputorientierte Wortbildung. *Zeitschrift für germanistische Linguistik* 30. 293–309.
Lappe, Sabine. 2007. *English prosodic morphology*. Dordrecht: Springer.
Libben, Gary, Martha Gibson, Yeo Bom Yoon & Dominiek Sandra. 2003. Compound fracture: The role of semantic transparency and morphological headedness. *Brain and Language* 84. 26–43.
Manova, Stela. 2016. Subtractive morphology. *Oxford Bibliographies Online*.
Marchand, Hans. 1960. *Categories and types of present-Day English word-formation*. Wiesbaden: O. Harrassowitz.

Mattiello, Elisa. 2013. *Extra-grammatical morphology in English: Abbreviations, blends, reduplicatives, and related phenomena* (Topics in English Linguistics). Berlin & Boston: Mouton de Gruyter.
McCarthy, John & Alan Prince. 1993. *Prosodic morphology I: Constraint interaction and satisfaction* (Technical Reports of the Rutgers Center for Cognitive Science 3). New Brunswick, Bolder: Rutgers University.
McCarthy, John & Alan Prince. 1996 [1986]. *Prosodic morphology* (Technical Reports of the Rutgers Center for Cognitive Science 32). New Brunswick, Bolder: Rutgers University.
Nooteboom, Sieb G. 1981. Lexical retrieval from fragments of spoken words: Beginnings vs. endings. *Journal of Phonetics* 9. 407–424.
Nübling, Damaris. 2001. *Auto–bil*, *Reha–rehab*, *Mikro–mick*, *Alki–alkis*: Kurzwörter im Deutschen und Schwedischen. *Skandinavistik* 31(2). 167–199.
Piñeros, Carlos E. 2000. Prosodic and segmental unmarkedness in Spanish truncation. *Linguistics* 38. 63–98.
Plag, Ingo. 2003. *Word-formation in English* (Cambridge Textbooks in Linguistics). Cambridge: Cambridge University Press.
Quirk, Randolph, Sidney Greenbaum, Geoffrey Leech & Jan Svartvik. 1985. *A comprehensive grammar of the English language*. London: Harcourt Press.
Reinisch, Eva, Alexandra Jesse & James McQueen. 2010. Early use of phonetic information in spoken word recognition – lexical stress drives eye movements immediately. *The Quarterly Journal of Experimental Psychology* 63(4). 772–783.
Ronneberger-Sibold, Elke. 1992. *Die Lautgestalt neuer Wurzeln – Kürzungen und Kunstwörter im Deutschen und Französischen*. Freiburg: University of Freiburg unpublished habilitation thesis.
Ronneberger-Sibold, Elke. 1995. Die Optimierung von Lautgestalten durch Wortkürzung und durch langfristigen Sprachwandel. In Norbert Boretzky, Wolfgang U. Dressler, Janez Orešnik, Karmen Teržan-Kopecky & Ulrich Wurzel (eds.), *Beiträge zum internationalen Symposium über 'Natürlichkeitstheorie und Sprachwandel' an der Universität Maribor vom 13.5.-15.5.1993*, 31–44. Bochum: Universitätsverlag N. Brockmeyer.
Ronneberger-Sibold, Elke. 2001. On useful darkness: Loss and destruction of transparency by linguistic change, borrowing, and word creation. In Geert Booij & Jaap van Marle (eds.), *Yearbook of Morphology 2000*, 97–120. Dordrecht: Kluwer.
Ronneberger-Sibold, Elke. 2010. Word creation: Definition – function – typology. In Franz Rainer, Wolfgang U. Dressler, Dieter Kastovsky & Hans C. Luschützky (eds.), *Variation and change in morphology*: Selected papers from the 13th International Morphology Meeting, Vienna, February 2008 (Current issues in linguistic theory 310), 201–216. Amsterdam & Philadelphia: John Benjamins.
Ronneberger-Sibold, Elke. 2015a. Word-creation. In Peter O. Müller, Ingeborg Ohnheiser, Susan Olsen & Franz Rainer (eds.), *Word-formation. An international handbook of the languages of Europe* (Handbooks of Linguistics and Communication Science 40.1), 485–499. Berlin & New York: De Gruyter.
Ronneberger-Sibold, Elke. 2015b. Word-formation and brand names. In Peter O. Müller, Ingeborg Ohnheiser, Susan Olsen & Franz Rainer (eds.), *Word-formation. An international handbook of the languages of Europe* (Handbooks of Linguistics and Communication Science 40.2), 2192–2210. Berlin & New York: De Gruyter.
Ronneberger-Sibold, Elke & Sabine Wahl. 2014. Associations in German brand names: Current trends. In Joan Tort i Donada & Montserrat Montagut i Montagut (eds.), *El noms en la vida*

quotidiana. Actes del XXIV Congrés Internacional d'ICOS sobre Ciències Onomàstiques, 582–593. Barcelona: Annex.

Schäfer, Martin. 2017. *The semantic transparency of English compound nouns*. Jena: Friedrich-Schiller-Universität Jena habilitation thesis.

Schneider, Klaus P. 1993. Pragmagrammar and the case of German diminutives. In Theo Harden & Cliona Marsh (eds.), *Wieviel Grammatik braucht der Mensch?*, 158–173. München: Iudicium.

Schneider, Klaus P. 2003. *Diminutives in English* (Linguistische Arbeiten 479). Tübingen: Niemeyer.

Scullen, Mary E. 1997. *French prosodic morphology: A unified account*. Bloomington: University of Indiana dissertation.

Segui, Juan, Uli H. Frauenfelder, Jaques Mehler & John Morton. 1982. The word frequency effect and lexical access. *Neuropsychologica* 20(6). 615–627.

Soto-Faraco, Salvador, Nuria Sebastián-Gallés & Anne Cutler. 2001. Segmental and suprasegmental mismatch in lexical access. *Journal of Memory and Language* 45. 412–432.

Spradlin, Lauren & Taylor Jones. 2016. A morphophonological account of totes constructions in English. Paper presented at the 2016 Annual Meeting of the Linguistic Society of America. Washington, D.C. http://opencuny.org/laurenspradlin/the-morphophonology-of-totes (accessed 07 September 2017).

Steinhauer, Anja. 2000. *Sprachökonomie durch Kurzwörter. Bildung und Verwendung in der Fachkommunikation* (Forum für Fachsprachen-Forschung 56). Tübingen: Gunter Narr Verlag.

Steinhauer, Anja. 2007. Kürze im deutschen Wortschatz. In Jochen A. Bär, Thorsten Roelcke & Anja Steinhauer (eds.), *Sprachliche Kürze – Konzeptuelle, strukturelle und pragmatische Aspekte* (Linguistik – Impulse & Tendenzen 27), 131–158. Berlin & New York: De Gruyter.

Steriade, Donca. 1999. Lexical conservatism in French adjectival liaison. In Jean-Marc Authier, Barbara E. Bullock & Lisa A. Reed (eds.), *Formal perspectives in Romance linguistics. Selected papers from the 28th Linguistic Symposium on Romance Languages (LSRL XXVIII), University Park, 16–19 April 1998* (Current Issues in Linguistic Theory 185), 243–270. Amsterdam: John Benjamins.

Vroomen, Jean, Monique van Zon & Beatrice de Gelder. 1996. Cues to speech segmentation: Evidence from juncture misperceptions and word spotting. *Memory and Cognition* 24(6). 744–755.

Wierzbicka, Anna. 1984. Diminutives and depreciatives: Semantic representation for derivational categories. *Quaderni di Semantica* 5(1). 123–130.

Wiese, Richard. 2001. Regular morphology vs. prosodic morphology? The case of truncations in German. *Journal of Germanic Linguistics* 13. 131–178.

Zuraw, Kie. 2010. A model of lexical variation and the grammar with application to Tagalog nasal substitution. *Natural Language & Linguistic Theory* 28(2). 417–472.

III **Ludicity**

Angelika Braun
Approaching wordplay from the angle of phonology and phonetics – examples from German

Abstract: The present contribution seeks to outline what a phonetic approach can contribute to the study of wordplay. Therefore, it is confined to the analysis wordplay at the syllable level of language. To this end, a taxonomy of wordplay based on structural elements of the syllable is proposed. It emphasizes the distinction between wordplay relying on existing lexical items as opposed to creating new ones. Various mechanisms of "classical" wordplay are examined with respect to their effect on syllable structure. A quantitative study involving 213 items intended for a German audience is presented. Specifically, the following questions are addressed: (1) what is the distribution among the various types of wordplay at the syllable level; (2) which part of the syllable is played on, and (3) which mechanisms are most frequently used in this type of wordplay. Results show that paronymy and blending are the most frequent types of wordplay. Furthermore, there is a clear preference for the syllable onset to be played on. *

1 Introduction: Verbal humor, wordplay, puns, and soundplay

When trying to describe wordplay phenomena at a sublexical level, one is confronted with a plethora of terms which are usually not even used in the same way by different researchers. One point which seems reasonably uncontroversial is that "verbal humor" is the most general term to denote ludicity in language and speech (cf. e.g. Winter-Froemel 2016; Attardo and Raskin 2017). Things become more confusing when the relationship between "punning" and "wordplay"[1] is concerned. Hempelmann (2014: 612), whose work is based on the General Theory of Verbal Humor (GTVH) (cf. Attardo and Raskin 1991) defines

---
* I am indebted to two anonymous reviewers and my colleagues Esme Winter-Froemel and Sabine Arndt-Lappe for many very useful suggestions and discussions.
1 Some authors draw further distinctions between various types of puns (cf. e.g. Hempelmann and Miller 2017) or between "wordplay in a broad sense" and "wordplay in a narrow sense" (cf. e.g. Winter-Froemel 2016; Thaler 2016).

"pun" as "[...] a type of joke in which one sound sequence (e.g., a word) has two meanings and this similarity in sound creates a relationship for the two meanings from which humor is derived".

He draws a clear distinction between puns on the one hand and what he repeatedly terms "mere wordplay" on the other (Hempelmann 2004: 386): "[...] a text lacking the playful resolution of the SOp [semantic opposition; AB] created by the LM [logical mechanism; AB] will be mere wordplay rather than humor." In other words, his concept of "puns" is limited to what is called homophony and near-homophony in the present contribution. The subject of blends, which form a major element in phonological wordplay is neither addressed nor discussed in his overview (cf. Hempelmann and Miller 2017). The lack of semantic opposition turns "wordplay" into a "bad pun", called *Kalauer* in German (Hempelmann and Miller 2017: 99). In an earlier publication, Hempelmann (2004: 388) adds "word play", "play with words" and the terms "Sinnspiel" ('play with meaning') and "Klangspiel" ('soundplay') to his definition of punning:

> In sum, punning includes word play, but play with words cannot work at the sound level alone as mere 'Klangspiel' (play with sounds) if it strives to be humor as well. But it must be accompanied by 'Sinnspiel' (play with meaning; cf. Hausmann 1974: 20) [...]. [...] the belief on the part of a joker that he or she can get away with pure 'Klangspiel' is what earns bad puns a pariah status in the family of jokes.

The term "soundplay" (or *Klangspiel* in German), in turn, has been used by other researchers to denote a very small and well-defined subcategory of wordplay in a broad sense (Winter-Froemel 2016: 42). Soundplay thus understood encompasses tongue-twisters (1), alliterations (2), lipograms[2] (3), palindromes (4) and the like. Examples are

(1) *Blaukraut bleibt Blaukraut, und Brautkleid bleibt Brautkleid.*
(Well-known German tongue-twister which literally translates as *Red cabbage remains red cabbage, and bridal gown remains bridal gown.*)

(2) *Hinter Hermann Hansens Haus hängen hundert Hemden raus.*
(This tongue-twister is based on alliteration. The literal translation is *Behind Hermann Hansen's house one hundred shirts are hanging out(side).*)

(3) Friederike Kempner (1995), *Gedichte ohne r*. 'Poems without r'.

(4) *Die Liebe geht, hege Beileid.* 'love goes, be sympathetic'.

---

2 A lipogram is a kind of constrained writing which avoids one or more letters.

At the same time, not all soundplay involves wordplay. The former also includes instances of infant babble, serving to explore the human articulatory possibilities. For a long time soundplay was not even considered a "legitimate" subtype of wordplay (Heibert 1993: 12). This has changed somewhat in the past decades (but see Hempelmann 2004: 388 as quoted above), and soundplay in the sense of "combining elements selected according to a formal criterion which is defined on a sublexical level [...] and identifies paradigmatically similar items [...] [is] presently considered a major subtype of wordplay in a broad sense" (Winter-Froemel 2016: 38). Still, although it seems intuitive to use the term "soundplay" as a descriptor when dealing with wordplay on a phonological level, that would just add to the confusion of terms.

Thus we are faced with the problem that the term "pun" is in some ways too narrow to be used in the present contribution. The definition of "wordplay" as a "bad pun" as in Hempelmann (2004) does not meet with general acceptance either. "Wordplay" in a broader sense, on the other hand, has been defined in many different ways, reflecting the research interests of the respective authors. They range from rhetorical aspects (e.g. Plett 1979) to literary (e.g. Wagenknecht 1965) and linguistic ones including the translation of wordplay (e.g. Heibert 1993).

A "common denominator" is sought by Winter-Froemel (2009: 1429), who defines wordplay as follows:

> [...] eine Gruppe rhetorischer Sinn- und Klangfiguren, bei denen 'spielerisch' die Bedeutungen lautähnlicher oder lautgleicher Wörter überraschend gegenübergestellt werden.
> [[...] a group of rhetorical plays on sound or content, ludically and surprisingly contrasting the meanings of similar sounding or homophonous words. (Translation: AB)]

The present contribution narrows down this definition to phonological and also phonetic phenomena and adopts the following working definition: Wordplay from a phonological / phonetic perspective encompasses a range of phenomena operating at syllable level which involve lexemes sounding and / or spelled identically or alike in a way which surprises the listener and is therefore perceived as ludic. In this approach, wordplay is considered to be a deliberate speech act with the aim of amusing, but also intellectually challenging the listener and creating complicity between speaker and listener (cf. Winter-Froemel, this volume).

Thus, a constituting factor of wordplay is that it presents the listener with a riddle. In this context, one of the delicate tasks of the creator of a wordplay is to make the riddle neither too easy nor too difficult to solve[3]. The former amounts to stating something which is immediately obvious to the listener and may be perceived as boring by the intended audience (5); in the latter case the audience will possibly not get the point or take quite some time to process the riddle, thus potentially missing the subsequent punch line if the riddle forms part of a sketch comedy program (6).

(5) *Kraft auf den Teller, Knorr auf den Tisch*
(A parallelism in advertising Knorr instant soup products, which translates into 'power into the (soup) dish, Knorr onto the table'; a commercial featuring German soccer player Franz Beckenbauer dating back to 1966, where *Kraft* 'power' is represented both by the product and the athlete.)

(6) *Cinzano* [tʃɪnˈtsaːno]
(Brand name of Italian sweet wine; near-homophonous with German *Jeans a no*; [tʃiːnˈsaːno] 'Jeans in addition' as pronounced in Bavarian only. The pun was part of a sketch by the German comedian Willy Astor which was broadcast on German regional television (WDR) on 01 July 2017. The punchline had to be repeated in the show because the audience – originating from outside Bavaria – did not get the joke in the first instance.)

The latter example underlines the need for a usage-based approach to studying wordplay, involving both the speaker and the listener perspectives as well as the interaction between the two (cf. Zirker and Winter-Froemel 2015: 10).

Wordplay has been studied from a wide range of perspectives (for an overview, cf. Winter-Froemel 2009). The sound level was occasionally mentioned in classical wordplay research (e.g. Wagenknecht 1965: 15–22; Hausmann 1974: 76–80; Plett 1979: 36–39), but the focus was on rhetorical rather than phonetic / phonological aspects. Plett (1979) establishes what he terms "similarity classes" from a phonetic and a semantic point of view. He distinguishes "total similarity" (=identity) from "partial similarity" (36). Among the latter class, he lists the following subtypes (Plett 1979: 37–38):
– phonetic identiy + semantic difference (homophony / polysemy);
– phonetic similarity + semantic similarity (paronymy);
– phonetic difference + semantic similarity.

Of those, only the first two are of interest in the present context, the first subtype amounting to homophony or polysemy and the second to paronymy. These "phonetic" considerations do not extend beyond the broad typological level,

---

[3] The second point was first pointed out by Attardo (1994); cf. also Guidi (2012: 343).

though⁴. Recently, Thaler (2016) developed a taxonomy of wordplay which includes what she calls "Phonetic Techniques". Among these, she lists homophones, similarity of pronunciation, which she terms "homoephonic [sic!] play", permutation of sounds, rhythm and rhyme, and finally alliteration and assonance. She considers the first two to be wordplay in the narrow sense, the third one as either wordplay in either a broad sense or a narrow sense and does not become specific on the classification of the latter two. Based on the taxonomy developed by Winter-Froemel (2016: 42), they would fall into the category of wordplay in a broad sense.

Within the field of phonetics, publications covering the ludic use of speech (sounds) are not easy to find either. This is somewhat surprising considering the fact that wordplay can often be analyzed at the syllable level of language, cf. (7) and (8). Instead, most recent studies on the subject refer to the linguistic level of interest as phonological rather than phonetic (Binsted and Ritchie 1997; Hempelmann 2004; Hempelmann and Miller 2017). While this is certainly true for the most part, the phonetic level does come into play at the subphonemic level, be it in conjunction with analyzing near-homophones, especially from a cross-linguistic point of view or in relation to narrowing down phonetic processes like sound substitutions to their articulatory phonetic properties.

(7) *Ein Land röstet auf* with reference to the German verb *aufrüsten* with the nuclear vowel /ʏ/ 'gear up'. An analogy is created by the formation of a verb *aufrösten* 'roast up' with the nuclear vowel /œ/. The newspaper article refers to the growing number of coffee roasteries in some parts of the country. (*Welt am Sonntag* 46, 2016, NRW section, 10).

(8) *Ran an den Dreck* [ran ʔan den dʁɛkʰ] (literally 'go right at the dirt' with reference to spring cleaning; the saying played on is *ran an den Speck* [ran ʔan den ʃpɛkʰ], literally 'go right at the fat', meaning 'go right at it'; posted at a local drugstore (*dm*) in Trier, April 2017).

Guidi (2012) was probably the first researcher to introduce the syllable level as the one relevant to the sublexical analysis of wordplay. In a cross-linguistic study she analyzed a total of 209 puns from 15 languages. Given these numbers, her results cannot be interpreted quantitatively, but the analytic framework used in the present contribution is very similar to hers.

From a phonetic / phonological perspective, the syllable consists of three elements: the onset, the nucleus, and the coda. Of those, only the nucleus is

---

4 An example for semantic similarity and phonetic difference is German *Erdapfel* vs. *Kartoffel*, both meaning 'potato'.

mandatory, whereas the other two are optional. The phonotactic rules of each individual language determine not only the phonological constraints on the nucleus but also – and more notably – the phonological structure of both the onset and the coda.

All three constituents of the syllable lend themselves to being played on in wordplay. In many cases, the ludic forms will create minimal pairs with the original wording (cf. 7). In instances like (8), however, the whole onset cluster is replaced. In this context, the question of whether wordplay complies with the phonotactic rules is an important one. German, e.g., is known for displaying extensive consonant clusters in the onset as well as the coda (cf. *schrumpfst* [ʃʀʊmpfst]). On the one hand, it might be argued that a "forbidden" syllable structure such as /ʃtʃ/ as an onset in a German syllable might impede listener acceptance; on the other hand, it has been argued that "the violation of structural well-formedness rules" may render the new form more playful (Renner 2015: 126–127).

Most of the time, wordplay at the syllable level works on both a phonological and a graphemic level cf. e.g. (7) or (8). Sometimes, however, it rests primarily on the graphemic strand[5]. Whereas the former type may be presented orally or in writing, the latter type lends itself to be written.

The present contribution attempts to outline an analytic framework of sublexical wordplay[6] and subsequently presents a quantitative analysis of a small set of data which has been collected by this author. By focusing on formal characteristics of wordplay at the syllable level, it is in a way complementary to Winter-Froemel's (2016) discussion which is primarily concerned with semantic and communicative issues related to wordplay.

---

[5] In rare cases, the wordplay will rely on graphemic more than phonemic similarity, e.g. *Make America sweat again* (*NDR extra* 3 on June 10 2017 with reference to Donald Trump), where <sweat> and <great> resemble each other more closely than the pronunciations [swɛtʰ] and [gɹɛɪtʰ] do. Another example is *Horst case scenario* (alluding to *worst case scenario*; referring to the fear within the German Christian Social Party that its leader Horst Seehofer would cling to his office). There is no phonetic similarity in the onset or the nucleus ([hɔʁstʰ] vs. [wɜːstʰ], assuming a rhotic variety of English), but *Horst* and *worst* form a "minimal pair" on the graphemic level, which is called *eye pun* (Hempelmann and Miller 2017: 96).
[6] Obviously, complete homophones fall into this category only ex negativo, i.e., they are characterized by the absence of any such process.

2 Wordplay analyzed at the syllable level

When looking at examples of wordplay at the syllable level, one is confronted with a major dividing line:
- Wordplay drawing on existing lexical items (i.e. recontextualizing them), and
- Wordplay creating new lexical items

Examples for the former process are (7) and (8); examples for the latter are (9) and (10):

(9) *Staycation* to denote a trend in Germany to spend one's vacation at home; *Frankfurter Allgemeine Sonntagszeitung* 31 of 07 August 2016, p. 65.

(10) *Earbags*
(Trademark for frameless ear warmers, creating an analogy to *airbags*).

Examples (7): *Ein Land röstet auf* and (8): *Ran an den Dreck* can be classified as horizontal wordplay, i.e. involving more than one word, the latter (9): *Staycation* and (10): *Earbags* may be called vertical, i.e. involving only one lexeme (Wagenknecht 1965: 21; Hausmann 1974: 76). The status of compounds in this context is unclear, though. Wagenknecht (1965: 15) argues that compounds form a horizontal wordplay from a structural point of view whereas blends are to be considered as vertical.

If wordplay makes use of existing lexical items, the surprise effect which is intended to intellectually challenge and amuse the listener is generated by placing them in an unexpected co(n)text. In the case of homophones, it is up to the listener to create the unusual interpretation. If that endeavor is successful, he or she will "get" the pun, if not, the pun is lost on the listener. Thus, in a way, wordplay at the syllable level is selective in that its success largely depends on listener ability to reconstruct the process of punning.

Wordplay creating new lexical items will often take on the form of blends (see 2.2 below). Following Winter-Froemel (2016: 42), ludic innovations like e.g. *Stubentiger* ('cat'; literally *room tiger*) are not considered to constitute wordplay here but are regarded as verbal humor instead (cf. Winter-Froemel, this volume; Moulin, this volume).

Drawing a distinction between recontextualizing existing lexical items as described above and creating new ones is of potential interest from a cognitive point of view. The task for the listener is different: In the former case the element of surprise (and humorous effect) is generated by an unexpected sequence or combination of lexemes, whereas in the latter case, new lexemes are generated which are expected to conform to phonotactic rules of a given variety, may or may not become conventional and may even make it into the dictionaries. A good example is the German blend *Ostalgie* (11).

(11) *Ostalgie*, a blend created from *Nostalgie* 'nostalgia' and *Osten* 'east', describing the "Sehnsucht nach [bestimmten Lebensformen] der DDR" (longing for [certain aspects of living in] the GDR; translation mine; AB); cf. DUDEN online (2017).

It is open to debate whether the cognitive processing between those two subgroups of wordplay at sublexical level really is all that different. One might argue that a phrase like *Ein Land röstet auf* is processed as an entity just as the blend *Staycation* is. I will keep them separate for the time being, though, in order to be on the safe side, because the phonetic implementation of the two categories may differ (see 3 below), and this difference should not be lost in the analysis.

2.1 Recontextualization of existing lexical items

This type of wordplay uses a recombination of existing lexical items, i.e., the lexical items used are not "funny" on their own, but the pun is produced by embedding them into a context which creates an element of surprise. This is known as horizontal wordplay (Wagenknecht 1975: 21). This process may leave the phonological and / or phonetic structure of the lexeme intact, putting it in a different context. This is what happens in the case of homophones. Alternatively, slight changes to the syllable structure may be made, thus creating minimal pairs in a strict sense or near-minimal pairs[7]. These mechanisms are considered here from a descriptive phonetic point of view.

---

[7] The larger the phonological overlap, the easier the detection of wordplay (e.g., *Ostalgie*, see above). A borderline case of phonological similarity is *Almer Nordwand*, where three out of five phonemes as well as the spelling differ [ʔeɪgɐ] vs. [ʔalmɐ]. The pun refers to the excellent performance of the Austrian goalkeeper Almer during the World Championship in 2015, comparing him with the almost invincible *Eiger Nordwand* in the Alps (*Deutschlandfunk* on 19 June 2016).

2.1.1 Homophony

One very popular way of creating wordplay at the syllable level is certainly the use of homophones. This contribution distinguishes between complete homophony (or perfect puns in the terms of Hempelmann and Miller (2017) and near-homophony (or imperfect puns in the terms of Hempelmann and Miller 2017). Complete homophony includes homonyms as well as polysemes. They may or may not be homographs. Examples are (12) and (13), and many more are to be found in Winter-Froemel (2016). It seems that certain languages like e.g. French, which display a many-to-one relationship between spelling and pronunciation[8], lend themselves to wordplay by homophony much more than languages like e.g. Spanish do, in which this relationship is closer to a one-to-one ratio. This is a mere hypothesis at this point in time but certainly seems to merit looking into in future studies[9].

(12) *Unsere Sommerreifen* [ˈʔʊnzəʁə ˈzɔmɐʁɐɪfən]
(Slogan advertising fresh produce sold by a German chain of supermarkets. It translates either as 'Our summer-ripe (produce)' playing on the homophonous 'our summer tires')

(13) Greatest Hitz [ˈgɹɛɪtəst hɪts]
(literally 'greatest heat' and, of course, 'greatest hits'; Jan Böhmermann on 29 September 2016 in his ZDF show, commenting on a heat wave in Germany)

If we are dealing with complete homophony in oral speech (as opposed to heterography[10]), there is definitely a need for signaling the wordplay to the listener as long as the wordplay is presented orally only. This may be achieved by a wide variety of mechanisms which have yet to be analyzed in detail. On a phonetic level, pausing, raising one's voice, articulating carefully, voice quality and slowing down are probably the ones which are used most frequently. Another way of signaling wordplay is obviously the graphemic level, which may in turn reveal a blend (cf. *alternatief*,[11] discussed by Ronneberger-Sibold 2006: 167).

---

8 A famous example is French [oː], which may be written <au>, <aux>, <haut>, <hauts>, <eau>, <eaux>, <aulx>, or <oh>.
9 This, by the way, opens up a whole new field of wordplay research, which might relate typological features of languages to their (preferred) mechanisms of wordplay.
10 E.g., *Nuhr im Ersten*, where *Nuhr* is the last name of a German comedian whose show is broadcast on German television's Channel One as opposed to homophonous *nur im Ersten* 'only on Channel One'.
11 This blend (*alternativ* + *tief* 'alternative + low') is pronounced [ʔaltɛɐnaˈtʰiːf] and refers to a bad option.

2.1.2 Near-homophony (homeophony)

From a strictly phonetic perspective, complete homophony has to be distinguished from quasi- or intended homophony or "homoephonic play [sic!]" according to Thaler (2016: 53). As is evident from the database analyzed for the present study (see 3. below), homeophonic wordplay often involves either bilingual punning (Stefanowitsch 2002) or punning across linguistic varieties[12] which show different realizations of nearly identical phonemes. The speaker may rely on the mismatch going unnoticed by German listeners as in (14) or (16), depending on whether the borrowing has been integrated into the German phonological system or the donor language is used as a reference:

(14) *Funtastisch*
([fʌn] vs. [fan]; advertizing slogan for Swatch watches, seen in Trier in February 2017; Knospe 2015: 173 lists a different source)

On the other hand, the mismatch may add to the ludic impression, creating an extra challenge to the listener to solve the riddle, cf. examples (15) and (17):

(15) *Karl mag's. Du auch?*
('Karl likes it. Do you, too?' Billboard advertizing for the automobiles manufactured by Mini, seen in Chemnitz (eastern Germany) on 29 June 2013. The homophony [kʰaːl maːks] with *Karl Marx* will work best for those parts of Germany where /r/ following /a/ is realized through vowel lengthening only, i.e. primarily the north. In areas where postvocalic /r/ is pronounced as a consonant, the pun might just go undetected.

(16) *We* kehr *for Vienna* ('we sweep for Vienna') where the first element of the diphthong is oscillating between (British) English [ɛ] in *care* and Austrian German [e] in *kehr*[13].

(17) *Am Arsch* ([ʔamaʁʃ] 'to be fucked', playing on Macron's "en marche" [ãmaʁʃ]; *NDR extra 3* on 15 May 2017)

---

12 From a structural point of view, there is no difference between historical languages and, say, regional varieties thereof. They will therefore be treated equally here.
13 Knospe (2015: 174) lists the slogan "We kehr for you" as originating in Berlin. The present author saw the above version in Vienna in June of 2016.

Fig. 1: Advertizement banner seen in Chemnitz on 29 June 2013 (© Angelika Braun)

As Knospe (2015: 172–173), who studied press examples of German / English puns, puts it,

> Only rarely are diamorphs [i.e., identical elements of different language indexing; AB] full homonyms, i.e. both interlingual homonyms and homographs. Rather, partial German / English homonyms, which either constitute (near-)homophones or homographs, predominate. As a consequence, most bilingual puns which appear in written texts also involve the level of orthography.

Near-homophones can be expected to go largely unnoticed by the untrained listener if the difference is located at a subphonemic level, as is the case in (14) and (16). If there is a difference at the phonemic level as in e.g. (17), the inter-language seems to render the wordplay more challenging and thus more attractive to listener intellect. Generally speaking, its detection is quite a demanding task because it will always depend on the extent to which the listener knows the languages or varieties involved. Among the languages utilized in wordplay directed at German recipients, English clearly plays a dominant role in the data studied here. Knospe (2015: 170) supports this view:

> [T]he attractiveness of bilingual puns resides in two aspects, namely in the prestige of English, which is bound to a gradual bilingualism, as well as in the specificity of bilingual puns that [...] require an additional cognitive effort, which leads to a particular sense of achievement if the addressee succeeds in understanding the pun.

2.1.3 Suprasegmental wordplay

It is, however, worthwhile to extend the perspective beyond the segmental level of speech. Wordplay may be implemented by suprasegmental means just as well, the segmental level being homophonous. The two mechanisms to be considered in this context have to do with stress and juncture. Homophones on a segmental strand may be turned into wordplay by shifting the stress pattern and / or by dintroducing juncture. Examples are:

(18) *Miss **Bildung***[14] [mɪs ˈbɪldʊŋ] vs. [ˈmɪs bɪldʊŋ]
(literally either 'Miss Education' as a nickname for Margot Honecker, the wife of the late Erich Honecker, who held the post of secretary of education in the GDR from 1963 to 1989, or 'deformity').

(19) *Du darfst keinen Gott neben mir haben außer **Mar** # got.*
('Thou shalt have no other gods before me – except Mar-god'; popular saying in the former GDR referring to Margot Honecker, who was ill-reputed for her neo-Stalinist views.)

(20) *Jan Josef # **Liefers**!*
(literally 'Jan Josef – deliver it!' as part of a comedy sketch by comedian Willy Astor on German television. The name of the popular German actor Jan Josef Liefers is played on. The context is an order to a pizza service, and a certain Jan Josef is urged to deliver it. Willy Astor; Promi WG; https://www.youtube.com/watch?v=osHEsa5OUAc).

The pun in these last examples primarily rests on the introduction of juncture, i.e., a pause. It is very clear that in these cases, pausing forms an indispensable element of the wordplay, i.e., it would not be understood without the pause.

---

14 The stressed syllable is marked by boldface characters.

Shifted stress patterns and junctures are obviously sufficient indications of wordplay, and they often constitute it. However, in some cases it may prove useful to exaggerate the juncture in order to make sure that the listener really gets the point. Therefore, signaling suprasegmental wordplay is often a matter of degree rather than of kind, i,e., the pause accompanying the juncture may be longer than linguistically necessary in order to make sure that the wordplay is recognized.

Suprasegmental mechanisms of speech have also been used in poetry to signal wordplay. It is precisely what the verbal humor in the following poem by Christoph Schwarz (*1947) relies on (Dencker 2002: 330).

(21) be, B [bə beː] b, B

ich schreibe, [ʔɪç ˈʃʁeɪbə] 'I write',
ich schrei "B". [ʔɪç ʃʁeɪˈbeː] 'I scream "B"'.

ich beschreibe, [ʔɪç bəˈʃʁeɪbə] 'I describe',
ich, B., schrei "B". [ʔɪç ˈbeːʃʁeɪˈbeː] 'I, B, scream "B"'.

ich beschreibe B, [ʔɪç bəˈʃʁeɪbə ˈbeː] 'I describe B',
ich, B., schreibe "B". [ʔɪç ˈbeːʃʁeɪbəˈbeː] 'I, B, write "B"'.

ich bebe, schrei "B", [ʔɪç ˈbeːbə ʃʁeɪ ˈbeː] 'I tremble, scream "B"',
ich, B., beschreibe. [ʔɪç ˈbeː bəˈʃʁeɪbə] 'I, B, describe.'
(Translation: AB)

2.1.4 Paronymy

This paper argues that analyzing the changes are made at the syllable level of a lexeme which is then placed in a new and unexpected context will provide further insight into differences in punning mechanisms across languages (cf. Guidi 2012 for an example) and into the acceptability of puns to various listener groups. Paronymy is the textbook example of wordplay (see 3.1 below). The distinction between paronymy and homeophony is quite clear-cut: whereas homeophony operates in an interlinguistic context paronymy does not. Another defining element of paronyms is that the newly introduced lexical items constitute minimal pairs or near-minimal pairs with the items which they are derived from. Examples besides (7) and (8) are:

(22) *Bin Baden* as a nickname for the German politician Rudolf Scharping, who had himself and his partner photographed in a swimming pool as part of a home story. It literally translates as 'gone for a swim', but the allusion to Bin Laden is evident[15].

(23) *Vater, Sohn, eiliger Geist* 'Father, son, and hurried ghost'.
(*Süddeutsche Zeitung* of 16 May 2016) on the occasion of Max Verstappen's first Formula 1 victory. His father, Jos Verstappen, was also a famous Formula 1 driver.

2.2 Wordplay creating new lexical items

The creation of a new lexical item by way of wordplay can – and will most of the time – happen through blending. Even though there is no general agreement on a definition of blending (Bauer 2012), the following definition by Ronneberger-Sibold (2006: 157) is adopted here: "A blend here is defined as a deliberate creation of a new word out of two (or more) previously existing ones in a way which differs from the rules or patterns of regular compounding."

Few researchers have taken the trouble to look at blending processes from a phonological, let alone a phonetic perspective (e.g. Kubozono 1990; Kelly 1998; Gries 2004a, b; Wright et al. 2005; Arndt-Lappe & Plag 2013; Renner 2015). Kubozono (1990) formulates phonological and phonotactic constraints for the formation of blends. Kelly (1998: 586) points to the "playful" and "teas[ing]" character of blends. He argues that the phonemes at the boundary tend to be similar, which has an effect on how they are processed by the listener: "By constructing the blend so that the onset of word two sounds similar to the expected continuation of word one, the speaker postpones, however momentarily, the listeners' recognition that they have been sidetracked" (Kelly 1998: 587). Gries (2004a) argues that it does not suffice to look at similarity at the breakpoint but makes a case for analyzing the overall phonetic similarity of the source words instead. He proposes carrying out a detailed phonetic analysis extending to the feature level (Gries 2004a: 652–653).

In the context of the present study, which focuses on the processes at the syllable level, only a fraction of blends are of immediate interest, i.e. those which create minimal pairs or near-minimal pairs with one of the constituents of the blend, the prosodic structure remaining intact. This implies that one of the constituents will remain unchanged. These blends fall into the category of "contour blends" as defined by Ronneberger-Sibold (2006: 170), and they are known to retain the prosodic structure of the longer source word (Renner

---

15 All of this took place well before the times of Al Qaida and 9 / 11.

2015: 125) or matrix word (Ronneberger-Sibold 2006). Some researchers will not even consider these new word creations as blends (Bauer 2012: 15). They are included here, however, because they are quite frequent and are distinct from the use of minimal pairs in lexical recontextualization as discussed above. Examples from our database are

(24) *Zauderkünstler: Zaudern + Zauberkünstler* ('hesitate' + 'magician'; *Welt kompakt* of 09 January 2017, 4)
This wordplay refers to the former head of the German Social Democrats, Sigmar Gabriel, who hesitated for a long time before announcing that he would not run for Chancellor in 2017.

(25) *Scheinmeier: Schein + Steinmeier* ('appearance' + Steinmeier)
This wordplay makes reference to allegations that the German President plagiarized in his PhD dissertation.

(26) *Muttivationsseminar: Mutti + Motivationsseminar* ('Mom' + 'pep talk'; heute-show of 15 December 2016)
"Mutti" ('mom') is a nickname for Chancellor Merkel; the blend *Muttivationsseminar* refers to a meeting of Merkel with political leaders of her own party in order to prepare for the 2017 elections.

Irrespective of whether or not these newly formed words are considered to be blends by various authors, they merit consideration in the present context, because they may follow the same rules as paronymy as discussed in 2.1.4 above.

The reason why this is relevant to the present contribution is that while blending relatively rarely operates at the level of individual sounds, it will create minimal pairs if it does (cf. also Kubozono 1990).

(27) *Electile Dysfunction*
(Title of a book by Alan Dershowitz on the US presidential campaign 2016. Obviously the allusion is to *erectile dysfunction*.)

(28) *Saarmageddon (Saar + Armageddon)* as a comment on the outcome of the 2017 elections in the German State of Saarland (ZDF heute-show on 06 April 2017).

(29) *Teuro (Teuer + Euro)* as a satirical comment on the fact that many businesses used the establishment/introduction of the Euro to raise their prices.

(30) *Weinsinnig (Wein + wahnsinnig)* (name of a wine bar in Trier).

It might be argued that the phonetic processes which lead to minimal-pair-type blends resemble those discussed above in the context of paronymy. But even though they may turn out to be similar from a descriptive angle, they seem to differ from a cognitive point of view. Whereas paronymy is reliably signaled to the hearer by co-text, this condition being mandatory for its perception, as well as by context, this condition being optional, the newly created lexical items by way of blends speak for themselves.

2.3 The phonetics of wordplay at the syllable level

From an analytic point of view, it does not seem sufficient to take into account homeophony, paronymy or blending only when analyzing wordplay. Instead, the phonetic description of what exactly is "played on" and how this is done may add to our knowledge about the detailed mechanisms used in wordplay. The crudest difference to be taken into account is that between the phonetic and phonological levels. From a systematic point of view, there is a total of four options:

Tab. 1: Structural properties of homophones

Structure of homophones	Phonological identity	Phonological difference
Phonetic identity	total homophony	final consonant devoicing
Phonetic difference	juncture	(impossible by definition)

Identity on the phonetic as well as the phonological level will result in complete homophony. Differences on both these levels, on the other hand, run counter to the definition of homophony. Phonetic differences combined with phonological identity seems highly unlikely, unless one chooses to consider juncture and stress to be phonetic features only.[16] Final consonant devoicing forms a prototypical example of phonological difference and at the same time phonetic identity:

(31) *Radhaus* /radhaus/, phonetically ['ʁaːtheʊs] to denote a bicycle station; creating a homophone with *Rathaus* /rathaus/ 'town hall' on a phonetic level only

A very frequent case is obviously constituted by homophony on both the phonological and phonetic levels, as is the case in the following examples:

---

16 In this case, (18) and (19) conform to this description.

(32) *Nuhr im Ersten*
(Name of a comedy program on German TV hosted by Dieter Nuhr; the title will also translate as 'only on Channel One')

(33) *Nur für Busse*
(Name of a comedy program on German TV hosted by Jochen Busse; the title will also translate as 'buses only')

(34) *The Importance of Being Earnest*
(Title of a comedy by Oscar Wilde), drawing on the homophony between *Earnest* as a first name and *earnest* as an adjective.

The relationship between pronunciation and writing may form an additional factor in wordplay. In cases of homophony combined with heterography the graphemic level may serve to signal the pun (*Nuhr im Ersten*). If, on the other hand, heterophony (['ʔybɛzɛtsən] vs. [ʔybɐ'zɛtsən]) is paired with homography <übersetzen>, this constitutes a different phenomenon which has to be discussed separately.

Wordplay as defined above will not always affect its "target" in the same way. A major distinction should be made between stressed and unstressed syllables being played on. Given the need to successfully communicate a pun for it to be effective, the expectation would be that mainly stressed syllables are affected by wordplay.

Within the syllable category, phonetic analysis calls for a further distinction between its elements: onset, nucleus, and coda. In the syllable onset and coda, different phonetic processes may occur. An onset or a coda may be inserted, deleted substituted, or modified. *Insertion* means that an onset is added where there used to be none. The possibility of onset *deletion* in German depends on how the phonemic status of the glottal stop is assessed. If the glottal stop were considered to have phonemic status, there would effectively be no syllable without an onset, and consequently there could be no onset deletion. Yet Hall (2011: 65) reports that "Die meisten Phonologen, die das Konsonantensystem des Deutschen untersucht haben, [...] zu dem Schluss gekommen [sind], daß [sic!] der glottale Plosiv [ʔ] kein Phonem des Deutschen ist. [Most phonologists who have studied the consonant system of German have come to the conclusion that the glottal stop is not a phoneme of German. (Translation: AB)]"

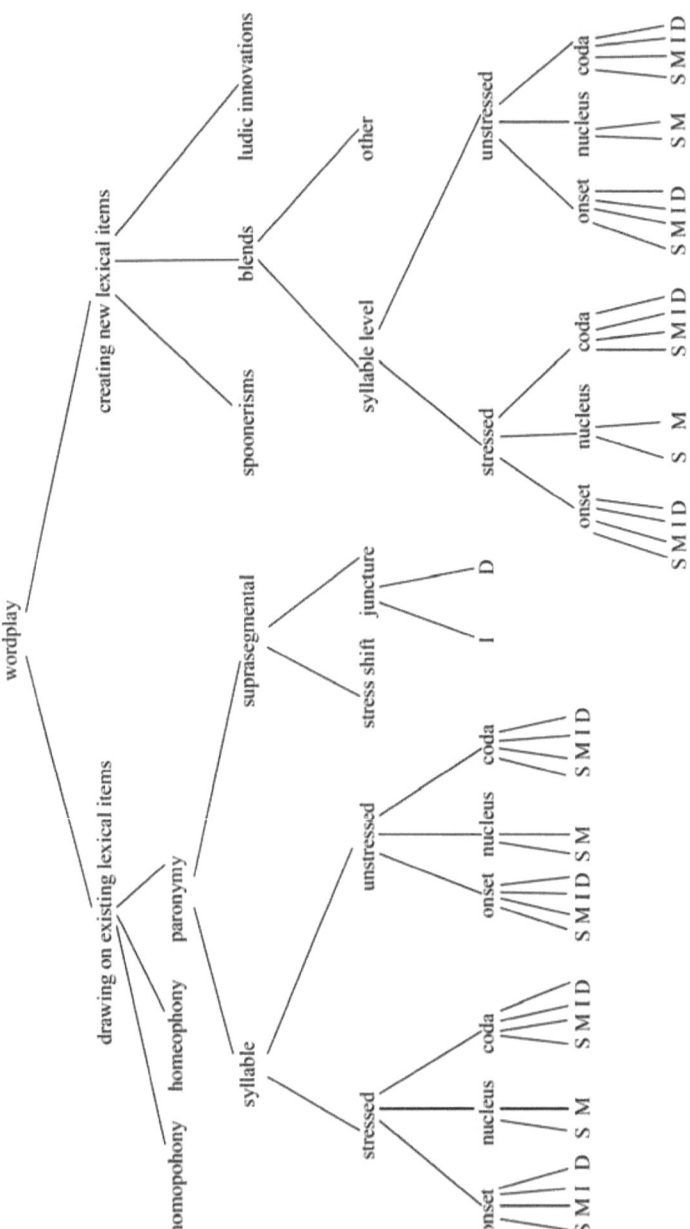

Fig. 2: A taxonomy of wordplay from the angle of phonology (I = insertion; D = deletion; M = modification; S = substitution)

Thus, the glottal stop is not regarded as having phonemic status in this contribution, i.e. examples like *Vater, Sohn, eiliger Geist* (23) are considered to show onset deletion. Another process to be taken into account is *substitution*, i.e. one consonant replacing another. Finally, onset or coda *modification* has to be taken into account. This may entail the expansion or reduction of a consonant cluster. The nucleus, on the other hand, can only be modified, e.g. by replacing a diphthong with a monophthong or vice versa, or substituted, e.g. replacing a monophthong with a different monophthong.

Based on these structural considerations, a taxonomy of formal, sublexical aspects of wordplay in a narrow sense according to Winter-Froemel (2016: 42) could look as shown in Figure 2.

Examples for the types of wordplay mentioned in Figure 2 are:

(35) Onset – Insertion
Ein Mann, kein Wort. 'One man, not a word'; ZEIT online 7 July 2011 with reference to the phrase *Ein Mann, ein Wort* "one man, one word". This refers to the mayor of Duisburg, Germany, who failed to express his regret over a number of fatalities at a local pop concert.

Onset – Deletion
Cf. (23) above: *Vater, Sohn und eiliger Geist*

(36) Onset – Substitution
Bin baden; (literally: 'gone for a swim'), referring to the former leader of the Social Democratic Party, Rudolf Scharping, who had himself photographed with his partner in a swimming pool. The allusion is, of course, to Bin Laden.

(37) Onset – Modification: Cluster reduction
Wahlverbrechen, (literally: 'election crime') referring to Donald Trump being elected POTUS; NDR extra 3 on 2 February 2017. The term played on is *Wahlversprechen* ('pre-election promise').

(38) Onset – Modification: Cluster expansion
Jack the Dripper. Nickname for Jackson Pollock for throwing bags of paint at the canvas; playing on *Jack the Ripper*.

(39) Nucleus – Modification: Expansion
Doppelt heilt besser (literally: 'double will cure better', playing on the proverb *doppelt hält besser* 'double will hold (together) better'; *NDR* Series on two sisters who are animal healers).

(40) Nucleus – Modification: Reduction
BonnGiorno [bɔn ˈdʒɔrno]; near-homophony with Italian *buon giorno* [buɔn ˈdʒɔrnɔ] 'good day'; Name of a restaurant in the Sinn Leffers department store in Bonn, seen on 24 November 2016.

(41) Nucleus – Substitution[17]
Keine Macht den Drögen (literally: 'no power to the boring'), playing on the slogan *Keine Macht den Drogen* 'no power to drugs'; *ZDF heute-show* of 05 May 2017 with reference to the lack of profile in the candidates running in a state election.

(42) Coda – Insertion
Carmorra; (NDR extra-3-spezial of 12 May 2016, referring to potentially criminal activities by the German car manufacturers in conjunction with the exhaust measurement scandal).

(43) Coda – Deletion
Verstehen Sie Spa? (Article in the *Deutsche Bahn* Journal DB mobil of 28 January 2017, advertising weekend wellness trips; the reference is to the German equivalent to *Candid Camera* called *Verstehen Sie Spaß*; literally 'Can you take a joke').

(44) Coda – Substitution
Kopfpit[18] (literally 'head pit'); *NDR extra 3 Das Beste*, seen on German TV's Channel One on 23 April 2017; the reference is to *cockpit*; the sketch dealing with a pubertal boy who is sitting inside Donald Trump's head and steering his actions).

(45) Coda – Modification: Cluster reduction
Irren ist männlich [ˈʔɪʁən ʔɪst ˈmɛnlɪç] ('to err is male'; title of a German comedy film of 1996; the pun is on *irren ist menschlich* [ˈʔɪʁən ʔɪst ˈmɛnʃlɪç] 'to err is human').

(46) Coda – Modification: Cluster expansion
Last Vegas (Title of a 2013 American comedy film featuring three friends who travel to Las Vegas to hold a bachelor party for their last remaining single friend.)

As far as vowels are concerned, stressed ones seem to be the prime candidates for wordplay. Rare examples of unstressed vowels being affected are the following:

(47) *Gewichtstsunami* (literally 'weight tsunami', playing on *Gewichtszunahme* 'weight gain'; alluding to a large weight gain; *Welt am Sonntag* 45 of 06 November 2016, 24).

---

17 Nucleus insertion and deletion are not listed because neither is compatible with German phonotactics.
18 *Kopfpit* is an outright blend (*Kopf* + *Cockpit*). Depending on whether affricates are considered as monophonemic or biphonemic, this might alternatively be interpreted as a cluster expansion.

(48) *Dubai sein ist alles* (playing on *dabei sein ist alles* 'participating is everything' in an advertisement for trips to Dubai in a Trier travel agency)

(49) *Sahra Waggonknecht* [vaˈgɔnknɛçtʰ] (literally 'waggon servant', playing on the name of communist politician Sahra Wagenknecht [ˈvaːgənknɛçtʰ]; literally 'car servant' in conjunction with Deutsche Bahn; *NDR extra3* on 02 February 2017)

3 Quantitative analysis

In an attempt to quantify the various kinds of wordplay at the syllable level, a total of 213 samples taken from a multilingual (German, English, French, Italian) database on wordplay were analyzed. This database has been compiled by the present author since 2016, largely relying on TV shows, newspapers, posted advertisements, and – to a very limited extent – applicable examples from previous publications (Ronneberger-Sibold 2006; Winter-Froemel 2009). The selection was confined to examples which were intended for a German audience. This includes items which are in part (see example 16 above) or completely (cf. example 27) in English. Interestingly enough, in some of these examples, the pun will work for a German-speaking audience only, cf. e.g. (51) below. The latter example will completely elude monolingual speakers of English. Puns which are bilingual or even completely in English may be considered to present listeners with an extra challenge and thus establish some kind of a group spirit between the speaker and the hearers.

(50) *The winner fakes it all* (*ZDF heute-show* of 23 February 2017 on Donald Trump).

(51) *Maut* [mɐʊtʰ] *Rushmore* (*ZDF heute-show* of 15 December 2016 on the impending toll ('Maut') for privately owned cars in Germany); the allusion here is to Mount [mɐʊntʰ] Rushmore.

Table 2 shows the overall distribution of the types of wordplay at the syllable level. In some rare cases, it is difficult to make a clear distinction between homeophony and blends. Normally, homeophony will be confined to interlinguistic use, and blends are generally monolingual. An area of overlap emerges where interlinguistic blends occur which form a minimal pair with one of the source words as in the case of *funtastisch*. The latter example was counted as a near-homophony in the present contribution. This decision was made under the assumption that *fun* almost has loan-word status in German. However, it could arguably have been made in a different way.

Tab. 2: Distribution of types of wordplay at the syllable level (N = 213)

phonetic mechanism	paronymy	blending	complete homophony	near-homophony (homeo-phony)	suprasegmental	total
no. (percent)	91 (43%)	61 (29%)	22 (11%)	27 (13%)	12 (6%)	213 (100%)

The table shows that paronymy and blending are by far the most frequent processes in wordplay at the syllable level in German. Complete homophony and homeophony are each used much less frequently, homeophony being slightly more frequent than homophony. This does not come as a surprise considering that complete homophony between languages and varieties is not particularly widespread. – In a relatively small number of incidents of wordplay at the syllable level, the suprasegmental level is affected. This includes stress shift and / or an insertion / deletion of juncture.

3.1 Paronymy

Of the items studied, 91 (43%) can be categorized as paronyms. Based on these results, the question arises of whether all elements of the (stressed) syllable are equally susceptible to wordplay or if there is a preference. For this reason the number of paronymic instances was analyzed according to syllable position (cf. Table 3).

Tab. 3: Distribution of paronyms (N=91) across the syllable (numbers and percentages)

syllable position	onset	nucleus	coda	total
phonetic processes	53 (58%)	22 (24%)	16 (18%)	91 (100%)

As far as syllable position is concerned, it is quite obvious that in German there is a clear preference for the syllable onset to be played on. This covers more than half of the total number of items analyzed. The nucleus is affected in one in four of the cases, whereas the coda is played on only 18% of the time. Given that chance level is at 33%, the preference for the onset position is even more evident.

In order to narrow down the phonetic processes even further, they were broken down according to the taxonomy outlined above (cf. Table 4).

Tab. 4: Types of phonetic processes within the syllable in paronyms (N=91). + / - *str* refers to stressed vs. unstressed syllables

syllable position	onset		+str	-str	nucleus		+str	-str	coda[19]	
phonetic process										
substitution	33	(61%)	28	5	14	(67%)	8	6	3	(19%)
deletion	4	(7%)	4	0	0	(0%)			2	(13%)
insertion	8	(15%)	8	0	0	(0%)			5	(31%)
modification	9	(17%)	7	2	7	(33%)	4	3	6	(38%)

If one takes a closer look at where the phonetic wordplay mechanisms occur most frequently, i.e. in the onset position, it emerges that substitutions are the preferred process by a large margin. Considering the onset position alone, close to two thirds (61%) of the items consist of substitutions, followed by modifications and insertions (17% and 15%, respectively), whereas deletions (7%) play a minor role. As far as the overall results are concerned, more than one third of all paronyms present in the corpus (36%) consist of onset substitutions alone.

In the syllable nucleus, which is affected much less frequently than the onset, substitutions dominate over modifications, i.e., the nuclear element tends to be replaced rather than expanded or reduced.

The coda is played on even less frequently than the nucleus, modification and insertion being the most frequent mechanisms. This means that one element of the coda tends to be replaced or deleted, or that a coda is added.

A further distinction which turns out to be crucial for the distribution of phonetic wordplay is syllable stress. As Table 4 shows, the onset processes affect stressed syllables almost exclusively, whereas the nuclear processes are almost evenly distributed between stressed[20] and unstressed syllables. The latter cases merit a closer look at the perception side, specifically the question of whether an audience is able to grasp the pun despite the unstressed vowel.

---

19 In view of the small number of tokens, it did not seem appropriate to distinguish stressed and unstressed realizations.
20 Since the vast majority of lexemes studied contain no more than three syllables, only primary stress is taken into account.

The general results are quite clear-cut, and despite the limited size of the database there can be little doubt about the preferred phonetic ludic mechanism intended for German listeners: replacing the (stressed) syllable onset. The substitution of the nuclear vowel also plays a major part, but is far less frequent. The coda is clearly of lesser importance to this type of wordplay.

A further question to be addressed is whether the phonotactic constraints of the language in question are respected by the wordplay, and if so, whether there are exceptions. If the latter turns out to be true, this might on the one hand affect the acceptability for listeners or on the other hand increase the intellectual challenge to the listener because it renders solving the riddle more difficult. Renner (2015: 126–127, 130–131) calls this "structural transgression". As far as our German data is concerned, wordplay at the syllable level always concurs with the phonotactic constraints of German[21]. There is not a single violation of those rules, which is, by the way, also true for the remaining instances of ludic wordplay which were analyzed, e.g., the blends. This result is in accord with Guidi's (2012) findings on puns in 15 different languages. She observes that "[...] strings do not generally violate phonotactic constraints [...]" (Guidi 2012: 361).

3.2 Blends

The question of whether a recontextualized paronymy will be subject to the same underlying cognitive process as a blend remains as yet unsolved. However, the approach taken here is descriptive, and thus, the same descriptive framework which was outlined above (see 2.3) for paronymy will be applied in the empirical study concerning blends. Specifically, 61 (29%) out of the 213 items analyzed consist of blends. In 21 of these, the blend forms a minimal pair with one of the constituents of the blend. An example is

(52) *Kurlaub (Kur* 'rehab' + *Urlaub* 'vacation' the implication being that for many, rehab amounts to a kind of vacation.

---

[21] Taking phonotactic considerations into account when looking at wordplay is by no means new. In 1651, Georg Philipp Harsdörffer developed a so-called *Denckring* (literally: *thinking ring*) as a means of creative use of language (cf. Moulin, this volume). It consists of a concentric array of five different rings on which the prefixes, syllable-initial clusters, nuclear vowels, syllable-final clusters, and suffixes of German are listed. By turning each ring individually, a total of 82,944,000 linguistic items can be created. The *Denckring* was intended for ludic word formation, and it was by no means the first such device (Dencker 2002: 425). What is particularly remarkable is that Harsdörffer was evidently well aware of the phonotactic constraints of German since he lists all possible prenuclear and postnuclear consonant clusters.

The following table shows the distribution of phonetic processes across the syllable.

Tab. 2: Distribution of phonetic processes in blends (N=67) across the syllable (numbers and percentages)[22]

syllable position	onset	nucleus	coda	total
phonetic processes	44 (64%)	12 (19%)	11 (16%)	67 (100%)

In those blends which involve wordplay at the syllable level, the syllable onset is by far most often played on (cf. Table 5). Nucleus and coda are affected in about one in five instances. This distribution is quite comparable to that for paronymy in Table 3 above.

A detailed look at the phonetic wordplay mechanisms is given in Table 6. It reveals that where they occur most frequently, i.e. in the onset position, modifications, insertions, and substitutions are fairly evenly distributed. On the other hand, there were no instances of onset deletions. As far as the overall results are concerned, about one in four of all the ludic variations (41%) occurs in the form of modifications (i.e. expansions or reductions) of the syllable onset alone. All phonetic processes occur much more often in the onset of stressed syllables than in unstressed ones. Substitutions and modifications of the nucleus are too infrequent to draw firm conclusions, but the results indicate that syllable stress may not be as crucial a factor here as it is in the onset.

If one compares Tables 3 / 5 and 4 / 6, respectively, the similarities are striking at first glance. The syllable onset forms the preferred object of wordplay in both. However, there are some differences with respect to the favored processes. Whereas substitution predominates in the paronyms, modification is most frequent in blend onsets. In the nuclear position, substitutions are the preferred process in both paronyms and blends. Differences between the two kinds of wordplay emerge regarding the coda. While substitutions, insertions and modifications are about evenly distributed in blends, modifications predominate in the paronyms.

---

[22] The total number of phonetic processes is larger than the number of items because in some cases there was more than one process, i.e. one element of the syllable onset may have been replaced and a second one added.

Tab. 3: Distribution of phonetic processes across the syllable in blends (N=67)

syllable position / phonetic process	onset	+str	-str	nucleus	+str	-str	coda
substitution	14 (33%)	11	3	8 (62%)	5	3	3 (27%)
deletion	0 (0%)			0 (0%)			0 (0%)
insertion	12 (28%)	12	0	0 (0%)			4 (36%)
modification	17 (40%)	11	6	5 (38%)	3	2	4 (36%)

The fact that paronymy and blending (as understood here) do not follow the same patterns especially as far as syllable onset is concerned justifies keeping those two mechanisms of wordplay separate. Still, it seems as if – irrespective of context – the phonetic processes utilized will primarily affect the onset of a stressed syllable and will most likely involve a replacement or modification of the syllable-initial consonant.

3.3 Fine phonetic detail

It is conceivable to break down the analysis even further, i.e., towards a feature-based phonetic description (as expressed by 3-term labels; Abercrombie 1967: 52) of sounds which have been substituted or modified. For example, in *Electile Dysfunction* (27), a (central) voiced alveolar approximant /ɹ/ is replaced by a voiced alveolar lateral approximant /l/. These two sounds differ in one respect only, i.e. manner of articulation, i.e., /ɹ/ being a central approximant and /l/ a lateral approximant. They are identical with respect to voicing and place of articulation and are both classified as approximants. Strictly speaking, the difference between the two can be narrowed down to central vs. lateral airflow. They are thus much more similar than, e.g., the two phonemes played on in *Ich lease Dich* (53), i.e. the voiced bilabial plosive /b/ and the voiced alveolar fricative /z/, which differ with respect to place (bilabial /b/ vs. alveolar /z/), and manner of articulation (plosive /b/ vs. fricative /z/). This kind of analysis allows for a subsegmental description of the processes which are employed in wordplay. It is applicable to homeophony as well as paronymy and blends. Once sufficient data is available, it will be possible to narrow down the preferences on the part of the sender like e.g. playing on the voicing of a plosive as opposed to its place of articulation. This will help to unveil fine phonetic detail of wordplay. The data can be used to establish patterns of wordplay at the syllable level and thus serve to differentiate between languages, genres, or media. For instance, it is quite obvious that the syllable onset is most frequently played on in German, but the question of whether this is the same for other languages remains to be answered. Mechanisms specific to the advertizing business or to political satire could be identified. Finally, written wordplay which is meant to hit the eye rather than the ear may follow patterns which differ from those of oral wordplay. Perception studies will be able to show which processes are most easily acceptable to listeners and thus contribute to the discourse-related understanding of wordplay.

(53) *Ich lease Dich* [ˈʔɪç liːzə dɪç] (advertizement for the car leasing company *smart cars;* the reference is to German *ich liebe Dich* [ˈʔɪç liːbə dɪç] 'I love you').

4 Discussion and perspectives

The present study constitutes a first attempt at establishing a taxonomy of wordplay at the syllable level. For wordplay intended for a German audience,[23] a very clear pattern emerges with respect to syllable position (onset of stressed syllable). The preferred processes vary: substitutions predominate in paronyms, whereas modifications are most frequent in blends. This may serve as an argument for studying those two categories separately.

Further quantitative studies are lacking. These would be needed in order to determine the fine phonetic detail which is played on in a given language and allows for a comparative approach once sufficient material has been collected. There remains a lot to be unveiled about language specificity of phonetic wordplay (Guidi 2012).

Another research field which would merit attention in the present context is the perception of wordplay at sublexical level. One of the very few studies in that subject area was carried out by Fuhrich and Schmid (2016). These authors show that fictitious monolingual slogans are recalled better than mixed-language ones, but they do not address the question of popularity of actual puns among listener groups. On a different strand, there have been attempts to establish a maximum number of segments differing in target and pun for a tar-

---

23 As was mentioned earlier on, the items analyzed in this study were used in a German language context, but many lexical items played on are not originally German but English. Discretion should therefore be exercised when drawing conclusions with respect to German phonology.

get to still be recognizable. This limit was originally determined by Hempelmann (2003) to be N=5 phonemes based on English puns, and Guidi (2012:343) confirmed this number for examples from numerous other languages. It remains to be seen, however, if a solely quantitative approach to this issue is sufficient. It might turn out that a more detailed phonetic analysis taking into account not just the number but also the kind of differences will prove more promising.

Studies on the acceptability and, in addition, on the criteria for the "success" of wordplay remain to be carried out as part of determining the pragmatic dimension of wordplay. It would be highly desirable to establish which mechanisms used in the encoding process meet with acceptance[24] on the part of the hearers and which ones fail to evoke the complicity between speaker and hearer which is so crucial to the success of wordplay. This may involve (re)determining a degree of phonetic similarity beyond which a pun is no longer easily decipherable (for an audience to be defined). The whole area of speaker-hearer interaction is clearly an aspect of wordplay which is worthy of future attention.

5 References

Aarons, Debra. 2017. Puns. Taxonomy and phonology. In Salvatore Attardo (ed.), *The Routledge Handbook of Language and Humor*, 80–94. New York: Routledge.

Arndt-Lappe, Sabine & Ingo Plag (2013): The role of prosodic structure in the formation of English blends. English Language and Linguistics 17(3). 537–563.

Attardo, Salvatore. 1994. *Linguistic Theories of Humor* (Humor Research 1). Berlin & New York: De Gruyter.

Attardo, Salvatore & Victor Raskin. 1991. Script theory revis(it)ed: Joke similarity and joke representation model. *Humor. International Journal of Humor Research* 4(3/4). 293–347.

Attardo, Salvatore & Victor Raskin. 2017. Linguistics and Humor Theory. In Salvatore Attardo (ed.). *The Routledge Handbook of Language and Humor*, 49–62. New York: Routledge.

Bauer, Laurie. 2012. Blends: Core and periphery. In Vincent Renner, François Maniez & Pierre J. L. Arnaud (eds.), *Cross-disciplinary perspectives on lexical blending* (Trends in Linguistics. Studies and Monographs 252), 11–22. Berlin & Boston: De Gruyter.

Binsted, Kim & Graeme Ritchie. 1997. Computational rules for generating punning riddles. *Humor. International Journal of Humor Research* 10(1). 25–76.

Dencker, Klaus Peter (ed.). 2002. *Poetische Sprachspiele. Vom Mittelalter bis zur Gegenwart*. Stuttgart: Reclam.

---

[24] "Acceptance" here describes the ability to resolve the riddle, assuming that listeners gain satisfaction from being able to get the pun and are not appreciative of riddles that are impossible to solve.

Fuhrich, Kerstin & Hans-Jörg Schmid. 2016. *Too Matsch for You?* Monolingual humorous slogans are recalled better than mixed-language ones. In Sebastian Knospe, Alexander Onysko & Maik Goth (eds.), *Crossing languages to play with words: Multidisciplinary perspectives* (The Dynamics of Wordplay 3), 135–156. Berlin & Boston: De Gruyter.

Gries, Stefan Th. 2004a. Shouldn't it be *breakfunch*? A quantitative analysis of blend structure in English. *Linguistics* 42(3). 639–667.

Gries, Stefan Th. 2004b. Isn't that *Fantabulous*? How similarity motivates intentional morphological blends in English. In Michel Achard & Suzanne Kemmer (eds.), *Language, culture, and mind* (Conceptual Structure, Discourse, and Language), 415–428. Stanford: CSLI Publications.

Guidi, Annarita. 2012. Are pun mechanisms universal? A comparative analysis across language families. *Humor. International Journal of Humor Research* 25(3). 339–366.

Hall, T. Alan. [2]2011. *Phonologie. Eine Einführung.* Berlin & New York: De Gruyter.

Harsdörffer, Georg Philipp. 1651. *Philosophische und mathematische Erquickstunden.* Nürnberg. [Reprint Frankfurt am Main 1990]. 517.

Hausmann, Franz Josef. 1974. *Studien zu einer Linguistik des Wortspiels: Das Wortspiel im "Canard enchaîné"* (Beihefte zur Zeitschrift für romanische Philologie). Tübingen: Niemeyer.

Heibert, Frank. 1993. *Das Wortspiel als Stilmittel und seine Übersetzung am Beispiel von sieben Übersetzungen des 'Ulysses' von James Joyce* (Kodikas, Code: Supplement 20). Tübingen: Gunter Narr.

Hempelmann, Christian. 2003. *Paronomasic puns: target recoverability toward automatic generation.* PhD Thesis: Purdue University.

Hempelmann, Christian F. 2004. Script opposition and logical mechanism in punning. *Humor. International Journal of Humor Research* 17(4). 381–392.

Hempelmann, Christian F. 2014. Puns. In Salvatore Attardo (ed.), *Encyclopedia of humor studies*, vol. 2, 612–615. Thousand Oaks, CA: Sage.

Hempelmann, Christian F. & Tristan Miller. 2017. Puns. Taxonomy and phonology. In: Salvatore Attardo (ed.), *The Routledge Handbook of Language and Humor*, 95–108. New York: Routledge.

Kelly, Michael H. 1998. To "brunch" or to "brench": Some aspects of blend structure. *Linguistics* 36(3). 579–590.

Kempner, Friederike. 1995. *Gedichte ohne r.* München: Matthes & Seitz.

Knospe, Sebastian. 2015. A cognitive model for bilingual puns. In Angelika Zirker & Esme Winter-Froemel (eds.), *Wordplay and metalinguistic / metadiscursive reflection. Authors, contexts, techniques, and meta-reflection* (The Dynamics of Wordplay 1), 161–193. Berlin & Boston: De Gruyter.

Kubozono, Haruo. 1990. Phonological constraints on blending in English as a case for phonology-morphology interface. *Yearbook of Morphology* 3. 1–20.

Plett, Heinrich F. 1979. *Einführung in die rhetorische Textanalyse.* Hamburg: Buske.

Renner, Vincent. 2015. Lexical blending as wordplay. In Angelika Zirker & Esme Winter-Froemel (eds.), *Wordplay and metalinguistic / metadiscursive reflection. Authors, contexts, techniques, and meta-reflection* (The Dynamics of Wordplay 1), 119–133. Berlin & Boston: De Gruyter.

Ronneberger-Sibold, Elke. 2006. Lexical blends: Functionally tuning the transparency of complex words. *Folia Linguistica* 40(1–2). 155–181.

Schwarz, Christoph. 2002. be, B. In Klaus Peter Dencker (ed.), *Poetische Sprachspiele. Vom Mittelalter bis zur Gegenwart*, 330. Stuttgart: Reclam.
Stefanowitsch, Anatol. 2002. Nice to *miet* you: Bilingual puns and the status of English in Germany. *Intercultural Communication Studies* XI(4). 67–84.
Thaler, Verena. 2016. Varieties of wordplay. In Sebastian Knospe, Alexander Onysko & Maik Goth (eds.), *Crossing languages to play with words: Multidisciplinary perspectives* (The Dynamics of Wordplay 3), 47–62. Berlin & Boston: De Gruyter.
Wagenknecht, Christian Johannes. 1965. *Das Wortspiel bei Karl Kraus*. Göttingen: Vandenhoeck & Ruprecht.
Winter-Froemel, Esme. 2009. Wortspiel. In Gert Ueding (ed.), *Historisches Wörterbuch der Rhetorik*, vol. 9, 1429–1443. Tübingen: Niemeyer.
Winter-Froemel, Esme. 2016. Approaching wordplay. In Sebastian Knospe, Alexander Onysko & Maik Goth (eds.), *Crossing languages to play with words: Multidisciplinary perspectives* (The Dynamics of Wordplay 3), 11–46. Berlin & Boston: De Gruyter.
Wright, Saundra K., Jennifer Hay & Tessa Bent. 2005. Ladies first? Phonology, frequency, and the naming conspiracy. *Linguistics* 43(3). 531–561.

Internet sources

Astor, Willy: Promi WG. https://www.youtube.com/watch?v=osHEsa5OUAc (accessed 08 August 2017)
DUDEN online. www.duden-online.de (accessed 05 September 2017)

Georgette Dal and Fiammetta Namer
Playful nonce-formations in French: Creativity and productivity

Abstract: Nonce-formations, conceived as "[n]ew complex word[s] created by a speaker / writer on the spur of the moment to cover some immediate need" (Bauer 1983: 45), have been a theme in Anglo-Saxon and Germanic studies for several decades now (cf. among others Lipka 1975; Bauer 1983; Hohenhaus 1996; Crystal 2000; Štekauer 2002; Kerremans 2015), but they have received very little investigation in the French domain. Although nowadays all the conditions are met for the capture of observable data with the use of large corpora, French morphologists tend to be suspicious of individual coinages, especially if they are playful and diverge from what they consider established word formation rules. In French studies, despite the emergence of corpus-based studies, context is rarely taken into consideration, and the generative distinction between competence and performance often remains active: nonce-formations are in the scope of performance, (socio-)pragmatics or stylistics; therefore, they are not to be taken into account in morphological studies. However, nonce-formations address some interesting morphological issues: do they have to be taken into account for productivity measures? What about the clear-cut distinction between productivity and creativity? In the vein of Dal and Namer (2016a), this paper focuses on patterns of emergence of playful nonce-formations in French. After a brief definition of nonce-formations (§ 1), we first identify several recurring patterns of emergence of nonce-formations (§ 2). We then use these patterns to build a continuum among playful nonce-formations (§ 3.1). Lastly, issues related to productivity are discussed (§ 3.2).

1 Introduction

Nonce-formations are "[n]ew complex word[s] created by a speaker / writer on the spur of the moment to cover some immediate need" (Bauer 1983: 45). By definition, a nonce-formation is a contextual coinage in a given communication situation, and the speaker / writer does not aim to impose her / his spontaneous coinage on everyone (Bauer 1983: 45; Crystal 2000: 219).

According to Hohenhaus, who has devoted a considerable amount of research to this topic (cf. 1996, 1998, 2005, 2007, 2015), the common feature of all nonce-formations is their newness, not with respect to any institutionalized[1] repertoire such as dictionaries but with respect to the speaker / writer:

> Formation is new in a psycholinguistic sense, i.e. formed actively (by whatever means) by a speaker – as opposed to retrieved ready-made from his / her storage of already existing listemes in the lexicon. (Hohenhaus 2005: 364)

As a result, even if previous studies are not always clear on this point, a well-established word can be regarded as new by the speaker / writer, because he / she has never been exposed to it; put another way, the word does not belong to his / her mental lexicon:

Nonce-formations can be regular according to productive Lexeme Formation Rules henceforth LFR (see Fradin 2003 for a justification for the use of this term instead of that of 'Word Formation Rules') like heroid in the following quotation from Time Magazine, or intentionally deviant with regard to them like *oid-y*:

> It's an oid-y world out there. Tabloids run factoids about humanoids on steroids. In a world gone synthetic, why should movies offer something as organic as a hero? Welcome, then, to the age of the Heroid. (Hohenhaus 2005: 363)

Despite their explicit or implicit rejection from the field of investigation by many morphologists on the grounds that they would be in the scope of performance, (socio-)pragmatics or stylistics, nonce-formations give some interesting indications on the speaker / writer's perception of the morphological system. They also address interesting theoretical issues: are they taken into account for productivity measures? Is there a clear-cut distinction between productivity and creativity? (See also the contribution by Arndt-Lappe, this volume).

In view of the above definition, a major problem with nonce-formations is their detection, because morphologists have no access to the speaker's mental lexicon: as mentioned by Kerremans (2015: 92), appealing to external native-speaker judgment of novelty is not reliable, because such a procedure gives rise to suboptimal results; automatic detection, based on the search for unknown forms such as the *Logoscope* project, which aims to provide means for observation of new words in an enlarged textual context (for a presentation, see Falk, Bernhard, and Gérard 2014; Gérard, Falk, and Bernhard 2014), can be helpful.

---

[1] Among others, see Hohenhaus (2005) for a presentation of the difference between 'lexicalization' and 'institutionalization'.

However, such (semi-)automatic systems are mostly based on filters, and, perhaps more problematically, they fail to catch the use of lexicalized words as nonce-formations by the speaker / writer.

One of the surest ways to detect nonce-formations is to rely upon clues furnished by the speaker / writer him- / herself to his / her own productions or to identify discursive schemas fostering the emergence of such coinages. This is the aim of the present paper. In section 2, recurring patterns of emergence of nonce-formations are identified. In section 3, after a summary, issues of nonce-formations in regard to theoretical morphology are discussed.

2 Patterns of emergence of nonce-formations

In what follows, we make use of examples collected on the Web (or on its avatar frWac[2]) for various morphological studies (cf. Dal and Namer 2010a, 2010b; Lignon and Namer 2010; Koehl 2010, 2012; Namer 2013b; Namer and Villoing 2015; Dal and Namer 2016a). When necessary, these examples are complemented by others.

Indeed, a very large amount of contextualized Web data has been collected since the early 2000s in the context of various research projects in morphology. Initially, this data was gathered by means of Web Search Engine API-based tools. These applications replace human users in performing Web searches. At least two programs using such APIs have been specifically developed to make Web search for word formation automatic: Webaffix (Tanguy and Hathout 2002) was designed to collect data with the Altavista engine, and WaliM (Namer 2013a) was initially used to work first with Yahoo, then with Bing. The user provides both systems with a list of words which have to be checked online, in order to assess his / her underlying intuitions and theoretical hypotheses. For each successful query, the program displays the global word count, and, for each indexed URL, a text sequence containing the searchword. From the results obtained, the morphologist can then construct new word-formation hypotheses and assertions (for a more detailed description, cf. Dal and Namer 2015).

---

[2] The WaCky project is an informal consortium of researchers who constructed four very large freely available language specific corpora from the Web for English, German, French and Italian (Ferraresi 2007; Ferraresi et al. 2008; Baroni, Guevara, and Zamparelli 2009). Each corpus size is approximately 2 billion words. The WaCky approach consists of a BootCat-style crawl using seed URLs. Each corpus has been obtained by limiting crawls to the country domains. Initial seed words come from two distinct sources: the language's basic vocabulary and lexical items from well-established large resources. Each corpus is tagged for part of speech and lemmatized.

In our corpus, several patterns of emergence can be identified. The most obvious pattern is the case when the speaker / writer flags his / her nonce-formation with quotation marks and / or (meta-)discursive comments (section 2.1). A second general case (section 2.2) is the insertion into discursive patterns such as parallels, chiasmas, outbursts and affix swappings.

The examples displayed throughout the article originate from any kind of Web document: forums, blogs, and electronic versions of newspapers or scientific articles. We have not annotated the exact source of our examples, since the original Webpage is often no longer available.

2.1 Quotation marks and / or (meta-)discursive comments[3]

When he / she coins (what he / she considers) a new word, the speaker / writer can use quotation marks as in (1):[4]

(1) a. Ce n'est pas tant par ce qu'on pourrait appeler son "iranianité" que l'œuvre de Narmine Sadeg s'inscrit dans une problématique d'exil.
[It is not so much because of what one might call its "Iranian-ity" that the work of Narmine Sadeg is part of an exile problematic.]
b. Je ne peux m'empêcher de m'inquiéter pour des enseignants, qui se font embarquer, interroger et "juridictionner".
[I cannot help but worry about teachers, who get drawn in, interrogated and "jurisdic tion$_V$".]
c. Ma terre étant loin d'être argileuse, il n'était pas question de creuser une petite mare... Jamais eu de "verdâtrerie" en une saison...!
[My soil being far from clayey, there was no question of digging a small pond... Never had "greenish-ery" in one season...!]

In our corpus, a second recurrent case is the use of (meta-)discursive comments. When he / she uses one of the most frequent formulas *Je sais pas si ça se dit* 'I don't know if it is the right word' (or any variant of it), the speaker / writer announces his / her insecurity with respect to the adequacy of the sequence (cf. Dal and Namer 2012):

---

[3] For metalinguistic comments and lexicographic marks pointing to the speakers' perception of ludic items, see also the contributions by Kremer and Stricker, this volume; Moulin, this volume, and Winter-Froemel, this volume.
[4] The present analysis is based on a written corpus. It would be interesting to work on oral data, and study prosody and para-verbal markers such as spatio-gestural quotation marks.

(2) a. Est-ce que les brévistes (je sais pas si ça se dit) sont obligés de faire des chutes à chacune de leurs brèves?
[Are news headliners (I don't know if that is the right word) obliged to end each of their headlines with a punchline?]
b. Il est visitable (je sais pas si ça se dit).
[It is visitable (I don't know if that is the right word).]
c. Mais son visage est reconnu pour sa juvénilité (je sais pas si ça se dit)!
[But his face is known for its youthfulness (I don't know if that is the right word)!]
d. Alors si tu te plains pour 5 centimes [...], t'as un sérieux problème d'avarisme (chais pas si ça se dit).
[Then, if you complain about 5 cents [...], you have a serious problem of stingy-ism (dunno if that's what you say).]
e. Ah je pense que c'est dans l'écriture qui a été françaisisée (je sais pas si ça se dit).
[Ah, I think that it is through the writing that it has been French-ized (I don't know if you say that).]
f. Il existe des claviers souples, en matière caoutchouteuse (je sais pas si ça se dit ce mot).
[There are soft keyboards, in rubbery (I don't know if you say that, that word) material.]

Sometimes, the speaker / writer uses (meta-)linguistic comments to claim his / her inventiveness and / or to formulate an aesthetic judgement on his / her novelty:

(3) a. Aujourd'hui, incivilités et incourtoisies (ça n'existe pas ce mot, je viens de l'inventer mais ça se pratique, je vous assure!!) sont très usitées.
[Nowadays, incivilities and un-courtesies (that word, it does not exist, I've just invented it, but the practice does, I can assure you!!) are very frequent.]
b. un bouquin qui nous donne en quelque 250 grandes pages une vision élargie et différente de l'univers tolkienien (quel beau néologisme!).
[a book which gives us in some 250 pages an enlarged and different view of the Tolkienian (what a beautiful neologism!) universe.]
c. Peut-être un nouvel élément de réponse sur le rôle du biologique sur notre comportement progénitural (il est pas beau ce néologisme?)
[Perhaps a new element in the answer about the role of biology in our progeny-al (this neologism is nice, isn't?) behaviour.]

The two previous methods, quotation marks and (meta-)linguistic comments, can be associated, as in (4):

(4) a. Il évoque, me semble-t-il, des particules solaires dont il suppose la "supracélérité" (je sais pas si ça se dit).
[It evokes, it seems to me, solar particles, which he assumes have "supracelerity" (I don't know you say that).]
b. Les fils sont bien embrouillés et tous sont potentiellement "suspectables" (quel beau néologisme!).

[The threads are quite tangled and everybody is potentially "suspect-able" (what a nice neologism!).]

c. Machin indigeste et totalement "inimplicatif" (j'ai pas trouvé mieux que ce néologisme moche).
[Both indigestible and absolutely "unimplicative" (I didn't find anything better than this ugly neologism) gizmo.]

In the above examples, lexical innovations, from the point of view of the speaker / writer, may occur only infrequently. For example, *iranianité* 'Iranianity' (1a), *juridictionner* 'jurisdiction$_V$' (1b), *verdâtrerie* 'greenish-ery' (1c) have fewer than ten occurrences on the Web. However, others are well on the way to becoming institutionalized or are already in current use in a given specialized language: for example, *bréviste* 'news headliner' (2a), which occurs about 650 times on the Web, is the usual way of referring to a journalist who writes short news items. Some of them have been fully lexicalized, sometimes for a long time: for example, *visitable* (2b), *juvénilité* 'youthfulness' (2c), *caoutchouteux* 'rubbery' (2f) are long-established French lexemes which appear in dictionaries. However, what matters is the impression of novelty for the speaker / writer.

In this first pattern, nonce-formations mainly involve productive patterns: in our dataset, suffixations in *-able, -al, -eux, -ien, -iser, -iste, -isme, -ité*, prefixations in *dé-, in-*, and conversion from noun to verb are very frequent. The nonce-formation itself is rarely formally problematic: in the previous examples, only *irianianité* and *tolkienien* 'Tolken-ian' do not respect the dissimilatory constraint (Grammont 1895), which prevents two identical or similar (mainly consonantic) phonemes at the stem-affix boundary.[5] We agree here with Štekauer (2002), who claims that, from an inherent word-formation point of view, such nonce-formations are (mainly) regular coinages generated by productive word-formation rules. They are coined by the speaker / writer in order to satisfy a semantic need.

2.2 Insertion into discursive patterns

In our dataset, we identified three recurrent discursive patterns in which nonce-formations appear: parallel and crossed structures (§ 2.2.1), outbursts (§ 2.2.2) and swapping *in praesentia* and *in absentia* (§ 2.2.3).

---

5 On the avoidance of /njanite/–/mjanite/ sequences in French property nouns in -ité based on toponyms, cf. Dal and Namer (2010a).

2.2.1 Parallels and chiasmas

In our corpus, the use of parallel structures (henceforth: parallels) and crossed structures (henceforth: chiasmas) fosters the emergence of nonce-formations, mostly for rhyme purposes.

These two figures are based on the repetition of at least two words or phrases A and B. The repeated form may or may not be identical to the original one. In what follows, A' (resp. B') indicates the repetition of A (resp. B). Parallels correspond to a schema ABA'B', where the A' / B' pair presents the same syntactic structure as A / B (cf. 5); chiasmas correspond to a schema ABB'A' (cf. 6):

(5) Une vie sans avenir est souvent une vie sans souvenir
     A   B   A'   B'
    [A life with no future is often a life without memories]

(6) Il faut manger pour vivre et non pas vivre pour manger
     A   B   B'   A'
    [One must eat to live and not live to eat]

Dubremetz (2013) proposes a classification of parallels and chiasmas, following the literature dedicated to this issue (cf. among others Nordahl 1971; Rabatel 2008). Both are stylistic devices relying on the comparison of the sequences X and X'. They can be strictly identical as in (6), they can rhyme, as *avenir* 'future' and *souvenir* in (5), or be semantically related, but formally unconnected, and share no phonological similarity, as in (7): in the chiasma (7a), X and X' are co-hyponyms (*bouche* 'mouth' and *main* 'hand' refer to body-parts, while *bâillon* 'gag' and *clou* 'nail' can be treated as instruments); in (7b), they are in opposition (*ajoutez* 'add' / *effacez* 'delete'; *quelquefois* 'sometimes' / *souvent* 'often'):

(7) a. Un bâillon pour la bouche et pour la main le clou.
       A   B   B'   A'
     [A gag for the mouth and for the hand the nail.]
   b. Ajoutez quelquefois, et souvent effacez.
       A   B   B'   A'
     [Add sometimes, and often delete.]

Chiasmas and parallels usually combine rhyming properties, semantic relations, formal resemblance and morphological parenthood between X and X', as shown by chiasmas in (8). Rhyme's effect in (8a) is due to both the morphological relation between *entière* 'entire' (B) and *entièrement* 'entirely' (B') and the formal identity of A and A' (A = A' = *part*). In (8b), the figure combines semantic and formal similarities: B and B' (*morts / mortes*) are inflectional variants of the same adjective *mort* 'dead', and A (*désespoirs* 'despair') and A' (*douleurs* 'pain') are (quasi-)synonyms[6]:

(8) a. Les Réunionnais sont des Français à part entière... ils sont entièrement à part.
                  A   B   B'   A'
       [The Réunionese are entirely French citizens ...   they are entirely apart.]
b. Les désespoirs sont morts, et mortes les douleurs.
          A   B   B'   A'
      [Despair   is dead   and dead is pain.]

The function of rhyme creation and semantic relatedness are two defining properties of chiasmas and parallels that derivational morphology makes a large contribution to. Therefore, achieving rhyme patterns is a motivation for speakers to coin nonce-formations. When X and X' belong to the same derivational family, rhyme creation consists of creating Y', where Y' is morphologically related to Y and belongs to the same derivational series of either X or X'. This is what happens with the chiasma in (9). In order to ensure a rhyme with A (*moderniser* 'modernize'), morphologically related to A' (*modernité* 'modernity') the speaker coins *islamiser* 'islam-ize' (B'), which belongs to both the derivational family of *Islam* (B) and the derivational series of A (both B' and A' are verbs derived in *-iser*):

(9) Moderniser l'Islam plutôt qu'islamiser la modernité.
     A   B   B'   A'
    [Modernize Islam rather than Islam-ize modernity.]

Let us add that parallels and chiasmas are important rhetorical devices which strengthen the sense of contrast or similarity in (especially written) speeches. Not surprisingly, a wide range of parallels and chiasmas are found in the vast virtual marketplace of the Internet, where rythming, rhyming, and semantic effects are guaranteed by the creation of a derived word X' morphologically related to the word X and / or semantically connected to the word Y or Y', and thus contribute to the power of conviction of the whole figure (whose terms are X, X', Y and Y').

The following examples have been collected on the Web among Google low-frequency results, within the context of various studies aiming at identifying regular properties of morphologically complex neologisms found in online French written texts. Each study being devoted to a particular derivational pattern, automatic collections of wordforms from the Web were affix-driven (see Namer 2013a for the search methodology applied to extract newly coined words from the web used as a corpus). The aim in Lignon and Namer (2010), for instance, was to

---

6 Examples (5) to (8) are borrowed from Dubremetz (2013).

investigate the reasons for the co-occurrence of long-term stored verbs X (*converser* 'converse$_V$') with Xionner verbal neologisms (*conversationner* 'conversation$_V$'), both related to a Xion noun (*conversation* 'conversation$_N$'). Likewise, Lignon (2013) and Namer (2013b) questioned the formal, semantic and quantitative aspects of the competition between *-iser* and *-ifier* suffixed verbs. The specificity of these search tasks is the reason why the chiasmas and parallels below contain verbal nonce-formations mainly suffixed in *-iser, -ifier* and *-ionner*.

Examples (10–13) are instances of different sorts of parallels and chiasmas according to two parameters: the place of the nonce word in the schema, and the nature of its relation (semantic, formal, derivational) to the three other components.

In (10), nonce-formations correspond to the item B' (10a, c, d) or A (10b) in chiasmas ABB'A'. In (10a, b, c) A / B' form derivational series where both are suffixed with *-iser* (*chienniser / humaniser* 'dog-ize / humanize', *contemporaniser / archéologiser* 'contemporan-ize / archaeologize', *architecturiser / végétaliser* 'architecture-ize / vegetalize'). In (10a, b), the echo effect is total, because both pairs A / A' and B / B' are morphologically related. In (10a), the opposition between the concepts (human / dog) is reinforced by a double syntactic negation. There is no derivational parenthood in (10c) between X and X', but the concepts are synonymous (A: 'perform archaeology' / A': 'past', and B: 'nowadays' / B': 'make contemporary'). Moreover, X and X' are in the 'nowadays vs. formerly' temporal opposition with both Y and Y': A with B and with B', B with A and with A'.

In (10d), the A / B' pair embodies two close concepts: creation (*accomplir* 'achieve') and transformation (*miraculiser* 'transform into a miracle'), counterbalancing the *miracles / faits* 'miracles / facts' semantic opposition in B / A'.

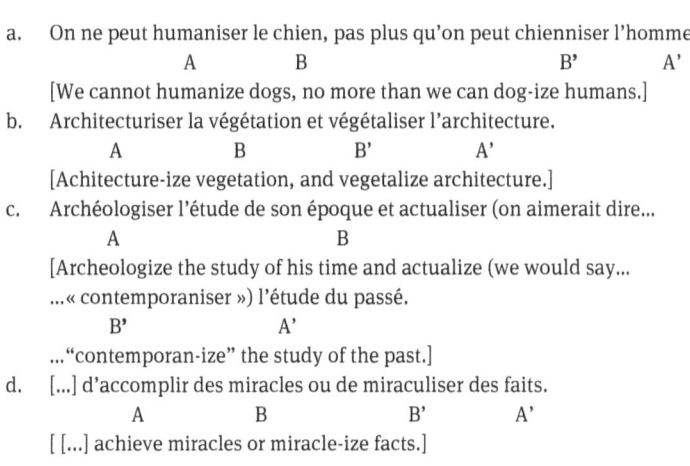

Examples (11) illustrate various realizations of parallels AA'BB'. The variation concerns the position of the nonce word X (it may correspond to any of the items A, A', B, B', or even to two of them), and the kind of relation between X and X' (semantic relation, derivational relatedness, or belonging to the same derivational series).

In (11a) and (11b), the nonce word is in B. In (11a), its connection with the prime A is semantically motivated: *(re)sucrer* 'provide with sugar (again)' is opposed – physiologically – to *insuliniser* 'provide with insulin'. The contrast between A' ('the ones') to B' ('the others') strengthens the opposition. In (10b), the opposition value is enhanced by morphological relations: A and B belong to the same derivational family, the possessive pronouns *mon* 'my' and *le tien* 'yours' are inflectional and syntactic variants of each other.

In (11c), the neologism, in B', is a relational adjective based on the patronym *Valls* (a French center-left politician), corresponding to the adjective A', derived from the patronym of Sarkozy, a French right-wing politician. Both adjectives result from competing adjectivizing suffixes. So, in this chiasma, there is no rhyme. The rhythm in the figure is achieved by the contiguity relation of similarity between A and B (reinforced by the repeated quotation marks, expressing the distance of the writer with respect to the marked words), which, in turn, affects also A' and B', and, consequently, Sarkozy's and Valls' political actions, in the writer's opinion. The parallelism in (11d) is derivationally and semantically grounded: both A and B are action nouns, related respectively to the verbs A' and B', the latter being coined for the occasion. Moreover, both A and B (as well as A' and B') are related notions in the field of economics. Note however that the A / A' vs B / B' likeness is offset by the negation marker in the B / B' structure.

In (11e), the parallelism is supported by the semantic resemblance between speech (represented by A and A') and eating (in B and B'). The newly coined word is A, morphologically related to A'. The similarity with the elements of B / B' is derivational (A' and B' are suffixed with -*able*) and semantic (both A' and B' are negatively marked, the former by morphology, the latter, by syntax).

The A / A' and B / B' organization in (11f) makes this rhyming parallel structure both semantically and derivationally motivated: A' is a verb derived from the noun A, as B' is from B, A' and B' are both suffixed with -*iser*. The original aspect of this example is the fact that both A' and B' are nonce-formations:

(11) a. Resucrer les uns, insuliniser les autres.
         A   A'   B   B'
   [re-sugar the ones, insulin-ize the others.]

b. Et pour exemplifier mon propos, et contre-exemplifier le tien
          A   A'   B   B'
[And to exemplify my remarks, and counter-examplify yours]

c. de « simplification » sarkozyenne en « assouplissement » vallsique
     A   A'   B   B'
[from "simplification" Sarkozy-ianA to "easing" Valls-icA]

d. Le ralentissement on peut le ralentir, la récession on peut pas la récessionner.
     A   A'   B   B'
[Deceleration can be decelerated, recession cannot be recessionned.]

e. [...] vous narrationner l'inénarrable et vous faire digérer le pas mangeable
     A   A'   B   B'
[[...] you narration$_V$ the unnarratable, and to make you digest the uneatable]

f. [...] les équipiers pour équipiériser et le leader pour leaderiser.
     A   A'   B   B'
[[...] the crewmen to crewman-ize, and the leader to leader-ize.]

Parallel structures can be multi-levelled, as shown in the examples below. In (12a), the series of nonce-formations is driven by contiguity relations: all the verbs X' are derived from nouns whose relation with X stems from the same extralinguistic field, that of terrorist attacks. The same is observed with (12b), where the three created verbs A, A' and A'' belong to the area of ethnicity. Moreover, the echo provided to *hispaniser* 'Hispanicize' (A') by its derivational base, expressed by the inflected form *Espagnols* 'Spaniards' (B') gives the structure the cross feature of chiasmas:

(12) a. [...] sariner le métro, avioniser des buildings, grenader des touristes
       A   B   A'   B'   A''   B''
[[...] to sarin the subway, airplane-ize buildings, grenade tourists]

b. Mais l'objectif est bien d'hispaniser les ouvriers français...
                          A   B
[But the aim is that to Hispanicize the French workers...
...comme ont été turkisés les Espagnols...
              A'   B'
...as have been Turkized the Spaniards...
...avant de maroquiniser et d'algérianiser tout ce petit monde.
      A''   A'''   B''
... before Moroccan-ing and Algerian-ing everybody.]

In fact, combinations of parallels and chiasmas are not uncommon. In (13a), A / B / C and B' / A' / C' are parallel structures from a syntactic point of view, and are marked by a dual relation: contiguity (*moyen-orientaliser / libaniser* 'Middle-East-ize / Lebanon-ize') and antonymy (*conflit / paix* 'conflict / peace'). Meanwhile, (13a) is also an ABB'A' chiasma, where the nonce verbs B and A' are derived, respectively, from B' and A.

Likewise, a chiasma (BCC'B') and a parallel figure (ABA'B') overlap in (13b). The parallel structure involves antonymy with AA' (*vieux / jeune* 'old / young'), and register-switching synonymy with B / B' (*graillent* 'munch' / *mangeantes* 'eating'), where B' is the nonce word. The chiasma implies a semantic contrast between *graillent* (B) and *pètent* 'fart' (C'), a derivational connection (C / C': *pétantes / pètent* 'farting$_A$ / fart$_V$') and a rhyme with *pétantes* (C) and *mangeantes* (B'), *pétantes* meaning here 'on the dot':

(13) a. le Liban s'est moyen-orientisé (par le conflit), il aurait été mieux que ...
        A   B   C
[Lebanon has Middle-East-ized itself (through the conflict), it would have been better if...
... le Moyen Orient se libanise (par la paix).
        B'   A'   C'
...the Middle East had Lebanon-ized (through peace).]
b. les vieux graillent à 19h pétantes. Les jeunes pètent à 19h mangeantes.
    A   B   C   A'   C'   B'
[The old munch at farting 7 o'clock [= 7 o'clock on the dot]. The young fart at 7 o'clock eating.]

To sum up, rhetorical figures are suitable triggers for nonce-formations. Moreover, all these creations consist of denominal verbs either converted or suffixed with *-iser* or *-ionner* and adjectives suffixed by *-ien* or *-ant*, which are all productive word-formation patterns. However, we must bear in mind that these results may be methodologically biased due to the principles of data collection. To our knowledge (also according to Dubremetz 2013), there is no way to automatically extract chiasmas and parallels from very large corpora, which would be the right method in order to allow a meaningful statistical assessment of the preferred word-formation rules used to coin new words for this stylistic purpose.

2.2.2 Outbursts

Tanguy (2012: 104) defines suffixal outbursts as sequences containing a series of suffixed terms. However, the notion can be extended to any series containing prefixed and compound lexemes, as well as lexemes formed by a process of what Jespersen (1928) called "secretion" (see also Fradin 2000). The detection threshold is here established at three.

Outbursts facilitate the emergence of nonce-formations. In our corpus, they often involve deverbal nouns. Other morphological types may nonetheless be involved. When they contain nonce-formations, outbursts often begin with one or more well-established complex lexemes, which serve as baits or primers and with which the nonce formations rhyme, as in (14) where *discussion* in (14a), *matheuse* 'maths brain$_{FEM}$' in (14b), *papotage* 'chattering' and *copinage* 'boy- / girlfriending' in (14c), *elegance* 'elegance' and *prestance* 'poise' in (14d) are (very) common French nouns. *Workaholic* in (14e) is perhaps less frequent in French (approximately 250 occurrences are found on the French Web), but writers consider it common. Sometimes, the first term of the outburst is a nonce-formation: in (15a), only *coloriser* 'colorize' belongs to the French institutionalized lexicon (in fact, it belongs to movie terminology, which increases the comic effect produced by the series). More rarely in our dataset, the outburst consists exclusively of nonce-formations, as in (16) where the baits do not belong to the same morphological series as the nonce-formations, but to their morphological family:[7]

(14) a. Je vaque aux petites occupations du matin: *discussion* avec Filip, **douchation, maquillation, habillation, coiffation**.
[I go about my everyday activities: discussion with Philip, shower-ation, makeup-ation, dress-ation, hair-style-ation.]
b. Scientifique, littéraire et manuelle à la fois! *Matheuse*, **physiqueuse, informateuse**, écrit des (mauvais) poèmes, **philosopheuse** et **perleuse**.
[A scientist, a woman of letters and good with her hands all at once! Maths brain$_{FEM}$, physics-er$_{FEM}$, computer science-er$_{FEM}$, writer of (bad) poems, philosophy-er$_{FEM}$ and pearl-erFEM.]
c. *Papotage, copinage*, **discutage, mangeage**...et **reposage**.
[Chatting, cronyism, discuss-age, eat-age...and rest-age.]
d. Niveau *élégance, prestance*, **classance** et **distinctance**, je reste sur mes positions.
[In terms of elegance, poise, class-ancy and distinct-ancy, I maintain my stance.]
e. Le "*workaholic*" est bien connu et l'on voit partout ses ravages! Et les **footingholics** et les **pétanqueholics**.
[The "workaholic" is well known, and his / her ravages can be seen everywhere! And jog-aholics and boules-aholics.]

(15) a. Il faut **déboucletiser**, *coloriser* et **blanchitiser** et **batailliser** attention pas décoifferiser.
[It is necessary to de-curl-ize, colorize and whiten-ize and battle-ize, caution: do not de-hairstyle-ize.]
b. Montée au col de la Temple (2h00 du refuge)...**Bouffade**, *balade* (encore!) et pas de **gerbade**.
[Climbed to the La Temple pass (2h from the hut)...Pig-out-ade, walk (again!) and no puke-ade.]

---

7 In examples (14) to (28), primers are given in italics and nonce formations in boldface.

(16) « Autour d'une *confiance*, d'une *ambition* et d'un *espoir* partagés »...C'est beau. Du coup, je me sens tellement **confianceuse, ambitionneuse** et **espoireuse**.
["Around a common trust, ambition and hope"...how beautiful. As a result, I feel so trusty, ambition-y and hope-y.]

Outbursts consist more frequently of lexemes belonging to a unique morphological series as in the previous examples. However, they may also consist of lexemes formed by concurrent patterns, such as suffixation in *-iser* and conversion in (17a), or suffixation in *-iser* and conversion again, and suffixation in *-ifier* in (17b):

(17) a. Quelques-uns d'entre vous se sont manifestés pour *chanter*, **guitarer, accordéoniser, batterir, flûter.**
[Some of you came forward to sing, guitar$_V$, accordion-ize, drum$_V$, flute$_V$.]
b. Bref, continuez de sciencier, scienciser, scientifiser!
[In short, continue to science$_V$, scienc-ize, scientif-ize!]

Unlike the above quotation marks or (meta-)discursive comments where the speaker / writer notifies that he / she does not know if the sequence is used or belongs to any institutionalized lexicon, outbursts form a rhetorical perspective of obstinate repetition (which recall parallelisms). Moreover, this playful use satisfies the requirements of rhyme. As already stated in Winter-Froemel (2016), who developed the concept of "ludic deformation", where unexpectedness and deviation as a source of verbal humour are concerned, we see that comic effects are enhanced when the nonce-formation replaces a frequent lexeme which obviously belongs to his / her mental lexicon (see also the contributions by Braun, this volume; Moulin, this volume; Winter-Froemel, this volume). Compare (14a) repeated under (18a), and (18b), where each nonce-formation is replaced by its corresponding lexicalized lexeme. The more frequent the lexicalized lexeme, the greater the comic effect:

(18) a. Je vaque aux petites occupations du matin: discussion avec Filip, **douchation, maquillation, habillation, coiffation.**
b. Je vaque aux petites occupations du matin: discussion avec Filip, *douche, maquillage, habillage, coiffage.*

LFRs involved in outbursts can be highly productive, such as suffixation in *-age* in (14c) or *-iser* in (15a), and nonce-formations can be perfectly well-formed. Constraints, however, can sometimes be violated. Such is the case with French suffixation in *-ion*, which is productive only with bases in *-iser* or *-ifier* (cf. Dal et al. 2008): in such cases, what matters is the compliance with the pattern of the bait, more than its availability.

2.2.3 Affix swapping in praesentia and in absentia

A final recurring pattern in our corpus of playful nonce-formations consists in exchanging suffixes between two or more well-established complex lexemes. Examples below (19)–(28) show that this playful mechanism is reminiscent of chiasmas and parallelisms. And as with outbursts, moreover, lists play an important role.

Permutation is performed more frequently *in praesentia*, and the two lexemes involve concurrent LFR. For example, in (19), the two expected property nouns *finesse* 'finesse' and *légéreté* 'lightness' exchange their suffixes:

(19) Ces filles qui apporteraient **fineté**, **subtilesse**, douceur et poésie.
 [These girls who would bring fine-ity, subtle-ness, gentleness and poetry.]

Exchanges can also be done *in absentia*, as in (20) where another property noun *bêtesse* (vs. lexicalized *bêtise*[8]) results from the permutation of the expected suffix *-ise* with *-esse*:

(20) Mdr, je suis d'une **bêtesse**...
 [Lol, I am of such an idiot-ness...]

Exchanges *in praesentia* and *in absentia* can coexist. For example in (21), *-ion*, present in the expected noun *expansion*, is replaced by *-itude* in the first nonce-formation, but present in the second one, instead of the expected *-isme*:

(21) L'**expansitude** contraste beaucoup avec l'**amateuration** de la première.
 [Expans-itude contrasts a lot with the former's amateur-ation.]

Such a domino permutation can also be observed in (22) (French lexicalized lexemes corresponding to nonce-formations in bold are: *démocratie* 'democracy', *syndicalisme* 'unionism', *corporation* 'corporation' and *copinage* 'cronyism'):

(22) Mélange de **démocrature** et de **syndicalerie**, de **corporatage** et de **copinerie**.
 [Mix of democrat-ure and union-ery, corporat-age and crony-ery.]

---

[8] *Bêtise* is a well-established noun in the French lexicon, both diachronically (its first attestation dates back to the 15th century) and in contemporary use (there are 2 million occurrences on the Web).

Of course, *démocrature* could also be analysed as a blend of *democraty* and *dictature*. But it is more likely for each nonce-formation in this series to follow the same model, that is suffix exchange.

Our dataset also contains some cases where permutation does not involve the exponent, but the stem, for example *ambitionneuse* (vs. the expected *ambitieuse* 'ambitious$_{FEM}$') in (23):

(23) Plus **ambitionneuse**, comme le titre le laisse entendre.
[More ambition-ous$_{FEM}$, as suggested by the title.]

The speaker / writer can also substitute the lexicalized form with a synonymous nonce-formation, and graft the LFR involved in the first nonce-formation onto the base of the second one, which, in turn, gives rise to another nonce-formation. In (24), *interruptionner* is used instead of *interrompre* 'interrupt$_V$' (cf. Lignon and Namer 2010), and *travaillationnage*, which implies *travaillationner*, replaces the usual noun *travail* 'work'). Several clues allow us to argue in favor of deliberate speaker switchings, and not simple acquisition or performance errors. One is the fact that substitutions involve high-frequency words – which, in all likelihood, belong to everyone's mental lexicon (on this topic, see below § 3.1). The fact that two deviant forms are combined, as e.g. in (22) or (24), is also a strong indication of an intentional use:

(24) Désolé de vous interruptionner pendant votre travaillationnage.
[Sorry to interruption$_V$ you during your work-ionage.]

Previous substitutions can of course be combined with each other or with other patterns. For example, (25) cumulates suffixal and radical permutations in *impressionneuse* (vs. the expected *imprimante* 'printer$_N$') while *reconfigurationner* replaces the lexicalized French verb *reconfigurer*:

(25) C'est un gros problème de reconfigurationner l'impressionneuse.
[This is a big problem, reconfiguration$_V$ the print-ationer.]

As above in outbursts, the aim of the speaker / writer is not to impose his / her nonce-formations on anyone. On the contrary: the dissemination of these nonce-formations in general use would lead to the annihilation of any comic effect. The loss of this special pragmatic effect of deviant forms if items are diffused in the speech community does not occur only with nonce-formations: see for instance Onysko and Winter-Froemel (2011), which discusses a fundamentally different group of marked items: 'unnecessary' borrowed items.

As we showed previously in (18), this effect can be evaluated by replacing the nonce-formations with the corresponding lexicalized lexeme. For example, comparing (a) and (b) in (26) to (28):

(26) a. L'**expansitude** contraste beaucoup avec l'**amateuration** de la première.
b. L'*expansion* contraste beaucoup avec l'*amateurisme* de la première.
[Expansion constrasts a lot with the former's amateurism.]

(27) a. Désolé de vous **interruptionner** pendant votre **travaillationnage**.
b. Désolé de vous *interrompre* pendant votre *travail*.
[Sorry to interrupt you while you are working.]

(28) a. C'est un gros problème de **reconfigurationner** l'**impressionneuse**.
b. C'est un gros problème de *reconfigurer* l'*imprimante*.
[This is a big problem, reconfiguring the printer.]

3 Discussion

3.1 A continuum in playful nonce-formations

Summarizing the above results, we obtain a continuum in types of playful nonce-formations identified by the use of clues, from the speaker / writer's perspective:
– At one extreme, we find cases where the speaker / writer bridges a lexical gap (or what he / she considers to be one in regard to his / her mental lexicon). In our dataset, this is the main function of nonce-formations labelled as such by means of quotation marks or discursive (meta-)comments. The aim of the speaker / writer is less to coin a playful word than to coin a word *tout court*. Most of the time, he / she uses an available process with a high productivity index (Baayen 1992), such as suffixations in *-age*, *-ité*, *-iser*, etc. (cf. Dal et al. 2008); the nonce-formation is semantically and formally transparent and satisfies most if not all linguistic constraints. As a consequence, the reader / hearer does not need context to understand it (for a similar conclusion, see Renouf and Bauer 2000). The nonce-formation, from the speaker / writer's point of view, can be either a really new word or a well-established lexical unit. However, what is important here is not the frequency of use, but the perception of novelty by the writer / speaker. Paradoxically, by using quotations marks or comments, his / her aim is not to draw the attention of the reader / hearer to his / her coinage, but rather to prevent any suspicion of using an inappropriate word. The particular relevance of this attitude for French relies on the fact that normativity has weighed heavily on the lexicon

content and its evolution since the creation of the Académie Française in 1635.
- At the other extreme of the continuum are affixal swaps *in prasentia* and *in absentia*, and radical substitutions. In this case, the nonce-formation is coined for a playful purpose. In affix swappings, the game consists in the distortion of the form of a well-established complex lexeme, more precisely the replacement of its suffix with a different one in order to surprise the reader / hearer and to force him / her to analyse the complex word. Following recent results in experiments on word comprehension (Baayen et al. 2017), one can assume that, above in (20) "Je suis d'une bêtesse", the intended meaning of the expected, well-established French property noun word *bêtise*, first becomes available to the speaker / writer as a whole, whereas parts of the word are sensed, but only later. That is, the reader will also see a large part of *bête* (and the listener will hear /bɛt/ before the /iz/ comes in). In other words, *bêtise* is probably not composing the meaning of "stupid act" from the meaning of *bête* 'beast' and *-ise* suffixation, but the hearer / reader cannot help co-perceiving this meaning. This openness to parts, even in high-frequency opaque words, is well-captured by the Discriminative Perspective approach described in Baayen et al. (2017). According to the authors, this approach highlights the many layers of meaning that come with complex words that explain how language mechanisms work to produce poetry and playfulness.[9] This is what explains that, in (20), the speaker / writer has access to the parts of the word *bêtise*, which enables the exponent *-ise* to be replaced with the yet unproductive property noun suffix *-esse*.[10]
- Chiasmas, parallel structures and outbursts are situated between the two poles of the continuum. In these cases, the aim of the speaker / writer is not to satisfy a denominative need, but to insert his / her coinage in a series, often (though not always) with comic effect. For example, by using *maquillation*, instead of the very common noun *maquillage* 'makeup', he / she aims at such a playful effect, but in cases such as *mangeage* 'eat-age' in (14c), he / she can also bridge what can be considered a lexical gap: the French lexicon has no process noun built on *manger* 'eat', and *mangeage* is often used in order to

---

[9] We thank the anonymous reviewer for bringing these new developments in psycholinguistics to our knowledge, and leading us to discover the concept of discriminative perspective, a very promising device for the understanding of language playfulness.
[10] Koehl (2012) shows that French suffixations in *-ise* and *-esse* are no longer productive in French except, for the former, with bases ending in *-ard* and, less frequently, in *-ant*.

bridge this gap.[11] Chiasmas, parallel structures and outbursts mostly resort to productive rules (such as suffixation in *-age*), but also to unproductive ones (such as suffixation in *-ion*, only available in contemporary French with bases in *-iser* and *-ifier*).

3.2 Nonce-formations and productivity

Nonce-formations, and among them especially playful coinages, have been the object of only little investigation by French morphologists. Despite the emergence of corpus-based studies in French in the past decade, co(n)text is rarely taken into consideration, and the generative distinction between competence and performance often remains active: nonce-formations are considered as being in the scope of performance, (socio-)pragmatics or stylistics, or as satisfying creative purposes. Therefore, they are not to be taken into account in morphological studies, which concentrate on collective and not on individual productions. However, nonce-formations address some interesting morphological issues, all in relation to productivity.

Since Schultink's (1961) seminal work, morphological productivity has been understood as the possibility for language users to unintentionally coin an in principle uncountable number of new morphologically complex words. Determining which processes are productive and which are not is thus a key issue in morphological research: "Morphological theory should account only for processes of word formation which are productive" (Baayen and Lieber 1991: 801–802).

Schultink's (1961) definition has been commented upon (cf., inter alia, Plag 1999; Evert and Lüdeling 2001; Dal 2003; Gaeta and Ricca 2003; Gaeta and Ricca 2015; Dal and Namer 2016b). The main points of criticism deal with unintentionality, newness and uncountability. We focus here on unintentionality and newness.

Eliminating intentional formations from observation means that the deliberate use of a given morphological process or pattern to coin new terms in a given domain says nothing about its availability. The same is true for nonce-formations studied in the present paper: in all cases, the speaker / writer is aware of his / her

---

11 On the Web, *mangeage* is often used with meta-discursive comments, even in outbursts. For example: « Je te dis un grand merci (...) pour ce très bel après midi de grande rigolade, papotage, mangeage (je sais pas si ça se dit ça hihihihi) » [Many thanks to you (...) for the wonderful afternoon with lots of laughter, small talk, eat-age (I don't know if you can say that hahahaha)].

coinage. So, if we apply Schultink's (1961) definition strictly, nonce-formations are not to be taken into account, even when they involve productive rules. In fact, as seen above in section 3.1 and as also mentioned by Štekauer (2002: 97), nonce-formations often involve productive rules:

> It is argued that from the inherent word-formation point of view nonce-formations are regular coinages generated by productive word-formation rules, and as such they are listed in the Lexicon as any other naming units.

More generally, if strictly applied, this criterion would amount to considering that, whenever speakers voluntarily coin a specific complex word appropriate in a given utterance context or in order to meet nomenclatural purposes, this new word could not illustrate the productivity of the morphological process it results from. Yet, on the contrary, intentionality says something about the speaker / writer's consciousness of the morphological system.

As regards the criterion of newness, the question arises as to what precisely should be considered a new formation: what is the reference of newness? If the reference is dictionaries or any institutionalized vocabulary, then we adopt a social perspective (that is, the lexicon as a sum of knowledge of an ideal speaker about what is or is not conventional); if the reference is the mental lexicon of users, then the perspective is more individual. For example, in our dataset, the use of quotation marks or (meta-)linguistic comments shows that, for the speaker / writer, even a well-established complex word such as *caoutchouteux* 'rubbery' in (2f) is a new formation, and that he / she productively uses suffixation in *-eux* in order to bridge what he / she considers a lexical gap. In such cases, the presence or absence of the complex word in any dictionary is irrelevant. We consider here that it is better for newness to be taken into account from the speaker / writer point of view than from any social perspective.

In quantitative approaches, in order to address the issue of productivity and to eliminate recourse to intuitive judgements, the major work is that of Baayen (1992) and the research initiated by its results. Apart from what he calls "realized productivity", which evaluates the presumable success of a morphological process or pattern in the past independently of its actual use, statistical measures of productivity are based on rare events. In productivity measures according to Baayen (1992), hapax legonema play an essential role. Expanding productivity P* (also referred to as the hapax-conditioned degree of productivity) and potential productivity P are ratios calculated in a text corpus C. They take as a dividend the number n_1 of hapax legomena (words formed by a given morphological process or pattern with a frequency 1 in C). The question here is whether nonce-formations, from the speaker / writer's perspective, have to be taken into account in statistical measures. In practice, it is impossible. If, in a given corpus C, the speaker / writer coins *caoutchouteux*, one can suppose that his / her coinage does not correspond to any hapax legomena in C. However, for him / her, this complex word *is* a hapax. In other words, productivity measures are well suited for the estimation of productivity from a social or collective point of view, but they provide no indication as to individual productivity. The problem is that nothing enables us to predict whether the sum of all productive uses of morphological processes or patterns by individual speakers / writers will actually correspond to the productivity of these processes / patterns for the entire language community as well or even in a given corpus.

A last issue in relation to nonce-formations is the difference between productivity and creativity. This distinction is connected with the disputed opposition between intentionality and unintentionality in word-formation (among proponents of such a distinction, see Lyons 1977; van Marle 1985; Bauer 2001; Štekauer 2005, 2009; Fernández-Domínguez 2010; Ronneberger-Sibold 2015). The term *creativity* is reserved for the case in which the (nonce) coined word obviously transgresses the morphological system, such as in poetry or playful creations. However, we have seen that even playful coinages, particularly in outbursts, use mainly productive processes.

4 Conclusion

Nonce-formations as individual productions are clearly within the scope of performance, (socio-)pragmatics or stylistics studies. Yet there is no reason to exclude them from morphogical studies. On the contrary: even when they are inserted in playful schemata such as affixal or root substitutions, chiasmas, parallel structures or outbursts, they demonstrate that the speaker / writer is aware of the morphological system: perhaps paradoxically, the more playful the nonce-formations, the greater his / her awareness.

The series of findings emerging from our analysis of the examples presented in this paper, and discussed in § 3 lead us to draw two conclusions:

- Firstly, nonce-formation defines a micro-system within the overall morphological system: it has its own grammar, is driven by particular needs, and results in a particular set of wordforms, part of which is included in the general language lexical network, the rest of which is more or less specific to playful purposes. This grammar can be construed according to two aspects: that of the triggering speech and syntactic structures, in which nonce-formations are preferably found, and that of the choice of word-formation rules selected by speakers / writers, and the way these processes are used. As far as specific structures are concerned, we have seen that they are insensitive to the classical descriptive and prescriptive principles: we have identified some of the patterns fostering their emergence (outbursts, chiasmas, parallels, suffix or stem swapping), and we have seen how speakers / writers can draw attention to their coinage.

- Secondly – and in a sense, this is a consequence of the first conclusion –, analysing nonce-formations requires a complete methodological reversal. It is clear that (1) expressing a meaningful message is not necessarily the speaker / writer's priority or, for that matter, his / her concern; (2) the well-formedness morpho-phonological constraints operating elsewhere are not relevant; and (3) it is less a matter of characterizing the formation patterns at the origin of the nonce-formations than of describing the forms themselves (even if we have noticed that the means used to coin these words are predominantly productive morphological processes). Quantitative issues are not the point either: as we have shown, nonce-formations exist only because their authors are convinced that they have invented these words, even those with a very frequent use. By contrast, our analysis was based on the identification and the use of tools fundamental to nonce-formation, but rarely summoned in morphology studies in general: (meta)discursive marking, recurring schemata, sequence inversions and syntactic patterns specific to certain stylistic devices.

By the use of nonce-formations, the speaker presents him- / herself as taking control of his / her language, even if sometimes in a paradoxical way: this is especially true when he / she feels the need to complete his / her production with a (meta)linguistic comment, inasmuch as the comment confirms his / her control of his / her language, while it also exempts him / her with respect to any external review ("I do not know if that's what you say"). However, he / she can accept to the fullest his / her inventions, without feeling the need to apologize to anyone, as does the author of the following statement, found online in December 2015 (https://alabergerie.wordpress.com/2012/02/20/deux-amis, accessed 12 September 2017):

> [C]'est tout de même plus intéressant qu'une lepénerie ou une sarkouillonnade même bien musquée aussi n'hésitons pas [...]
> [This is much more interesting than a Le Pen-crap-ery or a Sarko-moron-ery, even a strong-smelling one, so let us not be hesitant.]

5 References

Baayen, Harald. 1992. Quantitative Aspects of Morphological Productivity. *Yearbook of Morphology* 1991. 109–149.

Baayen, Harald & Rochelle Lieber. 1991. Productivity and English derivation: A corpus-based study. *Linguistics* 29(5). 801–843.

Baayen, Harald, Tino Sering, Cyrus Shaoul & Petar Milin. 2017. Language comprehension as a multiple label classification problem. In: Marco Grzegorczyk & Giacomo Ceoldo (eds.), *Proceedings of the 32nd International Workshop on Statistical Modelling (IWSM)*, 21–31. Groningen: Johann Bernoulli Institute, Rijksuniversiteit Groningen.

Baroni, Marco, Emiliano Guevara & Roberto Zamparelli. 2009. The dual nature of deverbal nominal constructions: Evidence from acceptability ratings and corpus analysis. *Corpus Linguistics and Linguistic Theory* 5(1). 27–60.

Bauer, Laurie. 1983. *English word-formation*. Cambridge: Cambridge University Press.

Bauer, Laurie. 2001. *Morphological productivity*. Cambridge: Cambridge University Press.

Crystal, David 2000. Investigating nonceness: Lexical innovation and lexicographic coverage. In Robert Boenig & Kathleen Davis (eds.), *Manuscript, narrative and lexicon: Essays on literary and cultural transmission in honor of Whitney F Bolton*, 218–231. Lewisburg: Bucknell University Press.

Dal, Georgette. 2003. Productivité morphologique: Définitions et notions connexes. *Langue Française* 140. 3–23.

Dal, Georgette, Bernard Fradin, Natalia Grabar, Fiammetta Namer, Stéphanie Lignon & Pierre Zweigenbaum. 2008. Quelques préalables au calcul de la productivité des règles constructionnelles et premiers résultats. In Jacques Durand, Benoît Habert & Bernard Laks (eds.), *Actes en ligne du 1er Congrès Mondial de Linguistique Française, Paris, 9–12 juillet 2008*, 1587–1599. Paris: Institut de Linguistique Française. https://www.linguistiquefrancaise.org/articles/cmlf/pdf/2008/01/cmlf08184.pdf (accessed 07 June 2017).

Dal, Georgette & Fiammetta Namer. 2010a. French property nouns toponymes or ethnic adjective: A case of base variation. In Franz Rainer, Wolfgang U. Dressler, Dieter Kastovsky & Hans Christian Luschützky (eds.), *Variation and change in morphology. Selected papers from the 13th International Morphology Meeting, Vienna February 2008*, 53–73. Amsterdam & Philadelphia: John Benjamins.

Dal, Georgette & Fiammetta Namer. 2010b. Les noms en *-ance* / *-ence* du français: Quel(s) patron(s) constructionnel(s). In Frank Neveu, Valelia Muni Toke, Thomas Klinger, Jacques Durand, Lorenza Mondada & Sophie Prévost (eds.), *Actes en ligne du 2ème Congrès Mondial de Linguistique Française, La Nouvelle Orléans, 12–15 juillet 2010*, 893–907. Paris: Institut de Linguistique Française. https://www.linguistiquefrancaise.org/articles/cmlf/pdf/2010/01/ cmlf2010_000154.pdf (accessed 07 June 2017).

Dal, Georgette & Fiammetta Namer. 2012. Faut-il brûler les dictionnaires? Où comment les ressources numériques ont révolutionné les recherches en morphologie. In Frank Neveu, Valelia Muni Toke, Peter Blumenthal, Thomas Klingler, Pierluigi Ligas, Sophie Prévost & Sandra Teston-Bonnard (eds.), *Actes en ligne du 3e Congrès Mondial de Linguistique Française, Lyon, 4–7 juillet 2012*, 1261–1276. https://www.shs-conferences.org/articles/ shsconf/ pdf/2012/01/shsconf_cmlf12_000217.pdf (accessed 07 June 2017).

Dal, Georgette & Fiammetta Namer. 2015. Internet. In: Peter O. Müller, Ingeborg Ohnheiser, Susan Olsen & Franz Rainer (eds), *Word-formation. An international handbook of the languages of Europe* (Handbooks of Linguistics and Communication Science 40.3), 2372–2386. Berlin & New York: De Gruyter.

Dal, Georgette & Fiammetta Namer. 2016a. À propos des occasionnalismes. In Frank Neveu, Gabriel Bergounioux, Marie-Hélène Côté, Jean-Michel Fournier, Linda Hriba & Sophie Prévost (eds.), *Actes en ligne du 5ᵉ Congrès Mondial de Linguistique Française, Tours, 4–8 juillet 2016*. https://www.shs-conferences.org/articles/shsconf/pdf/2016/05/shsconf_cmlf2016_08002.pdf (accessed 07 June 2017).

Dal, Georgette & Fiammetta Namer. 2016b. Productivity. In Andrew Hippisley & Gregory T. Stump (eds.), *The Cambridge handbook of morphology* (Cambridge Handbooks in Language and Linguistics), 70–90. Cambridge: Cambridge University Press.

Dubremetz, Marie 2013. Vers une identification automatique du chiasme de mots. In Emmanuel Morin & Yannick Estève (eds.), *Actes de la 15ᵉ Rencontres des Étudiants Chercheurs en Informatique pour le Traitement Automatique des Langues (RECITAL'2013), Sables d'Olonne (France)*, 150–163. New York: Curran Associates.

Evert, Stefan & Anke Lüdeling. 2001. Measuring morphological productivity: Is automatic preprocessing sufficient? In Paul Rayson, Andrew Wilson, Tony McEnery, Andrew Hardie & Shereen Khoja (eds.), *Proceedings of the Corpus Linguistics 2001 Conference*, 167–175. Lancaster University: UCREL Technical Papers.

Falk, Ingrid, Delphine Bernhard & Christophe Gérard. 2014. From non word to new word: Automatically identifying neologisms in French newspapers. *Proceedings of the 9th edition of the Language Resources and Evaluation Conference, May 2014, Reykjavik, Iceland*, 4337–4344. http://www.lrec-conf.org/proceedings/lrec2014/pdf/288_Paper.pdf (accessed 07 June 2017).

Fernández-Domínguez, Jesús. 2010. Productivity vs. lexicalisation: Frequency-based hypotheses on word-formation. *Poznań Studies in Contemporary Linguistics* 46(2). 193–219.

Ferraresi, Adriano. 2007. *Building a very large corpus of English obtained by Web crawling: ukWaC*. Bologna: University of Bologna MA Thesis.

Ferraresi, Adriano, Eros Zanchetta, Marco Baroni & Silvia Bernardini. 2008. Introducing and evaluating ukWaC, a very large Web-derived corpus of English. In Stefan Evert, Adam Kilgarriff & Serge Sharoff (eds.), *Proceedings of the 4th Web as Corpus Workshop (WAC-4) – Can we beat Google? Marrakech, 1 June 2008*. 47–54. http://www.lrec-conf.org/proceedings/lrec2008/index.html (accessed 07 June 2017).

Fradin, Bernard 2000. Combining forms, blends and related phenomena. In Ursula Doleschal & Anna M. Thornton (eds.), *Extragrammatical and marginal morphology* (LINCOM Studies in Theoretical Linguistics 12), 11–59. München: Lincom Europa.

Fradin, Bernard. 2003. *Nouvelles approches en morphologie* (Linguistique nouvelle). Paris: PUF.

Gaeta, Livio & Davide Ricca. 2003. Italian prefixes and productivity: A quantitative approach. *Acta Linguistica Hungarica* 50. 89–108.

Gaeta, Livio & Davide Ricca. 2015. Productivity. In Peter O. Müller, Ingeborg Ohnheiser, Susan Olsen & Franz Rainer (eds.), *Word-formation. An international handbook of the languages of Europe* (Handbooks of Linguistics and Communication Science 40.2), 842–858. Berlin & New York: De Gruyter.

Gérard, Christophe, Ingrid Falk & Delphine Bernhard. 2014. Traitement automatisé de la néologie: Pourquoi et comment intégrer l'analyse thématique? In Frank Neveu, Peter Blumenthal, Linda Hriba, Annette Gerstenberg, Judith Meinschaefer & Sophie Prévost (eds.), *Actes en ligne du 4ᵉ Congrès Mondial de Linguistique Française, Berlin, Allemagne, 19–23 juillet 2014*. 2627–2646. https://www.shs-conferences.org/articles/shsconf/pdf/2014/05/shsconf_cmlf14_01208.pdf (accessed 07 June 2017).

Grammont, Maurice. 1895. *La dissimilation consonantique dans les langues indo-européennes et dans les langues romanes*. Dijon: Imprimerie Darantière.

Hohenhaus, Peter 1996. *Ad-hoc Wortbildung – Terminologie, Typologie und Theorie kreativer Wortbildung im Englischen*. Frankfurt / M. u.a.: Peter Lang.

Hohenhaus, Peter. 1998. Non-lexicability as a characteristic feature of nonce-word-formation in English and German. *Lexicology* 4(2). 237–280.

Hohenhaus, Peter. 2005. Lexicalization and institutionalization. In Pavol Štekauer and Rochelle Lieber (eds.), *Handbook of word-formation* (Studies in Natural Language and Linguistic Theory 64), 353–373. Dordrecht: Springer.

Hohenhaus, Peter. 2007. How to do (even more) things with nonce words (other than naming). In Judith Munat (ed.), *Lexical creativity, texts and contexts* (Studies in Functional and Structural Linguistics 58), 15–38. Amsterdam & Philadelphia: John Benjamins.

Hohenhaus, Peter. 2015. Anti-naming through non word-formation. *Skase Journal of Theoretical Linguistics* 12(3). 272–291.

Jespersen, Otto. 1928. *An international language*. London: Allen & Unwin.

Kerremans, Daphné. 2015. *A web of new words. A corpus-based study of the conventionalization process of English neologisms* (English Corpus Linguistics 15). Frankfurt / M.: Peter Lang.

Koehl, Aurore. 2010. Nominalisation en *-erie* à partir d'adjectifs en français et construction du sens: De l'occurrence à la propriété. Paper presented at the international morphology meeting *Les Décembrettes 7*, Toulouse, 2–3 December 2010.

Koehl, Aurore. 2012. *La construction morphologique des noms désadjectivaux suffixés en français*. Nancy: Université de Lorraine dissertation.

Lignon, Stéphanie. 2013. *-iser* and *-ifier* suffixation in French: Verify data to verize hypotheses? In Nabil Hathout, Fabio Montermini & Jessie Tseng (eds.), *Selected Proceedings of the 7th Décembrettes: Morphology in Toulouse* (LINCOM Studies in Theoretical Linguistics 51), 109–132. München: Lincom Europa.

Lignon, Stéphanie & Fiammetta Namer. 2010. Comment conversionner les V-ion? ou: La construction de Vionner_VERBE par conversion. In Frank Neveu, Valelia Muni Toke, Thomas Klinger, Jacques Durand, Lorenza Mondada & Sophie Prévost (eds.), *Actes en ligne du 2ᵉᵐᵉ Congrès Mondial de Linguistique Française, La Nouvelle Orléans, 12–15 juillet 2010*. 1009–1028. https://www.linguistiquefrancaise.org/articles/cmlf/pdf/2010/01/cmlf2010_000095.pdf (accessed 07 June 2017).

Lipka, Leonhard. 1975. Re-discovery procedures and the lexicon. *Lingua* 37. 197–224.

Lyons, John. 1977. *Semantics*. Cambridge: Cambridge University Press.

Marle, Jaap van. 1985. *On the paradigmatic dimension of morphological creativity*. Dordrecht: Foris Publications.

Namer, Fiammetta. 2013a. WaliM: Valider les unités morphologiques complexes par le Web. In Georgette Dal & Dany Amiot (eds.), *Repères en morphologie. Édition en ligne de textes choisis parus dans Silexicales 1-3*, 171–181. http://stl.recherche.univ-lille3.fr/textesenligne/Reperes-Morphologie/Namer_Reperes_morphologie_p171-181.pdf (accessed 07 June 2017).

Namer, Fiammetta. 2013b. Adjectival bases of French *-aliser* and *-ariser* verbs: Syncretism or under-specification? In Nabil Hathout, Fabio Montermini & Jessie Tseng (eds.), *Selected Proceedings of the 7th Décembrettes: Morphology in Toulouse* (LINCOM Studies in Theoretical Linguistics 51), 185–210. München: Lincom Europa.

Namer, Fiammetta & FlorenceVilloing. 2015. Sens morphologiquement construit et procédés concurrents: Les noms de spécialistes en -ogue et –logiste. *Revue de sémantique et de pragmatique* 35–36. 7–26.

Nordahl, Helge. 1971. Variantes chiasmiques. Essai de description formelle. *Revue Romane* 6. 219–232.

Onysko, Alexander & Esme Winter-Froemel. 2011. Necessary loans – luxury loans? Exploring the pragmatic dimension of borrowing. *Journal of Pragmatics* 43(6). 550–1567.

Plag, Ingo. 1999. *Morphological productivity. Structural constraints in English derivation* (Topics in English linguistics 28). Berlin & New York: Mouton de Gruyter.

Rabatel, Alain. 2008. Points de vue en confrontation dans les antimétaboles PLUS et MOINS. *Langue française* 160. 21–36.

Renouf, Antoinette & Laurie Bauer. 2000. Contextual clues to word-meaning. *International Journal of Corpus Linguistics* 5. 231–258.

Ronneberger-Sibold, Elke. 2015. Word-creation. In Peter O. Müller, Ingeborg Ohnheiser, Susan Olsen & Franz Rainer (eds.), *Word-formation. An international handbook of the languages of Europe* (Handbooks of Linguistics and Communication Science 40.1), 485–499. Berlin & New York: De Gruyter.

Schultink, Henk. 1961. Produktiviteit als Morfologisch Fenomeen. *Forum der Letteren* 2, 110–125.

Štekauer, Pavol. 2002. On the theory of neologisms and nonce-formations. *Australian Journal of Linguistics* 22(1). 97–112.

Štekauer, Pavol. 2005. Onomasiological approach to word-formation. In Pavol Štekauer and Rochelle Lieber (eds.), *Handbook of word-formation* (Studies in Natural Language and Linguistic Theory 64), 207–232. Dordrecht: Springer.

Štekauer, Pavol. 2009. Meaning predictability of novel context-free compounds. In Rochelle Lieber and Pavol Štekauer (eds.), *The Oxford Handbook of Compounding* (Oxford Handbooks in Linguistics), 272–297. Oxford: Oxford University Press.

Tanguy, Ludovic. 2012. *Complexification des données et des techniques en linguistique: Contributions du TAL aux solutions et aux problèmes*. Toulouse: Université de Toulouse-Le Mirail Habilitation thesis.

Tanguy, Ludovic & Nabil Hathout. 2002. Webaffix: un outil d'acquisition morphologique dérivationnelle à partir du Web. In *Actes de la 9ᵉ conférence annuelle sur le Traitement Automatique des Langues Naturelles (TALN'02), Nancy, 24-27 juin 2002*, 245–254. http://www.atala.org/taln_archives/TALN/TALN-2002/taln-2002-long-022.pdf (accessed 07 June 2017).

Winter-Froemel, Esme. 2016. Approaching wordplay. In Sebastian Knospe, Alexander Onysko & Maik Goth (eds.), *Crossing languages to play with words. Multidisciplinary perspectives* (The Dynamics of Wordplay 3), 11–46. Berlin & Boston: De Gruyter.

Esme Winter-Froemel
Ludicity in lexical innovation (I) – French

Abstract: The aim of this paper is to explore the importance of the ludic dimension for linguistic innovations by combining synchronic and diachronic analyses of lexicographic sources from French and by reinterpreting the data from a usage-based perspective. I will discuss the possibilities and methodological challenges in tracing ludicity in the lexicon, taking into account contemporary and historical dictionaries, most importantly *Le Petit Robert* 2016 and different editions of the *Dictionnaire de l'Académie française*. Moreover, I will analyse how innovations are introduced and perceived by speakers, distinguishing different subtypes of innovation based on structural, semantic, and pragmatic features. Finally, I will turn to the diachronic evolution of ludic innovations in order to identify general tendencies and pathways of evolution and argue that markedness plays a key role for ludic innovation, which represents an important, albeit so far neglected, domain of lexical dynamics. *

1 Introduction: Ludicity as an important factor for lexical innovation

If we compare the target language equivalents of English *V.I.P.* (*very important person*) in French and German, we can observe an interesting difference: while the French dictionary *Le Petit Robert* 2016 (= PR 2016) indicates that this form is used in familiar French and in ludic contexts (see the lexicographic marks "fam[ilier]" and "plaisant"), the German dictionary *Duden* does not indicate any special value for this item.

(1) (French) **V. I. P.** [veipe; viajpi] nom invariable ETYM. avant 1959 ◊ sigle anglais de *Very Important Person* «personne très importante» FAM. et PLAISANT Personnalité de marque. *Une V. I. P.* (PR 2016)

---

* Some of the reflections of this paper and the following paper were presented in a "tandem talk" given together with Claudine Moulin at a linguistic colloquium at Trier University in December 2016. We would like to thank our colleagues at Trier for their valuable feedback. Moreover, we would like to thank Peter Kühn and two anonymous reviewers for their very helpful comments and suggestions. In addition, our thanks go to Martina Bross and Angela Oakeshott for the stylistic revision of our papers.

ə Open Access. © 2018 Esme Winter-Froemel, published by De Gruyter. [CC BY-NC-ND] This work is licensed under the Creative Commons Attribution-NonCommercial-NoDerivatives 4.0 License.
https://doi.org/10.1515/9783110501933-231

(2) (German) **VIP**, der oder die [vɪp] [Abkürzung für englisch *very important person* = sehr wichtige Person] wichtige Persönlichkeit [mit Privilegien] (Duden)

Given the common source language origin of the two borrowings, this difference appears surprising and raises the question of how the presence (or absence) of a ludic dimension of certain lexical innovations can be explained. The example thus points to ludicity as a specific and challenging dimension of lexical innovation, and this paper aims to explore the importance and diversity of ludic innovations in the context of lexical expansion. The following reflections will be mainly based on French, and they will be complemented by Claudine Moulin's survey on ludic innovations in German (this volume).

The term *ludic innovation* incorporates two basic concepts: ludicity and innovation.[1] The notion of ludicity, seen as the expression of a certain kind of verbal humour, will be used here to describe linguistic items which are used playfully in situations of speaker-hearer interaction. The notion of innovation, in turn, points to the domain of language change, and more specifically to lexical change and lexical expansion. We are concerned here with lexical items that are newly created or introduced and that can diffuse in the speech community and eventually become lexicalised (for general reflections on modelling language change, see Winter-Froemel 2011: 197–227). However, in theoretical reflections on lexical change, the ludic dimension is mostly passed over. "Classical" factors motivating lexical innovation are the need to name new concepts and referents, the need to account for cultural and social change, linguistic economy, social reasons such as taboo, and emotional markedness or expressivity (cf. e.g. Blank 1997; 2001: 95–100; on neology and neonymy, see also Sablayrolles 2000; 2003; Pruvost & Sablayrolles 2003; Luna 2014). Ludicity can be included in the category of expressivity; however, this notion is often used in a fuzzy and relatively unclear way[2], and the importance of a ludic dimension of

---

[1] In Winter-Froemel (2016a), I used this term to refer to a subset of innovations, namely ludic word formations and semantic innovations which are usually semantically transparent for the speakers. Following the lexicographic practice of the dictionaries consulted for this paper, which mark different types of lexical items and usage as being ludic, the following reflections will adopt a broader definition of the term 'ludic innovation' and include not only ludic word formation and semantic innovations / change, but also cases of ludic borrowing and ludic deformation (see e.g. the examples of French *coolos* and German *Atöljö* which will be discussed below). Furthermore, the ludic pseudo-translations included in the data can be linked to the ludic translations discussed in Winter-Froemel (2016a).

[2] It has been argued that the notion of expressivity has been used as a cover term including a broad range of different phenomena, and that it still needs to be discussed and defined in a more precise way (see e.g. Pustka 2015).

lexical innovation thus has not yet been sufficiently determined and integrated into a general framework of lexical innovation.

In previous research, the phenomenon of ludic innovation has been primarily approached in the context of literary studies, where it has been studied as a stylistic device used by individual (literary) authors (see the seminal study by Spitzer 1910; for more recent studies we can think of e.g. Kemmner 1972 on Raymond Queneau; Klein 2016 on Louis-Ferdinand Céline, André Martel, Jean-Pierre Verheggen and Valère Novarina; Arrivé 2016 on Alfred Jarry and Novarina; Galli 2016 on San Antonio, etc.). However, at least to my knowledge, up to now ludic innovations have not been systematically studied as a subtype of lexical innovation in linguistic and theoretical approaches.

First reflections in this direction have been exchanged in the scientific network "The Dynamics of Wordplay"[3] and in the Discussion Forum opened in the third volume of this series (Knospe, Onysko & Goth 2016). A basic observation made in this context was that ludic innovations are often intuitively assigned to the category of wordplay, but if we compare different kinds of innovations and linguistic usage with a ludic dimension, we can immediately see considerable divergences between these manifestations of verbal humour. Moreover, innovations such as French *V.I.P.* cannot be considered to fall into the category of wordplay proper if this latter notion is defined by a juxtaposition or manipulation of linguistic items, as illustrated by the following definition:

> Wordplay is a historically determined phenomenon in which a speaker produces an utterance – and is aware of doing so – that juxtaposes or manipulates linguistic items from one or more languages in order to surprise the hearer(s) and produce a humorous effect on them. (Winter-Froemel 2016a: 37)

For French *V.I.P.* there is no juxtaposition or manipulation, but only the introduction of a linguistic item into another language where it has a special communicative value. How this special ludic value arises, however, still needs to be explained.

Based on these observations, the aim of my paper is to contribute to defining and exploring this domain of investigation and to argue that ludic innovations should be recognized as a subtype of lexical innovation. More specifically,

---

[3] The academic network, funded by the German Research Foundation (DFG) since 2013, brings together 14 linguistic and literary scholars from Germany, Austria and France as well as international co-operation partners in order to confront different approaches and perspectives and establish an interdisciplinary dialogue on wordplay in the context of language contact, lexical innovation and speaker-hearer interaction (see www.wortspiel.uni-trier.de).

synchronic and diachronic analyses of lexicographic sources for French will be combined to gain insights into the importance of ludicity in different historical contexts. Occasionally, the data will be complemented by examples found in everyday communication in order to illustrate how the innovations are produced and perceived by the speakers.

The paper is structured as follows: section 2 will outline basic types of lexical innovation and show that ludicity plays a potentially important role across the different categories. Section 3 is dedicated to methodological reflections on the possibilities and challenges in tracing ludic innovations based on contemporary and historical dictionaries. In the next step, I will analyse how the lexicographic data can be reinterpreted from the perspective of the speakers. I will examine how ludic innovations are coined and interpreted, and which different subtypes of ludic and humorous innovation can be distinguished according to structural, semantic, and pragmatic features (section 4). Finally, section 5 will turn to the question of how the innovations evolve in diachrony, aiming to identify general cross-linguistic tendencies and pathways of evolution. Although these tendencies will need to be verified in further research, the analysis of ludic innovations in different historical contexts (and languages, see the following contribution by Claudine Moulin) sheds light on the complex interplay of markedness and ludicity: ludicity is often based on a relative markedness of the innovations, and otherwise marked forms can be ludically reused or reinterpreted, but we can also observe a general tendency of wearout effects that also applies to ludically marked items which thus tend to become unmarked in their diachronic evolution.

2 Delimiting the area under investigation: Ludicity in lexical innovation

One of the few previous studies in the domain of ludic innovation is the lexicographic analysis of comical forms in twentieth-century French presented by Preite (2007). Her study reveals considerable differences with respect to the proportion of comic forms in standard dictionaries: the search parameter used – the occurrence of expressions indicating a comic dimension (French *badiner, burlesque, comique, dérision, humoristique, ironie, moquerie, parodie, plaisanterie, raillerie, ridicule*) in the microstructure of the dictionary entries – identifies between 0.6% (for *Le Grand Robert* 1962[4]) and 4.2% (for the *Trésor de la Langue Française*) of the total number of entries. As these differences appear to be considerable, no clear picture of the importance of ludicity in the lexicon emerges. Moreover, it should be added that the search criterion used by Preite does not distinguish between items that are used to convey humorous effects (i.e. items that belong to the domain of interest of this paper) and other items with a lexical meaning which belongs to the semantic field of verbal humour (e.g. the items French *railler, humoristique, ridicule* are included in Preite's search, but do not represent ludic forms). In spite of these issues that would require further research, it seems possible to interpret Preite's results as a general confirmation of the potentially important role of ludic innovations.

However, ludic innovations embrace very different subtypes of innovations. To begin with, a potentially important role of ludicity can be observed for semantic change and word formation. Phenomena of this kind have already been discussed under the label of 'ludic innovation' in Winter-Froemel (2016a), and will be investigated in more detail in this paper. What appears to be central here is that the items are semantically motivated or transparent for the speakers. For borrowings, which can be analysed as another basic type of lexical innovation, we have already seen that borrowed items such as *V.I.P.* may also be interpreted as being ludic. In this case, the ludic effects are accounted for by structural features, the loanwords being to some extent different from native, or less marked items. Moreover, ludicity can also affect other subtypes of borrowings such as calques, and other types of contact-induced innovations (Winter-Froemel 2008b; 2009). In addition, structural manipulations (see also Dal & Namer, this volume) and certain phenomena of loanword integration (or non-integration) can equally be perceived as being ludic.

3 Tracing ludic innovations in lexicographic sources

To illustrate the challenges of tracing ludic innovations, I will first present some observations based on two case studies on French, the first focusing on ludic items in contemporary French according to the dictionary *Le Petit Robert* (2016)

---

4 Preite indicates 1962 for the year of publication. The volumes of the first edition of this dictionary were published between 1953 and 1964, the second edition was published in 1985 (see references section).

(see also Winter-Froemel 2016b), the second analysing ludic items in historical dictionaries of French. To identify ludic items, lexicographic marks were used as a search parameter in both surveys.

Generally, we are concerned here with diaevaluative marks, a subcategory of pragmatic marks in lexicography (see Ludwig 2009: 1585–1587). These marks form a less homogeneous group than diatopic or diastratic marks, which represent key topics in lexicography and metalexicography (see e.g. the contributions in Baider, Lamprou & Monville-Burston 2011). For *Le Petit Robert* 2016, the standard lexicographic marks used to signal ludic forms and usages are "plaisant" (PLAIS.) and "par plaisanterie" (PAR PLAIS.). The search for lexical entries containing the string "plais" yielded 347 items, which corresponds to about 0.64% of the total of 54,466 dictionary entries.[5] These entries can be illustrated by the following items:

(3) **réformette** [...] PLAISANT Réforme jugée superficielle, peu sérieuse (par ses adversaires). → aussi *mesurette*. *Une réformette sans lendemain.* (PR 2016)

(4) **antédiluvien, ienne** [...] FIG. (FAM. ou PAR PLAIS.) Très ancien, tout à fait démodé. → préhistorique. *«Figurez-vous une voiture antédiluvienne»* (Gautier). (PR 2016)

(5) **couvre-chef** [...] PAR PLAIS. Ce qui couvre la tête. → chapeau, coiffure. *Un curieux couvre-chef. Des couvre-chefs.* (PR 2016)

(6) **accoucher** [...] II. [...] FIG. 1. Tr. ind. PAR PLAIS. Élaborer péniblement. → créer, produire. *Il a fini par accoucher d'un mauvais roman.* (PR 2016)

Compared to the previous study by Preite (2007) mentioned in section 2, the number of ludic forms thus appears to be very low in the 2016 edition of *Le Petit*

---

5 In addition to the 347 ludic forms that were correctly identified, 45 false hits had to be excluded. These are either lexical entries containing the sequence "plus" which were equally identified by the search criterion (this can only be explained as resulting from a technical problem), or entries indicating near-equivalents where only the equivalents have a ludic dimension (e.g. "*néerlandais, aise* • adj. et n. PLAIS. *batave*"). These forms were manually checked and excluded from further analysis (the ludic equivalents such as *batave*, which were equally identified by the search criterion, however, were of course included). It should also be added that the results slightly diverge from the numbers given in the previous study by Winter-Froemel (2016b), the divergences being confined to the ludic items *mouillé,e* and *(en) titi* and the false hit *bise*, which were additionally retrieved in the new query conducted in May 2017. Although for both queries, the bibliographical references indicated in the electronic version of the dictionary are identical (i.e. PR 2016), these minor changes are probably due to updates in the electronic version of the dictionary.

Robert. However, a few sample surveys show that this is partly explained by the fact that not all lexical items which can be perceived as being ludic or ludically used are characterised by the lexicographic marks cited above. The basic definition given by *Le Petit Robert* for the mark "plaisant", «emploi qui vise à être drôle, à amuser, mais sans ironie» ('usage which aims to be funny, to amuse, but without irony'), also applies to items characterised by other lexicographic marks expressing pragmatic usage strategies or rhetorical techniques, as illustrated by ex. (7) to (13). Among these lexicographic marks are the following (the number of search results for each expression is given in brackets): ALLUSION (LITTÉRAIRE) (108), PAR ANTIPHRASE (36), PAR DÉNIGREMENT 'deprecative' (2), EMPHATIQUE (5), EUPHÉMISME (76), and HYPERBOLE (8). This means that in additon to the 347 lexical items retrieved, there is a certain number of other items in PR 2016 that are also potentially ludic. However, as the marks can also apply to forms which are not ludic, the items retrieved by additional searches require manual checking.

(7) **substantifique** [sypstɑ̃tifik] adjectif [...] ALLUS. LITTER. (Rabelais) *«La substantifique moelle»*: ce qu'il y a de plus riche en substance (III), dans un écrit. → quintessence. *«Cette substantifique moelle qu'est le fric»* (Queneau). (PR 2016)

(8) **dormitif, ive** [dɔʀmitif, iv] adjectif [...] ■ VIEUX MED. Qui provoque le sommeil. → soporifique. ▫ ALLUS. LITTER. *«Pourquoi l'opium fait-il dormir?... Parce qu'il a une vertu dormitive»* (Molière), cité pour ridiculiser une explication purement verbale. (PR 2016)

(9) **beau, belle** [...] PAR ANTIPHR. Mauvais, vilain. → 1. sacré. *Une belle coupure. Une belle bronchite.* → 1. bon, joli. *C'est du beau travail! Être dans de beaux draps*. C'est un beau gâchis. La belle affaire!* ce n'est pas si important. [...] (PR 2016)

(10) **culotte** [...] VIEILLI *Culotte de peau*, que portaient autrefois les militaires. FIG. et PAR DENIGR. *Une vieille culotte de peau*: un militaire borné. (PR 2016)

(11) **bout** [...] morceau. EMPHAT. *Ça fait un bout de chemin!* c'est loin. (PR 2016)

(12) **précaution** [...] LOC. FAM. (EUPHEM.) *Prendre ses précautions*: aller aux toilettes en prévision de situations qui ne le permettront pas. (PR 2016)

(13) **seau** [...] PAR HYPERB. *Il pleut à seaux*, abondamment. (PR 2016)

Another basic problem which immediately becomes clear from the examples is the difficulty of clearly distinguishing ludic items in the lexicon from ludic usage: Some of the entries containing the mark "plaisant" represent items for which a ludic effect appears to be regularly observed independently of specific contexts of use (e.g. *réformette, antédiluvien*), for other entries, in contrast, we are dealing with specific instances of ludic usage (e.g. *une belle bronchite*). Thus, a basic difficulty emerges from the fact that for some entries, the lexical item as a whole is marked as being ludic, while for others, only specific uses are involved. These latter uses may represent citations, i.e. uses that directly evoke individual discourse events, or complex items that are conventionalised to different degrees (see also Lecolle 2012, Rabatel 2016, Winter-Froemel 2016c, and the contributions in Anscombre & Mejri 2011). However, it seems difficult to establish a strict delimitation between ludic items pertaining to the lexicon and ludic usage, as there are different types of phenomena that suggest a continuum (see e.g. idiomatic expressions such as *vieille culotte de peau, il pleut à seaux*), and this is also confirmed by the phenomena investigated in the contributions by Moulin, Dal & Namer, Filatkina, and Stumpf (this volume). Moreover, from the perspective of language change, adopting a usage-based approach to language change implies that lexical change needs to be interpreted as going back to individual usage events, so that ludic usage represents a potential innovation initiating a process of diffusion and subsequent language change (see Winter-Froemel 2008a; 2011). This means that we are faced with a broad variety of items that form a continuum between ludic usage in the sense of individual discourse events (which may represent lexical innovations that can become lexicalised) on the one hand, and fully conventionalised elements of the lexicon, i.e. ludic innovations which have become part of the language system, on the other (on the difficulty of tracing lexical innovations, see also Walter 1991).

A further question that arises is whether ludic usage and irony are really mutually exclusive, as suggested by the definition given above. At least for the following examples it seems also possible to analyse them as cases of ludic usage. The 62 search results for entries containing the expression "iron." thus also need to be taken into account and checked with respect to their ludic character:[6]

(14) **ange** […] *Anges gardiens*, appelés à protéger chaque personne. […] FIG. *C'est son ange gardien*, la personne qui veille, guide et protège en tout une autre personne (par iron. garde du corps). (PR 2016)

(15) **sorte** […] VIEILLI *De (la) bonne sorte; de belle sorte*: comme il faut, et PAR IRON. sévèrement. (PR 2016)

---

[6] An additional difficulty arises from the fact that contrary to the other lexicographic marks cited above, "par iron." 'ironically' has a different lexicographic status, i.e. it is not part of the "marques d'usage et de domaine" used by *Le Petit Robert*.

In other cases, forms that can convey a ludic effect are characterised by yet other, more general marks, such as "fam." (*français familier*, e.g. *coolos* in ex. (16)). This means that we can assume a higher number of ludic items in the French lexicon than suggested by the first query, but for the moment no quantitative statement can be made (a query for "fam" yields 5,994 results, containing a high number of items that are not ludic or humorous).

(16) **cool** [...] FAM. (langage des jeunes) Agréable, excellent ; sympathique. *C'est trop cool, les vacances !* ◦ VAR. FAM. *coolos* [kulɔs] adjectif (PR 2016)

In addition, random native speaker judgements on the items and uses identified as being ludic / humorous ("plaisant") by *Le Petit Robert* have revealed a high degree of interindividual variation, i.e. the speakers' perception of the items as being (potentially) ludic diverges considerably. This adds to the methodological difficulties of tracing the items in the lexicon.

If we turn to historical dictionaries of French, we are faced with additional challenges. The second case study on ludic items in historical dictionaries of French was conducted using the ARTFL database "Dictionnaires d'autrefois". The queries included the following dictionaries (the years of publication and the abbreviations that will be used in the remainder of this paper are indicated for each dictionary):[7]

- Jean-François Féraud, *Dictionaire critique de la langue française* (1787–1788) [Fér]
- Émile Littré, *Dictionnaire de la langue française* (1872–1877) [Litt]
- *Dictionnaire de L'Académie française*, 1ère édition (1694), 4e édition (1762), 5e édition (1798), 6e édition (1835), 8e édition (1932–1935) [DAF 1 / 4 / 5 / 6 / 8]

A first observation to be made is that contrary to contemporary dictionaries, there is not yet a standard lexicographic mark that is used to characterise ludic items. The concept of being "plaisant" already prevails as a marker of ludicity in the earliest sources included in the survey, but we can find different expressions containing this lexical root in the dictionaries, and there are also other expressions which appear to be used as equivalents:

«par plaisanterie»   845 results
«en plaisantant»   339 results

---

[7] For Féraud, the database contains the three volumes of the dictionary issued in 1787–1788. The database also includes Jean Nicot, *Thresor de la langue française* (1606), which, however, did not yield any results for the queries made.

«pour plaisanter»	19 results
«en badinant»	72 results
«pour badiner»	9 results
Total:	1,284 results

Due to the overall less systematic manner of signalling special forms and restrictions of usage for the lexical items contained in the dictionaries, it is even more difficult to make quantitative observations about the importance of ludicity in the French lexicon for earlier periods of time.

From a qualitative point of view, the indications about the ludic character of the items and uses are more explicit in the historical dictionaries. Another notable difference with respect to the descriptions provided by PR 2016 consists in the importance of a normative dimension of metalinguistic reflection. This becomes clear if we compare different expressions that indicate a ludic dimension: these expressions range from primarily descriptive to strongly normative statements, where the latter admit the use of certain items in specific communicative contexts only. In this sense, ludic contexts appear to be a specific case of communication where special rules apply.

DESCRIPTIVE
«On dit en plaisantant» ('it is said in jest')
«Il ne se dit qu'en plaisantant» ('it [the lemma / expression] is only used in jest')
«Il ne se dit guère qu'en plaisantant» ('it [the lemma / expression] is rarely used and only in jest')
«On ne pourroit le dire qu'en plaisantant et en se moquant» ('it could only be used in jest and mockingly')
«Cela ne peut se dire qu'en plaisantant» ('this can only be said in jest')
«on ne doit l'employer qu'en plaisantant» ('it [the lemma / expression] may only be employed in jest')
NORMATIVE

Summing up the results of the two case studies on French, we can say that lexicographic marks offer a first way of approaching lexical items which are ludic or which can be used ludically. The queries yield some false positives, but these forms can be relatively easily and straightforwardly excluded from further research. Yet we can also assume that there is a high number of false negatives, i.e. of items in the lexicon which are also used in a ludic way, but which are difficult to retrieve (semi-)automatically, as they are indicated by other lexicographic marks and / or unsystematically characterised by lexicographic marks. Interestingly, the data retrieved from the dictionaries not only contains fully conventionalised lexical items, but also citational uses and collocations or complex units that are potentially on the way to becoming part of the French lexicon. Therefore, in spite of the dictionaries' primary focus on lexicalised forms, these sources also permit us to approach the domain of ludic usage.

4 Structural, semantic and pragmatic features of ludicity: Production and perception of ludic items in French

Having identified a set of ludic items and uses based on lexicographic sources, the following section aims to address the question of how ludic items and uses are characterised. I will take into account both the speaker's and the hearer's perspective[8] and consider both the production and perception of ludic forms. In this way, the following reflections also address the question whether we can identify typical innovation scenarios for ludic innovations, and how ludic innovations are introduced and interpreted. However, as we have already seen in the introduction, it appears difficult to identify ludic forms in a straightforward and unequivocal way. The following subsections will therefore combine reflections on structural, semantic, and pragmatic features of ludic items in the lexicon, based on the data from PR 2016 and the ARTFL dictionaries.

4.1 Structural markedness

Concerning the structural features of ludic items, we can first observe that a broad range of parts of speech is represented in the data sample of PR 2016 (see Table 1; as some of the items were counted in several categories, the total number of ludic items is 374 instead of 347 and the total number of items in PR 2016 on which the proportions are calculated is 64,860 instead of 54,466 [see section 2.1]). The quantitative order differs from the data collected by Preite (2007) with respect to the relative importance of verbs and adjectives (in Preite's data, there are more verbs than adjectives), but corresponds to the overall frequency of the parts of speech in PR 2016. Otherwise, the general results of both studies are quite similar and no special restrictions are observed, i.e. in principle, ludicity

---

8 Both terms are used in a broad sense here, including writers and readers.

seems to affect all parts of speech and roughly to the same extent as that to which the parts of speech are represented in the lexicon.[9]

Tab. 1: Proportions of ludic items in PR 2016

POS	Ludic items in PR		Total number of items in PR	
Noun	213	57.0%	41,181	63.5%
Adj.	82	21.9%	13,518	20.8%
Verb	53	14.2%	6,717	10.4%
Adv.	17	4.5%	1,749	2.7%
Interj.	3	0.8%	222	0.3%
Phrase	3	0.8%	221	0.3%
Pron.	3	0.8%	100	0.2%
Other	-	-	1,152	1.8%
Total	374	100%	64,860	100%

However, some ludic items are characterised by specific features that permit us to analyse the items as being structurally marked. A first type of markedness is markedness through rhyme effects and, more generally, repetition structures (see ex. (17) to (22)).[10] This feature concerns especially ludic usage, i.e. specific uses of otherwise unmarked lexical items in phrases or utterances that can have a citational value. For many cases, the uses can be characterised by the fact that a rhyming word is added to an otherwise unmarked and highly frequent routine formula (e.g. *À la tienne, Tu parles!, ¿me entiendes?*), the rhyming word being semantically unmotivated in the concrete context of use, but creating an effect of ludicity. The feature matches what Jakobson (1960) described as the "poetic" quality of messages (projecting the principle of equivalence from the axis of selection onto the axis of combination). The general framework proposed by Jakobson would require extensive further discussion (see Winter-Froemel 2016a; Kabatek 2015), which cannot be developed in more detail here. However,

---

9 The divergences that can be observed (especially the relative under- / overrepresentation of ludic nouns / verbs) would need to be investigated in further research.

10 It seems possible to analyse the interjection in (21) along the same lines as the other examples, even if a strong wearout effect can be assumed (i.e. today the item does not have a strong ludic effect, which is reflected by the fact that PR 2016 does not indicate a ludic dimension).

let us note that this "poetic" quality is not observed for other forms of ludic usage, i.e. it cannot be analysed as a necessary condition of ludicity.

(17) **tien, tienne** [...] ▫ FAM. *À la tienne!* formule accompagnant un toast (cf. *À ta santé!*). PLAISANT (pour l'assonance) *À la tienne, Étienne!* (PR 2016)

(18) **dilater** [...] 2. *se dilater* v. pron. Augmenter de volume. [...] PLAIS. «J'ai la rate qui s'dilate» (chanson). (PR 2016)

(19) PLAIS. *Ça roule ma poule!* (PR 2016 s.v. *rouler*)

(20) *Tu parles, Charles!* (PR 2016, s.v. *parler*: [...] ABSOLUMENT, FAM. (à la 2e personne de l'indic. seulement, avec une nuance de moquerie ou de colère, parfois d'admiration). *Tu parles! Tu parles, Charles! Sa reconnaissance, tu parles! Tu parles d'un idiot!, quel idiot!*)

(21) **patati, patata** [...] interjection ETYM. 1809; *patatin, patata* « bruit du cheval au galop » 1524 ◊ onomat., de *patt-* évoquant un coup, un choc [...] FAM. Onomatopée qui évoque un long bavardage. → blablabla. «*Comment va-t-il? Qu'est-ce qu'il fait? Pourquoi ne vient-il pas? Est-ce qu'il est content? [...] Et patati! et patata! Comme cela pendant des heures*» (Daudet). (PR 2016)

(22) [Spanish] *¿Me entiendes, Mendez? ¿o me explico, Federico?* [Do you understand me, Mendez? Or should I explain myself, Federico?] (Spanish catchphrase, personal communication by Dardo de Vecchi)

Another basic form of structural markedness arises from divergences from the structural features of the language system and / or from the expected realisation of the linguistic item. This leads us back to the domain of linguistic borrowing, as the deviations frequently concern the pronunciation and spelling of loanwords which differ from the "normal" degree of loanword adaptation that is considered to be adequate in a certain speech community. The deviations can be characterised by extremely weak or extremely strong loanword integration. Similar deviations are rarely attested in lexicographic sources, but can be observed in everyday communication. They have been commented on in the research literature on linguistic borrowing (see e.g. the potentially humorous dimension of anglicisms conveying a certain tone described by Galinsky,[11] i.e. arising from weak loanword integration; for strong loanword integration, see e.g. ludic spellings such as French *niouses* [*news*] attested on the internet as

---

[11] Among his list of basic stylistic functions of anglicisms in (post-war) German, he mentions "conveying tone, its gamut ranging from humorous playfulness to sneering parody on America and ‹Americanized› Germany" (Galinski 1967: 71, see also Winter-Froemel, in press).

well as ex. (23); cf. Winter-Froemel, in press). These ludic spellings can also be observed for native items which are "deformed" by substituting native segments with non-native segments, as illustrated by ex. (24) (see also the analyses of types of wordplay based on paronymy as discussed by Braun, this volume). This shows that the speakers may play on items and structures that are marked in the recipient language or that require additional linguistic knowledge of other languages.

(23) [German] *Atöljö* (deviation from the conventional spelling <Atelier> 'studio', see Figure 1

(24) [German] *El Kawé* (ludic deformation of the conventional abbreviation *LKW*, short for *Leberkäswecken* 'roll filled with a specific type of meat loaf popular in Germany and Austria', via hyperforeignisation into pseudo-Spanish [determiner *el* + noun, non-native grapheme <é>; however, these features clash with the graphemes <k> and <w>, which are part of German, but do not belong to the inventory of native Spanish graphemes; the same holds for the use of the capital letter <K>], see Figure 1)[12]

Fig. 1: Atöljö (Loretto-Areal, Tübingen, Germany, © Esme Winter-Froemel, 20 April 2014) / El Kawé (Advert for Truffner the butcher's, Wilhelmstraße 80, Tübingen, Germany, © Esme Winter-Froemel, 09 October 2017)

---

12 Due to the ambiguity of *LKW*, which can also be interpreted as an abbreviation for *Lastkraftwagen* 'heavy goods vehicle', the abbreviation itself already has ludic potential (however, neither the full form nor the abbreviation in the gastronomic meaning are indicated in *Duden*). Ex. (24) thus exhibits a secondary ludic innovation which points to a certain wearout effect of the ludic character of the abbreviation *LKW* for *Leberkäswecken*. Moreover, this example functions as a riddle for the passer-by, as the larger-than-life size of the original image in the advertisement hinders the immediate recognition of the object that is represented (we will return to this additional pragmatic function in section 4.3).

In addition to ludic deformations that play on pronunciation and spelling as well as on the grapheme-to-phoneme correspondence rules of the linguistic system, there are also ludic deformations of linguistic items that rely on the morphological level, e.g. by suffix alternation (see the contribution by Dal & Namer, this volume).

Another form of structural markedness can be observed for items characterised by an internal disparateness: polymorphemic ludic items may combine morphemes of different etymological origin, playing not only on the different structural patterns of the languages involved, but also on their different prestige, typically combining elements that can be perceived as being "high" with allegedly "low" items or contents (cf. Sablayrolles 2015: 204–205). This feature can be linked to the principle of *héroï-comique*, which has been identified as a general source of humour (see already Ducháček 1967: 118–119). It can be illustrated by the following examples, which combine Greek or Latin elements on the one hand, and items belonging to informal language (*français familier*) on the other (ex. (25) and (26); see also certain ludic word formations on -*itis* such as German *Flitzeritis* or *Scheißeritis* for 'diarrhea', cf. DO 2017), the combination of the native item *pipi* (belonging to child language) and the item *room*, borrowed from English, in ex. (27) as well as the pseudo-borrowing or pseudo-Latin translation in ex. (28) (playing on the phraseme *tiré par les cheveux* 'far-fetched' [literally, 'pulled by the hair']). The basic principle underlying these items cited is incongruity, which has been identified as a basic source of humour in various previous approaches (with different accentuations, see e.g. Bergson 1993 [1940]; Attardo 1994; Attardo, Hempelmann & Di Maio 2002).

(25) **flémingite** [flemɛ̃ʒit] nom féminin ETYM. 1879 *flemmingite* ◊ de *flemme*, avec finale de *laryngite, méningite...* ■ PLAIS. Flemme (considérée comme pathologique). *Crise de flemingite aiguë*. (PR 2016)

(26) **baisodrome** [bɛzodʀom] nom masculin ETYM. 1946 ◊ de 1. *baiser* et -*drome*, d'après *hippodrome*, etc. ■ FAM., PLAISANT Lieu réservé aux ébats amoureux. (PR 2016)

(27) **pipi-room** [pipiʀum] nom masculin ETYM. milieu xxe ◊ formation plaisante, de *pipi* et anglais *room*, d'après *living-room* ■ PLAISANT Toilettes (notamment d'un lieu public). *Aller au pipi-room. Où sont les pipi-rooms?* (PR 2016)

(28) **capillotracté, ée** [kapilotʀakte] adjectif ETYM. 1968 ◊ de *capillo-*, du latin *capillus* «cheveu», et *tracté* [...] ■ PLAIS. Amené d'une manière forcée et peu logique (cf. Tiré par les cheveux*). *Une histoire capillotractée*. (PR 2016)

Summing up, the structural features discussed here illustrate different kinds of structural markedness which characterise certain types of innovations having a ludic dimension. The structural features illustrate specific techniques of creating ludic innovations (which corresponds to the perspective of the speaker) and provide cues for recognising a ludic dimension of certain linguistic items (which corresponds to the perspective of the hearer).

4.2 Semantic features

Ludic innovations can also be produced and recognised on the basis of certain semantic features. Main aspects which clearly emerge from the data are negative contents, denigration, deprecative uses, and taboo concepts. Denigration and deprecative uses can be illustrated by the following items; as we can see, the examples may among others involve social criticism of individuals, political protagonists, or political measures. However, as observed in section 3, the definition of the lexicographic mark "plaisant" in PR 2016 excludes items expressing irony. The seriousness of the criticism expressed thus marks a limit of ludicity.

(29) **flémingite** [flemɛ̃ʒit] nom féminin ETYM. 1879 *flemmingite* ◊ de *flemme*, avec finale de *laryngite*, *méningite*... ■ PLAIS. Flemme (considérée comme pathologique). *Crise de flemingite aiguë*. (PR 2016)

(30) **roitelet** [...] ETYM. 1459 ◊ de l'ancien français *roitel*, diminutif de *roi* [...] 1. PEJ. ou PLAISANT Roi peu important, roi d'un petit pays. «*Les roitelets sont morts ou déchus*» (Sartre). (PR 2016)

(31) **réformette** [...] ETYM. v. 1960 ◊ de *réforme* ■ FAM. PLAISANT Réforme jugée superficielle, peu sérieuse (par ses adversaires). → aussi *mesurette*. *Une réformette sans lendemain*. (PR 2016)

(32) MUSEAU, s. m. [...] Cette partie de la tête du chien, et de quelques aûtres animaux, qui comprend la gueule et le nez. Par mépris ou par plaisanterie, on le dit des persones. "Elle est venûe montrer son museau. "On lui a doné sur le museau, sur son museau. [Fer]

(33) FROC, s. m. [...] C'est proprement la partie de l'habit monacal qui coûvre la tête; mais on le dit ordinairement de tout l'habit. "Porter, prendre, quiter le froc. On ne s'en sert guère que par plaisanterie et par mépris. [Fer]

Ludic innovations can also function as euphemisms or dysphemisms to refer to taboo concepts (on the role of euphemism, dysphemism, and playfulness in contexts of borrowing, see also Winter-Froemel, in press). In these cases, ludicity can arise from the fact that the taboo is deliberately violated by the speaker by choosing a dysphemistic expression. For euphemisms, a ludic effect can arise from the indirect way of expressing the respective concept, so that the speaker's utterance functions as a social game and a riddle to the hearer, creating an effect of complicity (or French *connivence*) between the speaker and hearer (potentially excluding other hearers) if the utterance is successfully decoded by the hearer (see ex. (34) to (36)). This means that semantic transparency / intransparency represents an important dimension in these cases, and this aspect immediately leads us to the pragmatic and social dimension of ludic innovations.

(34) **partie** [...] ▫ *Parties génitales*, (xve) VIEILLI *parties honteuses*. (1651) ABSOLUMENT, POP. ou PLAIS. *Les parties*: les organes génitaux externes de l'homme (cf. pop. Les organes) (PR 2016)

(35) **pipi-room** [pipiʀum] nom masculin ETYM. milieu xxe ◊ formation plaisante, de *pipi* et anglais *room*, d'après *living-room* ■ PLAISANT Toilettes (notamment d'un lieu public). *Aller au pipi-room. Où sont les pipi-rooms?* (PR 2016)

(36) **baisodrome** [bɛzodʀom] nom masculin ETYM. 1946 ◊ de 1. *baiser* et *-drome*, d'après *hippodrome*, etc. ■ FAM., PLAISANT Lieu réservé aux ébats amoureux. (PR 2016)

4.3 The pragmatic dimension: A social game of linguistic mastery

The discussion of structural and semantic features of ludic innovations has already revealed that certain items and uses are strongly marked by an interactional dimension. This aspect, which determines the production and perception of ludic items, can be formulated as follows: by using items that are to some extent "difficult" or marked and that require specific / additional knowledge in order to be correctly decoded, the speaker demonstrates linguistic mastery, and if the hearer equally possesses the required knowledge and succeeds in adequately decoding the speaker's utterance, an effect of complicity arises.

The difficulty of the items used can have different sources, the first being their obsoleteness and uncommonness / marginality (cf. Leclerc 2012). Based on the data collected in the two case studies on French, we can assert that obsolete forms lend themselves to ludic usage. This can be illustrated by the following examples; additional evidence is provided by the fact that the lexicographic marks "plaisant" and "vieux" 'obsolete' frequently cooccur, i.e. many items are characterised by both marks.

(37) **goutte** [...] *ne... goutte* Négation renforcée (avec les v. *voir, entendre, comprendre, connaître*) (milieu xiie) VIEUX ou PLAISANT *N'y voir goutte*: ne rien voir du tout. «*Quand il n'y*

voit goutte, le plus malin n'est pas fier» (Bernanos). *N'y entendre goutte*: ne rien comprendre (cf. **Pas* du tout**). (PR 2016)

(38) **occire** [...] Vieux ou plais. Tuer. «*Mais pourquoi qu't'as occis le mataf?*» (Genet). (PR 2016)

(39) NONNAIN [...] s. f. Synonyme, qui ne se dit plus que par plaisanterie, de nonne. [Litt]

A second way in which the social game of proving and testing linguistic mastery can be realised, are interlingual games, i.e. ludic items which are created by referring to patterns from other languages. This is explicitly commented on in the historical dictionaries of French for the items *platatim* and *durissime*:

(40) PLATATIM. Mot forgé par plaisanterie en manière latine, adverbiale, etc. qui signifie, *Plat à plat*. *On servit platatim*. [DAF 5]

(41) DURISSIME [...] adj. Très dur. Il ne se dit que par plaisanterie. Cette volaille est durissime. Étymologie Lat. *durissimus*, superlatif de *durus*, dur. [Litt]

Moreover, many ludic innovations function as riddles for the hearer. This can be illustrated by the innovation *personnel rampant*, introduced in the argot of aviators according to PR 2016, which clearly confirms this function. Other examples are provided by the various designations that have been introduced in German to refer to the concepts of GLASSES and BICYCLE in a creative and unexpected way (see also Winter-Froemel, in press). Likewise, we could cite again the items French *pipi-room* and *flémingite*.

(42) *personnel rampant*: Par plais. (1918 argot des aviateurs) *Personnel rampant, qui ne vole pas, employé à terre (opposé à personnel navigant). N. Les rampants.* (PR 2016 s.v. *rampant*)

(43) [German] *Intelligenzprothese* ('intelligence prosthesis'), *Nasenfahrrad* ('nose bicycle'), *Nasenquetscher* ('nose crusher'), *Spekuliereisen* ('speculating iron') for GLASSES (DO)

(44) [German] *Drahtesel* (or *Esel*) ('wire donkey' / 'donkey'), *Stahlross* (or *Ross*) ('steel steed' / 'steed'), *Hirsch* ('deer'), *Eierschaukel* ('nutsswing') for BICYCLE (DO)

An important feature which characterises all of these forms is the fact that they are relatively marked as well, as there are other expressions that are used more frequently to refer to the respective concept (e.g. French *souris (d'ordinateur)*, *personnel au sol*; German *Brille, Fahrrad*; see also French *capillotracté* vs. *tiré par les cheveux, pipi-room* vs. *toilettes, occire* vs. *tuer*; German *Atöljö* vs. *Atelier*, *El Kawé* vs. *LKW* (vs. *Leberkäswecken*)). The examples confirm that we are dealing with a very general characteristic of ludic items, and this leads us to another source of markedness, which is pragmatic markedness by virtue of the lexical items being different from more frequent and more established near-equivalents (see Winter-Froemel 2011: 295–319; Onysko & Winter-Froemel 2011; Winter-Froemel & Onysko 2012; Winter-Froemel, Onysko & Calude 2014; Winter-Froemel, in press). It has been shown that borrowings which are introduced alongside near-equivalent native items, i.e. non-catachrestic borrowings, systematically convey additional pragmatic meanings. This can be illustrated by the example of French *V.I.P.* as compared to *personnalité*, *célébrité* (however, the fact that German *V.I.P.*, which also competes with items such as *Persönlichkeit*, is not indicated as being ludically marked by the *Duden online* suggests that additional factors may come into play here).[13]

(45) French *V.I.P.* vs. *personnalité*, *célébrité*

A straightforward explanation of their specific communicative effect is provided by Levinson's theory of presumptive meanings (Levinson 2000), which is based on the assumption that "when we say something, we find ourselves committed to much more, just by virtue of choices between all the ways we could have said it" (Levinson 2000: 367). According to Levinson, this principle accounts for stable additional pragmatic meanings which are related to utterance types (Levinson 2000: 373) and to single elements of utterances. More specifically, we are faced here with one of the three basic types of generalised conversational implicatures as discussed by Levinson (Q-, I-, and M-implicatures, resting upon the principles of quantity, informativeness, and modality), viz. M-implicatures. These are based on the general heuristic assumed by the hearer: "What's said in an abnormal way, isn't normal; or Marked message indicates marked situation" (Levinson 2000: 33). According to this heuristic, if the speaker uses an uncommon, creative way of referring to a certain concept, thus choosing not the conventional expression, but a different expression which is more difficult to process, the hearer will assume that the speaker wants to convey an additional meaning, which can be an interactional meaning in the sense of an invitation to participate in a linguistic game of decoding a partly enigmatic utterance. The ludic innovations exhibiting this characteristic can thus be ranged into the general category of non-catachrestic innovations, i.e. of innovations that do not arise from a need to designate a new concept, but develop for other, interactional reasons (for a more detailed discussion of the notions of catachrestic /

---

[13] Nonetheless, a certain ludic potential can also be observed for uses of German *V.I.P.* in contexts where the native item *Persönlichkeit* would equally have been a plausible choice.

non-catachrestic innovation, see Winter-Froemel 2011: 295–315; Onysko & Winter-Froemel 2011; Winter-Froemel, in press).

Finally, for yet other items, the additional knowledge that proves the extensive linguistic and general knowledge of both the speaker and the hearer consists in being familiar with and recognising certain citations. We can thus also observe a complicity dimension here, which can be linked to Galisson's concept of *lexiculture*, coined to underpin the indissoluble links between lexicon and culture and to emphasise the existence of a certain cultural knowledge which is linked to particular linguistic items and shared by the speakers (Galisson 1988). In the dictionaries, the items concerned are sometimes marked as being ludic; in other cases, however, the entries only contain the lexicographic mark "allusion", sometimes with an indication of the original source of the citation.

(46) **dive** [...] Vieux ou plaisant Divine. — Allus. litter. *La dive bouteille*: le vin. «*on eût dit un prêtre de Bacchus officiant et célébrant les mystères de la dive bouteille*» (Gautier).

(47) **substantifique** [...] Allus. litter. (Rabelais) «*La substantifique moelle*»: ce qu'il y a de plus riche en substance (III), dans un écrit. [...] «*Cette substantifique moelle qu'est le fric*» (Queneau).

(48) **dormitif, ive** [...] ■ Vieux Med. Qui provoque le sommeil. [...] Allus. litter. «*Pourquoi l'opium fait-il dormir ?... Parce qu'il a une vertu dormitive*» (Molière), cité pour ridiculiser une explication purement verbale.

Similar effects can also be observed for more recent citational uses. For instance, French *mulot* 'computer mouse', which originates via semantic change from the meaning of 'field mouse', is marked as ludic ("plaisant") in PR 2016. The ludic effect can be explained by the fact that the conceptual and semantic relations established can be perceived as being surprising and showing the speaker's creativity. At the same time, the form *mulot* is unexpected and relatively marked compared to the conventional designation for the computer device *souris*, of which the original meaning is co-taxonomically related to the meaning of *mulot*. Moreover, as one of the reviewers of this paper points out, for many speakers this lexical item will recall specific uses, "for example, Jacques Chirac, not noted for his computer literacy, famously asked about using 'le mulot' (on *Guignols de l'information* and still brought up on television twenty years after the event)."[14]

(49) **mulot** • n. m. (1997) Plais. Souris d'ordinateur. (PR 2016)

---

14 I would like to thank the reviewer for this important observation.

Summing up, ludic innovations show a great variety of patterns and motivations. The items discussed appear to be generally characterised by being marked in a certain respect and / or by violating certain communicative rules and principles of "ordinary" communication. This markedness and these violations can be realised in different forms including a structural markedness which deviates from the rules and norms of grammar and usage as well as violations of the internal harmony of the linguistic items by combining structurally and / or semantically heterogeneous elements, producing a sort of clash for the hearer. Finally, we have seen that the interactional dimension is paramount to ludicity and that the use of ludic items in communication can be seen as (part of) a social game where the speaker's and hearer's linguistic mastery is at stake, potentially permitting a confirmation of social relations, complicity, and in-group / out-group structures.

5 Ludic innovations in diachrony: Pathways of evolution of ludic innovations in French

Let us now turn to the diachronic development of ludic and humorous items in the lexicon. I will first present some general observations on the lexicographic description of ludic items across the five editions of the *Dictionnaire de l'Académie française* contained in the ARTFL database (section 5.1). Then I will present some general patterns of evolution that emerge from the ARTFL data, including the dictionaries by Littré and Féraud (sections 5.2 to 5.5; for parallel observations on German, see Moulin, this volume).

5.1 General observations

Taking into account the five editions of the *Dictionnaire de l'Académie française*, there are altogether 238 items which are marked as being ludic ("plais" / *plaisant*) in at least one edition of the dictionary. If we look at the total numbers of ludic items in the *Dictionnaire de l'Académie française*, we can see that in the first edition, the lexicographic mark "plaisant" is not yet established and only a very low number of items is characterised as being ludic. In the following editions, the number of items marked as being ludic constantly increases until the 1835 edition, which clearly has the highest number of new ludic items. The number of items decreases again for the 1932–1935 edition (see Table 2). Moreover, the 1835 edition also clearly has the highest number of first occurrences of ludic items, i.e. of items newly marked as being ludic.

Tab. 2: Ludic innovations in different editions of the DAF

Edition	DAF 1 1694	DAF 4 1762	DAF 5 1798	DAF 6 1835	DAF 8 1932–1935	Total
Number of ludic items	8	70	75	161	93	407
First occurrences of ludic items	8	67	13	113	37	238

With respect to the diachronic stability of the items, Table 3 shows that the majority of ludic items is only registered as being ludic in one edition (which does not exclude of course their occurrence in other editions of the dictionary, but without the respective lexicographic mark). None of the 238 ludic items analysed occurs as a ludic item in all of the five editions of the dictionary. This means that the average life span of ludic innovations is reduced, and this observation already suggests that ludic items represent a highly dynamic domain in the lexicon. I will therefore discuss various developments that emerge as basic pathways of the diachronic evolution of ludic items in the following subsections.

Tab. 3: Occurrence of ludic items in several editions of the DAF

Number of editions indicating a ludic dimension	1	2	3	4	5	Total
Number of ludic items	132	62	25	19	0	238
Percentages	55.5%	26.1%	10.5%	8.0%	0.0%	100.0%

Before investigating these pathways of evolution, however, it has to be added that the results given above should be taken as approximative numbers only, as the lexicographic description of the items cannot be taken to represent a diachronically stable and objective analysis, but depends on a broad range of external factors influencing the lexicographic practice (for general reflections on this issue, see also Moulin, this volume). For instance, the general increase in marking ludic items until the 1835 edition goes along with a general increase in the use of lexicographic marks indicating pragmatic, rhetorical or stylistical features. For the first edition of the dictionary, there is a general reluctance to use lexicographic marks. This has been explained as being partly motivated by a relatively tolerant attitude (i.e. the Academy members' lexicographic practice is more tolerant than the puristic outline in the preface suggests; moreover, Popelar argues that in some cases, the lexicographic marks are used in a clearly unsystematic and even careless way in the first edition of the dictionary; cf. Popelar 1976: 202–220). For the second edition (issued in 1718), in turn, a much stricter puristic practice is already manifest.[15] Moreover, we have already seen in section 3 that the lexicographic descriptions become increasingly standardised, which means that the lower number of items retrieved for the first editions may also be partly explained by the fact that the analysis only included items identified by the search string "plais". Besides, for all of the editions, we have to take into account a certain influence of external factors, i.e. the lexicographic practice is strongly influenced by the historical context, by inter-individual variation between the different members of the *Académie française* elaborating the different editions of the dictionary, etc. It can be assumed that these aspects equally influence the ways in which the items are judged and described. And finally, the present survey does not allow us to evaluate the status of the linguistic items before the first edition of the DAF, i.e. for the items that are already marked as being ludic in the first edition, their possible preexistence as ludic forms is not taken into account.

5.2 Ludic usage of catchphrases and citations

Concerning the question of how ludic items and uses are introduced, a first pattern to emerge from the diachronic (and synchronic) data are cases in which individual utterances (i.e. individual discourse events) are repeated by other speakers and become part of the linguistic knowledge of the members of the speech community. This has already been commented on with respect to the lexicographic mark "allusion" in PR 2016, and conventionalised phrases have also been looked at in 4.1 for ludic innovations having a "poetic" quality. In the diachronic case study, this pattern is also frequently attested and it is addition-

---

15 However, the second edition of the dictionary is not included in the ARTFL database and is thus not included in this survey.

ally confirmed by the frequent cooccurrence of the lexicographic marks "par plaisanterie" and "proverbialement":

(50) FARCE. s. f. Comédie bouffonne. On dit figurément et proverbialement, *Tirez le rideau, la farce est jouée*, pour dire, C'en est fait; et cela se dit ordinairement par plaisanterie. [DAF 5]

(51) BRETAUDER. v. a. Tondre inégalement. Prov. et par plaisanterie, *Bretauder les cheveux de quelqu'un*, Les lui couper trop courts. [DAF 6]

(52) CHOU.1 s. m. Plante potagère de la famille des crucifères. *Bête comme un chou*.... Cette locution viendrait-elle, par plaisanterie, de ce que le chou a une tête et ne pense pas? [Litt]

The examples show that additional aspects that explain the ludic dimension come into play here: ex. (50) can be seen as a more prolix, more difficult, and less straightforward way of expressing a given subject matter. In this sense, the expression is clearly marked and can convey an additional pragmatic meaning. At the same time, there can be an effect of complicity between the speaker and hearer if the latter succeeds in decoding the message. For (51) and (52), there is a clear dimension of denigration; for the latter example, the reflections put forward by Littré also hint at the partly enigmatic character of the utterance.

5.3 Conventional items > obsolete items > ludic items

Another tendency which can be observed in the data is represented by ludic reinterpretations of otherwise marginal items of the lexicon, i.e. of items which have become obsolete (cf. Ludwig 2009: 1577–1580). This can be illustrated by the examples of French *ne ... goutte* and *occire* (see section 4.3) as well as the following examples.

(53) BONNETADE. s. f. Coup de bonnet, salut qu'on fait en ôtant son bonnet. Il a vieilli, et ne se dit que par plaisanterie. [DAF 6]

(54) *Réponse congrue*, Réponse précise. *Phrase congrue*, Phrase correcte. Ces deux locutions ont vieilli et ne s'emploient guère que par plaisanterie. [DAF 6, s.v. *congru,e*]

(55) TÂTER s'emploie aussi intransitivement et signifie Goûter à quelque chose, goûter de quelque chose. Je tâterais volontiers de ce vin, de ce perdreau. Il vieillit en ce sens et ne se dit guère que par plaisanterie. [DAF 8]

(56) BEDON. s. m. Vieux mot, qui signifioit autrefois Petit tambour, mais qui n'est plus en usage que dans cette phrase, *Un gros bedon*, qui se dit par plaisanterie d'Un homme gros et gras. *C'est un gros bedon*. [DAF 5]

Based on these observations, we can assume the following steps of evolution: conventional and unmarked items become obsolete, but may then, instead of disappearing completely, be preserved as ludic items, as they permit the speakers (and hearers) to demonstrate their extensive linguistic knowledge which includes marginal items of the lexicon (see section 4.3).

5.4 Remaining stability of ludic innovations

The reflections above have shown how ludicity can arise; if the innovations and ludic uses are perceived as being communicatively efficient, they can diffuse in the speech community and become conventionalised. Another question which arises in this context, however, is the question whether there are additional tendencies in the diachronic evolution of ludic items. In spite of the general dynamics of ludic and humorous items, for some ludic innovations we can observe a relative stability. For the 19 items which are indicated as being ludic in four editions of the DAF, we can find a high number of items where only specific uses of the respective lemma are ludic. These lemmas include items of a very high frequency (see ex. (57)) and items where the ludic uses remain very stable (ex. (58)).[16] Besides, there are items which keep their ludic dimension, but for which different uses are indicated by the different editions of the dictionary (ex. (59) / (60) / (61)).

(57) BON. [...] Et dans le style familier, soit par injure, soit par plaisanterie, on dit, *C'est un bon coquin, un bon fripon, un bon débauché, un bon vaurien, une bonne ame, une bonne pièce, une bonne bête, un bon bec*. [DAF 4, see also DAF 5, DAF 6, which adds "On dit de même, par exclamation, La bonne pièce! la bonne langue! etc.", DAF 8]

(58) COMPAGNIE. Se dit aussi d'Un nombre de gens de guerre sous un Capitaine. On dit proverbialement & par plaisanterie, qu'*Un homme est bête de Compagnie*, pour dire, qu'il aime la société, & qu'il se laisse facilement mener où l'on veut. Il fera ce que vous voudrez, *il est bête de compagnie*. [DAF 4, see also DAF 5, DAF 6, DAF 8]

---

[16] For (57), we can assume that the expression *bon bec* cited in the entry evoked for many 18th century speakers the refrain of Villon's famous poem "Ballade des femmes de Paris", "Il n'est bon bec que de Paris" (as it still does for many speakers today).

(59) CROÎTRE. v.n. Devenir plus grand. On dit proverbialement & par plaisanterie, Des enfants qui croissent beaucoup, Mauvaise herbe croît toujours. [DAF 4, see also DAF 5]

(60) CROÎTRE. v. n. Devenir plus grand. Prov., *Mauvaise herbe croît toujours*, se dit par plaisanterie Des enfants qui croissent beaucoup. Prov., *Ne faire que croître et embellir*, se dit D'une jeune personne qui devient tous les jours plus grande et plus belle. *Cette jeune fille ne fait que croître et embellir*. On le dit, par plaisanterie, De certaines choses qui augmentent, soit en bien, soit en mal. *Il se débauche tous les jours de plus en plus, cela ne fait que croître et embellir*. [DAF 6]

(61) CROÎTRE v. intr. Se développer, en parlant des Hommes, des animaux, des plantes. Fig., Ne faire que croître et embellir, se dit d'une Jeune personne qui devient tous les jours plus grande et plus belle. [DAF 8]

5.5 Ludic innovations > unmarked items

In addition to the tendencies observed in 5.4, however, we can also observe wearout effects. Ludic and playful items can be considered to be marked items of the lexicon. This markedness may favour the usage of these items in order to attract the hearer's attention and to convey additional pragmatic effects and meanings; however, if more and more speakers use the items in this way, the special effect will increasingly get lost. This wearout effect has been described among others in the context of Keller's (1994) approach to language change (for a critical discussion of this framework, cf. Winter-Froemel 2011: 131–177, 2013–2014).

For the data studied in this paper, we can mention the example of German *Drahtesel*, which does not convey strong pragmatic effects in contemporary German. Similar wearout effects can be observed for the following examples; interestingly, these developments are often accompanied by a semantic generalisation (see ex. (63), which has made the example below an unmarked expression for excursions of any type, not only for excursions that convey the literal meaning of German *Flug* 'flight').

(62) PHÉNOMÉNAL, ALE [...] adj. Néologisme. Qui tient du phénomène. Familièrement et par plaisanterie, surprenant, étonnant. Voilà qui est phénoménal. [Litt]

(63) **Ausflug** Sm std. (13. Jh.), mhd. *uzvluc* [the correct form is *ûzvluc*, however, EWF]. Zunächst nur vom Ausfliegen der Vögel gesagt, dann (seit Luther) übertragen auf Menschen, spezialisiert auf 'Wanderung, kleinere Reise' im 17. Jh. [...] (EWDS) [At first, only for the birds' leaving their nest, then (since Luther) transferred to humans, with a specialisation on 'walking-tour', 'short journey' in the 17th century]

Such developments can also be accompanied by other semantic innovations in which the items are reused to express new concepts (e.g. in technical contexts, etc., see ex. (64) / (65)).

(64) CONVERTISSEUR. s. m. Celui qui réussit dans la conversion des âmes. Il signifie également, Celui qui s'efforce de convertir les autres à sa religion. Il est familier dans les deux sens, et ne se dit guère que par plaisanterie. [DAF 6]

(65) *convertisseur* [kɔ̃vɛʀtisœʀ] nom masculin 1 RARE Celui qui opère des conversions (1°). [...] 2 (1869) Cornue basculante où l'on transforme la fonte en acier par oxydation du carbone, en y insufflant de l'air comprimé. [...] 3 *Convertisseur (de devises, de monnaie)*: dispositif (calculette, tableau...) permettant de connaître l'équivalent dans une monnaie d'un montant exprimé dans une autre monnaie, et inversement. (PR 2016)

These examples thus confirm the observations made in the diachronic study of ludic items in the *Dictionnaire de l'Académie française*: ludic items represent a highly dynamic domain in the lexicon, as ludicity motivates lexical innovation, but is also subject to different tendencies with respect to the subsequent development of the ludic items.

6 Conclusion

I have argued that ludicity represents an important dimension of lexical innovation and expansion. Studying the information on ludic lexical items provided by contemporary and historical dictionaries of French, it has been shown that this dimension is indicated by nowadays established lexicographic marks. It can thus be assumed that ludicity is also an important aspect perceived by the speakers when using or interpreting the lexical items. At the same time, however, the lexicographic treatment of ludic items is still in part unsystematic, as the categorisations are at times intuitive, and lexicographic marks indicating ludicity overlap with other marks. The overall number of ludic items indicated in *Le Petit Robert* seems to underrate the importance of this dimension of lexical innovation. Another observation that has been made is that normative and evaluative statements about ludic items are still strongly present. In order to contribute to a descriptive approach to ludicity in lexical innovation, basic structural, semantic, and pragmatic features of ludic innovations have been investigated. In addition, I have identified various subtypes of ludic innovations and ludic usage. Diachronic analyses of the introduction and evolution of ludic items have finally revealed basic pathways of evolution and confirmed that ludic innovations represent a highly dynamic domain which offers interesting insights into processes of lexical change. Important issues that will need to be addressed in further research concern the aptitude and productivity of certain patterns and processes of lexical innovation for ludic innovation / reuse (e.g. compounding, blending, reduplication, abbreviation, truncation, borrowing; see also the contributions by Arndt-Lappe and Braun, this volume). Another interesting topic for further research are specific patterns such as French *un beau X / une belle Y*, where the adjective functions as a ludic (ironical) augmentative. Finally, it seems necessary to investigate in more detail the evolution of ludic expressions along the continuum of context-dependent ludic uses and stable lexicalised items as well as the boundaries between ludic innovations and other types of innovations.

7 References

Anscombre, Jean-Claude & Mejri Salah (eds.). 2011. *Le figement linguistique: la parole entravée*. Paris: Champion.
Arrivé, Michel. 2016. Alfred Jarry et Valère Novarina: aspects de la néologie littéraire. In Jean-François Sablayrolles & Christine Jacquet-Pfau (eds.), *La fabrique des mots français*, 141–157. Paris: Lambert-Lucas.
ARTFL, "Dictionnaires d'autrefois", https://artfl-project.uchicago.edu/content/dictionnaires-dautrefois (accessed 9 August 2017).
Attardo, Salvatore. 1994. *Linguistic Theories of Humor*. New York: Mouton.
Attardo, Salvatore, Christian F. Hempelmann & Sara Di Maio. 2002. Script oppositions and logical mechanisms: Modeling incongruities and their resolutions. *Humor* 15(1). 3–46.
Baider, Fabienne, Efi Lamprou & Monique Monville-Burston (eds.). 2011. *La Marque en lexicographie. États présents, voies d'avenir*. Paris: Lambert-Lucas.
Bergson, Henri. [10]1993 [1940]. *Le rire. Essai sur la signification du comique*. Paris: Quadrige / P.U.F.
Blank, Andreas. 1997. *Prinzipien des lexikalischen Bedeutungswandels am Beispiel der romanischen Sprachen* (Beihefte zur Zeitschrift für romanische Philologie 285). Tübingen: Niemeyer.
Blank, Andreas. 2001. *Einführung in die lexikalische Semantik für Romanisten*. Tübingen: Niemeyer.
DO 2017 = *Duden online*. www.duden.de (accessed 7 July 2017).
Ducháček, Otto. 1967. *Précis de sémantique française*. Brno: Universita J.E. Purkyně.
EWDS = Kluge, Friedrich. [24]2002. *Etymologisches Wörterbuch der deutschen Sprache*. Berlin & New York: De Gruyter.
Galinsky, Hans. [2]1967. Stylistic Aspects of Linguistic Borrowing. A Stylistic View of American Elements in Modern German. In Broder Carstensen & Hans Galinsky (eds.), *Amerikanismen der deutschen Gegenwartssprache. Entlehnungsvorgänge und ihre stilistischen Aspekte*, 35–72. Heidelberg: Winter.

Galisson, Robert. 1988. Cultures et lexicultures. Pour une approche dictionnairique de la culture partagée. *Annexes des Cahiers de linguistique hispanique médiévale* 7/1, 325–341.
Galli, Hugues. 2016. San-Antonio sur le ring: les mots mis K.O. In Jean-François Sablayrolles & Christine Jacquet-Pfau (eds.), *La fabrique des mots français*, 159–175. Paris: Lambert-Lucas.
Grand Robert = Robert, Paul & Alain Rey: *Le grand Robert de la langue française: Dictionnaire alphabétique et analogique de la langue française.* 1985. 9 volumes. Paris: Le Robert.
Jakobson, Roman. 1960. Linguistics and Poetics. In Thomas A. Sebeok (ed.), *Style in Language*, 350–377. New York: Wiley.
Kabatek, Johannes. 2015. Wordplay and Discourse Traditions. In Angelika Zirker & Esme Winter-Froemel (eds.), *Wordplay and Metalinguistic / Metadiscursive Reflection. Authors, Contexts, Techniques, and Meta-Reflection* (The Dynamics of Wordplay 1), 213–228. Berlin & Boston: De Gruyter.
Kemmner, Ernst. 1972. *Sprachspiel und Stiltechnik in Raymond Queneaus Romanen* (Dissertation, Universität Tübingen). Tübingen: Fotodr. Präzis.
Klein, Jean-René. 2016. Degrés de la créativité lexicale littéraire. Esquisse d'une typologie de la 'néologie' littéraire. In Jean-François Sablayrolles & Christine Jacquet-Pfau (eds.), *La fabrique des mots français*, 123–139. Paris: Lambert-Lucas.
Knospe, Sebastian, Alexander Onysko & Maik Goth (eds.). 2016. *Crossing languages to play with words. Multidisciplinary perspectives* (The Dynamics of Wordplay 3). Berlin & Boston: De Gruyter
Leclercq, Odile. 2012. Lexicographie et sentiment du vieillissement des mots au XVIIe siècle. *Diachroniques. Revue de linguistique française diachronique* 2 (Sentiment de la langue et diachronie). 107–130.
Lecolle, Michelle. 2012. Sentiment de la langue, sentiment du discours: changement du lexique, phraséologie émergente et 'air du temps'. *Diachroniques. Revue de linguistique française diachronique* 2 (Sentiment de la langue et diachronie). 59–80.
Levinson, Stephen C. 2000. *Presumptive meanings. The theory of generalized conversational implicature*. Cambridge, Mass. & London: The MIT Press.
Ludwig, Klaus-Dieter. 2009. Stilistische Phänomene der Lexik. In Ulla Fix, Andreas Gardt & Joachim Knape (eds.), *Rhetorik und Stilistik / Rhetoric and Stylistics*, 1575–1594. Berlin & New York: Mouton de Gruyter.
Luna, Rosa. 2014. Un acercamiento a la neonimia comparada: el buzón neológico peruano. *Debate Terminológico* 11. 47–61.
Onysko, Alexander & Winter-Froemel, Esme. 2011. Necessary loans – luxury loans? Exploring the pragmatic dimension of borrowing. *Journal of Pragmatics* 43. 1550–1567.
Popelar, Inge. 1976. *Das Akademiewörterbuch von 1694 – das Wörterbuch des Honnête Homme?* Tübingen: Niemeyer.
PR 2016 = *Le Petit Robert de la Langue Française. Version numérique du Petit Robert / Dictionnaire alphabétique et analogique de la langue française*, Nouvelle édition (version 4.2) – millésime 2016. http://pr.bvdep.com/ (accessed 31 August 2017).
Preite, Chiara. 2007. Le comique et son enregistrement lexicographique. *Publifarum* 6. http://publifarum.farum.it/ezine_articles.php?id=33 (accessed 14 June 2015).
Pruvost, Jean & Jean-François Sablayrolles. 2003. *Les neologismes*. Paris: Presses Universitaires de France.
Pustka, Elissa. 2015. *Expressivität. Eine kognitive Theorie angewandt auf romanische Quantitätsausdrücke*. Berlin: Erich Schmidt Verlag.

Rabatel, Alain. 2016. Jeux de mots, créativité verbale et/ou lexicale: des lexies et des formules. In Jean-François Sablayrolles & Christine Jacquet-Pfau (eds.), *La fabrique des mots français*, 233–249. Paris: Lambert-Lucas.

Sablayrolles, Jean-François. 2000. *La néologie en français contemporain. Examen du concept et analyse de productions néologiques récentes*. Paris: Champion.

Sablayrolles, Jean-François (ed.). 2003. *L'innovation lexicale*. Paris: Champion.

Sablayrolles, Jean-François. 2015. Néologismes ludiques: études morphologique et énonciativo-pragmatique. In Esme Winter-Froemel & Angelika Zirker (eds), *Enjeux du jeu de mots. Perspectives linguistiques et littéraires* (The Dynamics of Wordplay 2). 189–216. Berlin & Boston: De Gruyter

Spitzer, Leo. 1910. *Die Wortbildung als stilistisches Mittel: exemplifiziert an Rabelais; nebst einem Anhang über die Wortbildung bei Balzac in seinen "Contes drôlatiques"* (Beihefte zur Zeitschrift für romanische Philologie 42). Halle a. S.: Niemeyer.

Tableau des termes, signes conventionnels et abréviations du dictionnaire, Petit Robert 1993, http://pr.bvdep.com/aide/Pages/Abreviations.HTML et http://pr.bvdep.com/aide/Pages/pdf/abrevs.PD (accessed 14 June 2015).

Trésor de la Langue Française = Paul Imbs / Centre National de la Recherche Scientifique: *Trésor de la langue française: dictionnaire de la langue du XIXe et du XXe siècle (1789–1960)*. Paris: Éd. du Centre National de la Recherche Scientifique / Gallimard. 1971–1994. 16 volumes.

Walter, Henriette. 1991. Où commencent les innovations lexicales ? *Langue française* 90, Parlures argotiques. 53–64. doi: 10.3406/lfr.1991.6195; http://www.persee.fr/web/revues/home/prescript/article/lfr_0023-8368_1991_num_90_1_6195 (accessed 15 June 2015).

Winter-Froemel, Esme. 2008a. Towards a Comprehensive View of Language Change. Three Recent Evolutionary Approaches. In Ulrich Detges & Richard Waltereit (eds.), *The Paradox of Grammatical Change. Perspectives from Romance* (Current Issues in Linguistic Theory 293). 215–250. Amsterdam: Benjamins.

Winter-Froemel, Esme. 2008b. Unpleasant, Unnecessary, Unintelligible? Cognitive and Communicative Criteria for Judging Borrowings and Alternative Strategies. In Roswitha Fischer & Hanna Pułaczewska (eds.), *Anglicisms in Europe: Linguistic Diversity in a Global Context*, 16–41. Cambridge: Cambridge Scholars Publishing.

Winter-Froemel, Esme. 2009. Les emprunts linguistiques – enjeux théoriques et perspectives nouvelles. *Neologica* 3. 79–122.

Winter-Froemel, Esme. 2011. *Entlehnung in der Kommunikation und im Sprachwandel. Theorie und Analysen zum Französischen* (Beihefte zur Zeitschrift für romanische Philologie 360). Berlin & Boston: De Gruyter.

Winter-Froemel, Esme. 2013–14. What does it mean to explain language change? Usage-based perspectives on causal and intentional approaches to linguistic diachrony, or: On S-curves, invisible hands, and speaker creativity. In *Energeia. Online-Zeitschrift für Sprachwissenschaft, Sprachphilosophie und Sprachwissenschaftsgeschichte* 5: *Kausale und finale Erklärungen in der Linguistik*. 123–142.

Winter-Froemel, Esme. 2016a. Approaching Wordplay. In Sebastian Knospe, Alexander Onysko & Maik Goth (eds.), *Crossing Languages to Play With Words. Multidisciplinary Perspectives* (The Dynamics of Wordplay 3). 11–46. Berlin & Boston: De Gruyter.

Winter-Froemel, Esme. 2016b. Les créations ludiques dans la lexicographie et dans l'interaction locuteur-auditeur: aspects structurels, enjeux sémantiques, évolution diachronique. In Jean-François Sablayrolles & Christine Jacquet-Pfau (eds.), *La fabrique des mots français*, 251–267. Paris: Lambert-Lucas.

Winter-Froemel, Esme. 2016c. Répétitions et déformations ludiques de syntagmes linguistiques – entre parole, langue et traditions discursives. In Marie-Sol Ortola (ed.), *Varia. Transmettre, traduire, formaliser* (Aliento 8), Presses Universitaires de Lorraine. 237–255.

Winter-Froemel, Esme. In press. The pragmatic necessity of borrowing: Euphemism, dysphemism, playfulness – and naming. To appear in: *Taal en Tongval* 69/1 (2017).

Winter-Froemel, Esme & Alexander Onysko. 2012. Proposing a pragmatic disctinction for lexical anglicisms. In Cristiano Furiassi, Virginia Pulcini & Félix Rodríguez González (eds): *The Anglicization of European Lexis*, 43–64. Amsterdam & Philadelphia: Benjamins.

Winter-Froemel, Esme, Alexander Onysko & Andreea Calude. 2014. Why some non-catachrestic borrowings are more successful than others: a case study of English loans in German. In Amei Koll-Stobbe & Sebastian Knospe (eds.), *Language contact around the globe*, 119–142. Frankfurt et al.: Peter Lang.

Claudine Moulin
Ludicity in lexical innovation (II) – German

Abstract: The paper explores ludic innovations as a specific subtype of linguistic innovation at the lexical level. I will discuss the phenomenon of linguistic ludicity in the context of lexicographic sources in German, taking into account contemporary and historical dictionaries as well as Early New High German sources of metalinguistic reflection. Different types of lexical innovation will be analysed, with a special focus on structural, semantic, and pragmatic features underlying the process of ludic expansion of the lexicon. Firstly, I will reflect on methodological challenges encountered when exploring linguistic ludicity from a lexicographic point of view. Subsequently, I will analyse the linguistic and lexical marking of ludicity in dictionaries of contemporary German (most importantly *Duden online* 2017) and in selected sources of the (Early) Modern period (Harsdörffer, Kramer, Adelung), in order to investigate general metalinguistic and lexicographic lines of depicting wordplay and ludic innovation leading to language change. There will be a particular focus on Johann Christoph Adelung's *Grammatisch-kritisches Wörterbuch der hochdeutschen Mundart* ([1793–1801] 1970) and the tracing of relevant pathways of evolution of ludic innovations, especially in the predominant domain of nominal compounds. Overall, it will be shown that markedness plays a central role for ludic innovation and that the analysis of ludic use from a lexicographic point of view can uncover underlying dynamics of lexical expansion and change. *

1 Introduction: Exploring ludicity in the context of lexical innovation

Linguistic ludicity can be explored from different angles and has been the object of scientific reflection on both the theoretical and empirical levels (see for example different recent positions in Knospe et al. 2016: 11–94; Filatkina and Moulin, submitted). In the following, the focus is centred on *ludic innovations* as a

---

* As stated in the preceding contribution, Esme Winter-Froemel and I would like to thank the audience of our joint "tandem talk" at Trier University as well as Peter Kühn and two anonymous reviewers for their very helpful comments and suggestions. In addition, our thanks go to Martina Bross and Angela Oakeshott for the stylistic revision of our papers and for assisting us with the translations of the citations from historical sources of German.

specific subtype of linguistic innovation at the lexical level. The term – as introduced by Winter-Froemel (see the preceding paper in this volume) – links the aspects of *ludicity*, understood as the playful use of linguistic items (coined with humorous intentions in the speaker-hearer interaction) and of *innovation*, a dimension associated with language change and semantic transformations at the lexical level. The notion of ludic innovation thus opens up a path to the inherent *dynamics* of linguistic innovation in general and to its diachronic implications in particular, especially in the domain of wordplay. Wordplay as such has an inherent historical component that is profoundly culturally bound, interactive und highly functional: The following definition given by Winter-Froemel can be used as a starting point for our reflections:

> Wordplay is a historically determined phenomenon in which a speaker produces an utterance – and is aware of doing so – that juxtaposes or manipulates linguistic items from one or more languages in order to surprise the hearer(s) and obtain a humorous effect on them. (Winter-Froemel 2016: 37)

Regarding the different parameters mentioned here for the identification of this type of linguistic innovation, it can be pointed out that the dimensions of awareness on the part of the speaker, the juxtaposition / manipulation of linguistic items and the functional dimension of humorousness are not always essential prerequisites, notably from a diachronic point of view when it comes to explaining the emergence, coining and dynamization of ludic items (see Filatkina and Moulin, submitted; Winter-Froemel, in this volume). Research on ludic innovation and wordplay has up to now mainly focused on synchronic aspects of the phenomenon in question (both for modern languages and for historical stages of these); it thus seems necessary to broaden the scope of analysis by combining both dimensions. Turning to lexicographic sources in order to explore ludic innovation allows one to observe metalinguistic choices concerning ludic items and their treatment in contemporary and historical dictionaries. Furthermore, for historical stages of a language, contemporary metalinguistic comments are often the only tangible witnesses of relatively unfiltered explanatory power when it comes to the interpretation of linguistic evidence.

As far as the treatment of ludic items in lexicographic sources is concerned (for the state of the art, see the preceding paper by Esme Winter-Froemel), there has up to now been little research undertaken from a genuine diachronic point of view, let alone from a crosslinguistic perspective as intended by the two interlinked papers on French and German in this volume. Based on the general theoretical premises developed in the preceding paper, I will present selected case studies using German lexicographic data in order to explore the importance of ludic innovations as a subtype of lexical innovation, with the intention of opening up the field for further research. With this aim in mind, the analysis of lexicographic and metalinguistic sources from modern and New Early High German will be combined to explore the importance and the role of ludicity from a historical point of view. Wherever possible, my findings are crosslinked with results obtained by Esme Winter-Froemel (see the preceding paper in this volume).

The paper is structured as follows: Section 2 addresses methodological issues concerning the possibilities and challenges of identifying and exploring ludic innovations in lexicographic sources. Section 3 then traces ludic innovations in selected case studies in order to reveal underlying mechanisms in the lexicographic treatment of metalinguistic information on linguistic ludicity. I will analyse how ludic innovation is encoded and interpreted in the dictionary entries of contemporary German (most importantly *Duden online*) and relevant historical dictionaries from the Early New High German period and the Enlightenment (Matthias Kramer, Johann Christof Adelung). Section 4 explores pathways of evolution of ludic innovation with a case study of Johann Christoph Adelung's dictionary, highlighting i. a. the predominant group of items designated as ludic, namely nominal compounds, and other relevant phenomena found in the corpus (for example the role of diminutives for ludic use). In accordance with the findings for French, it can be observed that ludicity is often based on a relative markedness of the innovations and that these can be grouped in different subtypes. Formerly otherwise marked items can moreover often be reused in a ludic way, so that a coexistence of different varieties of use can be observed. Moreover, items once ludically reinterpreted or reused can also show a tendency towards wearout effects, so that ludically marked items may in turn become differently marked or unmarked in the course of diachronic evolution.

2 Dictionaries and ludicity: Setting the frame

Turning to dictionaries in order to explore ludic innovations in synchrony and diachrony implies preconditions that are bound to the historicity, materiality and textual organization of these sources. Nowadays, users (and dictionary makers) expect lexicographic reference works to have a certain layout and contain a minimum of specific types of information, i.a. the lexicon item itself in a precise (usually alphabetical) order, grammatical, semantic and perhaps etymological information, examples illustrating the use of the respective word and details about its conditions of use, for example concerning its stylistic or dialectal marking. This modern dictionary 'architecture' with relevant micro- and macrostructural properties is part of a long lexicographic tradition that has evolved through the centuries (see for the German tradition e.g. Stötzel 1970; Grubmüller 1990; Kühn and Püschel 1990). Apart from the lexical item, prototypically placed at the head of the entry, the exact positioning and structuring of these features can vary. Furthermore, certain features present in dictionaries today were unknown or not compulsory in former times. Besides bearing in mind differences on a functional level, a diachronic investigation of dictionaries will have to cope with challenges linked to the heterogeneity, multimodality and variability of the material in question. Moreover, dictionaries themselves are subject to diachronic change, not only from one edition to another, but also when, for example, they comprise several volumes produced within the framework of a lexicographic project conducted over a longer period of time, possibly over more than several decades if not centuries. Research has shown that elaborate dictionaries with longer production periods, such as for example Jacob and Wilhelm Grimm's *Deutsches Wörterbuch*, not infrequently reveal inconsistencies and changes in the presentation of their linguistic material (see e.g. Dückert 1987; Schares 2006). All these factors pose challenges when it comes to their subsequent analysis for linguistic purposes. Particularly digital representations of formerly printed dictionaries can differ significantly in the way the lexicographic material is presented in the digital format. This ranges from non-searchable or only poorly searchable image reproductions to highly encoded lexicographic systems in database form that include the detailed marking of subpositions and lexicographic features with high digital searchability of the sources (see e.g. Hildenbrandt and Moulin 2012; Moulin and Nyhan 2014). Similarly, born-digital dictionaries of modern stages of a language show differing degrees of online searchability, as the investigation in the following will show.

Ludic innovation in lexicographic sources can be traced by specific information given in the bodies of the entries, especially in the form of diaevaluative marks,[1] a subcategory of pragmatic marks in lexicography (see Wiegand 1981; Püschel 1989; Ludwig 2009: 1585–1587). These marks are of a different type and form a less homogeneous group than diatopic or diastratic marks, which is also reflected in high variance at the terminological level in lexicographic literature and the dictionaries themselves (see e.g. Corbin 1989; Ludwig 1991 and the contributions in Baider et al. 2011). Diaevaluative marks in dictionaries display – even for modern dictionaries – a high variability at the verbalization level in the

---

[1] Püschel (1989) uses the term *evaluative Markierungen* (evaluative marks).

dictionary entries themselves, with a range of quasi-synonyms for the symptom values of ludic use, as seen for French (see Preite 2007; Winter-Froemel in this volume) and shown below for German.

In his overview of diaevaluative marks in German, French and English dictionaries, Püschel (1989: 693) points out that diaevaluative marks display peculiarities of use that are not (yet) included in the intrinsic semantic explanation of the item and that are related to their profound pragmatic properties:

> Sie dienen also der weiteren Spezifizierung der Gebrauchsregel eines Wortes. Während in den sog. Bedeutungserklärungen beschrieben wird, wie man mit einem Wort prädizieren bzw. referieren kann, geben die evaluativen Markierungen Hinweise darauf, was man mit einem Wort bei normaler Verwendung unter normalen Umständen außerdem noch machen kann. Denn wenn wir Wörter äußern, dann prädizieren und referieren wir nicht nur einfach, sondern wir machen zugleich noch was anderes.
> [They [= evaluative marks] thus provide further specification for the rules of use of a word. Whereas the so-called meaning explanations describe how one can predicate or refer, evaluative marks point out what one can further do with a word in normal use under normal circumstances. Namely, when we utter words, we don't only predicate or refer, but at the same time, we also do something else.]

Diaevaluative marks such as 'familiar', 'playful', 'jocular', 'ironical' imply close relations to factors of style and accordingly fuzzy borders in their delimitation from other types of markers, for example diastratic ones. In consequence, when dealing with marking in dictionaries, Püschel (1989: 694) suggests an underlying "zero-marking" for the "normal" use of words showing a neutral use without marked features. The concept of unmarked (or zero-marked) forms in the lexicographic context can prove helpful for the further analysis, as words can be per se diaevaluatively marked (such as *Räuberzivil* 'casual dress' or French *réformette* 'insufficient, so-called reform', which show no neutral variant) or develop a secondary, marked use alongside or instead of an unmarked one (such as *Banane* 'banana / helicopter with two rotors' or French *mesurette* 'measuring spoon / insufficient, so-called measure'). In the course of language change, scales of markedness can be envisaged to trace the development, reduction or fading-out of the diaevaluative markedness of lexical items against the background of lexical innovation.

3 Tracing ludic innovations in lexicographic sources

In the following section, I will turn to the treatment of ludic innovation in German with case studies for modern and historical German lexicography. The first (section 3.1) focuses on the treatment of ludic items in the *Duden online-Dictionary* (DO 2017). Before turning to the treatment of ludic elements in selected dictionaries of German published between the seventeenth and the end of the eighteenth century (section 3.3), I will present some preliminary observations which are, from a metalinguistic point of view, linked to the topic of linguistic ludicity in Baroque times (section 3.2). The reason for the inclusion of metalinguistic considerations in this chapter is i.a. the fact that for the German language in the Baroque period there is a completely different situation where lexicography is concerned, as there was no large monolingual dictionary comparable to the *Dictionnaire de l'Académie française* in the sixteenth and seventeenth centuries (see e.g. Stötzel 1970: 3). Furthermore, not all extant historical lexicographic sources of German are digitized and searchable online in a similar way to the ARTFL database of French dictionaries.

3.1 Ludic innovations in Modern German

For *Duden online*, the prototypical lexicographic mark for signalling ludic items and usages in contemporary German is *scherzhaft* ('jocular, playful(ly), humorous(ly)'). The search for lexical entries containing "scherzhaft" revealed 1,558 items, which corresponds to about 0.78% of the total of approx. 200,000 dictionary entries. The number is comparable to that observed by Esme Winter-Froemel (see preceding paper in this volume) for the *Petit Robert* 2016. It should be noted that similarly to the findings for French, either the lexical item as a whole or a specific use of this item is marked as ludic, for example in a phrase or sub-meaning.

Besides *scherzhaft*, the dictionary team I consulted[2] also mentioned *spöttisch* ('mocking'), *salopp* ('slang'), *emotional übertreibend* ('emotionally exag-

---

[2] The *Duden online* corpus cannot be queried by complex search parameters (such as for example stylistic markers) directly on the internet. I thank Kathrin Kunkel-Razum and Thorsten Frank (both Bibliographisches Institut / Berlin) for providing me with detailed and extensive material harvesting the stylistic marker field of the underlying dictionary database for the

gerating'), *gehoben* ('elevated') and *ironisch* ('ironic') as being used to signal degrees of ludicity. This is a similar finding to that made for French, showing the "fuzzy borders" of a clear marking of ludic use, as the following examples illustrate:

(1) **Amtsmiene, die** [...] MEIST SPÖTTISCH übertrieben strenger Gesichtsausdruck einer Amtsperson (DO 2017)

(2) **Alphamädchen, das** [...] SALOPP durchsetzungsfähige, andere Menschen dominierende junge Frau (DO 2017)

(3) **Humanitätsapostel, der** [...] IRONISCH jemand, der in übertriebener, der Realität nicht Rechnung tragender Weise die Verwirklichung der Humantitätsideale fordert. (DO 2017)

(4) **Diebeshandwerk, das** [...] IRONISCH Betätigung fortgesetzten Diebstahls, ständiger Diebereien, mit der jemand seinen Lebensunterhalt bestreitet (DO 2017)

On the whole, the analysed corpus of the *Duden online* yielded 1,784 entries with such lexicographic marks, which have to be checked separately for their ludic use. The markers can be used alone or combined with diatopic, diastratic, diaphasic or diachronic features. For *scherzhaft* for instance, we find i. a. *umgangssprachlich scherzhaft* ('colloquially jocular/playful/humorous'), *familiär scherzhaft* ('familiarly jocular/playful/humorous'), *verhüllend scherzhaft* ('euphemistically jocular/playful/humorous'), *landschaftlich verhüllend scherzhaft* ('diatopically euphemistically jocular/playful/humorous'), *veraltend scherzhaft* ('obsolescently jocular/playful/humorous'), *österreichisch scherzhaft* ('jocular/humorous/playful use in Austrian German'), *Soldatensprache scherzhaft* ('jocular/humorous/playful in army language'), it may sometimes be combined with another lexicographic mark (*salopp scherzhaft* 'colloquially (slangily) jocular'; *oft scherzhaft, ironisch* 'often jocular, ironic').

(5) **Räuberzivil, das** [...] UMGANGSSPRACHLICH SCHERZHAFT nachlässige, legere, nicht dem Anlass angemessene Kleidung (DO 2017)

(6) **Hausfreund, der** [...] (2) SCHERZHAFT VERHÜLLEND Liebhaber der Ehefrau (DO 2017)

(7) **Kapazunder, der** [...] ÖSTERREICHISCH SCHERZHAFT Koryphäe, Kapazität (DO 2017)

---

analysis. My thanks go further to Doris al-Wadi (Institut für Deutsche Sprache / Mannheim) for insights into the data of the *online IDS Neologismenwörterbuch* (NWB).

(8) **Bibliotaph, der** [...] BILDUNGSSPRACHLICH SCHERZHAFT VERALTEND jemand, der seine Bücher an geheimen Stellen aufbewahrt und nicht verleiht; zu griechisch *táphos* = Grab, eigentlich = Büchergrab (DO 2017)

(9) **Affenschaukel, die** [...] 1. SOLDATENSPRACHE SCHERZHAFT Fangschnur, Schulterschnur, 2. UMGANGSSPRACHLICH zu beiden Seiten des Kopfes in Form einer Schlinge herabhängender Zopf (DO 2017)

The examples demonstrate that native speakers (and dictionary makers) may judge the stylistic-diaevaluative marking of the item in different ways from those indicated by the dictionary makers; *Affenschaukel* (in (9)) in the meaning 'pigtails, plaits' is marked for example as colloquial, but not jocular. Thus, similar methodological constraints can be observed to those made for French in the preceding paper in this volume. In comparison to the *Petit Robert* 2016, the *Duden Online Dictionary* seems to be more reluctant to include of new lexical items in its corpus; for example, it does not record neologisms like *Aufschieberitis, Carbikini, Seniorenazubi* or *Tofutier*, which are recorded in the online IDS *Neologismenwörterbuch* (NWB) and marked as "pleasant", "mocking" ("spöttisch") or "colloquial". The dictionaries can also differ in their assessment of one lexical item:

(10) **Schwachmatikus, der** [...] SCHERZHAFT VERALTEND 1. Schwächling, 2. Dummkopf; scherzhaft latinisierte Bildung – **Schwachmat, der** UMGANGSSPRACHLICH 1. Schwächling, 2. Dummkopf; scherzhaft latinisierte Bildung; verwandte Form: Schwachmatikus (DO 2017)

(11) **Schwachmat, der** [...] 1. SALOPP Person, die für beschränkt gehalten wird; Kurzwort zu Schwachmatiker; seit Anfang des ersten Jahrzehnts des 21. Jahrhunderts in Gebrauch (NWB 2017)

The example above also shows that the ludic dimension is not necessarily mentioned in the field for lexicographic marks, but may also (as in (10), *Schwachmat*) occur somewhere else in the body of the lexicon entry, for example in etymological explanations.

3.2 Ludic innovations and wordplay in Baroque metalinguistic reflection

In order to understand the role of the ludic dimension in German lexicography in early modern times, it is necessary to briefly turn to the context in which

German Early Modern dictionaries developed. The European process of what Sylvain Auroux[3] calls grammatisation led to a systematical increase in the production of vernacular grammars and lexicographic sources from the sixteenth century onwards. These sources are to be seen not only against the background of a growing use of the vernaculars in written, especially urban, communication, but also in the context of a theoretical, metalinguistically reflected approach to these languages themselves. The consequent debates on the nature and value of the mother tongue were also carried out on a poetological-philosophical level, for instance in systematical linguistic explorations of the internal structure of the respective linguistic systems. The vernaculars were considered "natural" languages of a "Golden Age", qualitatively no different from and thus intrinsically equal to the so-called "holy" languages – Hebrew, Latin, and Greek, and thus subject to observation and experimentation. For German, the quantitative and qualitative increase in these discussions starts a little later than in other languages (for example Italian or French). It can be observed particularly in the Baroque period against the background of the Thirty Years' War (1618–1648), notably in the context of linguistic societies such as the *Fruchtbringende Gesellschaft* (founded in 1617) and their main actors, such as Justus Georg Schottelius (1612–1676), Georg Philipp Harsdörffer (1607–1658), Philipp von Zesen (1619–1689), and Kaspar Stieler (1632–1707). In the promotion of the role of German as a fully developed, equally prestige-marked medium of poetry and science, linguistic, rhetorical and aesthetic norms are deliberated and these norms are reflected at a moral-ethical level and employed as an instrument of epistemic insight. Thus, the analysis and puristic fostering of German were considered a central task for linguistic and poetic purposes, anchored in the concept of *Spracharbeit* ('working with language'), a term coined particularly by Schottelius (1663) as a conscious act of language cultivation (see Hundt 2000; Filatkina and Moulin, submitted).

One of the core domains of the *Spracharbeit* was the analysis and development of a rich yet pure lexicon, with a virtually unlimited and ever-growing potency of its elements. This empowerment of word creation – and thus of lexical innovation – was considered a characteristic feature of the German language

---

[3] See the definition of the term by Auroux (1992: 28): "Par grammatisation, on doit entendre le processus qui conduit à décrire et à outiller une langue sur la base de deux technologies, qui sont encore aujourd'hui les piliers de notre savoir métalinguistique: la grammaire et le dictionnaire." Similar observations to those made in this paper for German (see also Moulin 2000) can be made for other European vernaculars.

in comparison to other vernaculars.[4] This immense lexical reservoir has a realised (as speech and norm) and a virtual status (as a system) and can be activated by the speakers as agents of their *Spracharbeit*. As a reflection of naturality and its divine quality, *Spracharbeit* is sophisticated, yet also effortless and entertaining in a ludic way. Language can thus be specifically defined and described in its ludic performance (see Filatkina and Moulin, submitted).

Wordplay, as developed especially by Harsdörffer, who was programmatically called "der Spielende" ('the player') in the *Fruchtbringende Gesellschaft*, can be conducted at all levels of a language system, ranging from phonology to syntax and the lexicon, in written or spoken use, serving equally every day communication, cultivated conversation, and poetical purposes (Moulin 2016; Filatkina and Moulin, submitted). Wordplay thus follows rules that can be described and consciously applied for the sake of linguistic creativity and entertainment. Under these premises, ludicity plays a formative role in lexical innovation, the cultivation and expansion of the lexicon becoming a central motor in the development of Baroque dictionaries.

It is revealing that early evidence of the compound *Wortspiel* ('wordplay') is to be found in seventeenth-century texts,[5] produced by precisely those actors mentioned above: Baroque linguists and poets. In his *Frauenzimmer Gesprächspiele* (FZG [1643–1657] 1968), an eight-volume title based i.a. on ludic conversation and linguistic games played by six protagonists, Harsdörffer uses the term several times, i.a. in the context of building logogriphs (FZG, 7: 427). He also uses it as a header ("Wortspiele") in his chapter on linguistic plays ranging from letter play, syllable play to word play, where the focus is particularly on compounds with indigenous elements (FZG, 8: 64–67). Over several pages, the protagonists choose for their witty dialogue examples playing with the lemma *Wort* as the first element of endocentric nominal compounds, forming common or more or less ad-hoc compounds according to the principle of analogy, among them *Wortspiel* itself (see Figure 1). These results could be regarded as lists of items for an as yet non-existent dictionary.

---

[4] This conception is well visualized on the frontispiece of Caspar Stieler's dictionary (1691), which shows a paradisiac garden with a huge tree as a symbol of the German language bearing an unlimited number of branches and single leaves symbolizing the unquantifiable number of "self-growing" elements of the German lexicon.

[5] DWB, 30: col. 1623 (http://www.woerterbuchnetz.de/DWB?lemma=wortspiel, accessed 31 July 2017).

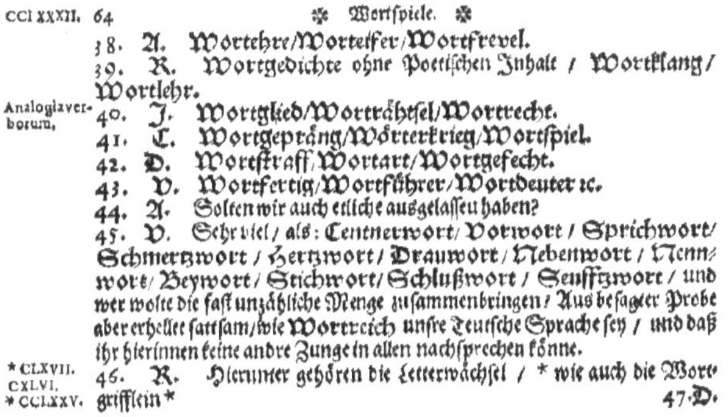

Fig. 1: Georg Philipp Harsdörffer, Frauenzimmer Gesprächspiele, VIII, 1649 (1969), 64 (header *Wortspiele* and compound example *Wortspiel* in the dialogue-part of the text)

Asking themselves if they have omitted results, the protagonists argue that this is the case and in inversion of the elements create further compounds with *Wort* as second element, culminating in the observation that German is so *wortreich* ('rich in words'), that no other language can compete ("ihr hierinnen keine andere Zunge in allen nachsprechen könne", FZG, 8: 64).

Harsdörffer offers no semantic description of what is meant with *Wortspiel* here, but the plural form of the header (*Wortspiele*) points towards the duplexity of the wordplay itself using *Wortspiel* as a metalinguistic phenomenon (a "state of mind") and an object-language use of the term in the play. In the German Dictionary founded by Jakob and Wilhelm Grimm (DWB, 30, 1960), where Harsdörffer is quoted as the first record for the item *Wortspiel*, the historical meaning of the lemma is described as follows, embracing the actual meaning as well as the figurative meaning of the compound for the seventeenth and eighteenth centuries:

> die lexikalische buchung des wortes um die wende vom 17. zum 18. jh. läszt sich über die allen anwendungen gemeinsame vorstellung 'spielerischer umgang mit dem wort oder den wörtern' hinaus im engeren sinne der bedeutung 1 'spiel mit bloszen worten' oder 2 'wortscherz' nicht immer sicher bestimmen, scheint aber bereits beide vorauszusetzen. (DWB 1960, vol. 30: 1622–1623)
> [the lexical entry for the word at the turn of the seventeenth to the eighteenth century cannot always be precisely determined beyond the concept of 'playful usage of the word(s)', which is common to all uses of the word; the narrower meanings 1 'play with mere words' or 2. 'jestful expression' can ultimately not be determined; though the word seems to already presuppose both.]

The Grimm Dictionary (DWB), whose article *Wortspiel* is well worth reading, then lists two entries taken from Baroque dictionaries. The first is from Kaspar Stieler's *Stammbaum* from 1691 ("rede- *sive* wortspiel *allusio verborum*", Stieler 1691: 2088), the second from the Italian-German dictionary by the foreign language teacher and linguist Matthias Kramer in its 1702 edition ("Wortschertz / wort- oder wörterspiel scherzo, giuoco di parole, bisticcio, motteggio", Kramer 1702, 2: 866c and 1397b; with the interesting synonyms *Redespiel, Wortspiel, Wörterspiel*, and *Wortschertz*).

The production of *Wortspiele* in seventeenth- and eighteenth-century German as a linguistic-cultural practice may not have been of liminal significance as the compound engendered a verbal derivate *wortspielen* ('to wordplay', DWB, vol. 30: 1625) and a nomen agentis *Wortspieler* ('word player', DWB, vol. 30: 1625) with both literal and figurative meanings, both terms (as opposed to the figurative *Wortspielerei* and the adjective *wortspielerisch*) no longer being common.

3.3 Ludic innovations in Early Modern dictionaries

These observations on the coining of the word *wordplay* in German allows us to move towards to the marking of ludic dimensions in the vocabulary described in the dictionary entries themselves. This lexicographic dimension is difficult to explore for German in an overarching way, as there is almost no comprehensive literature on the stylistic marking in dictionaries of the German language from a historical point of view (see e.g. Püschel 1989; von Polenz and Moulin 2013: 197). Furthermore, older dictionaries of German like those of Kaspar Stieler (1691), whose *Stammbaum* is in fact one of the first comprehensive dictionaries of the German language in early modern times, are, though available on-line in the form of images, not searchable as full texts or annotated data material. The same applies for bilingual or multilingual Early Modern dictionaries such as those of Levin Hulsius (1546–1606), Matthias Kramer (1640–1729) or Johann Leonhard Frisch (1666–1743). Thus, we are faced with additional methodological challenges. The first results of our findings are that dictionaries of the German language (both monolingual and bilingual ones) from the sixteenth and seventeenth centuries have no or only rather sparse stylistic or pragmatic indication as to the use of the lemmas they list. Levin Hulsius's popular bilingual and multilingual dictionaries, whose first editions appeared at the end of the sixteenth century (see Moulin-Fankhänel 1994: 96–105), and Kaspar Stieler's *Stammbaum* give no such pragma-stylistic or diaevaluative information.

Von Polenz and Moulin (2013: 197) mention that Matthias Kramer was the first to structure his dictionary entries with a semantic classification and to also provide markings for ludic word use. Kramer is the author of several bi- und multilingual dictionaries with i.a. German, French, and / or Italian, some of them also containing grammars of the respective languages (see Kühn and Püschel 1990: 2053; Moulin-Fankhänel 1997: 166–177; Bray 2000: 59–77). In the preface to his *Neu-ausgefertigtes, herrlich großes und allgemeines italiänisch-teutsches Sprach- und Wörterbuch* (1693), he explicitly explains how pragma-stylistic features are documented and marked with an asterisk, namely with phrases as lexicographic items:

> Etliche Phrases oder Redarten werden mit einem (*) bezeichnet/ welches dann andeutet/ daß dieselbige nicht wie die andere/ in Ernst/ sondern nur in Stylo Comico und in Kurtz-weil und Schimpff geredt werden: Dieweil aber dieses bis dato von keinem/ wie es sich gebührt hätte/ unterschieden worden/ haben nicht allein die gar Einfältigen/ sondern auch wol Geschicktere/ an statt einer ernstlicher Rede oder Concept/ zum öfftern die aller-lächerlichste Schwencke vorbringen/ und für halbe Schalcksnarren gehalten werden müssen. (Kramer, 1693, fol)( )( )(iv$^{r \cdot v}$)
>
> [A number of phrases or expressions are marked with a (*). This indicates that these items are not spoken in a serious way, but only in a stylo comico (a comic style) and for amusement and jest. Because this distinction has not been made by anyone as it should have been up to now, not only the really simple-minded but also more skilful speakers have – instead of putting forward a serious utterance or concept – occasionally uttered the most ridiculous stories and couldn't avoid being taken for more-or-less foolish jesters.]

Ludic use is thus marked for pragmatic purposes in order to prevent learners of German as a foreign language from using the lexicographic items erroneously in a serious ("in Ernst") – meaning unmarked – way. The same method is used in Kramer's German-French Dictionary (1712–1715), where lexical items as such can also be marked as "Schertz-Wort", see the following example explaining the use of French *épouseur* ('suitor') as a ludic creation and its parallels in German:

(12) **Epouseur,** [Schertz-wort] Heirater / Nehmer etc.
§ *tout amant n'est pas epouseur; beaucoup d'amans, peu d'epouseurs*, es ist nicht ein jeder Freyer ein Heirater; viel Freyer / wenig Nehmer.
un epouseur de la plus offrante & de la derniere encherisseuse, ein Heirater der jenigen Person so das meiste Geld hat.
**c'est un epouseur des onze mille vierges*, das ist ein Heirater der 11000. Jungfern (ein Uberall-Freyer.) (Kramer 1712, 1: 893)

A systematic analysis of these markers in all Kramer's dictionaries should certainly be addressed in further research, as soon as his oeuvre, which encompasses several thousands of pages, is searchable on-line; the same applies for example for the German-Latin and German-French dictionaries of Johann Leonhard Frisch (1666–1743).

Regarding monolingual dictionaries, the next milestone on the timeline is Johann Christoph Adelung's *Grammatisch-kritisches Wörterbuch der hochdeutschen Mundart*, which can fortunately be analysed regarding its pragmatic markers of ludic dimensions in its second edition (Adelung 1793–1801).[6] The author's grammatical and lexicographic work closes the Baroque grammaticographic and lexicographic tradition (Jellinek 1913: 329–385) and opens the path to descriptive metalinguistic theories indebted to insights of Enlightenment thinking. Adelung's definition of wordplay (*Wortspiel*) in the corresponding item entry of his dictionary serves to illustrate the more modern approach to the description of linguistic evidence. He carefully draws up a distinction between form and content in the ludic use of words and points out its pragmatic functions; for Adelung, wordplay is

> [...] eine bloß auf Belustigung abzielende Beschäftigung mit Wörtern und ihren Bedeutungen; z. B. wenn man aus der wahren oder erzwungenen appelativen Bedeutung eigener Nahmen den Stoff zu einer Gedankenreihe entlehnet. In engerer Bedeutung ist das Wortspiel, wenn Wörter und deren Bedeutungen, ohne eine Wahrheit von einiger Erheblichkeit zu erhalten, bloß zur Belustigung einander entgegen gesetzet werden. [Adelung, 4: 1616]
> [[...] an occupation with words and their meanings merely aiming to amuse, for example when one borrows from the real or contrived appellative meaning of actual names the material for a set of thoughts. Wordplay means in a narrower sense that words and their meanings are placed in contrast to each other solely for amusement, without obtaining a truth of any relevance.]

Furthermore, Adelung's Dictionary is one of the first dictionaries of German giving systematically pragmatic-diaevaluative information about the use of words in the approx. 58,500 entries it records (see Kühn and Püschel 1990: 2054–2057; Ludwig 1991: 55–102). Searching the online corpus with all combinations of *scherz** in the full text search, we obtain 494 entries; of these hits, 176 are not relevant for our question (false positives), leaving 318 hits indicating ludic use of the respective lexical item or one of its sub-meanings/uses. This corresponds to 0.54% of the listed vocabulary, a rate that lies under that determined above for the *Duden online* (0.78%). Similarly to the findings in French (see Esme Winter-Froemel in this volume), there is no standard stylistic

---

[6] This edition is available in a searchable database in an online edition available on the Trier dictionary portal (woerterbuchnetz.de). The later Vienna edition of 1811 is also available for full text search (http://lexika.digitale-sammlungen.de/adelung/online/angebot, accessed 31 July 2017). The results are similar to those of the second edition.

mark for ludic items and also no fixed position for this information in the entry sections of the four volumes of Adelung's dictionary. The most common formulations are:

(13) "im Scherze" ('in jocular / playful / humorous use')
"im gemeinen / niedrigen / vertraulichen Scherze" ('in common / low / familiar playful use')
"im figürlichen aber nur niedrigen Scherze" ('in figurative, but only low playful use')
„im Scherze und mit Verachtung" ('in jocular / playful use and with contempt')
"eine (übliche) scherzhafte Benennung" ('a (common) jocular / playful denomination')
"in der scherzhaften Schreib- und Sprechart" ('in the jocular / playful manner of writing and speaking')
"(nur) im figürlichen Scherze" ('(only) in a figurative jocular / playful use)
"ein nur im vertraulichen Scherze im figürlichen Verstande übliches Wort" ('a word, only used in a familiar jocular / playful manner with figurative meaning')
„nur noch zuweilen im niedrigen Scherze" ('only sometimes in a low jocular / playful use') [Adelung, 1–4]

The formulation patterns of the observed ludic use correlate with Adelung's overall approach to linguistic phenomena, which includes both normative aspects and elements of a descriptive approach (see e.g. Püschel 1982; Strohbach 1984; Kühn 1991: 108–109).

4 Disclosing pathways of evolution of ludic innovations in German (Adelung)

In the following section, I will concentrate on capturing ludic innovations as they can be traced diachronically in Adelung's dictionary (1793–1801). Given the constraints of a lack of annotated digital corpora of historical dictionaries from the sixteenth to eighteenth centuries, my case study focuses on Adelung and his treatment of diachronic change.

As seen above, Adelung's dictionary documents 318 lexical items with ludic use. Most of these items are products of word formation (compounds and derivations, 207 items), an observation that has to be placed in its historical context: For the German language, word formation patterns play a central role in the development of the lexicon in all linguistic periods. However, especially in the Early New High German period immediately preceding Adelung's dictionary, there is an increase in systematic metalinguistic reflection on the creative power of word formation and its use for puristic, poetic, lexicological and lexicographical purposes (see above section 3.2; e. g. Gützlaff 1989; Hundt 2000).

4.1 Ludic creations as nominal compounds

The predominant group of word formation structures in the Adelung corpus is made up of nominal compounds, namely 94 of the items in the list of results containing a ludic use marking (*scherzhaft* etc.) in the relevant entry:

(14) Der Abcschütz, das Amtsgesicht, das Augenpulver, der Bachhase, der Backfisch, der Becherstürzer, der Befehlshaber, die Beyschläferinn, der Blutegel, das Brustwerk, der Bücherjude, der Bücherwurm, die Butterbämme, der Degenkopf, der Denkzettel, der Ehekrüppel, der Ehrenmann, der Fehdebrief, der Fladenkrieg, der Fliegenfürst, die Flitterwoche, der Franzmann, der Freßsack, das Fußwerk, der Galgenstrick, der Gänsebauch, der Gänsewein, das Gartenhuhn, der Geiferbart, der Gesichtsgucker, der Gesundheitsrath, der Glücksritter, der Grabenfüller, der Grashecht, die Graswitwe, der Grillenfang, der Haarboden, der Haarmann, der Handgucker, die Handkrause, die Häringsnase, der Harnprophet, die Hausehre, die Haus-Postille, die Heckmutter, der Herrenbauch, die Herrenkranckheit, der Herzbeutel, die Himmelfahrt, der Hirsenpfriemer, der Hörnerträger, der Hosenflicker, das Hufeisen, der Kammerjäger, die Kammerjungfer, der Klopffechter, der Kohlgärtner, der Krähenfuß, der Kratzfuß, der Krippenreiter, das Küchen-Latein, der Kunstrichter, der Kuppelpelz, der Landläufer, der Langohr, das Luntenrecht, der Milchbart, der Milchbruder, die Pfaffengasse, der Poetenkasten, der Pumpernickel, der Salbader, der Sandmann, der Sandreiter, der Sauertopf, der Sausewind, die Schaflorbeere, der Schalksdeckel, die Schnabelweide, die Schneckenpost, der Schneiderfisch, die Schneiderkrankheit, der Schusterkarpfen, die Schweinsfeder, der Siebenschläfer, das Sitzfleisch, der Speicherdieb, die Staats-Dame, die Strohfiedel, die Strohwitwe, der Stuhlgang, der Stürzebecher, Das Weiberlehen, die Weindrossel [Adelung, 1–4]

The compounds in this list can be organized into different groups, displaying different systemic and diachronic features. A first pattern that emerges are cases in which diatopically unmarked compounds which already belong to a standard eighteenth-century lexical reservoir are endowed with a secondary, "new" ludic dimension. Generally, this new ludic use is encoded in the dictionary with a separate semantic entry:

(15) **Augenpulver, das** 1) Ein Pulver für Gebrechen der Augen. 2) Im ironischen Scherze, eine kleine Schrift, weil sie die Augen schwächet. [Adelung, 1: 564]

(16) **Blutêgel, der** 1) Ein kleiner länglicher Wurm, welcher sich in süßen Wassern aufhält, [...] 2) Im niedrigen Scherze, ein Vorgesetzter, der seine Untergebenen bis auf das Blut drücket. [Adelung, 1: 1093]

(17) **Bücherwurm, der** 1) Eigentlich, eine Made, welche aus dem Eye entstehet, welches ein kleiner Käfer [...] im August zwischen dem Pergamente und dem Deckel der Bücher leget. Die Made, die daraus entstehet, sucht sich einen Weg aus ihrem Gefängnisse zu bahnen, und verzehret darüber die prächtigsten Denkmähler des menschlichen Geistes. 2) Im figürlichen Scherze, ein Mensch, der immer über den Büchern liegt. [Adelung, 1: 1238]

From a diachronic point of view, the ludic use is of course generated from the unmarked, neutral one; the semantic relation between the main meaning and the secondary one is based on various semantic mechanisms, for example metaphorical transfer.

Another group of compounds are "ludically born", e.g. new nominal compound products that have been especially created for ludic use. Since they are not diatopically marked by Adelung, they can be counted as standard language variants of the time.

(18) **Amtsgesicht, das**. Im Scherze, ein ernsthaftes Gesicht, ein Gesicht, mit welchem man seine Amtsgeschäfte zu verrichten pfleget. [Adelung, 1: 256]

(19) **Bécherstürzer, der**. Im Scherze, ein starker Trinker. [Adelung, 1: 776]

(20) **Héckmutter, die**. Im vertraulichen Scherze, eine fruchtbare Person weiblichen Geschlechtes, welche fleißig hecket, d. i. oft gebieret. [Adelung, 2: 1049]

A further group consists of ludic compounds or ludic uses with a dialectal or regional scope. These are explicitly marked as such and can show both variants mentioned above, e.g. known compounds, with a new ludic (diatopically bound) meaning or "ludically born" (diatopically bound) compounds:

(21) **Báckfisch, der**. Eine allgemeine Benennung aller derjenigen Fische, welche man in den Küchen lieber zu backen, als zu kochen pflegt. Im Scherze nennt man in Niedersachsen, ein junges, zum Heirathen noch nicht tüchtiges Mädchen einen Backfisch. [Adelung, 1: 686]

(22) **Báchhase, der**. Im gemeinen Scherze einiger Gegenden, der Nahme eines Wassermußes oder Wasserbreyes, welcher auch wohl ein Landläufer genannt wird.' [Adelung, 1: 680]

(23) **Speicherdieb, der**. Eine im Niederdeutschen, vermuthlich nur im Scherze übliche Benennung des gemeinen Haussperlinges, weil er die Kornspeicher gern zu besuchen pflegt. [Adelung, 4: 179]

Ludic use in diatopically marked contexts can remain diatopically restricted, disappear or lose its diatopic mark through time as it becomes integrated into standard language (as for example *Backfisch*). At this point, we can note that for language evolution paths, the different types of markedness form a complex matrix showing certain degrees of permeability between their elements (see also section 4.3).

4.2 Reflecting ludicity in the dictionary: Diminutives and ludic use

In some of the entries in his dictionary, Adelung gives longer linguistic explanations, especially with lexical items displaying grammatical functions, for example derivation suffixes. In one case, that of the diminutive suffix *-chen* in German nouns, the author explicitly notes a ludic potential, pointing out that ludic use occurs especially with derivations of a plural base ending on *-er*:

> Aber es gibt im Hochdeutschen auch einige Diminutiva, welche von dem Plural des Hauptwortes, welches verkleinert werden soll, gebildet werden. Kleine Lichterchen, artige Bücherchen, liebe Kinderchen, närrische Dingerchen, possierliche Männerchen, niedliche Wörterchen. So auch Häuserchen, Weiberchen, Geisterchen u. s. f. Diese Diminutiva finden nur bey solchen Wörtern Statt, die sich im Plural auf -er endigen; über dieß sind sie nur in der vertraulichen oder scherzhaften Sprechart üblich. [Adelung, 1: 1326]
> [But in High German, there are some diminutives that are formed from the plural of the noun that is to be diminutised. *Kleine Lichterchen, artige Bücherchen, liebe Kinderchen, närrische Dingerchen, possierliche Männerchen, niedliche Wörterchen*. Thus also *Häuserchen, Weiberchen, Geisterchen* etc. These diminutives only occur with such words that show a plural ending in *-er*; moreover, they are only common in a familiar or jocular style of speech.]

The generic use of such ludic diminutives (noun+PL on *-er+chen*) is illustrated by Adelung in the explanation above (e.g. *Lichterchen, Bücherchen, Kinderchen, Dingerchen, Wörterchen, Häuserchen*), showing their paradigmatic seriation and synchronic productivity.[7] The forms are transparent with regard to their morphological and semantic structure and are not recorded systematically with separate lexicon entries in the dictionary, a fact that indicates the *ad-hoc* and strongly pragmatically marked character of the contexts they are used in. On the other hand, other derivatives with *-chen* without this pattern *(-er-chen)* are noted in their ludic use, as for example *Hänschen* (< *Hans*), *Männchen* (< *Mann*), *Seelchen* (< *Seele*), *Stellchen* (< *Stelle*), *Thalerchen* (< *Thaler*) or *Tummelchen* (< *Tummel*). On the whole, ludic diminutives in Adelung's dictionary show close affinities with other pragmatic marks such as familiar or colloquial usage, so that fuzzy borders between the categories do indeed have to be taken into account. Adelung's early metalinguistic observations on the ludic potential of diminutives are noteworthy and can be placed alongside to the findings of

---

[7] See for similar patterns in modern German Fleischer-Barz (2012: 235), who note besides the generic, diminutive function of the suffix an additional "emotional connotation"; see also Dressler and Barbaresi (1994).

Dressler and Barbaresi (1994) on diminutives in modern languages, especially German and Italian, showing, as they do, the central role of the ludic character of playfulness for this type of word formation.[8]

4.1 Ludic items and diachronic change

Regarding language change and the evolution of ludic items, Adelung's dictionary has a number of entries with historical conjectures or explanations for the creation of unmarked lexical entries involving preliminary ludic use for their creation (with a subsequent path *ludic innovations > eighteenth-century unmarked item*; see also section 4.1):

(24) **ABCSchütz, der**. Der Grund der Benennung ist unbekannt. Vielleicht hat man sie aus Scherz gemacht, und dabey vornehmlich auf die Griffel und andere Werkzeuge der Abcschüler gesehen, welche man mit Waffen verglichen [Adelung, 1: 16]

In other cases,[9] Adelung seeks the potential for etymological explanation in ludic origins, but does not always find convincing explanations in the "Mährchen"[10] ('fairy-tale') the etymological narratives might bring with them, when no confirmed path can be generated. The example above, with a compound designating a young child just starting school, aims at motivating the compound as an entity: whilst the first component (ABC, cf. Engl. *abecedarian*) is transparent, the second one (*Schütz(e)* 'shooter') is opaque in the eyes of the lexicographer, who conjectures ludic use with metaphorical bridging of writing instruments and weapons. The compound is obviously already lexicalized and unmarked in eighteenth-century German, as it is today.

Several other items from the list in (14) however, when compared to modern German, have lost the ludic markedness which still existed in Adelung's time, thus providing lexicographic evidence for semantic change in the direction *eighteenth-century German +ludic > modern German -ludic [+neutral]*, as the following examples illustrate:

---

8 See Dressler and Barbaresi (1994: 197): "[...] one realization of the pragmatic features [fictive] and particularly [non-serious] is the ludic character that most diminutives have, at least to some extent. The ludic character is the dominant pragmatic meaning in case of playful interactions and is prominent in homileic discourse."
9 Well worth reading is the long article PUMPERNICKEL, der (Adelung, 3: 864) with two diachronic conjectures based on ludic use for the creation of this compound designating a typical sort of German black bread.
10 This termed is used by Adelung for the ludic speculations in the entry PUMPERNICKEL.

(25) **Befêhlshaber, der** [...] 2) Der andern zu befehlen hat, besonders von einem Vorgesetzten bey der Armee. Der Befehlshaber eines Kriegesheeres, eines Regimentes [...]. Daher befehlshaberisch, im Scherze für gebietherisch, auf eine befehlende Art. [...] [Adelung, 1: 790]

(26) **Kammerjäger, der**. Ein fürstlicher Jäger, welcher seinen Herrn auf der Jagd und im Jagdwesen bedienet, aber von einem Leibjäger zuweilen noch verschieden ist. Im Scherze wird auch ein Mäuse- und Katzenfänger ein Kammerjäger genannt. [Adelung, 2: 1486]

(27) **Flítterwóche(n), die**. Im Scherze, die ersten Wochen im Ehestande, wo sich die gegenseitige Zärtlichkeit noch in ihrer ganzen Stärke zeiget; in welchem Verstande man auch wohl der Flittermonath sagt, wenn anders diese Zärtlichkeit die Dauer eines Monaths erreicht. [Adelung, 2: 214]

In (25), the adjective *befehlshaberisch* 'imperious' has completely lost its ludic mark; and *Kammerjäger* (26) has, besides its main historical meaning ('a hunter serving a prince'), nowadays developed a second, regular unmarked meaning ('vermin exterminator') originating from its ludic use:

(28) **Kammerjäger, der** 1) (früher) im persönlichen Dienst eines Fürsten stehender Jäger, 2) jemand, der beruflich Ungeziefer innerhalb von Gebäuden vernichtet. [DO 2017]

As for "ludically born" *Flitterwoche(n)*[11] ('the first [particularly tender] week(s) after marriage'), it has developed a plurale tantum with an unmarked meaning generated from its original use and a second (also neutral) one designating the holiday of a newlywed couple (DO 2017). Another development is documented with *Backfisch* 'small fish for frying' (21) showing in its marked, ludic meaning ('female teenager') a path *+dialectal* (18th century) > *–dialectal* (New High German) > *+obsolete* (contemporary German, see DO 2017). Here, the evolution path leads to archaization, and possibly, the disappearance of the lexical item in question.

As Ludwig (2009: 1579) points out, formally neutral archaic elements or phrases can be reactivated in language use with diaevaluative features:

Distanzierend oder ironisierend/scherzhaft bzw. alltertümelnd werden sie [= Archaismen; CM] verwendet, z.B. *Beinkleid, Konterfei, alldieweil, hochgelahrte Festversammlung, des Diskutierens war zu viel, eine artige Empfehlung an den Herrn Gemahl.*

---

11 The first part of the compound is opaque today; cf. MHG *vlittern* ‚to whisper, fondle'. English *honeymoon* has experienced a similar diachronic change (see the entry in the OED online, http://www.oed.com/view/Entry/88181?rskey=UzEVs1&result=1, accessed 31 July 2017).

[They [= archaisms; CM] can be used in a distancing, ironizing/ludic or antiquating way, for example *Beinkleid, Konterfei, alldieweil, hochgelahrte Festversammlung, des Diskutierens war zu viel, eine artige Empfehlung an den Herrn Gemahl.*]

Many of the examples cited here can be actualised (or reused) in concrete language use with a path showing an evolution *–archaic –ludic > + archaic –ludic > +archaic +ludic*. For example, the nouns *Beinkleid* ('trousers') and *Konterfei* ('portrait') show different stages of this path in Adelung's dictionary, the former having neither an archaic nor a ludic marking (Adelung, 1: 823), the latter being marked as archaic, but not (yet) as ludic (Adelung, 1: 1348). For contemporary German, *Duden online* marks *Beinkleid* as "scherzhaft, veraltet" ('jocular, obsolete; it is not clear here how the comma is to be understood) and *Konterfei* as "veraltet, noch altertümelnd oder scherzhaft" ('obsolete, still antiquating or jocular'].

Tracing such pathways of evolution in ludic innovation simultaneously through a larger diachronic corpus of dictionaries from the sixteenth century until today, would certainly be a promising challenge for the issues tackled in this paper. This also concerns the building of complex digital lexicographic information systems (see e.g. Moulin and Nyhan 2014) that would enable research queries with algorithms capable of disclosing complex patterns of evolution in multidirectional ways and of coping with the existing heterogeneity and potential overlapping of lexicographic marks in lexicographic practice.

5 Conclusion

This paper explores linguistic ludicity as an important source of lexical innovation and expansion. Focusing on the analysis of lexical items marked as playful in contemporary and Early New High dictionaries of German, I have shown that information on ludic use has been recorded in lexicographic sources since the seventeenth century and that the marking of ludicity can today be considered a normal component of lexicographic practice. The dictionaries in question have developed for the description of ludic use a set of terminological instruments, that until today has displayed a certain heterogeneity around the concept of playfulness and ludicity and that overlaps with other diaevaluative or pragmatic marks. As a consequence, this also brings methodological challenges for the exploration of linguistic ludicity in lexicographic sources, whether they are contemporary or historical. It is worth noticing that the verbalisation of ludic use in both historical dictionaries (Adelung) and contemporary ones (*Duden online*) seems to play a quantitatively smaller role in comparison to the total of the vocabulary treated, a finding that is similar to that made for the quantitative analysis for French (see the preceding paper in this volume by Esme Winter-Froemel). By choosing a descriptive approach that takes into account structural, semantic, and pragmatic features of ludic innovations, different types and steps of ludic innovation have been identified, allowing first insights into the structural types, the importance of markedness and the steps of the emergence and evolution of ludic items. An important methodological issue for further lexicographic research on lexical innovation will be the availability and operationability of networked digital lexical resources enabling not only the identification and further analysis of pathways and patterns of ludic innovation, but also of other mechanisms underlying the expansion of the lexicon. Another point of interest will be drawing comparisons between the findings in dictionaries and those in larger historical text corpora, in order to trace divergences and similarities in the occurrence and treatment of lexical innovation from a diachronic point of view.

6 References

Adelung = Adelung, Johann Christoph. ²1793–1801. *Grammatisch-kritisches Wörterbuch der Hochdeutschen Mundart mit beständiger Vergleichung der übrigen Mundarten, besonders aber der oberdeutschen*. Zweyte, vermehrte und verbesserte Ausgabe, 4 vols. Leipzig: Breitkopf [reprint Hildesheim & New York: Olms 1970]. Online version: http://woerterbuchnetz.de/cgi-bin/WBNetz/wbgui_py?sigle=Adelung (accessed 31 August 2017).
ARTFL = *Dictionnaires d'autrefois. French dictionaries of the 17th, 18th, 19th and 20th centuries*, https://artfl-project.uchicago.edu/content/dictionnaires-dautrefois (accessed 31 August 2017).
Auroux, Sylvain. 1992. Introduction. Le processus de grammatisation et ses enjeux. In Sylvain Auroux (ed.), *Histoire des idées linguistiques, tome 2. Le développement de la grammaire occidentale*, 11–64. Liège: Mardaga.
Baider, Fabienne, Efi Lamprou & Monique Monville-Burston (eds). 2011. *La Marque en lexicographie. États présents, voies d'avenir*. Paris: Lambert-Lucas.
Bray, Laurent. 2000. *Matthias Kramer et la lexicographie du français en Allemagne au XVIIIe siècle. Avec une edition des textes métalexicographiques de Kramer* (Lexicographica. Series Maior 99). Tübingen: Niemeyer.
Corbin, Pierre. 1989. Les marques stylistiques / diastratiques dans le dictionnaire monolingue. In Franz Josef Hausmann, Oskar Reichmann, Herbert Wiegand & Ladislav Zgusta (eds), *Wörterbücher / Dictionaries / Dictionnaires. Ein internationales Handbuch zur Lexikographie / An International Encyclopedia of Lexicography / Encyclopédie internationale de lexicographie* (Handbücher zur Sprach- und Kommunikationswissenschaft / Handbooks of Linguistics and Communication Science 5.1), 673–680. Berlin & New York: De Gruyter.
DO 2017 = *Duden online*, www.duden.de (accessed 31 August 2017).

Dressler, Wolfgang U. & Lavinia Merlini Barbaresi. 1994. *Morphopragmatics. Diminutives and intensifiers in Italian, German, and other languages* (Trends in Linguistics. Studies and Monographs 76). Berlin & New York: Mouton de Gruyter.
Dückert, Joachim (ed.). 1987. *Das Grimmsche Wörterbuch. Untersuchungen zur lexikographischen Methodologie*. Stuttgart: Hirzel.
DWB= Grimm, Jacob & Wilhelm Grimm. 1854–1971. *Deutsches Wörterbuch. Erstbearbeitung*, I–XVI, Quellenverzeichnis. Online-version: http://woerterbuchnetz.de/cgi-bin/WBNetz/wbgui_py?sigle=DWB (accessed 31 August 2017).
Filatkina, Natalia & Claudine Moulin. Submitted. Wordplay and baroque linguistic ideas. In Esme Winter-Froemel & Verena Thaler (eds.), *The Dynamics of Wordplay* (working title). Berlin & Boston: De Gruyter.
Fleischer, Wolfgang & Irmhild Barz. ⁴2012. Wortbildung der deutschen Gegenwartssprache (De Gruyter Studium). Berlin & Boston: De Gruyter.
Grubmüller, Klaus. 1990. Die deutsche Lexikographie von den Anfängen bis zum Beginn des 17. Jahrhunderts. In Franz Josef Hausmann, Oskar Reichmann, Herbert Wiegand & Ladislav Zgusta (eds), *Wörterbücher / Dictionaries / Dictionnaires. Ein internationales Handbuch zur Lexikographie / An International Encyclopedia of Lexicography / Encyclopédie internationale de lexicographie* (Handbücher zur Sprach- und Kommunikationswissenschaft / Handbooks of Linguistics and Communication Science 5.2), 2037–2049. Berlin & New York: De Gruyter.
Gützlaff, Kathrin. 1989. *Von der Fügung teutscher Stammwörter: Die Wortbildung in J.G. Schottelius' "Ausführlicher Arbeit von der Teutschen Haubt-Sprache"*. Hildesheim: Olms.
Harsdörffer, Georg Philipp. 1643–1657. [1968]. *Frauenzimmer Gesprächspiele*, 8 vols. Reprint Nurenberg, Tübingen: Niemeyer. Digital facsimilies of all original volumes: http://www.die-fruchtbringende-gesellschaft.de/index.php?category_id=6&article_id=18 (accessed 19 August 2017).
Hildenbrandt, Vera & Claudine Moulin. 2012. Das Trierer Wörterbuchnetz. Vom Einzelwörterbuch zum lexikographischen Informationssystem. *Korrespondenzblatt des Vereins für niederdeutsche Sprachforschung* 119. 73–81.
Hundt, Markus. 2000. *"Spracharbeit" im 17. Jahrhundert. Studien zu Georg Philipp Harsdörffer, Justus Georg Schottelius und Christian Gueintz* (Studia Linguistica Germanica 57). Berlin & New York: Mouton de Gruyter.
Jellinek, Max Hermann. 1913–1914. *Geschichte der neuhochdeutschen Grammatik von den Anfängen bis auf Adelung*, 2 vols. Heidelberg: Winter.
Knospe, Sebastian, Alexander Onysko & Maik Goth (eds.). 2016. *Crossing languages to play with words. Multidisciplinary perspectives* (The Dynamics of Wordplay 3). Berlin & Boston: De Gruyter.
Kramer, Matthias. 1693. *Neu-ausgefertigtes, herrlich großes und allgemeines Italiänisch-Teutsches Sprach- und Wörterbuch*. Nürnberg: Endter.
Kramer, Matthias. 1702. *Das herrlich Grosse Teutsch-Italiänische Dictionarium*. Nürnberg Endter.
Kramer, Matthias. 1712–1715. *Das recht vollkommen Königliche Dictionarium Französisch-Teutsch*. Nürnberg: Endter.
Kühn, Peter. 1991. "... wir wollen kein Gesetzbuch machen". Die normativen Kommentare Jacob Grimms im Deutschen Wörterbuch. In Alan Kirkness, Peter Kühn & Herbert Ernst Wiegand

(eds.), *Studien zum Deutschen Wörterbuch von Jacob Grimm und Wilhelm Grimm*, vol. 1, 105–167. Tübingen: Max Niemeyer.

Kühn, Peter & Ulrich Püschel. 1990. Die deutsche Lexikographie vom 17. Jahrhundert bis zu den Brüdern Grimm. In Franz Josef Hausmann, Oskar Reichmann, Herbert Wiegand & Ladislav Zgusta (eds.), *Wörterbücher / Dictionaries / Dictionnaires. Ein internationales Handbuch zur Lexikographie / An International Encyclopedia of Lexicography / Encyclopédie internationale de lexicographie* (Handbücher zur Sprach- und Kommunikationswissenschaft / Handbooks of Linguistics and Communication Science 5.2), 2049–2077. Berlin & New York: De Gruyter.

Ludwig, Klaus-Dieter. 1991. *Markierungen im allgemeinen einsprachigen Wörterbuch des Deutschen. Ein Beitrag zur Metalexikographie* (Lexicographica. Series Maior 38). Tübingen: Niemeyer.

Ludwig, Klaus-Dieter. 2009. Stilistische Phänomene der Lexik. In Ulla Fix, Andreas Gardt & Joachim Knape (eds.), Rhetorik und Stilistik / Rhetoric and Stylistics. Ein internationales Handbuch historischer und systematischer Forschung / An International Handbook of Historical and Systematic Research (Handbücher zur Sprach- und Kommunikationswissenschaft / Handbooks of Linguistics and Communication Science 31.2), 1575–1594. Berlin & New York: De Gruyter.

Moulin, Claudine. ²2000. Deutsche Grammatikschreibung vom 16. bis 18. Jahrhundert. In Werner Besch, Anne Betten, Oskar Reichmann & Stefan Sonderegger (eds.), *Sprachgeschichte. Ein Handbuch zur Geschichte der deutschen Sprache und ihrer Erforschung* (Handbücher zur Sprach- und Kommunikationswissenschaft / Handbooks of Linguistics and Communication Science 2.2), 1903–1911. Berlin & New York: De Gruyter.

Moulin, Claudine. 2016. "Nach dem die Gäste sind, nach dem ist das Gespräch". Spracharbeit und barocke Tischkultur bei Georg Philipp Harsdörffer. In Nina Bartsch & Simone Schultz-Balluff (eds.), *PerspektivWechsel oder: Die Wiederentdeckung der Philologie. II. Grenzgänge und Grenzüberschreitungen. Zusammenspiele von Sprache und Literatur im Mittelalter und Früher Neuzeit*, 261–287. Berlin: Erich Schmidt Verlag.

Moulin, Claudine & Julianne Nyhan. 2014. The dynamics of digital publications: An exploration of digital lexicography. In Péter Dávidházi (ed.), *New publication cultures in the humanities. Exploring the paradigm shift*, 47–62. Amsterdam: Amsterdam University Press.

Moulin-Fankhänel, Claudine. 1994. *Bibliographie der deutschen Grammatiken und Orthographielehren*, vol. 1: Von den Anfängen der Überlieferung bis zum Ende des 16. Jahrhunderts (Germanische Bibliothek N.F. 6. Reihe: Bibliographien und Dokumentationen 4). Heidelberg: Winter.

Moulin-Fankhänel, Claudine. 1997. *Bibliographie der deutschen Grammatiken und Orthographielehren*, vol. 2: Das 17. Jahrhundert (Germanische Bibliothek N.F. 6. Reihe: Bibliographien und Dokumentationen 5). Heidelberg: Winter.

Polenz, Peter von & Claudine Moulin. ²2013. *Deutsche Sprachgeschichte vom Spätmittelalter bis zur Gegenwart. Band II: Das 17. und 18. Jahrhundert* (De Gruyter Studienbuch). Berlin & Boston: De Gruyter.

PR 2016 = *Le Petit Robert de la Langue Française*. Version numérique du Petit Robert / Dictionnaire alphabétique et analogique de la langue française, Nouvelle édition (version 4.2) – millésime 2016. http://pr.bvdep.com/ (accessed 31 August 2017).

Preite, Chiara. 2007. Le comique et son enregistrement lexicographique. *Publif@rum* 6. http://publifarum.farum.it/ezine_articles.php?art_id=33 (accessed 19 August 2017).

Püschel, Ulrich. 1982. Die Berücksichtigung mundartlicher Lexik in Johann Christoph Adelungs "Wörterbuch der hochdeutschen Mundart". *Zeitschrift für Dialektologie und Linguistik* 40. 28–51.
Püschel, Ulrich. 1989. Evaluative Markierungen im allgemeinen einsprachigen Wörterbuch. In Franz Josef Hausmann, Oskar Reichmann, Herbert Wiegand & Ladislav Zgusta (eds), *Wörterbücher / Dictionaries / Dictionnaires. Ein internationales Handbuch zur Lexikographie / An International Encyclopedia of Lexicography / Encyclopédie internationale de lexicographie* (Handbücher zur Sprach- und Kommunikationswissenschaft / Handbooks of Linguistics and Communication Science 5.1), 693–699. Berlin & New York: De Gruyter.
Schares, Thomas. 2006. *Untersuchungen zu Anzahl, Umfang und Struktur der Artikel der Erstbearbeitung des Deutschen Woerterbuchs von Jacob Grimm und Wilhelm Grimm*. Trier: Trier University dissertation. http://ubt.opus.hbz-nrw.de/volltexte/2006/359/ (accessed 19 August 2017).
Stieler, Caspar. 1691. *Der Teutschen Sprache Stammbaum und Fortwachs / oder Teutscher Sprachschatz*. Nürnberg, Altdorf: Hofmann – Meyer.
Stötzel, Georg. 1970. Das Abbild des Wortschatzes. Zur lexikographischen Methode in Deutschland 1617–1967. *Poetica* 3. 1–23.
Strohbach, Margrit. 1984. *Johann Christoph Adelung: Ein Beitrag zu seinem germanistischen Schaffen mit einer Bibliographie seines Gesamtwerkes* (Studia Linguistica Germanica 21). Berlin & New York: De Gruyter.
Wiegand, Herbert Ernst. 1981. Pragmatische Informationen in neuhochdeutschen Wörterbüchern. Ein Beitrag zur praktischen Lexikologie. In Herbert Ernst Wiegand (ed.), *Studien zur neuhochdeutschen Lexikographie I*, 139–271. Hildesheim & New York: Georg Olms.
Winter-Froemel, Esme. 2016. Approaching wordplay. In Sebastian Knospe, Alexander Onysko & Maik Goth (eds.), *Crossing languages to play with words. Multidisciplinary perspectives* (*The Dynamics of Wordplay* 3), 11–46. Berlin & Boston: De Gruyter.

Appendix

List of Abstracts / Liste des résumés

The Dynamics of Wordplay 5

The edited book series *The Dynamics of Wordplay* is open for volumes in English and French. The following section provides French translations of the titles and abstracts of the contributions contained in this volume.

La collection *The Dynamics of Wordplay* regroupe des volumes en anglais et en français. On trouvera dans la section suivante une traduction française des titres et résumés des contributions dans ce volume.

Partie I: Innovation linguistique
Part I: Linguistic Innovation

Natalia Filatkina: L'expansion du lexique par les modèles formulaïques: l'émergence de la formulaïcité dans l'histoire de la langue et dans l'usage moderne
Expanding the lexicon through formulaic patterns: The emergence of formulaicity in language history and modern language use

La contribution a pour but d'étudier le rôle de modèles formulaïques dans l'expansion du lexique. La notion de modèles formulaïques est expliquée dans la partie 1, et on argumentera que le caractère conventionnel de la communication humaine inclut les mots isolés, les unités polyléxicales, les phrases et les textes. Utilisés en tant que combinaisons libres de mots, les modèles formulaïques sont une partie constitutive de l'interaction humaine et, par conséquent, aussi de l'expansion de lexique. La partie 2 donne un bref aperçu des découvertes de la recherche antérieure (cet aperçu sera surtout basé sur des données de l'allemand standard) concernant l'interaction des modèles formulaïques et des produits de formations des mots, qui ont été jusqu'ici considérés comme l'outil principal de l'expansion du lexique. J'argumenterai qu'en adoptant la nouvelle conception des modèles formulaïques proposée ici, le rôle de ces derniers dans l'expansion du lexique doit être révisé. La partie 3 fournit des exemples de l'apparition de modèles formulaïques dans l'histoire de la langue et dans l'usage contemporain pour montrer qu'ils constituent un outil supplémentaire de l'expansion du lexique. Contrairement à la formation des mots, les modèles formulaïques ont été relativement peu étudiés jusqu'à présent. Dans la partie 3, les analyses seront effectuées en partant des théories du changement linguistique. Des "éléments moteurs" du changement linguistique comme la variation / la modification créative, la régularité / l'irrégularité, la codification / la normatisation, le rôle de traditions culturelles et contextuelles / discursives et la fréquence sont appliqués à l'apparition de modèles formulaïques. On démontrera que les critères habituels des théories existantes du langage et du changement linguistique ne s'appliquent pas aux modèles formulaïques de la même façon qu'ils ne le font par exemple au changement phonétique, grammatical ou même lexical. Les résultats de l'étude sont récapitulés dans la partie 4.

Anette Kremer and Stefanie Stricker: Les mots complexes dans les *Leges Barbarorum* du début du Moyen Âge et leur contribution à l'expansion du lexique du vieux haut allemand

Complex words in the early medieval *Leges Barbarorum* and their contribution to expanding the Old High German lexicon

Cette contribution étudie une sélection de mots complexes (mots composés, dérivés) pris des premières *Leges barbarorum* et illustre comment ces mots ont étendu le lexique de l'ancien haut-allemand. Les exemples sont pris des lois en allemand supérieur (*Lex Baiuuariorum*, *Lex Alamannorum*, *Leges Langobardorum*) qui forment une tradition relativement homogène. Dans le domaine de la composition sont examinés des mots complexes non attestés en dehors de la tradition des *Leges* et exposant des relations spécifiques entre leurs premiers et deuxièmes éléments. Dans le domaine de la dérivation, l'accent est mis en particulier sur des lexèmes résultant d'un processus de formation des mots qui est productif dans le type de texte examiné, mais que l'on voit à peine ailleurs dans l'ancien haut-allemand et qui n'est plus productif aujourd'hui. Les données présentées dans cette contribution viennent de la base de données LegIT qui a été établie depuis 2012 dans le cadre d'un projet de recherche à l'Université de Bamberg.

Sören Stumpf: L'utilisation libre de composants uniques en allemand: perspectives de la linguistique de corpus, de la psycholinguistique et de la lexicographie
Free usage of German unique components: Corpus linguistics, psycholinguistics and lexicographical approaches

Dans la recherche phraséologique, les composants uniques sont des mots qui apparaissent seulement dans des phrasèmes (par exemple dans *jmdn. an den Pranger stellen* METTRE QQN A UC [= *unique compound* / composant unique] (*Pranger* PILORI) 'mettre qn au pilori' et *im Handumdrehen* EN UN UC (*Handumdrehen* TOUR DE MAIN) 'immédiatement, en un clin d'œil'. Cependant, les analyses des emplois réels du langage montrent que des composants apparemment uniques peuvent aussi être (ré-)utilisés indépendamment des contextes phraséologiques et qu'ils peuvent contribuer à l'expansion du lexique. Cette contribution traite de cette utilisation libre de composants uniques en se focalisant sur des approches de la linguistique de corpus, de la psycholinguistique et de la lexicographie. On abordera les questions de savoir comment l'utilisation libre de composants uniques peut être vérifiée à l'aide de la linguistique de corpus, comment on peut expliquer cette utilisation dans une perspective psycholinguistique, et dans quelle mesure les composants uniques librement utilisés sont enregistrés dans des dictionnaires allemands.

Partie II: Productivité morphologique
Part II: Morphological Productivity

Ingo Plag and Sonia Ben Hedia: La phonétique des mots nouvellement dérivés: l'effet de la segmentabilité morphologique sur la durée des affixes
The phonetics of newly derived words: Testing the effect of morphological segmentability on affix duration

Les mots morphologiquement complexes qui sont nouvellement dérivés ont joué un rôle important dans la recherche sur la productivité morphologique et l'innovation lexicale (par exemple Baayen 1989, 1996; Plag 1999; Mühleisen 2010). La majeure partie de l'attention concernant les propriétés de tels mots a été consacrée à leurs propriétés phonologiques, morphologiques, sémantiques et syntaxiques (voir, par exemple, Bauer et al. 2013 pour de telles analyses). Cette contribution jette un coup d'œil sur les propriétés phonétiques de mots affixés, testant 'l'hypothèse de segmentabilité' de Hay (2003), selon laquelle les mots nouvellement dérivés montrent moins d'intégration phonétique (donc moins de réduction phonétique) de l'affixe, que les formes établies. Cette hypothèse est basée sur l'idée que la segmentabilité morphologique corrèle négativement avec l'intégration phonologique. Jusqu'à présent, il y a seulement une étude qui a clairement confirmé l'hypothèse de segmentabilité (i. e. Hay 2007), tandis que d'autres études ont échoué à reproduire l'effet (voir Hanique et Ernestus 2012 pour une vue d'ensemble). Notre contribution examine cette question en partant des données du corpus Switchboard pour cinq affixes anglais: *un-*, *in-* locatif, *in-* négatif, *dis-* et *-ly* adverbial. En utilisant différentes mesures de segmentabilité morphologique, nous démontrons que les durées des deux préfixes *un-* et *dis-* (contrairement aux durées de *in-* et *-ly*) soutiennent l'hypothèse de segmentabilité en grande partie. Pour les mots avec les préfixes *un-* et *dis-*, les préfixes qui sont plus facilement segmentables ont des durées plus longues.

Marcel Schlechtweg: Comment l'accent reflète la signification. L'interaction de la proéminence prosodique et de la (non-)compositionnalité sémantique dans les combinaisons non-lexicalisées du type adjectif+substantif en anglais

How stress reflects meaning: The interplay of prosodic prominence and semantic (non-) compositionality in non-lexicalized English adjective-noun combinations

Le sujet de cet article est la relation entre la prosodie et la sémantique dans des constructions non-lexicalisées composées d'un adjectif et d'un nom (AN) en anglais. Dans un test de production, des locuteurs natifs de l'anglais américain ont été enregistrés pendant la lecture à haute voix de phrases contenant des constructions AN telles que *black tram* ('tramway noir'). Les constructions avaient un sens compositionnel (p.ex. un tram qui est noir) ou un sens non-compositionnel (p.ex. un tram qui ne roule que pendant la nuit). L'étude avait pour but d'examiner, premièrement, si les constructions non-lexicalisées dont la sémantique était non-compositionnelle avaient une prosodie différente de leurs équivalents compositionnels et, deuxièmement, si la présence de *called so because* ('appelé ainsi parce que'), une expression qui peut directement mettre l'accent sur la sémantique non-compositionnelle, influençait la prosodie des constructions non-compositionnelles. La durée, l'intensité et la fréquence fondamentale, des paramètres acoustiques de la prosodie, ont été mesurés et analysés. Globalement, les résultats montrent que les constructions non-compositionnelles (sans *called so because*) ont été produites avec l'accent tonique sur la première syllabe. Dans les constructions compositionnelles et les constructions non-compositionnelles (avec *called so because*), par contre, l'accent principal n'a pas été mis sur la première syllabe. L'article argumente qu'un accent tonique sur la première syllabe et *called so because* peuvent être utilisés pour souligner la sémantique non-compositionnelle des constructions. Cependant, quand des constructions non-lexicalisées sont produites, ces deux procédés ne se manifestent pas simultanément. Les résultats sont interprétés dans le contexte de l'interaction de la sémantique et de la phonétique dans la production du langage.

Sabine Arndt-Lappe: L'expansion du lexique par la troncation: variabilité, reconstitution des formes de départ, productivité

Expanding the lexicon by truncation: Variability, recoverability, and productivity

Deux problèmes ont constitué un défi pour les théories morphologiques visant à représenter comment et pourquoi les modèles de troncation de noms et d'abréviation sont si productifs en tant que moyens d'élargir le lexique dans beaucoup de langues. Ces problèmes ont alimenté les débats autour de la question de savoir si de tels modèles de troncation devraient être considérés comme des formations de mots régulières (p.ex. Lappe 2007; Ronneberger-Sibold 2010; Alber et Arndt-Lappe 2012; Mattiello 2013; Manova 2016). Les problèmes concernés sont (a) la variabilité des réalisations observées à la surface, et (b) leur indétermination fonctionnelle et leur manque de transparence sémantique. Cette contribution présente des études de cas sur l'italien, l'allemand et l'anglais afin d'éclaircir ces questions. En ce qui concerne (a), on démontrera que la variabilité résulte de l'existence de différents modèles systématiques de troncation aussi bien au sein des langues particulières qu'à travers différentes langues, et on discutera les données disponibles pour déterminer dans quelle mesure les distinctions formelles correspondent à la différenciation fonctionnelle des modèles. En ce qui concerne (b), j'argumenterai que les modèles de troncation productifs sont optimisés pour permettre de reconstituer les formes de départ, et à partir des analyses des données, je discuterai l'idée que le contexte du discours joue un rôle crucial dans l'établissement de relations transparentes entre les bases et les dérivés. À un niveau théorique, j'argumenterai qu'il pourrait être prématuré d'exclure la troncation de la morphologie grammaticale à cause l'ampleur de variation formelle dans les formes de surface et leur manque de transparence, et que cela n'est pas secourable pour représenter la productivité des modèles de troncation observés. Contrairement à de telles approches, les résultats de cette contribution suggèrent un programme pour des recherches futures qui étudieront de façon plus détaillée les modèles et l'usage de la troncation aussi bien dans des langues particulières que dans des perspectives comparatives.

Partie III: Ludicité
Part III: Ludicity

Angelika Braun: Une approche des jeux de mots dans une optique phonétique et phonologiques – exemples de l'allemand

Approaching wordplay from the angle of phonology and phonetics – examples from German

Cette contribution essaie de définir ce qu'une approche phonétique peut apporter à l'étude des jeux de mots. Pour cette raison, elle se limitera à analyser les jeux de mots au niveau linguistique de la syllabe. À cet effet, je proposerai une taxinomie des jeux de mots à partir des éléments structuraux de la syllabe. Je mettrai l'accent sur la distinction entre les jeux de mots jouant sur des unités lexicales existant déjà et ceux qui introduisent de nouvelles unités. Différents mécanismes de jeux de mots "classiques" seront examinés par rapport à leurs effets sur la structure de la syllabe. Je présenterai une étude quantitative de 195 exemples qui s'adressent à un public allemand, et je traiterai en particulier les questions suivantes: (1) Quelle est la répartition entre les différents types de jeux de mots au niveau de la syllabe? (2) Avec quelle constituante de la syllabe joue-t-on? (3) Quels sont les mécanismes les plus utilisés pour les jeux de mots? Les résultats montrent que la paronymie et les mots-valises sont les types de jeux de mots les plus fréquents. De plus, on note une préférence claire pour les jeux de mots s'opérant au niveau de l'attaque de syllabe.

Georgette Dal and Fiammetta Namer: Les occasionnalismes ludiques en français, productivité et créativité

Playful nonce-formations in French: Creativity and productivity

Les occasionnalismes définis comme de "[n]ew complex word[s] created by a speaker / writer on the spur of the moment to cover some immediate need" (Bauer 1983: 45), sont un thème récurrent dans les recherches anglo-saxonnes et germaniques depuis de nombreuses années (cf., entre autres, Lipka 1975; Bauer 1983; Hohenhaus 1996; Crystal 2000; Štekauer 2002; Kerremans 2015), mais ce thème a jusqu'ici peu retenu l'attention des morphologues du domaine francophone. En effet, bien que toutes les conditions soient désormais réunies pour faire de ces données langagières un objet d'étude à part entière, avec, notamment le recours de plus en plus fréquent aux données issues de corpus authentiques, les morphologues du domaine francophone demeurent majoritairement réservés quant à l'intérêt des créations individuelles, encore plus quand elles sont ludiques et qu'elles semblent enfreindre les règles de formation de lexèmes, au motif qu'elles relèvent davantage de la performance que de la compétence, donc du champ de la (socio-)pragmatique, de la stylistique, mais non de celui de la théorie morphologique. Or, les occasionnalismes soulèvent des questions théoriques intéressantes: entre autres, convient-il de les comptabiliser (et comment) lorsqu'il s'agit de mesurer la productivité des procédés? Existe-t-il une distinction nette en productivité et créativité?

Dans la suite de Dal et Namer (2016a), la présente contribution s'intéresse aux patrons d'émergence des occasionnalismes ludiques en français. Après une rapide définition de la notion (§ 1), nous mettons au jour quelques patrons d'émergence récurrents (§ 2). Ces patrons sont ensuite utilisés pour établir un continuum parmi les occasionnalismes, selon leur degré de ludicité (§ 3.1). Pour terminer, nous discutons de plusieurs questions toutes en lien avec la notion de productivité (§ 3.2), avant de conclure.

Esme Winter-Froemel: La dimension ludique dans les innovations lexicales (I) – Français

Ludicity in lexical innovation (I) – French

Cette contribution vise à explorer l'importance de la dimension ludique au sein de l'innovation linguistique à partir d'études synchroniques et diachroniques de sources lexicographiques du français, et en réinterprétant les données lexicographiques selon la perspective des locuteurs. On discutera les possibilités et les défis méthodologiques qui se présentent quand il s'agit de retracer la dimension ludique dans le lexique. Les réflexions seront basées sur des dictionnaires contemporains et historiques, surtout le *Petit Robert* 2016 et différentes éditions du *Dictionnaire de l'Académie française*. De plus, on analysera comment les innovations sont introduites et perçues par les locuteurs, et on distinguera différents types d'innovation à partir de critères structurels, sémantiques et pragmatiques. Finalement, on étudiera l'évolution diachronique des innovations ludiques afin d'identifier des tendances et chemins d'évolution généraux. On essaiera de démontrer que le caractère marqué est un trait fondamental de l'innovation ludique, qui représente un domaine important, mais jusqu'à présent négligé de la dynamique lexicale.

Claudine Moulin: La dimension ludique dans les innovations lexicales (II) – Allemand

Ludicity in lexical innovation (II) – German

Cette contribution explore les innovations ludiques comme sous-type spécifique de l'innovation linguistique dans le domaine lexical. On discutera le phénomène de la ludicité linguistique dans le contexte de sources lexicographiques de l'allemand, en se basant aussi bien sur des dictionnaires contemporains et des débuts du haut allemand moderne que sur des sources métalinguistiques. Différents types de l'innovation lexicale seront analysés, avec une mise en mire des critères structurels, sémantiques et pragmatiques sous-jacents au processus de l'expansion lexicale. Dans un premier pas, une réflexion sera entreprise sur les enjeux méthodologiques de l'analyse lexicographique du phénomène de ludicité linguistique. Ensuite, on analysera le marquage linguistique et lexical de la ludicité dans les dictionnaires de l'allemand contemporain (particulièrement le *Duden online* 2017) et dans une sélection de sources historiques des temps modernes (Harsdörffer, Kramer, Adelung), afin d'explorer les grandes lignes métalinguistiques et lexico-graphiques cernant le jeu de mots ainsi que l'innovation ludique menant au changement linguistique. Une attention particulière sera portée au *Grammatisch-kritisches Wörterbuch der hochdeutschen Mundart* (1793–1801) de Johann Christoph Adelung afin de retracer des chemins pertinents de l'évolution de phénomènes d'innovations ludiques, notamment dans le domaine de la composition. En tout, je montrerai que le caractère marqué joue un rôle fondamental pour l'innovation ludique et que l'analyse de l'emploi ludique du point de vue lexicographique peut dévoiler des dynamiques générales de l'expansion et du changement lexical.

List of Contributors and Editors

Sabine Arndt-Lappe (Universität Trier)
Sabine Arndt-Lappe is Professor of English Linguistics at the University of Trier. Her research interests particularly include morphology and its interfaces from both a theoretical and an empirical perspective. She has published in various international journals (e.g. *English Language and Linguistics, Journal of Linguistics, Language, Morphology*). A book that may be of interest to this volume is *English Prosodic Morphology* (Springer, 2007). She is also currently one of the editors of the *Zeitschrift für Sprachwissenschaft* and a member of the editorial board of *Morphology*.

Sonia Ben Hedia (Heinrich-Heine-Universität Düsseldorf)
Sonia Ben Hedia is a research assistant at Heinrich-Heine-Universität Düsseldorf and works in a project of DFG Research Unit FOR2373 'Spoken Morphology'. She is writing her PhD thesis on gemination and degemination in English affixation. An article on this subject has recently been published in *Journal of Phonetics* ('Gemination and degemination in English prefixation: Phonetic evidence for morphological organization', 2017)

Angelika Braun (Universität Trier)
Angelika Braun received her academic training in linguistics and phonetics at the University of Marburg, Germany. She took her Ph. D. in linguistics and phonetics in 1988. From 1986 to 2000, she worked as a full-time forensic phonetician. In July 2000 she earned her post-doctoral degree (Habilitation) from the University of Marburg. Later that year, she joined the faculty of that University. Since 2009, she has held the post of professor of general and applied phonetics at the University of Trier. Her main research interests include speaker characteristics and speaker variability as well as sociophonetics, specifically speech and emotion, non-actual speech (irony), and phonetic aspects of wordplay. From the beginning of her academic career, she has also maintained an interest in and published on the history of phonetics.

Georgette Dal (Université de Lille) and Fiammetta Namer (Université de Lorraine)

Georgette Dal and Fiammetta Namer are ordinary professors of Language Sciences in France (University of Lille for the former, University of Lorraine for the latter), both specialists in Word Formation, with a particular attention to real data and Internet, and especially with respect to creativity and productivity. They have been working together for more than fifteen years, exploring various fields of word formation: description, theory and Natural Language Processing. They have taken part in or (co-)organized several research projects aiming to the production of morphological resources for French, and have (co-)edited journal special issues or volumes devoted to key issues in Word Formation, such as quantitative aspects, emergence of new patterns, form-meaning discrepancies, or the role of paradigms.

Natalia Filatkina (Universität Trier)

Natalia Filatkina studied linguistics and intercultural communication at the Moscow State Linguistic University and at the Humboldt University of Berlin. She obtained her PhD in Germanic Linguistics from the University of Bamberg. Since 2003, she has been teaching Historical Linguistics of German at Trier University. Her main research interests include language change, formulaic and figurative language, standardization and normalization, historical dialogue, text and discourse studies as well as Digital Humanities.

Anette Kremer (Universität Bamberg)

Anette Kremer is a research assistant with the Chair of German Linguistics at the University of Bamberg, Germany, where she received her PhD degree in 2012. Since 2013, she has worked as a research assistant on the project *Database-supported documentation of the vernacular vocabulary of the Continental West-Germanic laws of the barbarians*, funded by the German Research Foundation (DFG). Her research interests include historical lexicology, historical lexicography, research on language contact, and morphology.

Claudine Moulin (Universität Trier)

Claudine Moulin holds the Chair of German Historical Linguistics at the University of Trier and is the scientific director of the Trier Centre for Digital Humanities. She studied German and English Philology in Brussels and Bamberg. After her PhD (1990) in the domain of Early New High German orthography, she was a researcher at the University of Bamberg, where she gained her Habilitation in 1999 in the field of German Linguistics and Philology. She was in Oxford (1995, 1997) for several research stays as a Heisenberg Fellow of the German Research Foundation (DFG), working on vernacular paratexts and marginalia in medieval manuscripts, and in 2002, professor for Linguistics at the University of Luxembourg. She has been visiting professor at the École Pratique des Hautes Études EPHE / Sorbonne in Paris and a research fellow at the Institut of Advanced Studies / Institut d'Études Avancées in Paris. Her research covers the fields of historical linguistics and language change, medieval languages and literature, grammaticography, lexicography, graphematics and digital humanities. She is also one of the editors of the journal *Sprachwissenschaft* and the *Germanistische Bibliothek*.

Ingo Plag (Heinrich-Heine-Universität Düsseldorf)

Ingo Plag is Professor of English Linguistics at Heinrich-Heine-Universität Düsseldorf. He has published extensively in various linguistics journals, is editor-in-chief of the journal *Morphology* and is a member of the editorial board of a number of international journals (*English Language and Linguistics*, *Journal of English Linguistics*, *Journal of Pidgin and Creole Languages*, *The Mental Lexicon*, *Zeit-schrift für Sprachwissenschaft*). His most recent books are *Introduction to English Linguistics* (2015), *The Oxford Reference Guide to English Morphology* (2013), and *Word knowledge and word usage: A cross-disciplinary guide to the mental lexicon* (2017).

Marcel Schlechtweg (Universität Kassel)

Marcel Schlechtweg is a Postdoctoral Research Fellow in Linguistics at the University of Kassel, Germany. His research interests include the mental representation and processing as well as the prosody of complex constructions, especially compounds and phrases. After his studies in Kassel and at Dartmouth College in Hanover, New Hampshire, he completed a doctorate in Linguistics at the University of Kassel. The dissertation *Memorization and the Compound-Phrase Distinction* will appear in the De Gruyter book series *Studia Grammatica* in 2018.

Stefanie Stricker (Universität Bamberg)
Stefanie Stricker is a research assistant and adjunct professor with the Chair of German Linguistics at the University of Bamberg, Germany. She currently supervises the research projects *Database-supported documentation of the vernacular vocabulary of the Continental West-Germanic laws of the barbarians* (since 2012), and *Catalogue of the Old High German and Old Saxon Glossed Manuscripts. A Primary-Source Based Analysis Providing Online Access to the Supplementary Manuscripts* (since 2013), both funded by the German Research Foundation (DFG). Her main research interests cover the fields of historical linguistics, Old High German glossography, historical word formation, lexicography, and contemporary German.

Sören Stumpf (Universität Trier)
Sören Stumpf studied German philology and history at Trier University from 2007 until 2012. After his final degree, he became a research assistant in German linguistics at the chair of Prof. Dr. Stephan Stein at Trier University and finished his doctoral thesis about formulaic (ir-)regularities in June 2015. Currently, he is working on his postdoctoral thesis, which deals with word formations in spoken and written German. Besides phraseology and word formation, his research interests are corpus linguistics, textlinguistics, discourse analysis, linguistic criticism and construction grammar.

Esme Winter-Froemel (Universität Trier)
Esme Winter-Froemel is Professor of Romance Linguistics at the University of Trier. Her fields of teaching and research include wordplay and verbal humour as well as linguistic ambiguity and language change, Romance lexicology, and pragmatic and cognitive aspects of linguistic borrowing. She currently chairs the scientific network "The Dynamics of Wordplay: Language Contact, Linguistic Innovation, Speaker-Hearer-Interaction" and is a member of the Graduate Research Training Group "Ambiguity: Production and Perception" (GRK 1808, Tübingen University).

Index

Adelung, Johann Christoph 9, 261, 263, 274ff.
adjective-noun combinations 6, 117
affixal swap *See* affixation: affix swapping
affixation
- affix 49, 93ff., 103ff., 111f.
- affix duration 93, 99, 106
- affix swapping 206, 217, 220
- prefix 5, 93, 95f., 98ff., 103ff., 196, 208
- prefixation 50
- suffix 44, 50, 53, 58, 60f., 98f., 104ff., 111f., 120, 142, 148, 166, 196, 212, 217f., 220, 224, 243, 278
- suffix derivative 55
- suffixation 50, 53, 55, 58f., 61, 216, 220ff.
ambiguity 48, 157, 242
analogy 22, 27f., 34, 121, 125, 177, 179, 270
anchoring 147ff., 151ff., 157f., 160, 165ff.

Baroque 9, 266, 268ff., 272, 274
blend 174, 179ff., 186f., 192f., 196ff., 218
borrowing 182, 229f., 233, 241, 243f., 247, 256
boundary strength 97f.

clipping 141f., 145, 153ff., 157f., 160ff.
coda 97, 177f., 189, 191, 194f., 197f.
codification 3, 15, 24, 30
complex word 3ff., 43f., 49ff., 61, 93ff., 96f., 103, 156, 203, 220ff.
complicity 9, 175, 200, 245, 248f., 252
compositionality 6, 74, 117ff., 121, 123f., 128f., 131, 133ff., 156
compound, compounding 3, 9, 20, 22f., 31, 43f., 47, 49ff., 55ff., 68, 85, 119ff., 127, 134f., 145, 163f., 179, 214, 256, 261, 263, 270ff., 275ff., 279f.
constraint 5, 178, 186, 196, 208, 216, 219, 224, 268, 275
constructional morphology *See* morphology
context 1f., 4, 6ff., 21, 23, 26, 28f., 33f., 46, 48ff., 54, 58, 60, 67ff., 72ff., 81f., 85, 95f., 117ff., 123f., 126, 135f., 141, 145, 156f., 161ff., 175., 178ff., 184f., 187, 198f., 203ff., 210, 219, 222, 229ff., 235, 238, 240, 244, 247, 251, 253ff., 261, 265, 268, 270, 275, 277f.
conventional wordplay *See* wordplay
conventionalisation 2, 20, 26, 29, 36, 161
corpus linguistics / analysis 4, 16, 23, 67f., 71ff., 79, 82, 85
creativity 2, 4, 7f., 27f., 203f., 223, 248, 270
culture 31, 35f., 46, 162, 248

debonding 4, 69, 82, 85
decomposability 75f., 103, 112
denigration 244, 252
diachronic evolution 2, 229, 232, 250, 253, 263
dialect, diatopic variation 27, 32, 62, 125
Dictionnaire de l'Académie française / DAF 9, 229, 237, 249, 255, 266
diminutive 9, 263, 278f.
discursive pattern 206, 208
duration 5, 93, 95ff., 102, 104ff., 108ff., 117, 120, 127f., 131, 134f., 160

Early New High German *See* German
English 2, 4ff., 8, 16ff., 25f., 34f., 67f., 93ff., 103, 105, 108, 112, 117f., 120f., 123ff., 134ff., 141ff., 151, 153ff., 178, 182ff., 193, 199, 205, 229, 243, 265, 280

formal transparency *See* transparency
formulaic (ir)regularity 36
formulaic pattern / expression / language 2f., 10, 15f., 18ff., 28ff., 67, 69f.
French 8f., 11, 17, 26, 70, 98, 143, 157, 181, 193, 203, 205, 207f., 210, 212f., 215ff., 229ff., 237ff., 241, 245ff., 252, 255, 262f., 265ff., 273f., 282
frequency 3, 5, 15f., 19, 24f., 29, 31, 33ff., 44, 95ff., 102f., 106ff., 164, 210, 218ff., 222, 239, 253
- fundamental frequency 117, 120, 128f.
Frisch, Johann Leonhard 272, 274
Fruchtbringende Gesellschaft 9, 269f.
fundamental frequency *See* frequency

German 2ff., 6ff., 15ff., 21ff., 33ff., 43ff., 57f., 60ff., 67ff., 74, 98, 119, 135, 141f., 144, 146f., 150ff., 155, 157f., 165f., 173f., 176ff., 180ff., 186f., 189, 192ff., 198f., 205, 229ff., 241ff., 246f., 249, 254, 261ff., 278ff.
– Early New High German 30, 261, 263, 275
– Old High German 2ff., 43ff., 50f., 53ff., 60f.
graphemic 62, 178, 181, 189

Harsdörffer, Georg Philipp 9, 196, 261, 269ff.
héroï-comique 243
historical word formation *See* word formation
homeophony 182, 185, 188, 193f., 198
homophony 174, 176, 181f., 188f., 192ff.
Hulsius, Levin 272

incongruity 243
innovation, lexical innovation 1ff., 33, 67, 80, 93f., 112f., 179, 208, 229ff., 236, 239, 242f., 246ff., 253, 255f., 261ff., 268ff., 275, 279, 281f.
– ludic innovation *See* ludicity
intensity 46, 117, 120, 127f., 133ff.
irony 235f., 244, 256, 265, 267
irregularity *See* regularity, irregularity
Italian 6, 17, 26, 141, 144, 146ff., 150, 152f., 155, 158, 165, 176, 192f., 205, 269, 272f., 279

Klangspiel 174
Kramer, Matthias 9, 261, 263, 272f.

language change 1, 3, 7, 15, 24, 33, 46, 230, 236, 254, 261f., 265, 279
Leges barbarorum 3, 43f., 46
lexical expansion 1ff., 10, 15, 43f., 61, 67f., 79f., 82, 85, 93, 141, 144, 230, 255, 261, 270, 281f.
lexicographic mark 206, 229, 234ff., 244f., 248ff., 255, 266ff., 281
lexicography 82, 234, 264, 266, 268
linguistic norm *See* norm
ludicity 1f., 4, 7ff., 173, 229ff., 237ff., 244, 249, 253, 255, 261, 263, 266f., 270, 278, 281

– ludic innovation 7, 9, 179, 229ff., 236, 239, 244ff., 249ff., 253ff., 261ff., 266, 268, 272, 275, 279, 281f.
– ludic item 9, 206, 233ff., 239f., 243, 245f., 249ff., 255, 262, 266, 275, 279, 282
– ludic translation 230
– ludic usage 7f., 10, 235f., 239ff., 245, 251, 255

markedness 9, 144, 229f., 232, 239ff., 243, 247, 249, 254, 261, 263, 265, 277, 279, 282
metalinguistic reflection 6, 9, 206f., 216, 219, 222, 224, 234, 238, 261ff., 266, 268, 271, 274f., 278
modification 10, 15, 24ff., 36, 69, 82, 119, 190ff., 195, 197ff.
morphology 5f., 93, 141, 144f., 205, 210, 212, 224f.

neologism 94, 96, 112, 207f., 210ff., 268
nonce-formation 8, 203ff., 208ff.
norm 3, 19, 26ff., 30, 36, 249, 269f.
normativity *See* norm
novelty 204, 207f., 219
nucleus 160, 177f., 189, 191, 194f., 197

obsoleteness 245
Old High German *See* German
onset 148, 173, 177f., 186, 189, 191, 194f., 197ff.

paronymy 173, 176, 185, 187f., 194, 196ff.
phonetic detail 94, 112, 198f.
phonetic reduction 93, 95f.
phonological integration 93
phraseological boundedness 68, 70, 73, 75f., 78ff., 84ff.
phraseology, phrasemes 4, 18f., 21ff., 25ff., 67ff., 74ff., 82, 85, 243
playfulness *See* ludicity
pragmatics 5, 25, 203f., 221, 223
prefix, prefixation *See* affixation
productivity 1f., 4ff., 21, 51, 93f., 141, 143, 145f., 203f., 219, 221ff., 256, 278
prominence 6, 105, 117f., 120, 127, 134, 159
prosody 118, 120, 126, 206

– prosodic prominence 6, 117, 134
psycholinguistics 4, 67, 69, 78f., 85, 102, 145, 154, 156ff., 166f., 204, 220

regularity, irregularity 1, 3, 6, 15, 18, 23f., 28, 36, 68, 146, 157
repetition 209, 216, 240
rhetorical 175f., 210, 214, 216, 235, 251, 269
rhyme 177, 209f., 212, 214ff.

Schottelius, Justus Georg 9, 269
segmentability 5, 93, 95ff., 102f., 106ff.
semantic change 25, 46, 58, 233, 248, 279
semantic decomposability 69, 74ff., 84f.
similarity 22, 27, 32, 144, 166, 174, 176ff., 180, 186, 200, 209f., 212, 282
– phonetic / phonological similarity 27, 176, 178, 180, 186, 200, 209
– semantic similarity 176
Sinnspiel 174
soundplay 173ff.
Spracharbeit 269
Stieler, Kaspar 9, 269f., 272
stress 6, 105, 117ff., 123f., 127, 134ff., 147ff., 151ff., 158ff., 184f., 188f., 192, 194f., 197ff.
– stress shift 194
stylistics 10f., 18, 21, 25f., 29, 167, 203f., 209, 214, 221, 223f., 230, 232, 241, 264, 266, 268, 272ff.
substitution 18, 25, 35, 144, 154, 177, 190f., 195, 197ff., 218, 220, 223
suffix substitution *See* substitution
suffix, suffixation *See* affixation

tradition 3, 15, 19f., 24, 29, 31ff., 36, 43ff., 53, 58, 60, 62, 264, 274
transparency 5f., 51, 102, 141, 145f., 156f., 166
– semantic transparency 5f., 97, 102f., 109f., 141, 145, 156, 167, 245
truncation 6, 141ff., 160f., 163ff., 256

unique component 2, 4f., 67ff., 71ff., 82, 84ff.
usage-based approach 7, 16, 18, 176, 236

variability 6, 78, 94f., 141, 145f., 154f., 165, 167, 264
variation 15, 24ff., 30, 35f., 53, 70, 118, 121, 141f., 145, 154, 167, 197, 212, 237, 251, *See also* dialect, diatopic variation
– interindividual variation 237, 251
– variant 31, 34, 72, 78, 125, 147, 166, 206, 209, 212, 265, 277
verbal humour 216, 230f., 233
vernacular inserts 45, 47

wearout effect 9, 232, 240, 242, 254, 263
word formation 4f., 15, 21, 43, 48f., 51, 55, 58, 61f., 79, 82, 85, 196, 203, 205, 221, 230, 233, 243, 275f., 279
word recognition 145, 154, 157ff., 165f.
wordplay 7, 9f., 27, 173ff., 184ff., 231, 242, 261f., 268, 270ff., 274
– conventional wordplay 27

Zesen, Philipp von 9, 269

www.ingramcontent.com/pod-product-compliance
Lightning Source LLC
Chambersburg PA
CBHW031723230426
43669CB00007B/225